The Nature of Love

1
Plato to Luther

Books by Irving Singer

The Nature of Love
  1. Plato to Luther
  2. Courtly and Romantic
  3. The Modern World
Mozart and Beethoven: The Concept of Love in Their Operas
The Goals of Human Sexuality
Santayana's Aesthetics
Essays in Literary Criticism by George Santayana (Editor)

The
NATURE
of LOVE

1
Plato to Luther
Second Edition

Irving Singer

The University of Chicago Press
Chicago and London

The University of Chicago Press, Chicago 60637
The University of Chicago Press, Ltd., London

© 1966, 1984 by Irving Singer
All rights reserved. First edition 1966
Second edition 1984
Paperback edition 1987
Printed in the United States of America
96 95 94 93 92 91 90 89 88   6543

Library of Congress Cataloging in Publication Data

Singer, Irving
    The nature of love.

    Vol. 1 : 2nd ed.
    Includes index.
    Contents: 1. Plato to Luther—2. Courtly and
romantic. 1. Love. I. Title.
BD436.S5   1984   128   84-2554
ISBN 0-226-76094-4 (v. 1, cl.); 0-226-76095-2 (v. 1, pbk.)
        0-226-76096-0 (v. 2, cl.); 0-226-76097-9 (v. 2, pbk.)
        0-226-76098-7 (v. 3)

april 2, 1993

To
J.F.S.

Contents

Preface to Second Edition

In Revising *The Nature of Love: Plato to Luther* for its second edition, I have altered the presentation, and sometimes the analysis, in many places. I have not hesitated to modify ideas of mine, as well as their stylistic expression, if they no longer satisfied me. Portions of the first and seventh chapters in particular have been considerably rewritten. The basic structure of the book remains the same—the concept of love analyzed in terms of appraisal and bestowal, and this distinction then employed to explicate philosophies of love in the ancient world and in the religious orientation of the Middle Ages.

In making this revision, I have not tried to answer criticisms of my philosophical approach. I will do so in the third volume of the trilogy, in chapters dealing with contemporary concepts. I there return to some of the issues mentioned at the beginning of this book. Here, however, I wish to make two methodological comments relevant to the entire work. First, the reader must realize that in this volume I have not sought to present my own philosophy of love in any comprehensive fashion. The distinction between appraisal and bestowal, and in general all of Part I, is designed primarily as a tool for the historical investigations in subsequent chapters. One should not expect this bit of theory to yield more than it can properly provide. Second, the labels I employ for concepts of love are not always the same as those found in philosophy or literature of the period in which the concepts occur. The concepts did not bear at every moment the names I have used in identifying them. One reviewer of the first edition remarked that, in religious documents of the Middle Ages, the word *philia* acquired the meanings I have specified only as late as the thirteenth century. Though interesting in itself, the comment is not germane to the philosophical history that I am writing. The concept of what I call religious philia originated long before the thirteenth century, despite the fact that other terms were used for it. Throughout the trilogy I try to make sense of ideas that mattered to people regardless of how confusing or inadequate their terminology may have been. If my conceptual analyses remain faithful to the ideas I discuss, while also helping the reader to develop his own critical insight, I will feel that I have succeeded in my major intention.

1984   I. S.

Preface to First Edition

In Stravinsky's Opera *The Rake's Progress*,* there is a scene in which the protagonist, Tom Rakewell, recites a mock catechism inspired by the devil and delivered before an audience of whores. He briefly expounds his moral code as a libertine and then gives definitions of beauty and of pleasure. But suddenly the catechism ends:

> Shadow:
>   One final question. Love is . . .
> Rakewell (aside):
>   Love!
> That precious word is like a fiery coal,
> It burns my lips, strikes terror to my soul.
> Shadow:
>   No answer? Will my scholar fail me?
> Rakewell (violently):
>   No,
> No more.

Though he is loved and would fain love in return, Tom Rakewell never clarifies his ideas about love. Despite the fictional setting, he is a "scholar" of the twentieth century; and in the last sixty years or so the analysis of love has been neglected more than almost any other subject in philosophy. Since we live in an age that romanticism has

*Libretto by W. H. Auden and Chester Kallman.

xi

permeated for two hundred years, the popular ideology of the Western world seems to concern itself with little besides love. Yet the precious word has been a fiery coal burning the lips of even our greatest philosophers. Thus far the twentieth century has been a stone age in which new tools, new methods of analysis, have been invented but hardly used. In pragmatism, psychoanalysis, analytical philosophy, and certain aspects of existentialism the ground has been cleared of much of what was worthless in earlier thinking. But relatively little has been done toward reconstruction, toward building attitudes of feeling and of action that might sustain a human being in the contemporary world. This part of the enterprise may take several generations to complete. Ultimate success will depend upon an army of technical philosophers addressing themselves to the logic of affective discourse and the phenomenology of affective experience (as, I fear, the subjects may be called). From their investigations, and from related work in science and the humanities, will emerge new ideals, new values, new patterns of experience. In returning to concepts such as love, the new philosophy may be more rigorous and more empirical than in the past. It need not be any less creative, or any less rewarding to heart or mind.

I write this book, then, as an offering to what I conceive to be the philosophy of the future. At the same time, it is written for readers in the present who wish to clarify their thinking about the nature of love. Its orientation is historical, but interpretive and not particularly recondite. I study the history of ideas for their contemporary relevance. La Rochefoucauld spoke better than he knew when he said that many people would never have been in love if they had not heard love talked about. Our attitudes cannot be separated from the ideas to which we are born and through which we express ourselves. The history of philosophy is man impregnating later generations with the ability to think by means of one concept or another. In this sense, the source of love is not God or the libido: it is rather ideas about love that have developed throughout the history of mankind, arising into prominence in one period and filtering down into the presuppositions of succeeding ones.

In every period, love (and most ideas about love) retains at least the residue of animal instinct. But in the case of man even the sexual instincts cannot be neatly demarcated. Human sexuality does not exist apart from thinking, feeling, doing—and, above all, the making of a system of values. That is why a word like "lust" suggests something beastly and atavistic, an instinct that has detached itself from all ideals and so become inhuman. By formulating a concept of love, man *re*-creates his instincts. He experiences them as part of his humanity, *relates* them to ideals, puts them into the class of things that can be good or bad, better or worse, and not merely necessary. Forces that may be indestructible are thereby tamed, repressed in part but also humanized and thoroughly transformed by the values to which they now contribute.

An adequate investigation would include much that goes beyond the scope of this book: a study of instincts themselves and the psychogenesis of feelings, a thorough analysis of valuation (the act or process of valuing), a systematic comparison of different uses of the term "love," a detailed account of how the various concepts of love evolved historically, a philosophical description of love in relation to sentiments such as hatred, anger, pity, sympathy. The present volume attempts nothing so ambitious. It draws a distinction between two types of valuing—appraisal and bestowal—and then shows how each is relevant not only to love but also to the philosophy of love in the ancient and the medieval world. In subsequent books I hope to use this volume as a basis for understanding courtly love, Romantic love, and love in the modern world. The following chapters may not solve any problems; but possibly they can serve as a prolegomenon to work that eventually will.

This book is not a solitary product. It has been sustained by friends and friendly influences too dear to mention in this place, by philosophical and literary models—both living and dead—that no acknowledgment by me can further dignify. From them and from the countryside in which I write, I have learned at second hand what the book is about. In the notes at the end of the volume I give credit for some of the specific ideas borrowed or stolen in the course of composition.

West Rindge, N. H.   I. S.
1965

Part 1
The Concept of Love

1
Appraisal and Bestowal

I START WITH THE IDEA THAT
love is a way of valuing something. It is a positive response *toward* the
"object of love"—which is to say, anyone or anything that is loved. In
a manner quite special to itself, love affirms the goodness of this
object. Some philosophers say that love *searches* for what is valuable
in the beloved; others say that love *creates* value in the sense that it
makes the beloved objectively valuable in some respect. Both assertions are often true, but sometimes false; and, therefore, neither
explains the type of valuing which is love.

In studying the relationship between love and valuation, let us
avoid merely semantical difficulties. The word "love" sometimes
means liking very much, as when a man speaks of loving the food he
is eating. It sometimes means desiring obsessively, as when a neurotic reports that he cannot control his feelings about a woman. In
these and similar instances the word does not affirm goodness.
Liking something very much is not the same as considering it good;
and the object of an obsessive desire may attract precisely because it
is felt to be bad. These uses of the word are only peripheral to the
concept of love as a positive response toward a valued object. As we
generally use the term, we imply an act of prizing, cherishing, caring
about—all of which constitutes a mode of valuation.

But what is it to value or evaluate? Think of what a man does when
he sets a price upon a house. He establishes various facts—the size of
the building, its physical condition, the cost of repairs, the proximity

to schools. He then weights these facts in accordance with their importance to a hypothetical society of likely buyers. Experts in this activity are called appraisers; the activity itself is appraisal or appraising. It seeks to find an objective value that things have in relation to one or another community of human interests. I call this value "objective" because, although it exists only insofar as there are people who want the house, the estimate is open to public verification. As long as they agree about the circumstances—what the house is like and what a relevant group of buyers prefer—all fair-minded appraisers should reach a similar appraisal, regardless of their own feelings about this particular house. In other words, appraising is a branch of empirical science, specifically directed toward the determining of value.

But now imagine that the man setting the price is not an appraiser, but a prospective buyer. The price that he sets need not agree with the appraiser's. For he does more than estimate objective value: he decides what the house is worth to *him*. To the extent that his preferences differ from other people's, the house will have a different value for him. By introducing such considerations, we relate the object to the particular and possibly idiosyncratic interests of a single person, his likings, his needs, his wants, his desires. Ultimately, all objective value depends upon interests of this sort. The community of buyers whose inclinations the appraiser must gauge is itself just a class of individuals. The appraiser merely predicts what each of them would be likely to pay for the house. At the same time, each buyer must be something of an appraiser himself; for he must have at least a rough idea of the price that other buyers will set. Furthermore, each person has to weigh, and so appraise, the relative importance of his own particular interests; and he must estimate whether the house can satisfy them. In principle these judgments are verifiable. They are also liable to mistake: for instance, when a man thinks that certain desires matter more to him than they really do, or when he expects greater benefits from an object than it can provide. Deciding what something is worth to *oneself* we may call an "individual appraisal." It differs from what the appraiser does; it determines a purely individual value, as opposed to any objective value.

Now, with this in mind, I suggest that love creates a new value, one that is not reducible to the individual or objective value that something may also have. This further type of valuing I call bestowal. Individual and objective value depend upon an object's ability to satisfy prior interests—the needs, the desires, the wants, or whatever it is that motivates us toward one object and not another. Bestowed value is different. It is created by the affirmative relationship *itself*, by the very act of responding favorably, giving an object emotional and pervasive importance regardless of its capacity to satisfy interests. Here it makes no sense to speak of verifiability; and though bestowing may often be injurious, unwise, even immoral, it cannot be erroneous in the way that an appraisal might be. For now it is the valuing alone that *makes* the value.

Think of what happens when a man comes to love the house he has bought. In addition to being something of use, something that gratifies antecedent desires, it takes on special value for him. It is now *his* house, not merely as a possession or a means of shelter but also as something he *cares about*, a part of his affective life. Of course, we also care about objects of mere utility. We need them for the benefits they provide. But in the process of loving, the man establishes another kind of relationship. He gives the house an importance beyond its individual or objective value. It becomes a focus of attention and possibly an object of personal commitment. Merely by engaging himself in this manner, the man bestows a value the house could not have had otherwise.

We might also say that the homeowner acts as if his house were valuable "for its own sake." And in a sense it is. For the value that he bestows does not depend upon the house's capacity to satisfy. Not that love need diminish that capacity. On the contrary, it often increases it by affording opportunities for enjoyment that would have been impossible without the peculiar attachment in which bestowal consists. Caring about the house, the man may find new and more satisfying ways of living in it. At the same time, the object achieves a kind of autonomy. The house assumes a presence and attains a dignity. It makes demands and may even seem to have a personality, to have needs of its own. In yielding to these "needs"— restoring the house to an earlier condition, perhaps, or completing its inherent design—the homeowner may not be guided by any other considerations.

In love between human beings something similar happens. For people, too, may be appraised; and they may be valued beyond one's appraisal. In saying that a woman is beautiful or that a man is handsome, or that a man or woman is good in any other respect, we ascribe objective value. This will always be a function of *some* community of human interests, though we may have difficulty specifying which one. And in all communities people have individual value for one another. We are means to each other's satisfactions, and we constantly evaluate one another on the basis of our individual interests. However subtly, we are always setting prices on other people, and on ourselves. But we also bestow value in the manner of love. We then respond to another as something that cannot be reduced to *any* system of appraisal. The lover takes an interest in the beloved as a *person*, and not merely as a commodity—which she may also be. (The lover may be female, of course, and the beloved may be male; but for the sake of brevity and grammatical simplicity I shall generally retain the old convention of referring to lovers as "he" and beloveds as "she.") He bestows importance upon *her* needs and *her* desires, even when they do not further the satisfaction of his own. Whatever her personality, he gives it a value it would not have apart from his loving attitude. In relation to the lover, the beloved has become valuable for her own sake.

In the love of persons, then, people bestow value upon one another over and above their individual or objective value. The reciprocity of love occurs when each participant receives bestowed value while also bestowing it upon the other. Reciprocity has always been recognized as a desired outcome of love. Since it need not occur, however, I define the lover as one who bestows value, and the beloved as one who receives it. The lover makes the beloved valuable merely by attaching and committing himself to her. Though she may satisfy his needs, he refuses to use her as just an instrument. To love a woman as a person is to desire her for the sake of values that appraisal might discover, and yet to place one's desire within a context that affirms her importance regardless of these values. Eventually the beloved may no longer matter to us as one who is useful. Treating her as an end, we may think only of how we can be useful to *her*. But still it is we who think and act and make this affirmative response. Only in relation to *our* bestowal does another person enjoy the kind of value that love creates.

In saying that love bestows value, I am not referring to the fact that lovers shower good things upon those they love. Gifts may sometimes symbolize love, but they never prove its existence. Loving is not synonymous with giving. We do speak of one person "giving love" to another, but what is given hardly resembles what we usually mean by a gift. Even to say that the lover gives himself is somewhat misleading. Love need not be self-sacrificial. In responding affirmatively to another person, the lover creates something and need lose nothing in himself. To bestow value is to augment one's own being as well as the beloved's. Bestowal generates a new society by the sheer force of emotional attachment, a society that enables the lovers to discard many of the conventions that would ordinarily have separated them. But such intimacy is only one of the criteria by which bestowal may be identified.

The bestowing of value shows itself in many different ways, not all of which need ever occur at the same time or in equal strength: by caring about the needs and interests of the beloved, by wishing to benefit or protect her, by delighting in her achievements, by encouraging her independence while also accepting and sustaining her dependency, by respecting her individuality, by giving her pleasure, by taking pleasures with her, by feeling glad when she is present and sad when she is not, by sharing ideas and emotions with her, by sympathizing with her weaknesses and depending upon her strength, by developing common pursuits, by allowing her to become second nature to him—"her smiles, her frowns, her ups, her downs"—by having a need to increase their society with other human beings upon whom they can jointly bestow value, by wanting children who may perpetuate their love. These are not necessary and sufficient conditions; but their occurrence would give us reason to think that an act of bestowal has taken place.

Through bestowal lovers have "a life" together. The lover accords the beloved the tribute of expressing *his* feelings by responding to *hers*. If he sends her valuable presents, they will signify that he too appreciates what she esteems; if he makes sacrifices on her behalf, he indicates how greatly her welfare matters to him. It is as if he were announcing that what is real for her is real for him also. Upon the sheer personality of the beloved he bestows a framework of value, emanating from himself but focused on her. Lovers linger over attributes that might well have been ignored. Whether sensuous or polite, passionate or serene, brusque or tender, the lover's response is variably fervent but constantly gratuitous. It dignifies the beloved by treating her as *someone*, with all the emphasis the italics imply. Though independent of our needs, she is also the significant object of our attention. We show ourselves receptive to her peculiarities in the sense that we readily respond to them. Response is itself a kind of affirmation, even when it issues into unpleasant emotions such as anger and jealousy. These need not be antithetical to love; they may even be signs of it. Under many circumstances one cannot respond to another person without the unpleasant emotions, as a parent cannot stay in touch with a wayward child unless he occasionally punishes him. It is when we reject the other person, reducing him to a nothing or expressing our indifference, that love disappears. For then instead of bestowing value, we have withdrawn it.

In general, every emotion or desire contributes to love once it serves as a positive response to an independent being. If a woman is *simply* a means to sexual satisfaction, a man may be said to want her, but not to love her. For his sexual desire to become a part of love, it must function as a way of responding to the character and special properties of this particular woman. Desire wants what it wants for the sake of some private gratification, whereas love demands an interest in that vague complexity we call another person. No wonder lovers sound like metaphysicians, and scientists are more comfortable in the study of desire. For love is an attitude with no clear objective. Through it one human being affirms the significance of another, much as a painter highlights a figure by defining it in a sharpened outline. But the beloved is not a painted figure. She is not static: she is fluid, changing, indefinable—*alive*. The lover is attending to a *person*. And who can say what that is?

In the history of philosophy, bestowal and appraisal have often been confused with one another, perhaps because they are both types of valuation.* Love is related to both; they interweave in it. Unless we appraised we could not bestow a value that goes beyond appraisal; and without bestowal there would be no love. We may speak of lovers accepting one another, or even taking each other as is. But this need not mean a blind submission to some unknown being. In love we *attend* to the beloved, in the sense that we respond to what *she* is. For the effort to succeed, it must be accompanied by justifiable appraisals, objective as well as individual. The objective beauty and goodness of his beloved will delight the lover, just as her deficiencies will distress him. In her, as in every other human being, these are important properties. How is the lover to know what they are without a system of appraisals? Or how to help her realize her potentialities—assuming that is what she wants? Of course, in bestowing value upon this woman, the lover will "accentuate the positive" and undergo a kind of personal involvement that no disinterested spectator would. He will feel an intimate concern about the continuance of good properties in the beloved and the diminishing of bad ones. But none of this would be possible without objective appraisals.

Even more important is the role of individual appraisal. The person we love is generally one who satisfies our needs and desires. She may do so without either of us realizing the full extent of these satisfactions; and possibly all individual value is somehow based upon unconscious effects. Be this as it may, our experience of another person includes a large network of individual evaluations continually in progress and available to consciousness. At each moment our interests are being gratified or frustrated, fulfilled or thwarted, strengthened or weakened in relation to the other person. Individual value is rarely stable. It changes in accordance with our success or failure in getting what we want. And as this happens, our perception of the beloved also changes. Though the lover bestows value upon the woman as a separate and autonomous person, she will always be a person in *his* experience, a person whom he needs and who may need him, a person whose very nature may eventually

*Though not of "*e*valuation." That word is usually reserved for appraisal.

9

conform to his inclinations, as well as vice versa. The attitude of love probably includes more, not fewer, individual appraisals than any other. How else could a lover, who must respond from his own point of view, really care about the beloved?

Love would not be love unless appraising were accompanied by the bestowing of value. But where this conjunction exists, *every* appraisal may lead on to a further bestowal. By disclosing an excellence in the beloved, appraisal (whether individual or objective) makes it easier for us to appreciate her. By revealing her faults and imperfections, it increases the importance of acting on her behalf. Love may thus encompass all possible appraisals. Once bestowal has occurred, a man may hardly care that his beloved is not deemed desirable by other men. Given a choice, he may prefer her to women who are sexually more attractive. His love is a way of compensating for and even overcoming negative appraisals. If it were a means of repaying the object for value received, love would turn into gratitude; if it were an attempt to give more than the object has provided, it would become generosity or condescension. These are related attitudes, but love differs from them in bestowing value without calculation. It confers importance no matter *what* the object is worth.

When appraisal occurs alone, our attitude develops in the direction of science, ambition, or morality. To do "the right thing" we need not bestow value upon another person; we need only recognize the truth about his character and act appropriately. Admiring a woman's superiority, we may delight in her as an evidence of the good life. We feel toward her what Hume calls "the sense of approbation." We find her socially useful or morally commendable, which is not to say that she excites our love. If she has faults, they offend our moral sensibility or else elicit our benevolence. In short, we respond to this woman as an abstraction, as a something that may be better or worse, an opportunity for judgment or for action, but not a person whom we love. Appraisal without bestowal may lead us to change other people regardless of what they want. As moralists or legislators, or as dutiful parents, we may even think that this is how we *ought* to behave. The magistrate will then enforce a distance between himself and the criminal, whose welfare he is quite prepared to sacrifice for the greater good of society. The parent will

discipline his child in the hope of molding him "in the most beneficial manner." On this moral attitude great institutions are often
built. But it is not a loving attitude. We are not responding affirmatively toward others. We are only doing what is (we hope) in their
best interests, or else society's.

When love intervenes, morality becomes more personal but also
more erratic. It is almost impossible to imagine someone bestowing
value without caring about the other person's welfare. To that
extent, love implies benevolence. And yet the lover does not act
benevolently for the sake of doing the right thing. In loving another
person, we respect *his* desire to improve himself. If we offer to help,
we do so because *he* wants to be better than he is, not because *we* think
he ought to be. Love and morality need not diverge, but they often
do. For love is not *inherently* moral. There is no guarantee that it will
bestow value properly, at the right time, in the right way. Through
love we enjoy another person as he is, including his moral condition;
yet this enjoyment may itself violate the demands of morality. Ethical attitudes must always be governed by appraisal rather than
bestowal. They must consider the individual in his relations to other
people, as one among many who have equal claims. Faced with the
being of a particular person, morality tells us to pick and choose
those attributes that are most desirable. It is like a chef who makes an
excellent stew by bringing out one flavor and muffling another. The
chef does not care about the ingredients as unique or terminal
entities, but only as things that are good to eat. In loving another
person, however, we enact a nonmoral *loyalty*—like the mother who
stands by her criminal son even though she knows he is guilty. Her
loyalty need not be *immoral*; and though she loves her son, she may
realize that he must be punished. But what if the value she has
bestowed upon her child blinds her to the harm he has done, deters
her from handing him over to the police, leads her to encourage him
as a criminal? Her love may increase through such devotion, but it
will be based on faulty appraisals and will not be a moral love.

Possibly the confusion between appraisal and bestowal results
from the way that lovers talk. To love another person is to *treat* him
with great regard, to confer a new and personal value upon him. But
when lovers describe their beloved, they sometimes sound as if she

were perfect just in being herself. In caring about someone, attending to her, affirming the importance of her being what she is, the lover resembles a man who has appraised an object and found it very valuable. Though he is bestowing value, the lover *seems* to be declaring the objective goodness of the beloved. It is *as if* he were predicting the outcome of all possible appraisals and insisting that they would always be favorable.

As a matter of fact, the lover is doing nothing of the sort. His superlatives are expressive and metaphoric. Far from being terms of literal praise, they betoken the magnitude of his attachment and say little about the lady's beauty or goodness. They may even be accompanied by remarks that diminish the beloved in some respect—as when a man lovingly describes a woman's funny face or inability to do mathematics. If he says she is "perfect" that way, he chooses this ambiguous word because it is used for things we refuse to relinquish. As in appraisal we may wish to accept nothing less than perfection, so too the lover calls perfect whatever he accepts despite its appraisal. The lover may borrow appraisive terminology, but he uses it with a special intent. His language signifies that love alone has bestowed incalculable worth upon this particular person. Such newly given value is not a good of the sort that appraisal seeks: it is not an attribute that supplements her other virtues, like a dimple wrought by some magician to make a pretty woman prettier. For it is nothing but the importance that one person assigns to another; and in part at least, it is created by the language. The valuative terms that lovers use—"wonderful," "marvelous," "glorious," "grand," "terrific"—bestow value in themselves. They are scarcely capable of describing excellence or reporting on appraisals.

If we have any doubts about the lover's use of language, we should listen to the personal appendages he usually adds. He will not say "That woman is perfect," but rather "To *me* she is perfect" or "*I* think she is wonderful." In talking this way, he reveals that objective appraisal does not determine his attitude. For objective appraisal puts the object in relation to a community of valuers, whereas love creates its own community. The men in some society may all admire an "official beauty"—as Ortega calls her. Every male may do homage to her exceptional qualities, as if the lady were a great work of art;

and some will want to possess her, as they would want to steal the crown jewels. But this is not the same as love, since that involves a different kind of response, more intimate, more personal, and more creative.

For similar reasons it would be a mistake to think that the lover's language articulates an individual appraisal. If he says that to him the woman is perfect, the lover does not mean that she is perfect *for* him. Unless the beloved satisfied in some respect, no man might be able to love her. For *she* must find a place in *his* experience; she must come alive for him, stimulate new and expansive interests; and none of this is likely to happen unless she has individual value to him. But though the beloved satisfies the lover, she need not satisfy perfectly. Nor does the lover expect her to. In saying that to him she is perfect, he merely reiterates the fact that he loves this woman. Her perfection is an honorific title which he, and only he, bestows. The lover is like a child who makes a scribble and then announces "This is a tree." The child could just as easily have said "This is a barn." Until he tells us, the scribble represents nothing. Once he tells us, it represents whatever he says—as long as his attitude remains consistent.

In being primarily bestowal and only secondarily appraisal, love is never elicited by the object in the sense that desire or approbation is. We desire things or people for the sake of what will satisfy us. We approve of someone for his commendable properties. But these conditions have only a causal tie to love: as when a man loves a woman *because* she is beautiful, or *because* she satisfies his sexual, domestic, and social needs, or *because* she resembles his childhood memory of mother. Such facts indicate the circumstances under which people love one another; they explain why this particular man loves this particular woman; and if the life sciences were sufficiently developed, the facts could help us to predict who among human beings would be likely to love whom. But explaining the occurrence of love is not the same as explicating the concept. The conditions for love are not the same as love itself. In some circumstances the bestowing of value will happen more easily than in others; but *whenever* it happens, it happens as a new creation of value and exceeds all attributes of the object that might be thought to elicit it. Even if a man loves only a woman who is beautiful and looks like his mother, he does not *love* her for these properties in the same sense in which he might *admire* her for being objectively valuable or *desire* her for satisfying his needs.

For what then does a man love a woman? For being the person she is, for being herself? But that is to say that he loves her for nothing at all. Everyone is himself. Having a beloved who is what she is does not reveal the nature of love. Neither does it help us to understand the saint's desire to love all people. They are what they are. Why should they be loved for it? Why not pitied or despised, ignored or simply put to use? Love supplements the human search for value with a capacity for bestowing it gratuitously. To one who has succeeded in cultivating this attitude, *anything* may become an object of love. The saint is a man whose earthly needs and desires are extraordinarily modest; in principle, every human being can satisfy them. That being so, the saint creates a value-system in which all persons fit equally well. This disposition, this freely given response, cannot be elicited from him: it bestows itself and happens to be indiscriminate.

To the man of common sense it is very upsetting that love does not limit itself to some prior value in the object. The idea goes against our purposive ways of thinking. If I wish to drink the best wine, I have reason to prefer French champagne over American. My choice is dictated by an objective goodness in the French champagne. If instead I wish to economize, I act sensibly in choosing a wine I value less highly. We act this way whenever we use purposive means of attaining the good life, which covers a major part of our existence. But love, unlike desire, is not wholly purposive. Within the total structure of a human life it may serve as a lubricant to purposive attitudes, furthering their aims through new interests that promise new satisfactions; but in creating value, bestowing it freely, love introduces an element of risk into the economy. Purposive attitudes are safe, secure, like money in the bank; the loving attitude is speculative and always dangerous. Love is not *practical*, and sometimes borders on madness. We take our life in our hands when we allow love to tamper with our purposive habits. Without love, life might not be worth living; but without purposiveness, there would be no life.

No wonder, then, that the *fear* of love is one of the great facts of human nature. In all men and women there lurks an atavistic dread of insolvency whenever we generate more emotion than something has a right to demand of us. In everyone there is the country bumpkin who giggles nervously at an abstract painting because it looks like nothing on earth. Man finds the mere possibility of invention and spontaneous originality disquieting, even ominous. We are threatened by any new bestowal. Particularly when it means the origination of feelings, we are afraid to run the usual risks of failure and frustration, to expose ourselves in a positive response that can so easily be thwarted. As a character in D. H. Lawrence says of love: "I am almost more afraid of this touch than I was of death. For I am more nakedly exposed to it." Even Pascal, who spoke of the heart's having reasons whereof reason does not know, seemed to think that love adheres to a secret, mysterious quality within the object that only feeling can discern. But Pascal was wrong. Love is sheer gratuity. It issues from the lover like hairs on his head. It can be stimulated and developed, but it cannot be derived from outside.

Love is like awakened genius that chooses its materials in accordance with its own creative requirements. Love does not create its object; it merely responds to it creatively. That is why one can rarely convince a man that his beloved is unworthy of him. For his love is a creative means of *making* her more worthy—in the sense that he invests her with greater value, not in making her a better human being. That may also happen. But more significantly, the lover changes *himself*. By subordinating his purposive attitudes, he transforms himself into a being who enjoys the act of bestowing. There is something magical about this, as we know from legends in which the transformations of love are effected by a philter or a wand. In making another person valuable by developing a certain disposition within oneself, the lover performs in the world of feeling something comparable to what the alchemist does in the world of matter.

The creativity of love is thus primarily a self-creation. Lovers create within themselves a remarkable capacity for affective response, an ability to use their emotions, their words, their deeds for bestowing as well as appraising value. Each enhances the other's importance through an imaginative play within valuation itself. Indeed, love may be best approached as a subspecies of the imagination. Not only does the lover speak in poetic metaphors, but also he behaves like any artist. Whatever his "realistic" aspirations, no painter can duplicate reality. The scene out there cannot be transferred to a canvas. The painter can only *paint* it: i.e., give it a new importance in human life by presenting his way of seeing it through the medium of his art and the techniques of his individual talent. These determine the values of his painting, not the external landscape that may have originally inspired him. The artist may vary the scene to his heart's content, as El Greco did when he rearranged the buildings of Toledo. What matters is his way of seeing as a function of the imagination, not the disposition in space of stones and mortar. Similarly, a lover sees a woman not as others might, but through the creative agency of bestowing value. He need not change her any more than El Greco changed the real Toledo. But he renews her personality by subsuming it within the imaginative system of his own positive responses. Through her he expresses the variety of feelings that belong to love. Artists, even the most abstract, do not create out of nothing: they re-create, create anew. So too, the lover re-creates another person. By deploying his imagination in the art of bestowing value, by caring about the independent being of another person, the lover adds a new dimension to the beloved. In relation to him, within his loving attitude, she becomes the object of an affirmative interest, even an aesthetic object. She is, as we say, "*ap*preciated"—made more valuable through the special media and techniques in which love consists.

Treating love as an aspect of the imagination enables us to confront problems I have thus far ignored. For instance, I said it was *as if* the lover were predicting that no appraisal would discover any significant fault. If we now inquire into the meaning of these "as ifs," I can only remind you how they operate in other situations involving the imagination. Think of yourself as a spectator in the theater, watching an engrossing drama. The hero dies, and you begin to weep. Now for whom are you crying? Surely not for the actor: you know that as soon as the curtain falls, he will scramble to his feet and prepare for a great ovation. Is it then the character in the play? But there is no such person. You are fully aware that Hamlet (at least Shakespeare's Hamlet) never existed. How can his death, which is purely fictional, sadden you? Yet it does, more so perhaps than the death of real people you may have known. What happens, I think, is that you respond *as if* the actor were really Hamlet and *as if* Hamlet really existed. The "as if" signifies that although you *know* the actor is only acting and Hamlet only fictitious, your imaginative involvement causes you to express feelings appropriate to real people. At no point are you deluded. The "illusion" of the theater is not an illusion at all. It is an act of imagination—nothing like a mistake of judgment, nothing like the derangement that causes Don Quixote to smash the cruel puppet show in order to save the unfortunate heroine. On entering the theater, you have entered the dramatic situation. You have allowed your imagination to engage itself in one specific channel. With the assistance of the realistic props, the surrounding darkness, the company of other people doing the same imagining, you have invested the actors and the characters they represent with a capacity to affect your feelings as real persons might.

In love the same kind of thing occurs. The as ifs of love are imaginative, not essentially delusional. Of course, the lover *may* be deluded about his beloved. That is the familiar joke about lovers: they live in constant illusion, Cupid is blinded by emotion, etc. That this often happens I do not care to deny. But that this should be the essence of love, that by its very nature love should be illusory, seems to me utterly absurd. Even if people frequently clambered on stage and acted like Don Quixote, we would not say that their behavior revealed what it is to be a theatrical spectator. We would say they did not know how to look at a play. Likewise, it is not in the acting out of illusions that people become lovers. Though lovers do commit errors of judgment and are sometimes carried away by their feelings, love itself is not illusory. Emotional aberrations are adventitious to it, not definitive. As love is not primarily a way of knowing, neither is it a way of making mistakes. Appraisal is a way of knowing, and emotions may always interfere with its proper employment. But love is an imaginative means of bestowing value that would not exist otherwise. To the extent that a man is a lover, rather than a person seeking knowledge or yielding to self-delusion (which he may also be), he accords his beloved the courtesy of being treated affirmatively regardless of what he knows about her. In refusing to let his appraisive knowledge deflect his amorous conduct, he bestows a tribute which can only be understood as an imaginative act. As one of Rousseau's characters says: "Love did not make me blind to your faults, but it made those faults dear to me." It is this kind of valuative gesture that the imagination uses for courtesy as a whole. A courteous man—what used to be called a "gentleman"—may show respect to all women alike, whatever their social rank. He does so as a loving gift to the female sex, the worst as well as the best, the lowest as well as the highest. He is not normally deluded about differences in society or among human beings. He does not think that women are all the same. Yet by means of his imaginative response he acts as if there were a universal excellence in them, regardless of what they actually merit.

There is another respect in which the analogy from the theater elucidates the lover's imagination. I refer to the phenomenon of *presence*. The spectator responds to the fictional character as if it were a real person. He can do so, in part, because the character has been *presented to* him by a real person. Talking, laughing, shouting, the actor *makes present* to the spectator the reality of a human being. The very artificiality of his surroundings—his being in a "play," a fiction, his being placed on a stage so that everyone can see and hear, his giving a performance scheduled for a particular time, in a particular building—all this accentuates the fact that the actor himself is not artificial, but alive. The spectator makes his imaginative leap by seeing the actor as a present reality framed within the aesthetic contrivances of the theater. The greater the actor's "stage presence," the more he facilitates the spectator's feat. But ultimately the phenomenon depends upon the spectator himself, upon his dramatic sensibility, his creative capacity to infuse a fictional character with the reality of the human being right there before him. As the Prologue to Shakespeare's *Henry V* tells the audience: "And let us, ciphers to this great accompt, / On your imaginary forces work. / . . . For 'tis your thoughts that now must deck our kings."

In a similar fashion the lover's attention fixes upon the sheer presence of the beloved. In that extreme condition sometimes called "falling in love," such attentiveness often approaches self-hypnosis. Freud was one of the first to recognize the kinship between hypnosis and certain types of love; but his analysis neglects the philosophical import of these occurrences, their linkage to valuation. For me the loving stare of one human being visually glued to another signifies an extraordinary bestowal of value, an imaginative (though possibly excessive) response to the presence of another person. The lover's glance illuminates the beloved. He celebrates her as a living reality to which he attends. As in celebration of any sort, his response contributes something new and expressive. He introduces the woman into the world of his own imagination—as if, through some enchantment, she were indeed his work of art and only he could contemplate her infinite detail. As long as they intensify her presence, the lover will cherish even those features in the beloved that appraisal scorns. Does the lady have a facial blemish? To her lover it may be more fascinating than her baby blue eyes: it makes her stand out more distinctly in his memory. Does she have a sharp tongue and a biting temper? Her lover may come to relish these traits, not generally but in this particular woman. They make the image of her vivid and compelling. Even the ludicrous banalities of Odette are endearing to Swann. They show him with unmistakable clarity what she is; and though he loathes the banal, as Proust himself hated the everyday world, he obviously enjoys this opportunity to compensate for his loathing by the imaginative bestowal of unmerited value.

Speaking of suitable subjects for literature, Flaubert said: "Yvetot [a provincial town in Northern France] is as good as Constantinople." Likewise, one might say that everything that distinguishes the beloved, even her lack of distinction, may contribute to the lover's art. For that consists of taking a woman as she is, in opening oneself to the impact of her presence, at the same time that one invokes aesthetic categories that give her a new significance. By his affirmative response alone, the lover places an ordinary stone within the costliest of settings. The amorous imagination bestows value upon a person as the dramatic imagination bestows theatrical import upon an actor. If, as sometimes happens, the beloved is put on a pedestal, this is comparable to the actor being put on stage: not necessarily for purposes of adoration, but in order to concentrate, in the most imaginative way, upon the suggestive reality of her presence. The lover knows the woman is not objectively perfect, as the audience knows the actor is not Hamlet; but in attending to her as she is, he imaginatively treats her as the presentation of (what is to him) incomparable Venus.

I am sure that the similarity between love and the theater could be pushed much further. Love is the art of enjoying another person, as theater is the art of enjoying dramatic situations. Because it inevitably suggests the possibility of *enjoyment*, love is the most frequent theme in all entertainments based on human relations: it is the only subject that interests everyone. Nevertheless, the analogy between love and the theater can also be misleading. The actor portrays a character; the beloved does not portray anything, though she may symbolize a great deal. The beloved is not an *image* of perfection in the sense in which an actor is an image or representation of Hamlet. The lover uses his imagination to appreciate the beloved as she is, to accept her in herself; but the audience uses the actor as a vehicle for the fiction. That is why an actor can only rarely look his audience in the eye. In so direct a communication his presence crowds out his aesthetic function, and we respond to him as the person he happens to be, not as the character he represents. On the other hand, lovers may well be stereotyped (as they are often photographed or painted) in a joint posture of immediate confrontation, face to face, each searching for the other's personality, each peering into the other's eyes: "Our eyebeams twisted, and did thread / Our eyes, upon one double string."

This fundamental difference between love and the theater may help to explain some of the emotional difficulties actors often feel. Like everyone else the actor wants to be loved for himself; but his audiences know him only through the roles he portrays. He senses that what they "love" is really the characters or at best his characterizations, certainly no more than that part of himself which goes into making the characters present. Succeeding as an actor, he may even identify with the type of character he best portrays. That may give him an opportunity to express much of his own personality, but the role he lives will often mask his deepest inclinations and make it difficult for anyone to respond to him as a person. For similar reasons, to which I shall return, I fail to see how Plato could be talking about the love of persons when he says that the lover sees in the beloved an "image" or "representation" of absolute beauty. Plato uses this idea to argue that all lovers are really in love with the absolute. Might we not also say that the lovers he has in mind are simply incapable of loving another person?

In love, as in the theater, imagination manifests itself in a particular set or disposition. A carpenter who happens to overhear a rehearsal may surely know that the man on stage is playing Hamlet. But he does not respond to the actor *as if* he were Hamlet. Preoccupied with his own work, the carpenter is not an audience: he has not put himself into a dramatic channel. Neither does an experimenter affirm the being of a person whom he observes with scientific detachment. He devotes himself to the experiment, not to the individual under observation. He may take the subject as is, but only in the sense of being impartial about his data. By detaching himself, the scientist refuses to enter into the relationship required for love. Through love one person *attaches* himself to another, and in ways that reveal his own personality as well as the other's. The reality of the beloved glows with a sense of importance that emanates from the lover and increases dynamically when love is reciprocal. Or is glow too vibrant a word? Love is not always ecstatic; and even its poetry is often prosaic. There are quiet, comfortable, humdrum loves as well as the rhapsodic ones that seem to accompany inexperience. Love has infinite modulations, all possible degrees of intensity, and endless variety in its means of imaginative expression.

It is even through the amorous imagination that one person becomes sexually attractive to another. Our instincts alone would not enable us to love or even to lust in the way that human beings do. At least not the *obvious* instincts, e.g., the mechanism of genital excitement. Possibly the bestowing of value is itself instinctive. It need not be learned, and it would seem to be universal in man. Everyone feels the need for some loving relationship. All people crave a society of their own making, different from the one to which they were born. That is why love is always a threat to the status quo, and sometimes subversive. Lovers create their own affective universe. When the amorous imagination ricochets back and forth—each person seeing himself as both lover and beloved—a new totality results, an interacting oneness. The human species could survive without the art of the theater, or of painting, or of literature, or of music; but man would not be man without the art of mutual love. In that sense, the amorous imagination, more than any other, shows us both what we are and what, ideally, we may become.

In the remainder of this book, I shall study the concepts of bestowal and appraisal as they have entered into the history of philosophy. I shall use them to explicate the nature of love as both a psychological attitude and a moral ideal, but above all, as an artifact of the human imagination.

2

Idealization in Freud
and Santayana

Iɴ Dɪsᴄᴜssɪɴɢ Lᴏᴠᴇ Aꜱ Aɴ imaginative use of both appraisal and bestowal, I have been analyzing the attitude itself. Let us now put it into relation with the rest of life. Once we do that, we see that *the* attitude of love turns into a *range* of attitudes having a different suitability for different persons. Though it combines bestowal and appraisal, love varies with the individual and objective values of the object as well as with the nature of the lover's bestowal. For most men it is easier to bestow value upon a beautiful rather than an ugly woman. But would it not be better to love an ugly one if that enabled us to satisfy a greater network of needs and desires? This is the moral of a Calypso song: "Therefore, from a logical point of view, / Always marry a woman uglier than you." The song justifies its disdain for objective beauty by enumerating the personal advantages that ugly women provide and beautiful ones do not. The argument implies that these benefits outweigh those that beautiful women provide and ugly ones do not. Even if this were not the case, however, an ugly woman might still be preferable for a man who enjoyed bestowing value on her. Love itself alters the beloved's individual value, and sometimes very considerably.

None of this will surprise us if we think of love not as an abstract possibility but as a practical reality requiring decisions about oneself and about one's environment. To assume that all acts of bestowal are equally good would be sheer lunacy. There is a scene in which Don

Quixote makes a helmet, which he then tests to see whether it can withstand a blow. The helmet immediately comes to pieces. The Don patches it together and tests no more: "Instead, he adopted it then and there as the finest helmet ever made." Don Quixote is not mad in making the helmet. That is an act of imagination, and so creative. But in pretending that the helmet is perfectly functional, he shows an eagerness to delude himself. To think that a bestowal, *any* bestowal, is justifiable without testing would be madness of a similar sort. A character in Byron says that to a man love is something apart, to a woman her entire existence. But love can also exist in the company of many attitudes that contribute to the good life. Love need not be—and should not be—either separate or exclusive. If it does not belong to a larger pattern of purposiveness, love is not worth having. For *no* interest, not even the enjoyment of other persons, is self-validating. Each must be subjected to a moral appraisal that, looking before and after, estimates its effect upon the well-being of one's life as a whole. Loving a person may be desirable in some circumstances, catastrophic in others. What is beneficial to a particular lover at a particular time might be extremely harmful at all other times—to him, to the beloved, and sometimes to the society at large.

In raising such problems, we consider whether and how the attitude of love may or may not be worth cultivating. We examine love as an ideal for human beings. In pursuing ideals generally, we commit ourselves to a way of life and try to become a particular kind of person. We foster certain interests and withdraw from others, praise actions that sustain our aspiration, and discourage the rest. If love were the highest ideal, it would take precedence over every other guide to conduct. To the extent that one became a loving person, one would feel a completeness in life; to the extent that one failed, no other achievements would count for very much.

But if love is to function as an ideal, particularly the highest ideal, we must have criteria for succeeding in this aspiration. Given the diversity of the attitude, we need to know wherein its desirability consists for each individual case. We need answers to various questions. For instance, is there a "true" as opposed to a "false" or "specious" love? If so, how do we make the distinction? Is there an object uniquely appropriate to love? In talking first about houses and then about people, I have implicitly distinguished between the love of things and the love of persons. To these we shall presently add the love of ideals. Now, are these three types of love reducible among themselves; and if so, which remains as ultimate? If they are not reducible, which one is best or most desirable? And what are their relations to each other? Furthermore, the attitude of love being composite, how are we to order the elements within it? To make ourselves into loving persons, how much importance must we give to bestowal as against individual and objective appraisal? Is that love superior or inferior which bestows itself upon objects of great objective value? Or great individual value? And how are we to determine which these are since bestowal itself affects the object's value? Finally, why should the attitude of love be singled out as the highest ideal? Is it even defensible as *an* ideal? Is even the truest love really worth cultivating?

These are questions about the *ideal* of love. In answering them, however, philosophers have rarely separated the ideal from the attitude. Perhaps this was inevitable, given the semantic confusions in the use of words like "love." As I have remarked, the term is notoriously ambiguous: sometimes honorific and morally positive, denoting an ideal condition that may fall short of perfection but can never be bad; at other times neutral, morally uncommitted, refer-ring to a wide spectrum of responses—everything from sexual yearning to ascetic renunciation—regardless of good, bad, or in-different. Traditionally philosophers have employed both mean-ings without admitting the fact of ambiguity. Indeed they have often tried to reduce the different senses of the word "love" to a single meaning that best suited their doctrinal position. To the Platonists "real love," being a search for absolute beauty or goodness, must be good itself; to the Freudians (for they, too, are philosophers in this area) love is "really" amoral sexuality, though usually sublimated and deflected from its coital aim. There would be no confusion if each thinker limited himself to whatever meaning he preferred, clearly demarcating his verbal convention. But philosophers are too ambitious for that. The Platonist argues that even sexuality belongs to a search for the ideal, and otherwise would not be called love in *any* sense. The Freudian derives all ideals from attempts to satisfy organic needs, so that whatever Plato recommends must also be reducible to love as sexuality.

Both types of philosophers do well to be ambitious. If one *could* reduce the ideal to the attitude, or vice versa, the problems of life would be much simpler. I shall not try to resolve the issue here, but I shall argue that Platonists and Freudians alike have misinterpreted *both* the attitude and the ideal. Each approach effects a reduction through a concept of "idealization." By examining the senses they give that word and then suggesting an alternative usage, I hope to construct something more defensible than any reductivism.

In our age Platonism survives in the philosophy of George Santayana. For Santayana, as for Plato, all love worthy of the name must have an "ideal object." Lovers seek in one another the embodiment of "an ideal form essentially eternal and capable of endless embodiments." This "form," or "essence" as Santayana was later to call it, is the abstract possibility of some perfection. If a man falls in love with a fair-haired woman, he does so because his heart has been captured by the ideal of a perfect blonde. It is this ideal object, not the woman "in her unvarnished and accidental person," that the man truly loves. And as the man loves a woman for the sake of an ideal that she suggests, so too does he love ideals for the sake of "the principle of goodness" that gives all goods their ultimate meaning.

This much of Santayana's philosophy is clearly Platonistic, though in some ways it sounds more like Renaissance interpretations of Plato than like Plato himself. In any event, Santayana supplements his Platonism with a naturalistic theory of value. Unlike Plato, he refuses to accord the ideal objects of love an independent status in reality. They are all essences, and so eternal as possibilities, but their ideality consists in the fact that men *use* them to guide human conduct. Like other naturalists, Santayana analyzes value in terms of human desire: men want certain things in order to survive or satisfy an interest, and these they call "good." By extrapolating beyond the goods that are actually available in nature, humanity brings ideals into existence as part of its struggle with the environment. Through the imagination, as Santayana shows in various books, man envisages possibilities that would endlessly delight if only they could be had. According to Santayana, however, these perfections must always remain unattainable. For they are merely essences that lead us on; they cannot be realized and would not be perfect if they were. In effect, the ideal objects are but the offspring of aspiration itself. They issue from the imagination of creatures who live in the realm of matter as well as in the realm of spirit. Expressing a natural impulse but seeking perfections that transcend all existent beings, love is—in different ways—both Platonistic and naturalistic: "There can be no philosophic interest in disguising the animal basis of love, or in denying its spiritual sublimations, since all life is animal in its origin and all spiritual in its possible fruits."

In the course of this book I shall be studying other (and purer) versions of Platonism; but Santayana's I find especially useful at this point because of its reliance upon the imagination. Without the imagination, in Santayana though *not* in Plato, there could be no love. Imagination not only fabricates human ideals but also enables one to subsume the beloved under them. This latter function Santayana calls "idealization." In accordance with its animal base, love originates in instinct; but instinct falls short of what Santayana means by love. He says that love always requires a process of idealization, the idealizing of what otherwise would merely be an object in nature. Santayana speaks of men and women being propelled toward one another by material forces that control their appetites, their desires, their sexual inclinations. He then goes on to show how different all this is once love intervenes. In an imaginative act the lover uses the beloved as a reminder of some ideal object that she approximates. His love expresses a dual devotion: first to the ideal object, itself an effect of man's imagination; and second to the beloved, whom he appreciates as the partial embodiment of beauty or goodness. By seeing the woman as the epiphany of some ideal, the lover dignifies the beloved beyond those accidental properties that constitute her natural condition. In Santayana's terminology he *idealizes* her—and does so by means of the imagination.

For Santayana, then, love is an imaginative search for unattainable ideal objects. No human being—or even the Venus de Milo—can *perfectly* exhibit the qualities that have evolved as an ideal of female beauty. This ideal object does not exist. It belongs to the imagination, where it has been nurtured by a formal genesis that transmutes the natural into the perfect. But when a man loves a woman, Santayana says, his imagination idealizes her in the sense that it allows her to represent the ideal, ignoring her shortcomings for the sake of enjoying whatever perfections she imperfectly embodies. In this fashion love changes a sexual object into an idealized one. What was formerly a striving for instinctual gratification now becomes an imaginative yearning for perfection; and in further transmutations the instinctual interest may even disappear. After all, it was only an animal prod, though in the order of nature a necessary prelude to love. In the final analysis, Santayana remains a Platonist at heart. As he defines it, love may idealize another person, but *really* it is only the ideal objects that anyone loves.

At the opposite extreme, Freud too characterizes love as "idealization." But he means something very different from what the Platonists have in mind. Freud equates idealization with "overestimation" or "overvaluation" of a sexual object. Words like "sex" and "sexual" he uses very broadly. Occasionally they signify instinctual and overt desire for coitus; more often, however, they refer to interests that may conduce to sexuality in the narrow sense but need not be genital in themselves. Through sublimation the erotic instinct may even be directed toward an aim quite remote from sexual intercourse. The motivation will still be sexual in the narrow sense, Freud maintains, but since the instinctual aim has been deflected or inhibited, its true character may never show itself. The objects of a sublimated interest are most easily idealized, and Freud thinks of love as generally aim-inhibited to some extent. Even when the sexual instinct has not been sublimated, the overestimation of the object is "only in the rarest cases" limited to the genitals. Overvaluation applies to every aspect of the body and personality of the beloved, to "all sensations emanating from the sexual object." The phenomenon itself Freud describes as follows: "Idealization is a process that concerns the [sexual] *object*; by it that object, without any alteration in its nature, is aggrandized and exalted in the subject's mind"; "The same overvaluation spreads over into the psychological sphere: the subject becomes, as it were, intellectually infatuated (that is, his powers of judgment are weakened) by the mental achievements and perfections of the sexual object and he submits to the latter's judgments with credulity"; "overvaluation—the fact that the loved object enjoys a certain amount of freedom from criticism, and that all its characteristics are valued more highly than those of people who are not loved, or than its own were at a time when it itself was not loved. If the sensual impulses are somewhat more effectively repressed or set aside, the illusion is produced that the object has come to be sensually loved on account of its spiritual merits, whereas on the contrary these merits may really only have been lent to it by its sensual charm. . . . The tendency which falsifies judgment in this respect is that of *idealization*."

In order to explain why idealization occurs, Freud introduces the concept of *narcissism* as the primal condition underlying all states of love. To the infant the first sexual object is himself, his own body, his own vital functions as an organism trying to stay alive. At a time when Freud distinguished between sexual instincts and ego-instincts (those concerned with self-preservation), he argued that the former must initially depend upon the latter. The infant would then really have two sexual objects: himself and whoever took care of him, whoever preserved and protected him—the mother or her substitute. Eventually the sexual instincts would separate from the ego-instincts, but in a way that normally retained the original protective objects. The fact of narcissism would thus remain constant: "We postulate a primary narcissism in everyone." In cases of perversion the sexual object is nothing but oneself, oneself to the exclusion of everything else, as it is for the infant. But even when an object has been chosen on the model of the mother, the motivation is still fundamentally narcissistic. The individual loves another person on the basis of his own need for protection, his own need to be tended and preserved, his own need to be satisfied in every respect—in short, his own need for *being* loved. According to Freud, all love is reducible to a desire *to be* loved: every interest in another object is just a circuitous device for satisfying self-love.

In this connection Freud argues that idealization, the overvaluation of the beloved, must have originated when the child's narcissistic love was first transferred from the self to another sexual object. Since it is really oneself one wishes to love, sexual overvaluation of something else appears to Freud as "a state suggestive of a neurotic compulsion, which is thus traceable to an impoverishment of the ego as regards libido in favor of the love-object." The libido itself Freud describes as a quantity of energy (sexual in the broadest sense) that may be piped to any object. The more it is channeled away from the self, as in sexual overestimation of another person, the less there remains for the ego of the lover. Normal love, what Freud calls "true object-love," must therefore be an impoverishment of the self. It is not only an "illusion" and a "logical blinding" about the reality of the beloved, but also a waste of energy—as if indeed it were a neurotic compulsion.

Analyzed in these terms, love would seem to be psychologically hopeless. But Freud also believes that the libido may flow back through other people as well as out to them. This opens new, and more constructive, possibilities. As the self develops, the pressures of external realities force it to give up its primary narcissism. The child comes to realize his relative unimportance in the world. He learns that other people—particularly the parents—expect him to change in many ways. As the child identifies himself with these outside demands, he constructs what Freud calls an "ego ideal"—his conception of what he would like to be. Since the ego ideal originates as a yielding to repressive forces in the environment, it drains away libido much as the loved object might; but as the child internalizes the ego ideal, he uses it to afford himself a new kind of narcissistic love. By fulfilling his ideals, a man restores to himself the sense of importance, even omnipotence, which the infant originally had. Furthermore, the ego ideal causes one to choose just those sexual objects that promise to reinstate the primary narcissism. To realize that promise is to meet the requirements of self-love through an object that gratifies doubly: for it satisfies the ego ideal as well as the sexual instinct. The circuit of libido is then complete; one's desire to be loved has been accomplished through loving someone else; and adult happiness now becomes possible: "The return of the libido from the object to the ego and its transformation into narcissism represents, as it were, the restoration of a happy love, and conversely an actual happy love corresponds to the primal condition in which object-libido and ego-libido cannot be distinguished."

The notion of coalescence between object- and ego-libido doubtless owes much to Platonistic ideas about union, to which we shall recur; but no Platonist could accept the Freudian doctrine as it stands. Freud himself merely confused matters when he claimed that what psychoanalysis calls sexuality in the wider sense coincides with "the all-inclusive and all-preserving eros of Plato's *Symposium*." For Platonic eros is the desire for that absolute good or beauty which Plato considered objectively real, logically prior to everything that exists, eternal, unchanging, and perfectly unitary. Platonic eros searches for *the* ideal, of which there can only be one, as there is only one universe and one reality. Freudian eros, however, is just libidinal energy programmed by biological necessity, generating whatever ego ideals the environment requires, polymorphously perverse except as repression channelizes it, similar to instinct in other animals and in no sense transcendental.

Santayana mediates between Freud and Plato. He resembles Freud in owing more to nineteenth-century romanticism than either he or Freud (reacting against it) realized. Like Freud, Santayana considers values as data within the world of nature; and like him too, Santayana derives all ideals from human interest in the sense that nothing could be an ideal except in relation to *some* need or desire. Santayana's ideal objects are just imagined satisfactions, and authoritative only as human beings choose to make them so. At the same time, the Platonistic side of Santayana's philosophy separates it from Freudian analysis. Once they have been chosen, Santayana's ideal objects function as goals that cannot be reduced to any other kind of satisfaction. They emanate from the imagination much as Freud's ego ideals emerge from the libido, but they are not devices for restoring a primal condition of narcissism. Nor are they really dependent upon the imagination for their being. As essences, they enjoy the same timeless independence as all logical possibilities. The imagination lights upon them, making them graphic to aspiration and so enabling them to *serve* as ideals; but they are what they are, like the Platonic forms, whether or not someone wishes to follow their guidance. The ideal objects are discovered perfections, relative to some interest without being reducible to any. They are certainly not reducible to self-love.

According to Freud, ideals are *merely* substitutes for the lost omnipotence of early childhood. As such, they make no sense apart from their psychogenesis in the development of individual human beings. They are not imagined perfections, but only techniques for instinctual satisfaction. They do not disclose what man really wants, only what his struggle with a hostile environment has forced upon him. According to Santayana, ideal objects are the irreducible ends of spirituality, the perfections to which man devotes himself insofar as he belongs to the realm of spirit as well as to the realm of matter. They are not objective in the way that Plato thought, for Santayana allows each man to choose his own ideals as determined by his own interests. But neither are they substitutes for anything else. They are not explicable in terms of infant needs, and only in the order of causation do they depend upon anything like the libido. The satisfactions they offer are not instinctual, but distinctively human nevertheless.

As a result, Santayana's concept of idealization is really very different from Freud's—despite the superficial similarity. Freud makes it quite clear that only persons who fulfill infantile conditions of narcissism, either directly or indirectly, can be idealized. That the beloved should be uniquely irreplaceable he explains by reference to the child's experience: "For no one possesses more than one mother, and the relation to her is based on an event that is not open to any doubt and cannot be repeated." From this it follows that loving anyone other than the mother can only be idealization in the sense of *over*estimation, *over*valuation, blinded judgment, excessive credulity, etc. No one can bring back the goddess of his childhood; and since that is how the Freudian lover must envisage his beloved, love can only involve illusion, even delusion—in any event, some fault of reasoning.

For Santayana, however, love need not be irrational. As an act of the imagination, it enables us to see the beloved under the aspect of an ideal, to respond to her as an image or symbol of perfection without necessarily being deceived. As in Plato love is the striving for ultimate goodness, so too does Santayana use it to illustrate how "human reason lives by turning the friction of material forces into the light of ideal goods." Where Freud is a debunker, concerned to show that values have no significance beyond the libidinal circumstances in which they arise, Santayana accords reason and the imagination—in general, the life of spirit—an ambiguous autonomy. They evolve in the course of nature and depend upon it for material support; but in revealing ideal objects relative to some human interest, they disclose new perfections, conceivable goods not reducible to any prior condition, possibilities that may at any moment become the goals of future developments in mankind. What Santayana calls the "pure heart" says: "I love, I do not ask to be loved." On the Freudian analysis, such dedication to an ideal can only be a disease of the mind, an intellectual confusion cunning in its ecstasies but obscuring one's real desires. If Freud were to counter Santayana's remark, he would have the *real* heart reply: "I ask to be loved and cannot love for any other reason."

The adequate study of love in either Freud or Santayana I must leave for its proper place within the history of modern thought. I have introduced them here as a way of approaching the concept of idealization. In each case, the analysis of idealization offers an insight into love as an attitude as well as an ideal. The analyses being different, so too are the resultant insights. But in one crucial respect the formulations are alike: they both reduce the love of persons to something else. For Freud, loving another person comes down to self-love, and every beloved must be a mere substitute for that person who loved us when we were incapable of loving anyone but ourselves. For Santayana, the beloved is a replica of some chosen perfection to which we dedicate ourselves and for the sake of which we submit to the accidental person through whom it shines. And as

Freud wishes to disintoxicate us from an overvalued object that can only befuddle the intellect, so too does Santayana recommend that "abstraction from persons" which is essential for loving the ideal: "Too much subjection to another personality makes the expression of our own impossible, and the ideal is nothing but a projection of the demands of our imagination." Both Freud and Santayana address themselves to the same question: "What is it that the lover really desires in another person?" Freud thinks it must be access to primal narcissism; Santayana thinks it must be approach to imagined perfections.

I myself have no alternative answer to offer. At least not as the question is formulated. Instead I suggest there is something wrong with the question itself. It seems to ask about love but is really limited to desire. And—as I have already argued—loving is not the same as desiring. We desire things or persons for what they can give us, for satisfactions we hope they will provide. In loving anyone, however, we take an interest in that person *himself*, as a person and not merely as a vehicle to something else. Unless the beloved satisfied needs and desires, we might never have come to love her. Yet love itself does not duplicate these interests: it adds a new one, an interest in the object as an independent being whose separate importance we now affirm. However much we may go *through* the beloved, as Freud and Santayana suggest, we *love* her as an opaque reality arresting our attention, forcing our imagination to find the appropriate manner of responding to *her*.

Each in his own way, Freud and Santayana neglect the role of bestowal. They perceive the relationship between love and valuation, but they assume that valuation must be appraisal. Thus, when Freud equates love with idealization, he falls back on stock ideas about the irrationality of lovers. He observes that erotic emotions often cause mistaken judgments about the excellence of another person, that sensuous charms are frequently rationalized as spiritual attainments, that people under the spell of passion behave with infinite and unjustified credulity. These are undeniable facts, attested to by everyone who has ever written about human nature. But it does not follow that idealization *in this sense* defines the nature of love. Freud thinks that it must because he never ventures beyond the concept of appraisal. He is rightly appalled to see how badly some people who are said to be "in love" appraise one another's qualities. From this he concludes that love must be illusory, an emotional distorting of appraisal, an autistic way of judging the beloved to be better than she really is.

What Freud misses is the play of imagination in love and its creativity, its ability to bestow a new value apart from any that may be correctly or incorrectly appraised. Freud describes how one of his children used to listen to fairy tales and then ask, "Is that a true story?" Learning that the story was not true, the child would turn away with an air of disdain that Freud approvingly calls a "marked sense of reality." But what an unimaginative child! And *do* we have a sense of reality if the logic of fiction or the playfulness of emotion eludes our comprehension? What a diminished reality Freud would leave us! Even what he calls "happy love" would have to be illusory: for though self-love would then triumph via love for someone else, we would merely have a double dose of idealization—overvaluing ourselves through narcissism at the same time that we overvalued someone else through object-love. The idea that happy love depends upon massive self-deception Freud inherits from Romantic thinkers who considered love a peculiar way of knowing, remarkably given to erroneous appraisals since it always follows the joyous but unreliable feelings of the heart. For them love is good emotion, whatever its defects as science or metaphysics. That part of their belief Freud finds unacceptable, but he retains the assumption that love is illusory.

For his part, Santayana understands the nature of imagination as well as anyone. Yet he restricts it to an area in which appraisal dominates to the exclusion of bestowal. His "ideal object" is an imagined perfection and therefore a standard against which to test the relative excellence of something. If one were appraising objective value, one might conceivably keep such standards in mind. In a beauty contest the judges *could* reach their decision by comparing each contestant with some ideal type of femininity. They would use the imagination both in choosing the ideal and in determining how each woman approached it. But theirs would not be the loving attitude. For the judges must *not* bestow a special value upon any of the contestants. In principle at least, they must keep their personal bestowals in abeyance and remain faithful to the ideal type. In treating the beloved as an end, however, the lover has no need to compare her with anything else. His love is not a way of ranking her in relation to the ideal: he cares about *her as a particular person* despite her imperfections, despite her inevitable distance from any or all ideals. The lover uses his imagination not to see an ideal object reflected through another person, but rather to find ways of acting *as if* that person were herself the ideal. What does this mean? Not that the beloved impersonates an ideal or even that she reminds the lover of it. It merely means that the lover has bestowed incalculable value upon her, that he responds to her with great and positive affirmation. His attitude is more than just appraisive. And even in appraisal, Santayana is wrong to think that decisions are made by determining the approximation to an ideal object. Our standards are rarely that precise. The judges in a beauty contest would be hard put to describe the qualities of the perfect female. And how many lovers could?

In one place Santayana claims that without idealization of *his* sort love would not be love; it would be only "a friendly and humorous affection." I disagree. What makes friendly affection into love is not a search for dubious ideal objects, but simply a greater and more extensive bestowal of value. In another place he says that love "penetrates to possibilities not to facts." But what are these possibilities? Are they real potentialities of the beloved or just abstract essences, logically self-consistent but unrelated to what the beloved *is*? If the latter, why call it love? The attitude sounds more like a subtle form of aggression against the reality of another person. In the endless realm of possibilities everyone can always be different, and infinitely better than he happens to be. But we do not show our love by imagining these ideal abstractions, except where they reveal what the other person actually is and what he himself desires. In this sense, possibilities cannot be separated from facts. The attempt to do so indicates that the supposed beloved is not really an object of love. Santayana's thinking about idealization may teach us how to use persons as a way of loving ideals, but not how to use ideals as a way of loving persons.

Thus, as analysts of love—attitude or ideal—I find Freud and Santayana somewhat deficient. Each espouses a different kind of reductivism, based however upon a similar mistake about valuation. But possibly there is another way in which their ideas may be taken. Perhaps we do best to consider Freud and Santayana as *moralists*. Not narrow-minded preachers to be sure, but men who are *making* ideals in the very process of analyzing them as they arise out of human attitudes. Freud and Santayana give us criteria for a life worth living. They answer questions about the desirability of love and so create new ideals to guide ethical choice. Quite obviously Freud is advocating, not merely describing, what he calls "mature love" or "fully normal" love. He sees a danger in love that does not satisfy our *deepest* needs and desires. He disapproves of love that will not submit to realistic appraisal. He minimizes the pleasures of bestowal because he thinks they are less conducive to human welfare than the satisfying of other instincts. But who is to define the nature of human welfare? This is not a psychological or a scientific concept, but a moral one. Freud's ideas about love belong to an orientation that generates its own morality—in his case, principles of sanity and healthy functioning in nature. Even to speak of love as *overvaluing* is to presuppose a standard of what is really worthwhile, to affirm a certain way of life as best for man. We may well agree with Freud, but to do so is to commit ourselves to comparable ideals as well as empirical analyses.

The same is true of Santayana. He too speaks as a moralist, advocating an ideal of love and not merely talking about it. In characterizing "true love," Santayana offers criteria for achieving the good life through a particular use of the imagination. In defining the word "love" as the search for embodied perfections, he reinforces his commitment to this as opposed to any other way of living. Romantic philosophers had often glorified a love of imperfections and the destructive element, as if appraisal had nothing to do with love, as if all bestowals were equally justifiable. Freud and Santayana rightly attack these ideas, each stressing his own kind of appraisal. Santayana tends to favor objective appraisal, just as Freud gives greater importance to individual appraisal. Santayana subordinates the love of persons to the love of ideals; Freud subordinates both to the love of self or self-gratification. Adhering to one or the other thinker, we would live different lives. For though in some respects the attitude of love might retain a similar structure, it would be used to serve different ideals. Within their historical context, Freud and Santayana have constructed these ideals for us.

The creating of an ideal of love, the giving (or expressing) of criteria that indicate the desirability of some type of love, I shall call "idealization." I use the same word as Freud and Santayana because I wish to incorporate their ideas within a more comprehensive approach. As appraisal is a part of love, overvaluing and the search for perfection may *sometimes* accompany it. Neither of these is definitive, however, and that has been the basis of my criticism. By introducing the concept of bestowal, I try to offer a more general theory of love than either Freud's or Santayana's. Correspondingly, I shall give a broader reference to idealization. I shall use it to describe not only what lovers do in devoting themselves to their beloved but also what philosophers do when they formulate theories about the nature of love. In both cases idealization will mean the *making* of ideals.

3

Love as Idealization

In Distinguishing Between appraisal and bestowal, I began with a discussion about the love of things, then persons, then ideals. Though very far from being identical, these concepts overlap. A house, a car, even a suit of clothes may seem to have a personality of its own; a person may embody a desired way of life, inspire emulation, and bear within himself the charismatic mana of a moral principle; ideals may harden into substantial presences, like things, and even assert their dignity by demanding proper names, as if they too were persons. And yet we easily recognize that the love of things is not the same as the love of persons and that the love of ideals differs from both. We do not expect things to respond to us in the way that we respond to them. Our love of things is never mutual and we know that a thing's "personality" has largely been bestowed by us. We therefore allow ourselves greater freedom in using things, subordinating their separate existence to our own desires with little or no compunction. If the object were *merely* instrumental, we could not be said to love it even as a thing. But in bestowing the relevant value upon such objects, we cannot hope to satisfy *them*; and so we do not think of their welfare or well-being—as we would in the love of persons.

It is the logic of this distinction that informs Shakespeare's wit in the wooing scene of *Henry V*. Katharine, the French princess, says (in broken English): "Is it possible dat I sould love de enemy of France?" To this Henry replies by playing upon the difference between the

39

love of things and the love of persons, thereby assuring Katharine that his love for her is not reducible to his love for the country he has just taken as a possession: "No; it is not possible you should love the enemy of France, Kate: but, in loving me, you should love the friend of France; for I love France so well that I will not part with a village of it; I will have it all mine: and Kate, when France is mine and I am yours, then yours is France and you are mine."

The love of persons and the love of ideals may also interweave, though they too must not be confused with one another. To the mythic mind they may *seem* to coalesce, as when the highest good is given a name and revered as a deity, or when a poet addresses his beloved as the personification of universal beauty. Even on these occasions the two types of love are distinguishable. At best they have occurred together, possibly reinforcing each other. At worst there is only one type of love, though the lover's sheer emotion may fool him into thinking there are two. Unlike persons, ideals are inherently elusive: for they must lead on to unforeseeable satisfactions. By their very nature they recede in the way that the horizon does. We project them as imaginary carrots before real donkeys. But persons are concrete: they loom before us as the *someone* to whom we must attend. When Mallory was asked why he climbed a mountain, he replied: "Because it is there." Well, human nature is such that persons are always *there*. The love of persons enables us to respond to them; the love of ideals often helps in this, but sometimes hinders.

As a generic concept idealization applies to all three types of love—though in different ways. The miser idealizes money, the lover idealizes some particular woman, the moralist idealizes a pattern of feeling or behavior (which we then call "an ideal"). Each abstracts a partial aspect of the world and orders his being in accordance with it. Each bestows value in a manner that gives the object pervasive power over human responses. Feelings, beliefs, actions—one's life itself—may receive a new orientation, a continual readjustment that keeps the lover in orbit about the object of his bestowal. To those who love the ideals of poverty or charity, the love of money may seem to be the root of all evil. To those who love another person (or themselves), the love of any ideal may well seem desiccated and inhuman. Nothing prevents the three types from cooperating; but since each is governed by its own idealization, they frequently conflict. In principle, however, all lovers do something similar: they idealize a portion of man's experience and use it to guide further responses. Within each attitude the chosen object will appear uniquely real and significant. In extreme cases it may be treated as more authoritative than anything else. Men sometimes speak the truth when they say that their beloved *is* their ideal. For love magnifies the object, giving it predominant importance in some or all of the lover's life and outlook. This may often be an overvaluation, but not necessarily.

Idealization is not limited to our relations with human beings. It also occurs in philosophical reasoning. It almost seems to be a constant in the history of philosophy, particularly the philosophy of love. Whether they are defining the attitude or the ideal of love, whether they prefer a love of persons or things or ideals, whether they speak as self-conscious moralists or quasi-scientists—in almost all cases, philosophers have *created* one or another ideal of love by giving criteria abstracted from their own experience. However objective their analyses, they idealize what matters most to them as human beings surrounded by their own emotional bestowals. Their words reverberate within a world constructed by idealizations that they themselves may never recognize. Possibly this is true of all philosophy: certainly it holds for metaphysics, probably for epistemology, perhaps even for logic and the philosophy of science. In the philosophy of love, idealization functions reflexively. For there philosophers talk about the very thing they are themselves enacting, idealization being (in different ways) both the form and the content of their discourse. Nor should this surprise us. After all, we live even in the process of talking about life.

When I say that philosophers idealize just as lovers do, I do not restrict myself to the "idealistic" tradition. Philosophers such as Plato, Plotinus, Augustine are idealists in believing that ultimate being sustains, indeed conforms to, human ideals. The so-called "realists"—e.g. Lucretius, Hobbes, Freud—find the universe too hostile to warrant such optimistic assumptions. They are realistic in approaching all morality as man's attempt to overcome the hazards of a nonpurposive environment. But the different traditions are alike in making new ideals of love while also investigating love; and frequently these idealizations turn out to be remarkably similar. As I have already suggested, Plato, Freud, and Santayana share many of the same idealizations. This does not prevent Plato from being an idealist, Freud a realist, and Santayana a combination of the two. It rather indicates that in the depths of their analyses even dissimilar philosophers may resemble one another more than they suspect.

Throughout this book I shall be studying love as idealization, both in life and in the writings of philosophers. At the same time, however, let us try to understand what these great men *thought* they were doing. Even if I am right in saying that they idealize, most philosophers had other intentions in their work. They sought to tell us truths about man and his environment, to show us the inner constitution of reality and how a good life might be managed. I do not diminish this aspect of their thinking; I merely wish to accommodate it within a larger framework. No philosopher does *just* one job. Neither should we.

In tracing philosophical idealization, I shall pursue a general hypothesis about love in the Western world. I suggest that the philosophy of love stems from two principal sources: on the one hand Plato, his followers, and his critics; on the other hand Christianity arising out of Judaism and merging with Greek philosophy begun by Plato. Beneath these two foundations, however, there existed an undeveloped mass of native ideas about both the attitude and the ideal of love. Greek and Christian thinking changed the character of these ideas immensely. What in primitive religions had served to idealize the natural functions of man now became a means of transcending nature. Love turned into a *super*natural device, and in Christianity it became the very essence of God. In the ancient and the medieval world philosophical idealizations were primarily transcendental. And possibly the concept of love could not have developed without passing beyond a purely naturalistic reference. But magnificent as they were, the idealizations of transcendental love could scarcely satisfy men who wanted to live in nature, to exercise their fullest capacities, to love one another authentically as human beings. At the very moment that religious love was reaching its apogee in the Middle Ages, a different type of idealization was also being created.

Beginning with the troubadours in Southern France, courtly love evolved over a period of five hundred years, from the twelfth to the seventeenth century. Like love in the ancient world and religious love in the Middle Ages, courtly love was an intricate network of diverse, even conflicting, idealizations. Through them all, however, love tended to return to its naturalistic origins. In various ways, courtly love is the humanization of Christian and Platonic love. What the transcendental idealizations had tried to achieve by getting beyond nature, courtly love duplicated on the level of human relations *in* nature. Not God or the Good but other men and women became the object of devotion. At a much later date and in a different context, Romantic love also humanized the ancient and medieval concepts of love. As with courtly love, the new idealizations were quite remote from primitive ideas about natural functions; they clearly showed the influence of Greek and Christian thinking; and yet they also continued the search for a *human* love—a love between human beings based upon the facts of human nature.

In this progression from primitive naturalism to transcendental idealization and then to humanistic love that synthesizes the other two, one might detect a Hegelian dialectic. As in all dialectical movements, each stage arouses critical antitheses with which it establishes some intimate union and generates new perceptions, new ideas, new values. (History is not a march, or even a waltz, but a game of love.) It is not surprising then that courtly love should have been criticized by Shakespeare, Montaigne, and many others who unknowingly contributed to the idealizations of Romantic love. These in turn engendered the twentieth-century attack on romanticism— as in Freud and Proust—that seems to be culminating with the "sexual revolution" in our day. Our age is one in which previous idealizations linger without being meaningful as once they were. A long tradition may be coming to an end. Or is it merely taking a new turn not yet apparent to us the participants? I myself am not pessimistic. I think we are entering a world in which new idealizations will arise from the ashes of the old. That is why the principal sources of love are still worth studying. Having mastered our heritage, we may possibly envisage a contemporary humanism more suitable to the post-Romantic world in which we live.

This sketch of what I call my general hypothesis needs several hundred pages of clarification. But in the meantime, it may answer the inevitable questions about my own idealizations. If all philosophers idealize in writing about love, am I not doing the same? Indeed I am. I do not offer a dispassionate history of ideas. I wish to *interpret* scholarly work in view of what I myself find real and important. The thinkers I examine are but a small selection from all those who have written about love; and I approach them from my own perspective. I explore the concepts of bestowal and appraisal as they have developed in the writings of earlier philosophers. I choose these concepts because I think they may be useful in constructing a new philosophy of love. I speak of a contemporary humanism "more suitable" to our age. But of course that means the present-day world as *I* experience it, the past as it has filtered through *my* system of values, the future as *my own* ideals would like it to be. However objective I may succeed in being, my thought inevitably reveals a preferential vision that is itself the making of new ideals and the revising of older ones. Let us now see exactly what this entails.

Part II
Love in the Ancient World

4

Platonic Eros

ALFRED NORTH WHITEHEAD
once wrote that all Western philosophy could be read as a series of
footnotes to Plato.* To some this remark will seem to minimize the
creative originality of later philosophy. To others it will need to be
amplified by comparing a footnote to a ball and chain: one immediately thinks of editions of the classics which scholars fill with
page after page of technical minutiae as if to obscure the text, like
bureaucrats who write out lengthy reports to compensate for the
loss of a valuable document. What Whitehead had in mind is not
entirely clear. In the philosophy of love, however, I am convinced
that every discussion must *start* with Plato. Courtly love, Romantic
love, and major emphases in religious love all take root in him. They
form a single tradition, albeit internally divided, that naturalistic
and realistic writers have attacked in a variety of ways. But even
among the latter, from Lucretius to Freud, Platonic elements often
contribute to the governing mode of expression.

In view of this continuity, the presence of Platonism throughout
all Western theorizing about love, what could be more astonishing
than the assertion by recent writers that our notions of love originate
with fanciful ladies in the medieval courts! *"L'amour? une invention du
douzième siècle."* That courtly love—at least one version of it—was

*"The safest general characterization of the European philosophical
tradition is that it consists of a series of footnotes to Plato."

47

developed under the inspiration of women like Eleanor of Aquitaine and the Countess of Champagne is certainly true. But their thinking was hardly original. It represented a timely synthesis of intellectual forces long at work within the Western world. Into the synthesis went many things, among them Moorish influences, Christian dogma, and popular folklore. And much of this can be traced to Platonic origins: Moorish idealism via Avicenna and Plotinus; Christian belief via St. Augustine; popular romances via Hellenistic fables that Ovid reproduced. The philosophical source was generally Plato. Even Romantic love, which (with its critics) has dominated the modern world, can be interpreted as a vulgarization of Platonic ideals. The path is long and sinuous, but it begins in ancient Greece.

Most of Plato's ideas about love occur in the *Symposium*, or as Shelley calls it in his translation, the *Banquet*. It ranks with the greatest works of literature as well as philosophy: so much so that its achievement makes all academic distinctions between these two disciplines seem arbitrary. As a work of philosophy the *Symposium* consists of a sequence of approximations, organized approaches to the truth about the nature of love. As a work of literature it is a portrait of the man Socrates, who—more than any other person known to Plato—exemplifies love as a way of life. The portrait of Socrates is not, however, a mere illustration of the Platonic doctrine. Socrates is used to *manifest*, embody, the truth about love: he shows it forth, like Christ in the Gospels. Just by existing as he does, Socrates serves as a living proof that the human condition Plato wishes to advocate is actually possible. For all the remoteness of his abstract thinking, Plato always returns to the personal touchstone of his own experience—Socrates as a concrete individual.

But what makes Socrates especially indicative of love? Does he feel compassion for the suffering of others? Does he make altruistic sacrifices? Does he pine for some beloved, write verses, broken-heartedly weep beneath the moon? No, for true love, as Plato conceives of it, is quite different from all this. Though sociable and well-mannered, Socrates is emotionally cool, unimpassioned, involved in the life about him but also at a distance from it. Toward the beginning of the dialogue, we are told how he has dressed himself in all his finery in order to attend the banquet given by Agathon. "One must look one's best," he explains, "when one is going to visit a good-looking man." Yet on the way to Agathon's house he lags behind, abandons himself to his thoughts, and finally arrives after the dinner is half-finished. He has fallen into one of his contemplative trances, and it is quite obvious that pursuing a philosophical argument means more to him than the company of the fine young men who await him.

Near the end of the *Symposium*, Alcibiades describes Socrates in ways that further accentuate the ambivalence of his character. In a society that was frankly homosexual, Alcibiades naturally interprets Socrates' interest in him as the routine expression of physical desire. Socrates himself speaks words that could have issued from the mouth of any lover in any Western romance (making allowance for the homosexuality of the relationship). "Be ready to protect me, Agathon," he says, "for I find that the love of this fellow [Alcibiades] has become no small burden. From the moment when I first fell in love with him I haven't been able to exchange a glance or a word with a single good-looking person without his falling into a passion of jealousy and envy, which makes him behave outrageously and abuse me and practically lay violent hands on me." But in fact the basis of Socrates' love is not at all physical. The excesses of Alcibiades, the intensity and the violence of his affections, bespeak confusion as much as jealousy. He cannot understand the love of a man like Socrates, one who spends the night with him in complete chastity, who seeks to improve his mind and rejects his sexual overtures.

In this age of psychologizing, one might try to explain Socrates' behavior in terms of repression or a sense of inadequacy. How facile that would be! And how inaccurate! For Socrates is not a timid schoolmaster of some post-Victorian era; he is not an aging don inhibiting and sublimating his attraction toward handsome youths. In the Greek society to which he belonged, love was generally assumed to be a male phenomenon. Heterosexual attitudes were respected as a biological device, not a spiritual opportunity; they could be refined and humanized, but they were not a means of idealization. The revulsion that some people nowadays feel toward homosexuality, many Greeks felt toward heterosexual passion. For them nothing could be more disgusting than the spectacle of a man wasting himself in the pursuit of women. I shall return to Plato's ideas about sex, but from the outset it should be clear that the oddness of Socrates in his society cannot be explained in terms that might apply to a twentieth-century man. He differed from his contemporaries in being dedicated to a kind of love, a kind of idealization, that no one had previously envisaged. Like all great men he begins with the preconceptions of his society, using them to the fullest but also transcending them in ways that could hardly have been foreseen. It is in this that his ambivalence consists.

Starting with this idea, the treatment of love in the *Symposium* takes on a unity it might otherwise have lacked. Before Socrates presents the Platonic doctrine there are five other speeches on love, which most scholars have discarded as mere preliminaries. As a matter of fact, however, there is very little in these earlier statements that Plato would have rejected out of hand; each serves to lay a foundation for the magnificent edifice Socrates will later construct. The early speeches emanate from the mythic and traditional conceptions prevalent in Greek society. Without spurning these ideas, indeed retaining as much of them as possible, Socrates transmutes the clay of his age into philosophical gold and silver.

For instance, consider the speech of the playwright Aristophanes. He describes the nature of love by recounting an ancient myth. In the beginning the human race consisted of three sexes—the male, the female, and the hermaphroditic (which combined characteristics of both male and female). Each of these primordial human beings was spherical and had four hands, four legs, two identical faces upon a circular neck, and a single head that could turn in opposite directions. They were very powerful, but also very proud. They attacked the gods, were defeated, and would have been destroyed but for the clemency of Zeus. In order to retain the honors and sacrifices afforded the gods, he allowed the human race to continue. But to preclude the possibility of future rebellion, he weakened the spherical beings by dividing each of them in two. He also let it be known that further insolence would cause him to bisect man again, leaving the unfortunates one leg to hop on and a face that resembled a bas-relief or a profile on a tombstone.

Among our spherical ancestors love did not exist. It came into being only after they were cut in two. For then each half yearned for the part from which it had been severed. Whenever the parts encountered one another, they embraced and sought to grow together again. Nor would they separate even to seek food. The race would have died of starvation had Zeus not taken pity upon the bisected creatures. He moved the reproductive organs around so that by embracing one another some of the mortals could beget new members of the race. Previously procreation had occurred without intercourse—"by emission onto the ground, as is the case with grasshoppers."

Ever since these prehistoric events, every human being has been only half of himself, each forever seeking the opposite portion that would make him whole again. Men who are halves of the hermaphrodites are lovers of women; adulterers come from this group, also promiscuous females. Women who are halves of a feminine whole are lesbians. Males who belong to the masculine whole are lovers of men in their youth and lovers of boys when they reach maturity themselves. "Such boys and lads are the best of their generation, because they are the most manly." Love itself "is simply the name for the desire and pursuit of the whole."

Here then is a myth about love that Aristophanes could have inherited from any number of primitive sources, some of them Hindu and Babylonian. It recounts a primordial Golden Age, an Age of Heroes, when men were supermen, double their present condition. In shape they resemble Indian deities with their multiple limbs and faces; for all we know, the myth may once have represented a struggle between Eastern and Western cultures. Not only were the losers titanically powerful, strong enough to threaten the Greek gods, but also they were *whole*. They were undivided—with all that that implies, particularly to Athenians, forever questioning themselves and squabbling with their neighbors. At the same time the original beings were brutish, like giants in fairy tales or like parental figures as they often appear to children. They were uncivilized. They had neither love for one another nor piety toward the heavenly powers. They were guilty of an original sin, and in words that remind us of the fallen angel, Aristophanes says "their pride was overweening." Once they have sinned, however, they become human beings who face a characteristic moral choice: either to achieve wholeness through love or to renew their insolence toward the gods and run the danger of being diminished further.

Finally, notice the relationship between love and sex in Aristophanes' myth. The two are not essentially connected. Love is the yearning for one's other half—the other self, or alter ego—and this occurs *before* Zeus moves the reproductive organs around to make sexual intercourse possible. For Aristophanes, as for Plato, sex is a physical makeshift. It is needed for procreation in our divided state; it may provide a rudimentary union with another person; but in itself it does not explain the nature of love. Far from being sexual, love is the search for that state of wholeness in which sex did not exist. This is the point that Freud misses. He sees the myth of Aristophanes as a poetic attempt to trace "the origin of an instinct to *a need to restore an earlier state of things.*" Strictly speaking, his interpretation is correct. What Freud ignores, however, is the fact that Aristophanes refers to *two* instincts: one is indeed the sexual instinct, but the other is not. Aristophanes calls it "innate love," by which he means an instinctual search for one's other self. *This* is the instinct that originates in a need to restore an earlier state of things. The sexual instinct is merely derivative from it. Psychiatrists who revise Freud by emphasizing a nonsexual instinct for oneness are actually closer to the myth of Aristophanes. Closer yet are those Romantic philosophers who speak of an elective affinity between the lover and his fated soulmate.

Though none of this analysis occurs in Plato, the myth of Aristophanes—like other speeches in the *Symposium*—serves a definite function within the final formulation. When his turn comes to speak, Socrates comments on an unascribed "theory" to the effect that lovers are people searching for the other half of themselves. He offers an emendation that seems to be minor but really changes everything. Love is not desire for either the half or the whole "unless that half or whole happens to be good. Men are quite willing to have their feet or their hands amputated if they believe those parts of themselves to be diseased." In making this point, Socrates moves far beyond the position of Aristophanes. For if love is desire for half or whole only as they are good, the motive force in love is a yearning for goodness, not just completion. From this Socrates concludes that love is always directed toward what is good, indeed that goodness itself is the only object of love. In loving something, man is really seeking to possess the goodness which is in it. Not temporarily but permanently, not casually but with that fervent longing men have always associated with love. And so, in brief compass, we start with the primitive myth of Aristophanes and end up with the first highly sophisticated conclusion of Plato's erotic philosophy: "Love is desire for the perpetual possession of the good."

In these few words all Platonic wisdom resides. Has there ever been a more suggestive definition or an epigram about love more stimulating to the imagination? Take the first three words: love is desire. This already articulates a fundamental presupposition. For Plato, as for all the Greeks—as well as Freud and many others—man is basically acquisitive. His life is a continuous search for things that will satisfy, things that fulfill his needs and provide happiness. Man striving, man in motion, man desiring and struggling to achieve the culminating objects of his desire—this is the prime category in Plato's psychology. But then one would seem to be saying very little in saying that love is desire. For many other things would also be desire, in fact everything else in human life. Plato himself recognizes this difficulty. He wonders how such a definition can account for the fact that all men are always in a state of desire, and that to desire something is to desire the goodness which is in it, and yet that we do not speak of all men being in love. He answers himself by saying that ordinary language is confusing. In popular usage we limit the term "love" to one particular *type* of love, which is merely an instance of a more generic condition. That condition manifests itself in ways that should be called love even though the nonphilosopher fails to do so. For instance, a man who loves wisdom may not be called a lover, but in principle his state does not differ from that of a man who dotes upon another person. Both are occasions of desiring, and there is something in the nature of desire which explicates the meaning of love.

This something is, for Plato, the fact that desiring always implies a desire to have what is good. No one desires anything unless he at least *thinks* it will do him good. Though people may act out of compulsion, the compulsion itself results from a distorted search for goodness. For Plato, and this too is common to all the Greeks, it makes no sense to ask whether a man might desire something for the sake of the badness in it. No one eats bread because it is bad. Bread is eaten because it is good as bread or good for the individual who eats it or because that man thinks it is good or because he is testing it for goodness or even because he is trying to get an enemy to poison himself by making a mistake about the goodness of the bread. Whatever anyone does, whatever he desires, whatever he strives for, Plato will always explain it as a direct or circuitous means of acquiring goodness.

This being so, it would follow that all human activity is motivated by love. Since Plato believes that everything—not just man—strives for the attainment of some good, the entire universe would seem to be continuously in love. And this is precisely what Plato suggests. It is love that makes the world go round; without love nothing could exist. But though all things love and all men are in some sense lovers, few of them recognize the object of their love, that which motivates their striving, that which underlies their every desire.

This supreme object—and there must be only one, since all things make a unity—Plato calls *the Good*. He also calls it *absolute beauty*. To the Greeks, beauty was a function of harmony. It arose from a harmonious relationship between parts that could not cohere unless they were good for one another. From this Plato concludes that what is truly beautiful must be good and what is truly good must be beautiful. One who recognizes the goodness of a so-called ugly person (Socrates, for instance) will see that he is really beautiful; and despite appearances, no one who is not good can attain beauty. As the supreme object of desire, the Good (or the Beautiful) must be present in all phases of human life. It is what everyone seeks, that for the sake of which everything is sought. But few people recognize it.

In the confusion of their lives men know that they have desires, but they do not know what will satisfy. The hungry man feels the pangs of hunger, which he alleviates by eating food. He thinks of the food as the object of his desire. But once he has eaten, he desires other things—and so on, until he dies. That all his striving is motivated by a search for beauty and goodness he may never realize. To that extent, a man lives in ignorance and is incapable of loving properly. In order to do so, he must find a method for clarifying his desire, for directing it overtly and authentically toward its real objective.

A great deal of Plato's philosophy concerns itself with the discovery of this method. Dozens of pages, in the *Republic* for instance, deal with nothing else. Moral training, scientific education, spiritual discipline—everything that can show a man what he really wants—is dedicated to this end. The culminating stages Plato refused to write about, though he is said to have delivered a lecture on the Good that baffled his audience. Success in love ultimately depends upon mysterious forces and they defy human comprehension. As a way of indicating the required direction, however, Plato outlines several stages through which the ideal lover must pass. In the *Symposium* he enumerates five of them.

At the outset the lover, being young, will apply himself to the contemplation of physical beauty. He will fall in love with one particular person, whose outward form he finds especially attractive. But attractive how? Sexually? Visually? Plato does not say, but the relationship cannot be merely sexual. For he speaks of the young lovers begetting noble sentiments, "fair thoughts," in the company of one another. In any event, the tie of love is ephemeral at this stage. By moving from one beautiful person to another, the lover comes to see that physical beauty is not limited to any one beloved. He will then become a lover of physical beauty in general, much as a painter might be. Not that Plato is interested in the growth of aesthetic sensibility for its own sake. He directs the lover toward all the occasions of physical beauty in order to liberate him more effectively from any one of them. The man who loves *all* physical beauty "will relax the intensity of his passion for one particular person, because he will realize that such a passion is beneath him and of small account."

At the next stage the lover comes to realize that beauty of soul is more valuable than beauty of body. This will enable him to appreciate men who are good and beautiful even if their external appearance is unattractive. In the company of these virtuous souls, the lover will move on to a still higher stage, which is the level of social and moral beauty. Here he will contemplate the beauty of institutions and noble activities. This in turn will lead him to the study of science and the acquisition of knowledge. At this fourth stage he will finally free himself from any undue attachment to an individual instance of beauty—whether of body, soul, or society. In his love of wisdom the man who has advanced this far will bring to birth "many beautiful and magnificent sentiments and ideas, until at last, strengthened and increased in stature by his experience, he catches sight of one unique science whose object is the beauty of which I am about to speak."

That beauty is absolute beauty. It culminates the mysteries of love as it also reveals the nature of the universe. Words cannot do it justice, and yet:

> This beauty is first of all eternal; it neither comes into being nor passes away, neither waxes nor wanes; next, it is not beautiful in part and ugly in part, nor beautiful at one time and ugly at another, nor beautiful in this relation and ugly in that, nor beautiful here and ugly there, as varying according to its beholders; nor again will this beauty appear to him like the beauty of a thought or a science, or like beauty which has its seat in something other than itself, be it a living thing or the earth or the sky or anything else whatever; he will see it as absolute, existing alone with itself, unique, eternal, and all other beautiful things as partaking of it, yet in such a manner that while they come into being and pass away, it neither undergoes any increase or diminution nor suffers any change.

This series of upward steps, this ladder toward perfection, the Middle Ages would have called an *ordo salutis*, an ordered progression toward salvation. In our study of Christian love we shall encounter various versions of it. The lover starts from his immersion in the world of sense, using one kind of love after another as a vehicle, always moving upward until he achieves the only object worthy of devotion. In Christianity the ultimate experience of love is unity with God; in Platonism it is the state of illumination provided by "the supreme knowledge whose sole object is that absolute beauty."

This absolute beauty—alone with itself, unique, eternal, and such that all beautiful things partake of it—how is one to understand such a way of talking? A complete answer cannot be given here: it would require a lengthy discussion of Plato's doctrine of forms. But one can say a little that will be useful. Plato's search for absolute beauty or goodness (*the* Beautiful or *the* Good) is related to what John Dewey called "the quest for certainty." In the ordinary world, the world of natural processes, nothing is constant, nothing is permanent, nothing endures. Nature is a flux. All things change, sometimes for the better, sometimes for the worse, but inevitably everything changes and becomes something other than what it was. In time the whitest birch will die and turn gray or brown. Where then are we to find the ultimate being of a thing, the essence of a color or a tree, that which makes it what it is and enables us to know it with certainty? The nature of a birch cannot be limited to any one tree, for it must be something all birches have in common. It is therefore a "universal" rather than a particular. It cannot be limited to any point in space or moment in time since all things in space and time are subject to change. Nor can it be a function of anyone's sense experience, since another observer with different senses or a different perspective will experience the object differently. Consequently, the being of a tree must be independent of all actual trees; it must be "outside" of nature. Still, nature would have no determinate character unless it could be subsumed under the essences, infinite in number, which explicate its being.

To understand what it is for something to be white or to be a birch tree, you must grasp the *form* of whiteness or birch treeness, the abstract universal shared by everything that *is* white or a birch tree.

Because they are merely abstract universals, these forms do not exist in the sense in which actual trees or patches of color exist. But unless they had some being of their own, Plato maintains, we could not conceive of things in nature as having just those characteristics which they do have. The forms are not created by us, just as we do not create white birch trees, and neither are they dependent upon the existence of actual birch trees. Even if no birch trees ever existed, the *being* of a birch tree would remain the same. The form of a unicorn, what it is that would enable us to recognize a unicorn, is not affected by the fact that this delightful animal has never existed. Existence is merely the actualization of a form; the form, however, is real whether or not anything does exist.

Scanty as this may be, perhaps it will help to explain what Plato means when he talks about entities that are "eternal" (i.e., independent of time and space), that neither come into being nor pass away (for they do not exist and therefore cannot cease to exist), that neither wax nor wane nor vary with beholder or relationship (for they simply are what they are, the abstract being of whiteness or birch treeness), unique and alone (for there can be only a single essence for each kind of entity), and such that actual things partake of them (for all things that exist must be instances of some universal). In effect, Plato is providing a theory about the nature of definition. He is explaining how we know the meaning of a word like "white" or "birch tree." No matter how many instances of whiteness you may see, you will not know what "white" means until you are capable of abstracting, sorting out what your observations have in common. On Plato's view it is the form or essence of whiteness that white things have in common; therefore, the realm of forms *is* the reality underlying our use of words. Existence being contingent, nature being in flux, sense-experience being relative, only the forms put us in touch with the permanent character of things. They reveal the structure of the universe. Acquaintance with their ineluctable whatness satisfies our quest for certainty: they are the ultimate reality.

If this much makes sense, it will not be too difficult to take a further step, one that leads to Plato's notions about absolute good or beauty. As we have seen, knowledge about the world is always knowledge about forms. But there are different degrees of knowledge, some higher than others. To know the being of a color or a tree is less important than to know a mathematical truth or a scientific law of nature. Even more important, however, is knowledge about the meaning and orderliness of everything. If, as Plato believes, the universe is not random but purposive, the highest knowledge shows us how everything strives to attain that which is good for itself and for the fulfillment of its being. Since all things participate in a single world-order, there must be a single good for which they yearn. This is the Good or the Beautiful, absolute goodness or absolute beauty, the highest of the forms, the pinnacle of being, the ultimate category in terms of which all other realities are to be explained. It is present to all existence in the sense that everything aims for it; but its being is not limited to anything in nature or to nature itself, and the height of love consists in knowing it in its metaphysical purity. Lovers are often carried away by a sense of beauty in the beloved. Would not the greatest love disclose the secret beauty in everything, that hidden harmony which directs all being toward the best of all possible ends? The very thought of it fills the heart with joy. We all wish to elope with absolute beauty (or so Plato thinks); but to reach it we must first mount the ladder of perfection.

In the *Symposium* Plato describes the stages of ascension. In other dialogues he locates the ladder within a more general doctrine about human nature. The *Phaedrus*, for instance, considers the search for absolute good or beauty in terms of problems that the soul faces in becoming mortal. Being immaterial and indestructible, the soul is in itself immortal. But once it descends to the world of nature, it is enclosed within the material casing of a mortal body. In its original state the soul lived among the gods, enjoying the true being of the eternal forms. As they become men, most souls forget their divine origin. Immersion in matter blunts the awareness of their spiritual source. Nevertheless, that remains as the state of wholeness to which all men secretly aspire. Their longing has been forced into a Platonic, as opposed to a Freudian, unconscious. Though it may act with confusion, the soul wishes to reunite itself with the realm of essences, particularly that absolute good or beauty which shimmers through the world of sense but can be properly enjoyed only in its own domain.

In the *Phaedrus* these ideas are presented through a colorful myth of love. Since it is only a myth, Socrates warns us not to take it *too* seriously. He freely admits that his account is "possibly true though partly erring." Obviously Plato has taken the myth from religious mysteries to which he does not wish to bind himself. All the same, he does not hesitate to use it fully.

In this myth human nature is represented as a pair of winged horses and a charioteer. One of the horses is black, the other white. The black horse, belonging to the world of sense, tries to pull the charioteer toward bodily pleasures at the expense of everything else. The white horse wants to soar upward, toward the world of ideals from which the soul originated. In Plato's conception the nature of man is double, an unstable composition of body and soul, each separable from the other, each governed by contrary impulses, each struggling to move the human being in its own direction. Both horses are impelled by the dictates of love, but love for different kinds of objects.

A similar idea is expressed in one of the earlier speeches of the *Symposium*. Pausanias maintains that two loves exist and seek to rule the universe: the heavenly Aphrodite and the earthly or common Aphrodite. Heavenly Aphrodite sprang from Uranus, the father of Zeus, but without a mother—clearly, women are not needed for this kind of love. Common Aphrodite issued from one of Zeus' sexual escapades among the mortals. As might be expected, common Aphrodite is physical rather than spiritual, concerned merely with the gratifications of bodily impulse, reckless about the means she uses to gain her materialistic ends, and generally interested in keeping the beloved servile and unintelligent. This type of love is directed toward women, for whom it is presumably sufficient, as well as toward unfortunate or corrupt young men. By contrast, heavenly Aphrodite cares only about the achievement of excellence. Hers is a pure, noble, spiritual relationship that enables both lover and (male) beloved to improve themselves in their search for virtue. Heavenly

Aphrodite is love moving the soul upward toward its home among the eternal forms, while common Aphrodite is love that has forgotten its divine source and allowed carnal temptations to drag it down into the mire of sensuality.

This dualism is characteristic of all Platonic philosophy. And so sharply does Plato distinguish the white horse from the black, the aspiration of spirit from the gravitational pull of matter, that one is not really surprised to find him associating true love with madness. For is not psychosis an impossible conflict between ideals and the inclinations of nature? Needless to say, Plato's account is somewhat different. Though heavenly Aphrodite directs man toward his authentic reality, human nature finds it easier to follow the lure of common Aphrodite. When the enlightened spirit finally wrenches itself from this debasing but pervasive influence, it seems to have lost all sense of equilibrium. Actually, it is only regaining freedom and the *true* sanity of man.

This upward thrust, love bursting the shackles, Plato calls "the divine madness." He likens it to all creative inspiration and ends up by arguing that madness is really of two kinds. One is, as we would say, pathological; it results from "human infirmity." But the other is "a divine release of the soul from the yoke of custom and convention." True love is madness of the latter, and highly desirable, sort. It is confused with the former only by persons who are so thoroughly debased as to misunderstand the nature of heavenly Aphrodite. In his usual fashion Plato starts with the popular notion that lovers are mad, refines it, reconstructs it, and puts it to his own idealistic use.

He does something similar in the parable of the cave, which appears in the *Republic*. We are asked to imagine a race of men who have grown up in a deep subterranean cave, chained to the ground and unable to move their heads. The sunlight never reaches them, but behind their backs a fire glows. It throws shadows on the walls of the cave and the prisoners come to treat these shadows like real objects. Suddenly one of the men breaks his chains, climbs out of the cave, and finds himself aboveground, looking at the world in sunlight. At first he is so dazed and dazzled that he does not believe his senses. Eventually he realizes what has happened. If he returns to the cave, however, and tries to convey his discovery to the others, they will revile him as a madman. Instead of admitting that they are being systematically deceived, they will assume that the renegade has simply gone out of his mind. The true lover is like the man who has broken his enchainment. That his radical experience has deranged him from ordinary life Plato does not deny. Indeed, that is why he uses the metaphor of madness. But it is a divine madness, and violent because spirit cannot free itself from the bonds of matter in any other way.

The major description of love as madness occurs in the *Phaedrus*. In the *Symposium* love generally appears calm, peaceful, serene—like the character of Socrates and like the orderly advance toward absolute beauty. In the *Phaedrus* it is turbulent, agitated, overwhelming. This applies to the heavenly Aphrodite as well as the common, to the white horse as well as the black. For the sight of beauty, which the soul encountered in its previous state but quickly forgot, stirs the spirit anew whenever it appears before the lover. In a way that seems to refer to the lowest of the five spiritual stages, Plato describes the excitement of a lover who sees in another person an expression of divine beauty: "At first a shudder runs through him, and again the old awe steals over him; then looking upon the face of his beloved as of a god he reverences him, and if he were not afraid of being thought a downright madman, he would sacrifice to his beloved as to the image of a god; then while he gazes on him there is a sort of reaction, and the shudder passes into an unusual heat and perspiration."

With the cleverness of the clinic, we may of course interpret the reaction and the shudder as sexual response. Plato, at least, does not have that in mind. He is not here speaking of carnal appetite, the black horse. He is rather describing how the soul grows wings—an image to which we shall return—and doing so through the language of emotion. Many Christian mystics will speak in a similar vein, except that they really do reverence their beloved as a deity. For the Platonist such adoration is merely the beginning, not the end, of love. And once Plato ascends beyond this level, the element of emotion seems to fall away. Or perhaps we should say it is reinterpreted. For instance, in the original definition of love as "desire for the perpetual possession of the good," the idea of *possession* must indicate something equivalent to an emotional bond. Certainly Plato does not think that the Good can be possessed in the sense in which a house may be possessed. More likely he is talking as we ordinarily do when we say that a man is *in* possession of himself, meaning that his faculties are functioning harmoniously. There is also, however, an inkling of possession in the religious sense. The *Phaedrus* explicitly relates the divine madness to the infusion of the Godhead into the trembling soul of some devout believer. The true lover possesses the Good by enabling the Good to take possession of *him*. When that happens, the lover attains knowledge of reality, though possibly this too needs to be reinterpreted. The Bible speaks of a man "knowing" a woman when he possesses her in sexual intercourse. The oneness and intimacy of that relationship is quite obvious. In possessing the Good, the Platonic lover undergoes something comparable but without being limited by the world of ordinary experience. Such at least is his objective.

So important is the notion of "perpetual possession" that in the *Symposium* Socrates feels the need to modify his earlier definition. For to love beauty is to wish to bring forth in beauty; to possess it perpetually would be to re-create it endlessly. Consequently, love must by its very nature be the love of immortality as well as the Beautiful. That is why love is associated with the reproduction of the species. Love issues into a desire to procreate because procreation is a mortal's nearest approach to perpetuity. Human beings cherish their progeny as the means by which the parents may partake of the future. Likewise, the self-sacrifice of heroes derives from a love of fame and reputation that can itself be traced to the love of immortality. On the highest level, at the uppermost rung of the spiritual ladder, the philosopher's love puts a human being as close to immortality as possible. The man who raises himself to that elevation, who contemplates absolute beauty with an unfettered soul, will finally be in contact with the eternal in a way that *assures* perpetuity. Though he may never create children or works of art, and though he may never enact a deed of great importance, his achievement in life will be supreme: "Having brought forth and nurtured true goodness [i.e., in living as he does] he will have the privilege of being beloved of God, and becoming, if ever a man can, immortal himself." In the *Republic* the philosopher, the lover of wisdom and perpetual possessor of the Good, is described as follows:

> He contemplates a world of unchanging and harmonious order, where reason governs and nothing can do or suffer wrong; and like one who imitates an admired companion, he cannot fail to fashion himself in its likeness. So the philosopher, in constant companionship with the divine order of the world, will reproduce that order in his soul and, so far as man may, become godlike; though here, as elsewhere, there will be scope for detraction.

No wonder Socrates states in several places that his lord is love and that this is the only subject he understands.

Having hewed so closely to the Platonic doctrine, let us now step back and reformulate its major themes. This will prepare us for understanding their importance in the history of ideas about love, as well as their difficulty for a contemporary philosopher.

Perhaps the most interesting theme is the emphasis upon union. Throughout the ages it reappears in fascinating variations, sometimes dominant in the definition of love and sometimes not, but always present. When a twentieth-century theologian like Paul Tillich defines love as "the dynamic reunion of that which is separated," he touches the chord that has been resounding ever since Plato.

As in Tillich's version, there are four elements that need to be articulated: the idea of a dynamic process, a state of separation, and an ultimate oneness that is not merely union but also *reunion*—the reestablishing of a previous oneness. All of these elements are clearly present in the myth of Aristophanes. The bisected human beings are driven by a sense of alienation from the other half, with which they seek to reunite; and they achieve their oneness through a process of searching, yearning, striving. Similar elements reappear in Plato's final doctrine. Love remains a seeking for that which eliminates separation. But now the object of love is a philosophical entity, and therefore the union must be spiritual rather than physical. Platonic love is not a return to the body of a bisected creature, any more than to the womb of the Freudian mother. Instead, it is the soul's dynamic effort to achieve oneness with the source of its being, a state of wholeness from which it was separated by descending into the material world. If that can be restored, Plato thinks, the lesser reunions of man's estate—oneness with nature, homeland, parental origins, sexual mate—will establish themselves automatically. If they do not, they will be sacrificed for the greater love of the Good, which matters most in any event.

But though Platonic love aspires toward oneness, it is hard to know exactly what Plato means by this. Is the ultimate union a *wedding* of diverse entities or an actual *merging*? When blue and yellow combine to make green, their union is a kind of merging. They do not merely touch one another or stick together; nor do they attain a superficial likeness. Their union is, so to speak, more intimate than that. It is a loss of identity but also a continuation of influence: neither color will appear as itself any longer, but each will contribute chemically to the whole that supplants them both. The same kind of union results when hydrogen and oxygen become water, or simultaneously struck notes make a chord, or the yolk and the albumen of an egg change into an omelet. But if these are instances of merging, what are we to say about a conversation between people who speak the same language, or partnership in business, or membership in a club, a profession, an army? Here the union is less of a merging and more of a wedding. The components join identities instead of losing them. They agree to devote themselves to similar ends and their agreement creates a bond; but their kind of union will not have the homogeneity or the uniformity of merging.

In the myth of Aristophanes the oneness of love is explicitly identified as merging rather than wedding. This in turn reinforces Plato's distinction between love and sex. In romanticism sex often serves as a vehicle of merging; but that is not Plato's view. For him, as for Freud, the coital union is an interpenetration of bodies, not the mingling of properties. Even the sense of sexual fulfillment, the waves of emotion so dear to the oceanic mind, would be for him the releasing of individual tension rather than an actual merging. Aristophanes makes precisely this point when he denies that mere physical enjoyment can give lovers what they really want. He imagines Hephaestus, the Vulcan of the Greeks, coming upon a couple in the act of love and asking them: "What is it, mortals, that you hope to gain from one another? . . . Is the object of your desire to be always together as much as possible, and never to be separated from one another day or night? If that is what you want, I am ready to melt and weld you together, so that, instead of two, you shall be one flesh; as long as you live you shall live a common life, and when you die, you shall suffer a common death, and be still one, not two, even in the next world. Would such a fate as this content you, and satisfy your longings?" Aristophanes assures us that it would and that melting into the beloved, becoming one instead of two, perfectly expresses the universal inclination toward love. In a sense, romanticism is following his lead, since he too describes sexual intercourse as an *effort* to achieve the desired merging. But unlike the Romantics (Wagner in *Tristan and Isolde*, for instance), Aristophanes is also showing the futility of sex. For he knows that it does *not* enable the lovers to melt into one another; and though Hephaestus serves the same function as the magic love potion, Aristophanes hardly pretends that the god will carry out his beneficent promise.

Instead, Plato himself redeems the promise by transferring it to the metaphysical realm for which the true lover yearns. There the philosopher does not merge with the body or soul of another human being. But he does merge—or so it would seem—with absolute beauty, the highest of the forms, the ultimate category of being. When Plato speaks of the philosopher as remaining "in constant union" with the Good or Beautiful, he means something more than superficial contact. The Platonic lover fashions himself in the likeness of his transcendental object; not only is he dyed with its tincture, becoming good and beautiful, but also he is totally transformed by being engulfed in it. Since reunion presupposes a prior communion, man must have had a divine source in the realm of forms—the Platonic myths about the soul's prehistory are designed to establish this—and since oneness requires an indissoluble bond, the soul must achieve its spiritual reunion by merging with the highest form. What else can Plato mean when he says that the true lover becomes "godlike" and "immortal" through oneness with absolute (eternal) beauty? How else are we to understand the philosopher's experience at the pinnacle of wisdom, at the moment of purest insight and deepest contemplation?

Unfortunately Plato never discusses the matter. But his frequent references to the rational character of true love, to the final state as intellectual, to the forms as philosophical categories pertaining to the search for wisdom—all this must give us pause. For that is not the language of oceanic feeling. It is the language of science or dialectic seeking to unify the world through the proper employment of reason. Knowledge may in *some* sense forge a oneness between the knower and the known, but it does not fuse them into a single entity. It clarifies differences, demarcates identities, organizes apparent diversity into an underlying pattern. This is basically the job of administration, and that is why philosophers must be kings. If he had wished to describe the ends of love in terms of merging, Plato could easily have drawn upon the religious beliefs of his time. Orphic mysteries, as well as Eastern religions from which they sprang, cultivated various means of melting into the Godhead and losing one's own identity. But however ambiguously, Plato transcends these practices as he also transmutes the other commonplaces of his age. The search for the whole he justifies only as the whole is good; but it is not at all certain that one can merge with the Platonic Good in the same sense in which the Hindus, for instance, wished to merge with the whole of the universe.

In either event, whether Platonic union is a merging or a wedding, it is always a return to the *same* object; and this too needs further examination. We are all so thoroughly imbued with confused ideas about love and fidelity that we scarcely appreciate the enormity of Plato's assumption. Even if love does consist in some kind of union, why must it be union with a single object? For Plato that object is not, of course, another person. It is neither God nor a human being. On the contrary, Plato scorns all fixations upon individuals. He would have had little tolerance for that latter-day romanticism which maintains that one life has only one love or that—in a monogamous society—love and marriage go together like a horse and carriage:

you can't have one without the other. Even Christian love, which at least chooses a transcendental object, would have struck Plato as overly romantic in thinking that the object must also be a person. With respect to persons in general, his philosophy is thoroughly promiscuous. Plato resembles a tenacious mother who encourages her son to sleep with many women in the hope that he will never become attached to any of them. We condemn such mothers because we know they really want their sons for themselves. In Plato, however, promiscuity is a means of liberation: the supreme technique by which men free themselves of everything in the empirical world. Insofar as all things participate in the beauty of the universe, the aspiring lover will feel himself drawn to one beloved after another; but as he clarifies his love, he will realize that none of them can satisfy his longings for perfection. As Santayana says of Platonic love: "All beauties attract by suggesting the ideal and then fail to satisfy by not fulfilling it." Through promiscuity—approached philosophically, not licentiously—we are to achieve absolute fidelity, and in relation to the only object that is ultimately worth it.

What the modern reader finds hard to accept is the idea that this object must be nonempirical. Moreover, his doubts will be reinforced by glaring non sequiturs. For instance, after criticizing the myth of Aristophanes, Socrates leads the discussion as follows:

> ". . . The only object of men's love is what is good. Don't you agree?"
> "Certainly I do."
> "May we then say without qualification that men are in love with what is good?"
> "Yes."
> "But we must add, mustn't we, that the aim of their love is the possession of the good for themselves?"
> "Yes."
> "And not only its possession but its perpetual possession?"
> "Certainly."
> "To sum up, then, love is desire for the perpetual possession of the good."
> "Very true."

Now, from the statement that men love only what is good, it does not follow that love is exclusively directed toward *the* Good. It might be true that love never happens unless one person discovers goodness in another; but this gives us no basis for concluding that the object of love is goodness itself. Though men may love only women who are under ten feet tall, we would never argue that love is really directed toward a certain height.

Plato makes little effort to defend his position. That the highest form is absolute beauty or goodness and that only it can be the ultimate object of love—these are articles of faith with him. He sees in all the varieties of love a unitary search for perfection, which he then assumes to be more important than the things or persons that are actually loved. But this is only an assumption, the kind that typifies most idealistic philosophy. At the same time Plato differs from many others who also belong to this tradition—the Romantics, for instance—inasmuch as he believes in the prior being of perfection. In searching for goodness or beauty, the Platonic lover is not trying to create perfections that would not have come into being without his love. On the contrary, he is seeking union with an object of metaphysical analysis whose being precedes his own, as it also precedes the being of everything else. This "object" is not, of course, a *thing*; and if it is an "entity" (another fruitless term), it is only an "abstract entity." Instead of "object" perhaps we should speak of "objective," as Aristotle does when he refers to the highest form as the goal or final end. Even so, Platonic perfection remains as something independent of the lover, prior to love itself, a specific terminus or target for human striving, that which elicits love and indeed the only thing capable of doing so.

To say, then, that love is the search for perfection, meaning by this what Plato does, is to say that none of the *apparent* objects of love can be authentic. We cannot love another person for himself, but only as a vehicle and partial embodiment of what we really want—the Good. By seeing that this is the real object of his love, the Platonic philosopher disintoxicates himself from the interest in persons as such. For what is a person but a conglomeration of accidental properties that chance and nature have thrown together? No, Plato would say, to love anyone is really to love the goodness which is in him. That is why even the most vulgar recognize the association between love and a beautiful body. For in that body, beauty—which stands for all perfection—has deigned to manifest itself. And though in our ignorance we may *think* our love is directed toward a man or woman who happens to partake of beauty, the real object of love is perfection itself. The true Platonic lover detaches his love from the limitations of one or another body, person, community, or activity. He goes *through* everything in the empirical world, but gives his heart to nothing. Though he detaches his love, however, the philosopher need not detach *himself*. He may live with and for other people, even ruling them as the voice of reason. He may enjoy the company of his fellows, delighting in their beauty and goodness. As one who reveres the absolute, he will automatically act for that which is best in man. But since the empirical world is radically imperfect, he knows that nothing on earth can satisfy his longing for the ideal. Only perfection can make the lover perfect in himself.

Seen from this point of view, as man's greatest effort toward self-perfection, Platonic love belongs to that aretaic strand which virtually defines Greek culture. "Aretaic" comes from the Greek word *aretē*, variously translated as virtue, honor, manliness, self-respect, dignity. None of these words renders the concept accurately; nor even a loose combination of them. The term was used by the Greeks to signify that condition of a man's soul or character without which life was not worth living. The man without aretē was better off dead; but the man who died in the quest for this inner excellence had nothing to fear from death. As a directive to action, the content of the ideal changed from age to age. In the *Iliad* aretē means warrior courage, physical heroism and the nobility of spirit that accompanies it. Achilles avenges Patroclus and goes to his death at the end of the poem for the same reason that he sulks in his tent and refuses to fight for Agamemnon at the beginning. On both occasions he acts out of a sense of honor, aretē. This involves recognition of his military status and respect for his exceptional powers as well as fidelity to an intimate companion. In the *Odyssey* aretē becomes an ideal of shrewd public policy. The cunning of Odysseus, his intelligence, his artfulness, his ability to solve the problems of domestic authority—these are the virtues now glorified. They pertain to a time of peace rather than war; they exalt the values of home life rather than aggressive marauding. Once we get to the fifth century B.C., aretē depends upon allegiance to the immediate environment of the city-state. Though Socrates was charged with impiety toward the Athenian gods, his crime really consisted in threatening the accepted interpretation of aretē. He, and Plato after him, proposed so unworldly a concept of human excellence that one can hardly blame a crumbling civilization for treating it as out-and-out treachery.

Throughout these variations in the content of Greek aretē there remains as a constant the idea of man struggling for self-perfection. Aretē is "egocentric" in the sense that salvation begins with individual effort and ends with individual achievement. It requires that each man search for his own personal excellence, putting his own honor and the purification of his soul before any other consideration. By nature man is assumed to be selfish in the sense of being self-oriented, concerned with the acquisition of everything that will benefit himself. For Plato this means something quite different from selfishness in the usual connotation of that word. Platonic eros is not the warfare of each against all; it is not personal aggrandizement at the expense of other people. On the contrary, Plato postulates a unifying principle between the individual and the group. In the *Republic* he argues that nothing can really benefit one without also benefiting the other. The *truly* selfish man, desiring the best for himself, will act for the welfare of others also. This he does partly as a matter of prudence, for even Socrates cannot be a wholly good man in a bad society, but also through the realization that no one will be happy unless he is just. In Platonism the individual is organically linked to the world he lives in. The good man, the good society, and the good universe (as this one is presumed to be) are all constructed on the same purposive model. Each of them fulfills itself through conformity to the Good, and therefore what is best for one must be best for the others. In Plato the most elevated moral standards are always shown to be manifestations of the deepest self-interest, and vice versa. Both are merely aspects of the unitary search for goodness which binds all things to one another.

It is for this reason that Plato (unlike the Calvinists or the Freudians) never admits the possibility of ultimate conflict between loving oneself and loving ideals. When modern theologians criticize Calvin for thinking that self-love prohibits the love of God, when revisionists attack Freud for assuming that the libido is directed either toward the ego or toward others but not toward both at the same time, they subterraneously return to the position Plato takes for granted. He defines love as the search for the Good and justifies this conclusion by reminding us that men always desire what is best for *themselves*. Likewise, he recognizes that love causes people to act altruistically—to undergo hardship, self-sacrifice, even death—but in each case he thinks there will always be some greater good to be attained. Alcestis dies to save Admetus, and Achilles to avenge Patroclus, because they pursue a virtuous love of renown. They are motivated by a search for the superior values of fame and personal glory. Parents make sacrifices for their children, sometimes giving their own lives, in order to assure immortality through their progeny. For every outgoing act there will always be a motive originating in a desire for some egocentric good. The philosophic lover (and only he fulfills Plato's aretaic code) desires the principle of goodness itself. He seeks to possess it, thereby making himself infinitely good. This is what all men really want, and yet the search is paradoxical. For if the Platonic lover could possess the Good, he would become a god—which is to say, he would no longer desire anything. Is this the state of bliss? Or have we merely taken a long way round to self-destruction? Such questions emanate from various difficulties in the Platonic philosophy. Let us now address ourselves to them.

Though it little matters where we begin, I shall start with the idea that the highest love is really the search for knowledge. Since the object of all love pertains to a category of metaphysical explanation, Plato assumes that love fulfills itself through an exercise of reason. Far from associating love with feelings or illusions, as the Romantics might, Plato sees it as rationality and a craving after wisdom. To many of us in the twentieth century, this is sure to be a stumbling block. We think of love as a matter of emotion, a kinship of feeling, an excitement and a fever in the blood. Of course, there is in Plato considerable reference to love as turbulence and perturbation. But these are not definitive of "true love." They signify unacceptable states of mind or else conditions external to love, falsifying its nature not revealing it. In the *Symposium*, for instance, several speakers lament the passionate bondage of certain men for (of all things!) women; these attachments sometimes go by the name of love, but Plato definitely considers them to be a kind of mental illness. In the *Phaedrus* there occur similar descriptions of unwholesome relations between men, emotional intimacy devoid of wisdom and therefore quite remote from the true nature of love. The Platonic lover rises above all this by leaving emotionality behind: his love is not an attempt to express or purify sensuous feelings but rather to supplant them by sheer rationality. Even when true love is described as a divine madness, emotions merely attend the condition, bespeaking the eagerness of the soul to enter into relationship with absolute beauty. The relationship itself is intellectual, the attainment of wisdom, of knowledge about the highest form.

Wherever possible, Plato avoids the language of feeling. The preferred state of love he describes in the language of thought, as an intuition and a culmination of reason. When the senses are included in Plato's magnificent metaphors, they are always the senses of sight or sound—never the less intellectual ones of touch or smell. In a way that underlies courtly love hundreds of years later, Plato often compares true love to *seeing* an object. The Good or the Beautiful is symbolized by the sun, which illumines everything, but which we must learn to look at. To see something is to appropriate its essence without bodily contact. Sight is the beginning of knowledge; without it, wisdom could only be rudimentary. Thus, even as union with the Good all men seek, Plato's highest love is predominantly intellectual: possibly fervent but always a form of rational activity. Platonic eros is basically a love of abstract science more than anything else.

I list this as a difficulty in Platonism because it ignores so much that is important to love: not only the bestowing of value, which is not reducible to reason, but also such feelings as tenderness, warmth, and that caring about in which bestowing manifests itself. Moreover, the emphasis upon sight tends to eliminate physical intimacy. The whole question of sexual relations seems to be pushed aside. Indeed, it is not at all clear how sex enters into the Platonic philosophy. As I have suggested, Plato dissociates love from sexual desire insofar as the *definition* of love is concerned. Sex is an afterthought, a technological device for propagating the race; love is an impulse more basic to human nature, the desire for the Good. The lover of wisdom, as illustrated by Socrates in his relations with Alcibiades, transcends the animal interests of sexuality. Once we move beyond the definition of love, however, Plato's attitude toward sex becomes quite ambivalent. He seems to hold at least two different views, each diametrically opposed to the other.

The first of these views about sex may be called puritanical. It demands that sex be eliminated to the greatest extent possible. For sexuality distracts from the love of wisdom; and frequently it buries us in a bog of sensual interests wholly inimical to true love. This antisexual ideal Plato advocates in various contexts. In the *Republic* men and women are allowed to mate only at prescribed periods, sexuality being condoned as nothing but a reproductive necessity. In one place Sophocles, the aged poet, is quoted as saying of sexual desire: "I am only too glad to be free of all that; it is like escaping from bondage to a raging madman." For Plato it is obviously an advantage of old age, not at all a misfortune, that libidinal inclinations dwindle.

This side of Plato's philosophy gives to the phrase "Platonic love" that bodiless, ethereal, wholly transcendental character it was later to acquire in the Italian Renaissance. It leads us to think of Pre-Raphaelite ladies and gentlemen demurely seeking a "pure" and spiritual relationship untainted by the lures of matter. But this is Neoplatonism, not Plato himself. Some French scholars distinguish between *amour platonicien* and *amour platonique* in order to emphasize the differences between Plato and his followers. Where *amour platonique* is as sexless as a painting by Rossetti or Puvis de Chavannes, *amour platonicien* respects and seeks to harmonize the vital energies of sexuality. And certainly, within the total body of Plato's writings, the latter view predominates. In the *Phaedrus*, for instance, Plato never suggests that the black horse must be destroyed or the chariot driven by the white horse of spirituality alone. He tells us time and again that the senses must be controlled but not extirpated. However dangerous and distracting the black horse may be, he still belongs to the team. Physical impulse being an element in human nature, it must be given at least a modicum of satisfaction. As long as they are subordinated to man's higher aspirations, remaining under the control of the charioteer (reason), sensory desires will not lead one astray. Even in the *Laws*, that severe book of Plato's old age, various types of licentious love are condemned but sexual pleasure itself is permitted in moderation.

This other (healthier) side of Plato issues into a search for harmony between body and soul. And as harmony implies the inner workings of rationality, Socrates says of both black and white horses: "Their happiness depends upon their self-control." In the *Republic* the various facets of human psychology, and all classes within the state, are said to contribute to the good life by freely consenting to their own harmonious integration. Nor is it surprising that one of the earlier speeches in the *Symposium* defines love itself as harmony. That being the basic principle of beauty, the *harmonious* soul would be the beautiful one to which the lover aspires. As long as sex enters into this harmony, it cannot be eliminated. It must be subjugated, subordinated, even "enslaved"; but it is not necessarily evil nor, in its place, even harmful. Like harmony itself, this pole of Plato's ambivalence seeks to be what Aristotle would call a "golden mean," avoiding the extremes of either libertinism or self-mortification.

I speak of these two Platonic aspects as poles within an ambivalence because the tension between them never seems to be recognized by Plato. Both are present in his writings, but in different ways and in varying emphases. It is not merely a question of whether to condemn or to tolerate sexuality. Of greater importance is the relationship between sex and ideal love. And here, despite the French scholars, I find great confusion in Plato. Even in the *Phaedrus* and the *Laws*, where moderation is condoned as "the appointment of nature," the satisfaction of bodily desires contributes nothing to the *highest* love. But then, to that extent, sex is being treated puritanically even at the healthier pole of Plato's ambivalence. On the one hand the harmonious soul will not spurn its natural inclinations toward sexual pleasure; on the other hand *true* love is purely spiritual, transcending all sexuality. But in that event, how can true love—that which perfectly fulfills the Platonic definition—be harmonious? Without harmony there can be no beauty; without beauty, no love at all—at least not as Plato defines it.

This problem is part of the larger one relating to the nature of Plato's metaphysical dualism. As man is divided into body and soul, so too is the universe analyzed into matter and spirit. At times, in the *Phaedo* for instance, Plato seems to say that true being is spirituality, the disembodied soul contemplating the bodiless eternal forms. From this it follows that all things material, including sexual desire, are somehow unreal: in principle, one does best to eliminate them. At other times, however, Plato seems to say that true being is a composite of spirit and matter, the one more important than the other, but both equally real and worth cultivating. The first view resembles Hindu notions of appearance and reality, the material world being *maya*, a web of mere illusion. The second view is more distinctively Western, the material world being useful at least as a stepping-stone and possibly itself contributing to spiritual attainments.

I myself doubt whether any study of the text can resolve this ambivalence in Plato. Scholars have underlined sometimes one, sometimes the other, aspect of his thinking; Platonistic philosophers have regularly chosen whatever suited their own preferences. Both alternatives are open. Perhaps, then, it would be wiser to deal with the problem more concretely, in terms of Plato's ambivalence toward homosexuality. For regardless of how bodily desires are treated in Platonic love, it is clear that for Plato the bodies must always be male bodies. He never so much as intimates that true love can be experienced by women or really directed toward them. A man may desire a woman sexually; he may even devote his life to an overwhelming passion for the female sex. But none of this fits the Platonic ideal. Even if heterosexual desire were moderate and harmonious, it would seem to have no place within the hierarchy that leads to ideal love. But neither does Plato recommend physical homosexuality. In the *Phaedrus* and the *Symposium* he seems to admit the utility of sexual relations between men; but in the *Laws* he explicitly condemns physical homosexuality, calling it "unnatural" and a crime against the state. He there contrasts it with the "natural love" that exists between a man and his wife—"love" because it is based on sexual instinct, and "natural" because it leads to the propagation of children. It is not love in any other sense.

The Platonic relationship between love and sexuality thus turns out to be more complicated than one might have originally thought. Insofar as bodily impulses may be satisfied, libidinal ties must be heterosexual. These desires are the only natural ones. But they are not related to perfect love. That requires the company of males. The love between men must not be physically consummatory, however, at least not as one approaches the ideal. In the *Phaedrus*, where masculine friendship is described at length, the harmony of black and white must finally yield to a spiritual bond from which the craving for sexual gratification has been exorcised. The lovers are then united as companions jointly searching for the Good. In the *Laws* Plato enumerates three types of love between men: one is a love of the body, another of the soul, and the third is a mixture of these. The first and third types he prohibits by law. Into the ideal society he admits only the lover "that treats carnal appetite as out of the question, that puts contemplation before passion, he whose desire is veritably that of soul for soul, looks on enjoyment of flesh by flesh as wanton shame."

If we were to translate Plato's ambivalence into Freudian language, we would have to say that "true" love is always sexually aim-inhibited, homosexual desire being at best transitional and heterosexual aims being natural but not ideal. When Freud analyzes civilization as a masculine phenomenon, he uses virtually these terms to characterize the erotic forces at work. Of course, each believes in a different type of aim-inhibition: for Freud all sublimation is reducible to direct sexuality, whereas Plato finds in every desire an underlying search for the Good. Nevertheless, both of them accord to quasi-homosexual relations a unique function in the development of man's noblest ideals.

In the case of Plato this conception springs from the belief that all approaches to absolute beauty originate with a masculine object. I myself find nothing in the principles of Platonic philosophy to require this assumption; but the sociological *setting* of Platonism makes it almost inevitable. Greek civilization idealized masculinity;

the society was built upon the supremacy of the male. Not only were women kept indoors as virtual household slaves, but also they remained uneducated and politically insignificant. They were even thought to be biologically inferior. Since the female sex was not fully rational, no man could have an intellectual friendship with a woman. Love being the quest for knowledge, how could there be a *truly* amorous relation with such fickle and emotional creatures? Exceptions seem to have existed: for instance, the devotion of Pericles to Aspasia is often described in terms reminiscent of Greek homosexual love. But ordinarily women were thought to be incapable of an uplifting relationship. Even in modern times, one often hears it said that men can never be friends with the opposite sex. Plato idealizes this attitude, true love presupposing the friendship of men joined in an exclusive pilgrimage (to use Jowett's word) toward the highest good.

That this idealization is largely a product of masculine bigotry reveals itself in the accepted ideas about creativity and procreation. Only the male sex could be creative; and therefore it alone was capable of producing anything—even children. In this vein Plato tells us that men are always pregnant with life. In their semen they carry the fully formed homunculus of a new human being, which they deposit in the womb of a woman as if in an oven or incubator. The man creates the child, borne within his seed; the woman merely provides soil to help it grow. From ideas such as these to those of Platonic love, the transition is easy. In both cases the underlying motive is surely masculine aggression.

But in keeping with his profound ambivalences, Plato is very far from being a misogynist. Scholars often claim that medieval attitudes toward sex were largely influenced by the *Laws*. And it is true that from Plato (or his followers) the medieval church appropriated the attack on physical homosexuality, the subordination of all carnal desire, the conception of a natural love between man and wife based upon the needs of procreation, and even the defense of marriage as a unit of social stability. Yet neither in the *Laws* nor in any other Platonic dialogue does one find anything like the hatred of women that seems to have inspired the church fathers to their greatest efforts of spirituality. At times Plato gives women extraordinary powers, even making them the "overseers" of marriage; nowhere does he treat them like domestic chattel. In the *Republic* women are offered equality with men, encouraged to develop their unique talents, and completely liberated from the constraints of housekeeping and maternity. Finally, as the culminating confusion, what are we to say about the *Symposium* itself? No women are present; even the flute girls are dismissed, since the men wish to have a serious discussion. Yet Plato's ultimate philosophy of love is said to have originated with a woman—Diotima, whom Socrates quotes throughout his speech. And though Eros must be a boy, it is heavenly Aphrodite—his mother in mythology—who represents spiritual love. Plato certainly does not put women on a pedestal, but at least he allows them to hover above the field of battle.

In its later developments the Platonic tradition assumes a variety of attitudes toward women. But the separation between love and sexuality remains fairly constant. In effect, this separation amounts to that split within the self that Freud discusses so brilliantly in "The Most Prevalent Form of Degradation in Erotic Life." In that essay Freud speaks of "normal love" as a confluence between tender, affectionate feelings on the one hand, and sensual feelings on the other. The tender feelings, which come from the instinct for self-preservation, originally direct themselves toward the mother or anyone else who takes care of the child. Before puberty, Freud says, they absorb all sensual feelings, which thus become aim-inhibited. After puberty the sexual instinct asserts itself overtly; but factors of frustration and repression tend to thwart it. If the sexual instinct could be gratified with someone who substitutes for the mother and so elicits the affectionate feelings, normal love would be possible. But more often, the sensual feelings are forced to break away and seek a purely sexual object. In certain neurotic states the separation becomes extreme: "The erotic life of such people remains dissociated, divided between two channels, the same two that are personified in art as heavenly and earthly (or animal) love. Where such men love they have no desire and where they desire they cannot love. In order to keep their sensuality out of contact with the objects they love, they seek out objects whom they need not love."

Freud does not mention Platonism in this essay, but it seems to me that Platonic love always runs the danger of some such division in the soul. Nor are its effects merely limited to men. As long as women cannot participate in ideal love, neither can they be expected to fulfill the ideals of their society. Assuming that women are not inherently or biologically inferior, merely to exclude them from the noble companionship reserved for men prevents them from becoming the kind of person Platonism respects. One tends to question the sincerity of a philosopher who says (in the *Republic*) that women are the equals of men, but elsewhere (in the *Phaedrus*, the *Symposium*, the *Laws*, etc.) describes the highest love in terms that specifically exclude the female sex. Of course, Neoplatonism of the Renaissance will change much of this. But even then only very special women become eligible; and they often turn out to be symbolic abstractions, like Dante's Beatrice, or else boy-substitutes, like the transvestite characters in Shakespearean plays. Within the Platonic tradition women *as women* are never accorded the ideal possibilities available to men. What Plato calls the "natural love" between man and wife may serve to keep a woman contentedly at home, propagating children in a perfectly wholesome way. But it will not make women into soulmates or satisfy those extrabiological yearnings for the Good which they feel as strongly as men do.

Moreover, as long as women are relegated to an inferior status, the Platonic male is likely to be less ideal than Plato thinks. For he must still be born to a mother and reared in the company of many females, from whom he finally chooses a wife. Possibly he remains celibate, but still he grows up as a sexual creature within a world inhabited by women. In principle at least, he is discouraged from satisfying his instincts through physical homosexuality. Such a person may live a useful, courageous, and possibly inspiring life; but it is likely that his capacity for love will have shrunk, that it will have channelized itself into limited relationships rather than richly extensible ones. In all this it may matter less than most people think whether the Platonic lover takes a wife and whether he is physically homosexual, heterosexual, or bisexual. What really matters is the value that he bestows upon these alternative possibilities. If the sexual occasions of intimacy are treated as mere devices of nature, instinctual but relatively unimportant, the "ideal love" upon which he bestows total value can easily become a neurotic fixation. The noble companionship that Plato idealizes is not suspect in itself, but only in its separation from the rest of human nature. Insofar as Plato restricts true love to the idiosyncrasies of spiritual friendship, he prevents it from being a deep, or really pervasive, attitude toward the world. Even though the Platonic friends are joined in a search for the underlying principle of everything, their splendid dedication will not make them more loving persons if it impairs their ability to appreciate all else in life.

The Platonic lover may be willing to run such risks, and he may find his type of interest more satisfying than any other available to him. This is for each man to decide, though Plato thinks that all sensible decisions *must* be the same. He claims to have discovered a relationship that perfectly embodies the ideal of love. What he does, however, is to idealize an individual preference, a kind of life that matters most to *him*. There is no objective reason to think that Platonic love is higher or better or more desirable than every other possibility. If it were, one might be willing to undergo the division in the erotic life that Freud discusses. If only intellectual friendship were worth pursuing or if its inherent value far exceeded all other human ties, Platonic love could justify the exclusiveness of its interest. The Platonist may be able to argue this case, but surely the burden of proof must lie with him.

Though I refuse to idealize the Platonic attitude at the expense of all others, I do not doubt its limited authenticity. Quite independently of Freud, the man in the street assumes that all love is really sex and Platonic love is a mere ruse to hide degenerate passions. But whether or not it is based on aim-inhibited sexuality, Platonic love projects an ideal of friendship that cannot be reduced to anything else. On the contrary, physical homosexuality may itself be understood as an attempt (in part) to achieve the ideality of Platonic love. Consider the speech of Oscar Wilde, delivered at his first trial in 1895:

> The "love" that dare not speak its name in this century is such a great affection of an older for a younger man as there was between David and Jonathan, such as Plato made the

very base of his philosophy and such as you find in the sonnets of Michelangelo and Shakespeare—a deep spiritual affection that is as pure as it is perfect and dictates great works of art like those of Shakespeare and Michelangelo. . . . It is beautiful; it is fine; it is the noblest form of affection. It is intellectual, and it repeatedly exists between an elder and a younger man, when the elder man has intellect, and the younger man has all the joy, hope and glamour of life. That it should be so the world does not understand. It mocks at it and sometimes puts one into the pillory for it.

In some ways this speech is sadly ironic. Wilde's love for boys was at best what Plato calls the mixed type, not the sexually pure; and he was later sent to prison for having violated a legal code that could have been copied out of Plato's *Laws*. Nevertheless, one has no right to impugn Wilde's honesty in articulating the ideal to which he aspired. In practice he may have been as ridiculous as Gilbert and Sullivan's Bunthorne, who secretly confesses to a "vegetable love." But at least Wilde's dream was beautiful, and this is more than can be said of those who persecuted him.

Underlying all difficulties in Platonic love, there resides a fundamental paradox. Everything in nature is motivated by eros; but nothing can "really" gratify its love within the limits of nature itself. That is why the true Platonic lover must be a philosopher. In being the desire for the perpetual possession of the Good, love strives for union with a metaphysical principle that does not *exist* (in nature or anywhere else) and shows itself only to philosophic intuition. In Platonism true love and true rationality coincide. As the basis of both knowledge and valuation, the Good is the only object worthy of being loved or capable of giving knowledge about reality. Consequently, no search for *natural* goods could possibly satisfy the definition of love. That requires a highly intellectual, purely rational, nonsensuous striving for transcendental insight, a love of wisdom which may have little or no relation to a love of life. Starting with a vision of everything being in love, Plato ends up with the incredible suggestion that only the (Platonic) philosopher really is.

If we had world enough and time, we might try to chip away at the doctrine of forms as well as Plato's concept of reason. Obviously much depends upon the defensibility of these supporting pillars. For present purposes, however, we do better to limit ourselves to more immediate objectives. Even if the foundations of Platonic dogma could be salvaged, one might still deny that philosophy is the model of true love. Plato argues that only he who loves wisdom can love anything properly: for loving always means searching for something that only the lover of wisdom can recognize. It is only in knowing the Good that one really loves. Plato's argument takes the following form: Love of any sort means desiring the Good; only the philosopher, through intellectual intuition which he alone possesses, knows the nature of the Good; therefore, only the philosopher is capable of true love. Unfortunately the conclusion of this argument does not follow from its premises. To make the reasoning valid, a further assumption is needed: namely, that truly desiring the Good implies knowing the nature of the Good. But this would be quite an assumption for Plato to make. It would force him to admit that not everything in the world *truly* desired the Good. This, however, would contradict his general belief that everything anyone did was always motived by a desire for the Good.

There is a way in which Plato might answer my objection. He might distinguish between "desiring" and "truly desiring." He might say that everything desires the Good, but that one *truly desires* it only when such desire is based on knowledge. He could then claim that no one but the philosopher truly desires the Good, and his argument might easily be rendered valid. But this device would scarcely help. For it entails a distinction between "loving" and "truly loving," the philosopher being a man who truly loves. If, however, we then ask wherein loving differs from truly loving, Plato can only say that the latter is based on knowledge whereas the former is not. As far as the definition of "love" is concerned, truly loving adds nothing whatsoever. It is just a special kind of love. How then can it claim to be the model of love in general?

The difficulty can be put more simply. One turns to Plato in the hope of learning about human relations, specifically about the phenomenon known as love. In calling our attention to the element of valuation (man searching for the Good), Plato takes us part of the way. But instead of analyzing what happens when people value or evaluate, Plato singles out one type of love—the love of wisdom—and neglects the rest. At best Platonic love may claim to be the only kind that ever *succeeds* in satisfying the universal desire for perpetual possession of the Good. Clearly it is the type of love Platonistic philosophers prefer, and they *could* be right in thinking it better than all others. At its crudest, however, Plato's position seems to reduce sexual love, married love, parental love, filial love, love of humanity to mere imperfect approaches to the philosopher's love. In neither event does Platonic love really explicate the nature of love itself. The philosopher has simply affixed the honorific term "true love" to that variety which matters most to him.

This objection leads to others. Not only does one fail to see how philosophic love is a model for love in general, but also one begins to suspect that it makes other kinds of love impossible. In his search for the absolute, the philosopher cannot concern himself with the uniqueness and individuality of another person. At least as Plato presents his final formulation, the true lover rises above this or that embodiment of beauty in order to intuit the pure form alone. Even at the outset of his definition, Plato emphasizes that love for another person is primarily a desire for the goodness which is in him. In other words, it is not the other person *as* a person that the Platonic lover cares about. He loves his beloved, not in himself, but only for the sake of goodness or beauty. The Platonic lover does not love *anyone*: he loves only the Good, either in abstraction or in concrete manifestations. But then, I insist, there is at least one kind of love that Plato's philosophy neglects. That is the love of persons, the love between human beings who bestow value upon one another, each responding to the uniqueness of the other, each taking an interest in the other as a separate individual, regardless of imperfections and apart from satisfactions that also accrue. I myself consider the love of persons to be central within the entire attitude, a type of love that issues into most of the human interests that go by the name of love.

But even if I am wrong in this, the love of persons remains as one of the most important types. If Platonism fails here, its shortcoming is very great indeed.

Platonism does fail on this account. It ignores, or largely misrepresents, the love of persons. The key to Plato's failure lies in the paradox I have mentioned, which may also be approached through the principles of promiscuity and frustration. By loving everything for the sake of loving nothing in nature, Platonic promiscuity necessarily leads to one frustration after another. All beauties attract, but none can really satisfy. And like Plato, I believe this is how life must be if ours is the love of ideals as such. Since nothing in this world can be objectively perfect, a pure love of ideals would prevent us from resting permanently at one or another degree of satisfaction. Man transcends himself by a *lack of fidelity* to the objects of his present interest, which frustrate merely in being finite and thus incapable of satisfying his infinite appetite. This would be the tragedy of human existence were it not for the fact that loving ideals is only one type of love. Upon it depends all civilization perhaps, but ultimate happiness requires more than it alone can offer. In the love of persons we enjoy another human being regardless of ideals, and our interest is not inherently promiscuous or frustrating. For we are not using the other as a vehicle to moral growth, but simply bestowing value upon that individual himself. As we are all imperfect, both lovers and beloved, our love for some particular person may turn out to be more frustrating than satisfying, and we may move on to another object. Possibly the ideal of a *perfect* love of persons even requires this. But the love of persons itself, as a specific and irreducible attitude, is not based on either promiscuity or frustration. On the contrary, in seeking to enjoy another as he is, it involves a kind of single-minded fidelity not *entirely* different from what Platonic love reserves only for the Good. The difference is that other people are real, whereas the Good is a dubious abstraction.

Furthermore, when we analyze the nature of this abstraction, it becomes evident that Plato's definition is not really about love, but about the purposive life. Human purposiveness begins with the fact of desire, and Plato may well assume that nothing is desired except for the sake of some goodness it provides. When he then concludes that the only object of desire is the Good, he metaphorically indicates the ideal of purposive life: namely, to subordinate all actual satisfactions to the unending search for perfection. To one who is in love with this ideal, it may seem that nothing else can really be desired. And obviously nothing satisfies the true Platonist more than his idea of perfection. Lover that he is, the philosopher then bestows value upon his conception, treating it not only as the object of his desire but also as the Good that *everything* must desire.

In all this, Plato is more than just a lover of the ideal. He claims to be defining love, not enacting one of its varieties. But surely it is his devotion to the purposive life that causes him to identify love with desire. And perhaps it is this identification that leads him to speak (however ambiguously) of possessing the Good, as if it were indeed something that could be *had*. For desire is always acquisitive and its object a mere commodity designed to satisfy. As Platonic eros is the organism striving to overcome deficiencies, so too is desire an attempt to eliminate a state of need or want. Nor is Plato wrong to associate love with desire. The two are closely related. Without desire there would be no love. But loving something is not the same as desiring it, even though the element of bestowal itself entails various relevant desires: a desire to be with the object, a desire for its continued existence, its welfare, etc. These and other desires may be necessary conditions for love; but as an interest in the object itself, one that refuses to treat the object as merely a means to satisfaction, love is not reducible to *any* desire.

In a sense, Plato also recognizes that love includes more than desire alone. The Good is not like any other object. It is the principle of value and would retain its form whether or not anyone desired it. Consequently, desiring oneness with the Good inevitably differs from desiring an ordinary object for the sake of its goodness. Indeed, the union for which Platonic love aspires sounds more like an act of surrender, a yielding up of desire at the moment that one is possessed *by* perfection. If eros is just a striving to satisfy organic needs, it must die and all desires end once absolute fulfillment has been achieved. This would be the dark side of Plato, true love culminating in self-destruction, the philosophic quest being as suicidal as Socrates' later life often seemed to be. The view presupposes that only in extinction are desires fulfilled, which is a poetic way of expressing a love of death.

Within the structure of Platonism, however, these implications are barely developed. They tie in with the concept of merging and possibly reflect the influence of Eastern religions. They lead to problems that Plato did not wholly ignore, but which he left for Aristotle and the Christians to resolve. For Plato it is sufficient that life involves desire, and the good life a desire for perfection. By making this the ground of being, he idealizes what I have called objective value. Goods that are merely individual he calls "specious" or "false." The principle of goodness he allocates to a realm of metaphysical ultimacy in which the truly valuable is also the truly real. Since both must be approached through processes of reason, Plato may be said to idealize appraisal itself. Instead of treating it as an instrument that determines what human beings want and so consider "good," he accords it the ability to penetrate beyond man's glassy essence. For Plato objective appraisal must be grander than any expert opinion about some preferred society; it must be objective in the sense of revealing a preordained system of ultimate values. Certainly this makes the purposive life more significant in the universe than it would be as a local human adventure. Certainly this buttresses morality and furthers the pursuit of ideals with greater security than any empiricism could possibly muster. And yet, Plato's dedication to the Good is itself but an act of love, a metaphysician's way of bestowing value upon objective appraisal. It reveals the nature of all love, not in giving an adequate analysis but in presenting a most magnificent and imaginative instance of the very attitude its doctrine misconstrues.

5
Friendship in Aristotle

I N TURNING FROM PLATO TO
Aristotle, we move from the greatest poet of Hellenic philosophy to
its greatest legal mind. Where Plato is suggestive, probing, imaginative, and seminal, Aristotle is thoroughly commonsensical, cautious,
exhaustive in proof, more interested in analysis than original thinking. Still, the two are clearly teacher and pupil. Despite his sophisticated criticisms of Plato, Aristotle burrows within the shaft his master sank. Though he changes terminology, he continues the eros
tradition. He is a great systematizer. In the *Nicomachean Ethics* the
idea of love as a search for goodness receives its most rigorous, and
possibly its most convincing, presentation.

Discussing the Platonic doctrine, I argued that it could not
account for the love of persons. As if to answer any such criticism,
Aristotle shrewdly distinguishes among three kinds of love or
friendship. Assuming (just as Plato had) that bad or evil things
cannot be loved, Aristotle claims that the object of love is always
useful, pleasant, and/or good. To each there corresponds a type of
friendship. In friendships based on utility or pleasure each participant is primarily concerned with his own welfare. Friends of this sort
do not really care about one another as separate individuals. Their
relationship being governed entirely by self-interest, each loves the
other merely as a source of personal benefits: "Now those who love
each other for their utility do not love each other for themselves but

in virtue of some good which they get from each other. So too with those who love for the sake of pleasure; it is not for their character that men love ready-witted people, but because they find them pleasant." In the third type of friendship, however, men do love one another for what they are, as persons in themselves and not just instrumentalities. This relationship Aristotle calls "perfect friendship." For it most perfectly embodies the defining characteristics of all friendship. By definition a friend is one who cares about the welfare of another person, bearing a good will toward him, wishing him well and doing what seems good for this other person. But benevolence is not enough. Aristotle also sees that friendship ideally requires constant association between the friends. Living together, sharing interests, mutually recognizing each other's good will, they establish a community of love in which each benefits himself by benefiting the other. Such friends will be both useful and pleasant, but only accidentally. What matters most is the companionship of men who *delight* in one another and freely act in each other's behalf.

If this were all that Aristotle meant by perfect friendship, his analysis would be incontestable. Men cannot be friends without the traits I have listed; indeed, they are essential characteristics in every love of persons. For loving another person does mean enjoying him instead of merely putting him to use, delighting in what he is and wishing him well, creating a community in which mutual interests can be developed. In these and other ways, each bestows value upon the other. But Aristotle cannot leave the analysis there, any more than Plato would have. Investigating the ideal of perfect friendship, he wonders what kind of person could enter into so excellent a relationship. He concludes that only those who are *morally virtuous* can be friends in a way that does not reduce to utility or pleasure; the third type of friendship, perfect friendship, exists among good men and no one else. Only the virtuous, Aristotle says, can be interested in one another as persons. For only they can love each other's character as opposed to incidental benefits of pleasure or utility. And since one ought not to delight in anyone who is bad, only the good men are *worthy* of being loved for themselves. Perfect friendship is, therefore, "the friendship of men who are good, and alike in virtue; for these wish well alike to each other *qua* good, and they are good in themselves."

In thus limiting perfect friendship, Aristotle retains the guiding principles of Platonic love. That he really had no intention of departing from them is evident from his initial questions about the object of love. He asks: "Do men love, then, *the* good, or what is good for *them*? These sometimes clash." He quickly resolves the clash by pointing out that what is loved is only the lovable, that the good is lovable without qualification, and that for each man the lovable is that which is good for that man. Now, this need not commit Aristotle to the Platonic belief in the Good as an ultimate object of love. But it does mean that he, like Plato, assumes that nothing can be worthy of love unless it is good. If good in itself, like the virtuous man, it will be lovable without qualification; if good for some personal benefit, like the wine a man drinks, it will be lovable for that individual person. On this basis, Aristotle offers a primitive distinction between the love of persons and the love of things. One may speak of loving wine, he says, but not of having friendship with it: "for it is not mutual love, nor is there a wishing of good to the other (for it would surely be ridiculous to wish wine well; if one wishes anything for it, it is that it may keep, so that one may have it oneself)." In either event, love remains the search for an objective goodness in the object. That love might be a way of bestowing value *upon* the object, taking an interest in it regardless of how good or bad it may be—this conception is as foreign to Aristotle as it was to Plato. Aristotle rightly perceives that the wine we love proffers goods to us, whereas our friend is one for whom we wish to do good things. But he fails to see that *loving* wine means giving it a significance in our lives which cannot be reduced to gratifications the wine itself provides. Likewise, loving a friend means more than wishing him well or enjoying his noble character; it also means caring about him despite his imperfections, treating him in a way that is *incommensurate* with his actual goodness, assuming a virtue though he have it not.

But though Aristotle neglects bestowal much as Plato had, he does eliminate some of the confusions in Platonic love. He does so by analyzing appraisal as a practical, mundane activity of ordinary valuation. For both Plato and Aristotle objective good elicits love; but with Plato one is never sure exactly *what* has been elicited. In defining love as desire for the perpetual possession of the Good, Plato subordinates all human relationships to an ultimate state of union that can hardly be described. As we shall see, Aristotle ends up with something comparable. In the analysis of perfect friendship, however, he does show how good men may love each other as human beings within a small society of their own choosing. The Aristotelian friends are related to one another as something more than vehicles to the highest form. If theirs is not the love of persons, at least it is a love of good character in other persons. Platonic lovers live together in harmony and wish each other well, but their mutual interest is always geared to a metaphysical objective that transcends every human being. One pictures Plato's lovers marching side by side in the direction of the ideal, or else roped together like mountain climbers. They may pause occasionally to appreciate one another's perfections, but really they yearn for something "bigger than us both." Even in the *Republic* those illustrious philosopher-kings seem restless and somewhat dazzled after their vision of the Good. Bivouacked in the temporal world, theirs is the fellowship of a military campaign. In Aristotle, however, the virtuous men that he idealizes seem stable, serenely satisfied, secure within their mutual admiration. They delight in each other's character, the sheer goodness of good men being the basis of perfect human relations. Though Plato says man is political by nature, it is really Aristotle who understands the joys of sociability.

Nevertheless, these joys come at a very high price. Even more than Plato, Aristotle associates love with reason as against emotion. Platonic lovers were at least divinely mad and ambiguously sexual. One always feels that with Plato sexuality has been sublimated as a defense against its imperious demands. His lovers are enthusiasts yearning for the Good if not for one another, ardent in their intellectual companionship, tormented by the imperfections of a world they never made and must now transcend. For all its repressiveness, Platonic love speaks with the poetry of youth saddened by too much experience. A skylark like Shelley feels its allure no less than a Michelangelo burning with a gemlike flame. Aristotle is infinitely older. The fellowship he calls perfect is crisp with virtue and rationality. He even restricts the meaning of Plato's word *eros*, using it only for the lesser relationship of sexual love. For what he really wishes to recommend, friendship, he adopts the term *philia*. Not merely is perfect friendship wholly asexual; it is also cool and institutional. The Aristotelian friends are businessmen who share a partnership in virtue. They admire one another's goodness and they mutually benefit from overlapping interests; but their feelings rarely issue into emotional responses. However intimate it may be, their friendship is purely professional. Philia is rational through and through. Pertaining to emotion rather than reason, eros hardly counts as a virtue for Aristotle. In the *Eudemian Ethics* he slightingly refers to it as a desire for pleasure; in the *Nicomachean Ethics* he calls it "a sort of excess of feeling." In general he considers sexual love an extreme of which true friendship is the mean. When people are sexually in love, Aristotle argues, they try to establish an exclusive relationship, a union more intense than true friendship and limited to only one other person.

It is obvious that Aristotle has scant regard for the society that sexual love effects. Yet on his own premises he might have argued differently. For he says that eros binds only two persons at a time because it is very difficult to find many people who are good enough to elicit love from any one individual. (For this reason too one cannot hope to have many friendships of the perfect type.) But if eros is just a convenient arrangement for the eliciting of love, it *need* not be an excess of feeling. On some occasions it might function as a special case of perfect friendship. Needless to say, Aristotle never even considers this line of argument. Elsewhere in the *Nicomachean Ethics* he classifies (sexual) love with friendship based on pleasure, particularly among the young: "Young people are amorous too; for the greater part of the friendship of love depends on emotion and aims at pleasure; this is why they fall in love and quickly fall out of love, changing often within a single day." When he details the actual goods that lovers get from one another, he speaks only of the lover's pleasure in seeing the beloved and the beloved's pleasure in receiving attention. The expressing of emotion, the sharing of feelings, the enjoying of instinctual satisfaction—none of these components in sexual love seem to count as goods. And even if they did, Aristotle would always subordinate such love to a friendship based on virtue and the admiration of moral character. He does say that perfect friendship may exist between man and wife; but there too it seems to be wholly independent of the emotional, sexual love for which Aristotle reserves the term *eros*.

Perfect friendship being an idealization of rationality, Aristotle automatically assumes that it arises from deliberate choice. When good men or women discern the moral virtue in one another, they naturally decide to be friends. Where love is governed by feeling, Aristotle remarks, one can never be assured of reciprocity. Since friendship cannot exist unless it is mutual, it requires a joint use of reason. Each participant must consciously and deliberately recognize the goodness of the other: "Mutual love involves choice and choice springs from a state of character; and men wish well to those whom they love, for their own sake, not as a result of feeling, but as a result of a state of character." But why limit such decisions to the participants? Will not all reasonable, right-thinking persons reach the same conclusions about an objective state of character? If so, why not allow those who are *most* rational to determine who is capable of friendship or mutual love and who is not? Aristotle's wise and virtuous men do not claim such powers, but they become the models of countless authorities who will do so in later centuries. In both church and state, the Aristotelian assumptions about choice will support each generation's attempts to control the marital, the erotic, the amorous practices of the next one. In the neoclassicism of the seventeenth century, even the *stirrings* of love will have to come and go as reason commands. Thus Corneille tells us that "a decent man's love should always spring up at the bidding of his will" and that the beloved "is under far greater obligation to our love when this results from our choice and her qualities than when it arises from a blind attraction."

Aristotle cannot be blamed for all the uses to which his philosophy has been put. He was not himself a neoclassicist. Still, the rationalism of the seventeenth-century attitude is merely Aristotle writ large. The underlying mistake is identical in both. Pascal comes close to detecting it, I think, when he despairs of ever loving another person: "Does he who loves someone on account of beauty really love that person? No; for the small-pox, which will kill beauty without killing the person, will cause him to love her no more. And if one loves me for my judgment, memory, he does not love *me*, for I can lose these qualities without losing myself. . . . We never, then, love a person, but only qualities." This is quite a dire conclusion. In reaching it, Pascal assumes that a person is something apart from his "qualities," whereas he is just the totality of them. Making this change, however, would not affect Pascal's skepticism. He rightly senses that loving a person is not the same as loving attributes. But like everyone else who has been influenced by Plato and Aristotle, Pascal thinks that love is always directed toward *some* quality. Whether it be goodness or beauty (as in Plato) or moral virtue (as in Aristotle), the quality must be an objective value that reason best discerns. Can this explain the love of persons? Confused as he may be, Pascal realizes that it cannot. The beloved's attributes may be as nearly perfect as anyone could hope for; and yet we do not love someone *as* a person if we are merely in love with her perfections.

Aristotle believes that loving another in himself means loving that man's character. Like Pascal, I wish to argue that a man is much more than his (good) character. To love him for the sake of his virtue alone is to disregard a great deal that makes him the person he is. Loving another as a person means bestowing value upon his personality even if it is not virtuous. In principle I see no difference between loving a man *qua* good and loving him *qua* useful or pleasant. His goodness may be more important, more revealing, than any other attribute. But it is still one among many properties—just like utility or pleasantness. To love a man for these attributes is certainly not to love him as a person; but the same is true of loving him for his goodness. In short, Aristotle does not succeed in explaining the love of persons. What he calls perfect friendship is rather love within a class of special individuals, each of whom cares about the other's welfare but none of whom cares about anyone as just the person he happens to be. They are in love with virtuous human character, much as the Platonic lovers were in love with ideals.

As a further perspective upon Aristotelian love, one needs to relate it to Aristotle's ideas about justice. Throughout the discussion of friendship he frequently compares the two moral concepts. At the outset he says: "When men are friends they have no need of justice, while when they are just they need friendship as well." But as we read on, it becomes quite apparent that just as friendship is the model of love, so too is justice the model of friendship. For there to be a moral community, friendship and justice must both exist; and each actual society will "involve friendship just in so far as it involves justice." Perfect friendship is a state of justice because it enables good men to take cognizance of each other's character, thereby according one another the love that virtue deserves. For Aristotle this constitutes the truest form of justice. Both parties being alike in excellence, each warrants a similar good, and as friends each will be happy to give the other his due.

When persons are not alike, one being superior to the other, friendships may also occur. Between parents and children, man and wife, ruler and subjects—all of whom Aristotle assumes to be morally unequal—he allows the possibility of viable friendships that need not be limited to pleasure or utility. But in every relationship love must be proportioned to merit. This is what Aristotelian justice demands, and friendship cannot be authentic if it goes against justice. In the friendship of equally good men each gets from each "in all respects" the same benefits he gives. This is the perfect condition. In the friendship of unequals, however, the proportioning of love creates a kind of equalization. Those who are most worthy (presumably the parents, the husbands, the rulers, etc.) receive the most in honor and deference. Even if the child, for instance, cannot fully repay his parents for having given him life, he shows filial devotion by serving them to the best of his ability. This equalizes the relationship, according to Aristotle, providing each participant with the degree and kind of love that he deserves.

What Aristotle imagines therefore is human sentiment regulating itself in accordance with a code of social morality. By making love proportional to merit, a society may promise to the virtuous man the greatest of all possible rewards. And is it not *just* that this should be so? As only the brave deserve the fair, does not every good man *deserve* to be loved? The better a man is, the more fitting it seems that love should be bestowed upon him. Possibly so. But still Aristotle misses the fact that one must *bestow* love. It is a spontaneous gift of the lover, not a conditioned response. It is not elicited by goodness in the beloved, and human feelings cannot be governed by the sensible pattern that Aristotle uses to organize society. Reason may force us to recognize the virtuous character of a good man; but nothing can force us to love him. Perhaps it is to compensate for this gap that we heap honors on the worthy. The honors express our admiration, our gratitude, our respect, and sometimes—but not always or necessarily—our love. To some extent we all envy, and therefore hate, the good man. He is better than we are. Why should we love him? His virtue is his reward. To play the game of justice and encourage other heroes, we may lavish all the symbols of social benefit upon him. But our loving emotions we more often save for those who have no moral claims upon us, persons who happen to satisfy our needs and so facilitate the process of bestowal.

At the same time, Aristotle does perceive that love is often disproportionate to merit. But then he claims that it *ought* not to be. In correlating love and justice, he means that only the good being worthy of love, the best men have the greatest *right* to it. I myself find this hard to believe. I can imagine an Aristotelian antithesis arguing that only the bad are worth loving. For they have the greatest need of it. If, as Aristotle says, a friend wishes well to another, a true friend will care about the welfare of one who most requires his assistance—and that is usually not the good man, but the bad one. In a sense, it *is* unjust for good men to be denied the reward of love, which they have earned and probably desire more than any other. Yet in another sense it is also unjust for a bad man to be deprived of the one thing that might make him better. If this be so, it is never unjust to love *anyone*. From which it follows that love need not be proportionate to merit. Hamlet has the right idea when he castigates

Polonius, that arch-Aristotelian, for his attitude toward the actors (with whom Shakespeare undoubtedly identified himself):

> Hamlet: . . . Good my lord, will you see the players well bestowed?
> Polonius: My lord, I will use them according to their desert.
> Hamlet: God's bodykins, man, much better! Use every man after his desert, and who shall 'scape whipping? Use them after your own honour and dignity: the less they deserve, the more merit is in your bounty.

The less they deserve, the more is in your bounty. This, I think, is something Aristotle does not understand. He says it is better to love than to be loved, since loving is active and being loved a kind of passivity; he says the benefactor, who exists by virtue of his good deeds, is happier than the beneficiary, who merely receives another's love; but he never recognizes the creative, autonomous character of love. For him it is always a response to external merit. That it may also function as an imaginative mechanism that *makes* men moral, the lover if not the beloved, Aristotle never seems to notice.

In this respect, I find a deep-rooted kinship between Freud and Aristotle (also a biologist, and the son of a doctor). Both are sensitive to the duties love imposes, and neither feels that so great an expenditure of energy can be justified unless the object bears a corresponding excellence. Freud sounds like Aristotle when he writes: "A love that does not discriminate seems to me to forfeit a part of its own value, by doing an injustice to its object; and secondly, not all men are worthy of love." So valuable is love to Freud, in the sense that it costs dearly in sacrifice and self-restraint, that he can see no reason for squandering it on anything but a worthy object: "If I love someone, he must deserve it in some way." Spoken like Polonius! Of course, Freud speaks at a deeper level than Polonius; but in his own fashion he also perpetuates the Aristotelian attitude: "He deserves it [Freud says of his love] if he is so like me in important ways that I can love myself in him; and he deserves it if he is so much more perfect than myself that I can love my ideal of my own self in him."

Nor are the doctrinal bases of this agreement between Freud and Aristotle wholly dissimilar. When Aristotle explains why good men must live together, he introduces concepts that closely resemble Freudian ideas about identification. In his writings on group psychology, Freud takes identification as the prerequisite for all emotional ties with other persons. Wanting to *be* his father, the little boy sees him as his "ideal"; eventually each individual comes to identify with others who are likewise related to an object that embodies their ideal; from this, society arises. Freud thinks of the group as an entity within which all the members identify with one another as equals striving to achieve a similar perfection.

In various ways this analysis fits the outline of what Aristotle says about perfect friendship, though standing it on its head as Marx did with Hegel. In Aristotle as in Plato, the ideal is built into the objective structure of things and therefore cannot depend upon a process of psychogenesis. But otherwise, Aristotle's ideas about the psychological roots of perfect friendship are at least parallel to what Freud says about the development of civilization. Asking why virtuous men need each other, Aristotle replies that no one but God is morally self-sufficient. The greatest happiness consists in two things: living actively, which the good man does in exercising his virtues as a human being; and second, being aware of one's goodness in living as one does. The friendship of good men is needed for both conditions. Since good men merit love, we act properly (and so exercise our virtue) in wishing them well; and since they are like ourselves, we achieve awareness of our own character by contemplating theirs. Insofar as good men are equally dedicated to the same ideal of virtue, they are bound to one another as if they were one person: "As the virtuous man is to himself, he is to his friend also (for his friend is another self)." This identification Aristotle would not call an "emotional tie," as Freud does, and definitely not a sexual one. Nevertheless, his little world of perfect friendship is patterned in relation to its objective ideal very much in the way that Freudian society organizes itself with respect to ego ideals projected by the libido.

As for the social tie itself, neither Aristotle nor Freud does much to analyze it. Just how is one's friend another self? Later Aristotelians were to define friendship as "one soul in two bodies." But exactly what does this mean? And how can one identify with another? Literally speaking, the child does not want to *be* his father: he wants to be a father *himself*, to resemble his father in crucial ways and to possess certain of his desirable attributes. One may say that the child wishes to *imitate* the father; but how are imitation and identification related?

Aristotle does not tell us; nor does Freud. Both seem to have been influenced by Aristophanes' myth about the alter ego, but whether the relevant union is a merging or a wedding one can hardly determine in them any more than in Plato. All three limit their moral perspective to what Bergson calls "the closed society": a small, tightly integrated unit, close to the primitive family or clan, externally hostile toward everything foreign, internally homogeneous and uniform. Thus, Plato's ideal republic brooks no innovation or difference of opinion or anything else that might create dissension; Aristotle's perfect friendship establishes the company of men who are so completely similar that each may contemplate the other's character as if it were his own; Freud's archetypal group resembles an enormous family in which everyone submits to a communal Oedipus complex and feels bound to all social siblings by a unified system of identifications. When Freud says that love must be deserved and that this means choosing someone in whom I can love either myself or my ideal of myself, he is voicing the morality of the closed society just like Plato and Aristotle. Freud's remarks occur in a passage that condemns the Judaeo-Christian precept to love one's neighbor as oneself. Universal love, Freud argues, is wrong as well as unrealistic: if the neighbor is just another human being, a stranger who has not deserved my love, fearing and hating him seems more appropriate than loving him. Plato and Aristotle would say the same. In their preferred societies one loves friends or intimates as oneself; but the relationship must be circumscribed, closed not open, in principle precluding the love of strangers or of mankind as such.

Freud's ideas about narcissism also run parallel to those of Aristotle. Just as Freud claims that parental love is "nothing but" parental

narcissism reborn, the parents' own infantile self-love being reproduced in another object, so too does Aristotle say that parents love
their children as a product of themselves: "For their issue are by
virtue of their separate existence a sort of other selves." In general
Aristotle maintains that all friendship is an extension of a man's
relation to himself. The defining characteristics of friendship are
initially present in self-love; and being a friend to someone else
merely means loving a duplicated self, an extended version of oneself, in that person. From this there follow two conclusions that
Aristotle does not spell out, but which are certainly implied in what
he says: first, that one cannot love another without loving oneself;
second, that loving others is ultimately *just* a way of loving oneself.

But Aristotle does not stop there. He also believes that every man
"is his own best friend and ought to love himself best." In keeping
with his Platonic heritage, he distinguishes between two kinds of
self-love. People are often said to love themselves when they selfishly
seek the greater share of wealth, power, and physical pleasure. This
is what most people desire, Aristotle says, and they are to be re-
proved for loving themselves poorly. For this kind of self-love does
not give people what they really want. It gratifies their momentary
appetites but destroys their nature as rational beings. The man who
loves himself best lives in accordance with what is *noblest* in him. He
will act justly and cultivate a virtuous character because he thereby
achieves the greatest share of what is truly desirable. Far from being
selfish, this kind of self-love causes the good man to sacrifice all
superficial values. He will do anything that leads to human perfection, what Aristotle calls nobility: "It is true of the good man too that
he does many acts for the sake of his friends and his country, and if
necessary dies for them; for he will throw away both wealth and
honours and in general the goods that are objects of competition,
gaining for himself nobility . . . he is therefore assigning the greater
good to himself."

From this we may derive two conclusions in addition to the ones
previously mentioned: that loving oneself best means living in a way
that satisfies one's ideals of what one would like to be; and, finally,
that however good a man is, whatever sacrifices he may undergo for
the welfare of others, he loves himself best in the sense that he always

desires the greatest good for himself—"it is for himself most of all that each man wishes what is good." Unless I am very much mistaken, all four of these conclusions are common to Freud and Aristotle (possibly to Plato as well).

I have listed the four statements as separate conclusions not only because they are different, but also because they are logically independent. One may believe any one of them without accepting the other three. For instance, believing that one cannot love others *without* loving oneself does not force us to conclude that loving others is really *just* a way of loving oneself. Nor does thinking that one loves oneself best by living in accordance with one's ideals require us to believe that loving oneself best means wanting the greatest of goods (even moral goods) for *oneself*. In fact, the first and third conclusions are probably true, but the second and fourth are surely false.

Freud and Aristotle maintain all four conclusions because their conjunction tends to justify the morally closed society each of them idealizes. Erich Fromm has argued that Freud considers loving oneself and loving others to be mutually exclusive "in the sense that the more there is of one, the less there is of the other." But this does Freud an injustice. Though he cites an impoverishment of the ego in cases of obsession with an external object, Freud treats primary narcissism as the basis of *all* libidinal ties. This means, for Freud no less than Aristotle, that all love is really self-love, and therefore that justifiable love must be a way of loving oneself in other persons. This, however, requires a little world that reflects the lover's personality: for not many objects could be the extension of oneself. Only in the emotional confines of a society such as Jean-Paul Sartre portrays in *No Exit* could Freudian love be satisfied. Nor is the situation greatly changed if we stock the little world with perfect Aristotelian friends. The inhabitants would be less neurotic and more rationally serene, but they would still be living in a changeless hell. Looking into each other's eyes, they would love only the image of themselves and of what they would like to be in their blocked universe. They would love each other not as separate persons but only as *things*, as mirrors variously propped at points within concentric circles. Is this even self-love?

I do not think so. Both Freud and Aristotle neglect the joy of loving those who are not like ourselves, persons who are not extensions of our own personality, but are really different, separate, autonomous. In the closed society there are no individual souls: the children belong to the parents and everyone belongs to the group. To love others as persons, however, we must accept their independence. Our children are not possessions, and only in part are they projections of ourselves. They come through us, impregnated with the stain of our reality, but not as extensions or artifacts. A human being cannot be created in anyone else's image. In loving children, we bestow value and give them what we can; but we do not love them as persons unless we delight in their separateness. Likewise, an open society encourages a diversity of ideals, permitting each individual to work out his own destiny, if not with diligence, at least with freedom. In such a society no one can *belong* to the group because the group has no definitive structure. It varies with the human environment and freely admits anyone who allows himself to be loved.

Properly understood, that universal love which Freud scorns and Aristotle prohibits is really the love of persons. For if we love another as a person, we bestow value whether or not he is so like us that we can love ourselves in him, and despite those imperfections that prevent him from embodying our own ideal of ourselves. Freud and Aristotle are right to think that no one loves another unless he loves himself. (How could one enjoy others without also enjoying oneself, bestowing value upon one's own involvement, one's own loving attitude?) But they are wrong to think that loving others is really just a way of loving oneself. Similarly, they do well to identify the best love as one that chooses objects in accordance with ideals. For in the long run such an attitude contributes to the greatest possibility of enjoyment by integrating love with the demands of purposiveness. But this must not lead us to conclude that the best love is really the lover's way of getting the greatest goods for himself. We care about another's welfare simply because the act of loving is enjoyable. We do not make sacrifices in love with the idea of perfecting ourselves or of attaining a nobility which is better than what we give. The lover does what he does because the circumstances of his love require it. No man hath greater love than to die for his friends, perhaps; but in doing so, the martyr may fully realize that his survivors are gaining the greater good. Indeed, could he be said to have loved *them* if his martyrdom turned out to be a device for getting the best for himself?

Throughout their respective analyses, both Freud and Aristotle describe the state of love in metaphors drawn from economics. Possibly this is their fundamental mistake. Even to ask whether the lover gets more good than he gives is already to misinterpret the situation. I leave aside Aristotle's references to friendship as a human "partnership" and his saying that children owe their parents a "debt" of life, etc. More important is the way in which he describes friendship as a condition of equality in the sense of "equal returns." Thus, in perfect friendship men who are alike in virtue benefit equally from one another. In loving his friend, each man loves what is good for himself and becomes a reciprocating good to the other. With respect to good will, utility, and also pleasure, the friends make an equal exchange. "Each gets from each in all respects the same as, or something like what, he gives; which is what ought to happen between friends." Other relationships are inferior precisely because the participants, not being alike in virtue, have greater difficulty in equalizing the flow of goods. The instability of such friendships can be rectified only through proportionality, the worthier men receiving more love in payment for the benefits they give just in being virtuous.

In Freud the comparable metaphors appear whenever he speaks of the libido. He refers to the libido as a specific quantity (like money in the bank) that may be invested either in the self or in other objects. When it is "withdrawn" from the ego, the self remains "depleted" until the libido "re-enriches" it by returning from the external object. In happy love object-libido and ego-libido cannot be distinguished inasmuch as the quantity that leaves is always balanced by an equal amount returning. This libidinal state, like the primal narcissistic one, is perfectly stable. In both cases, one pertaining to infancy, the other to ideal maturity, the *economy* of love is sound.

I criticize this as a basic mistake because love cannot be quantified, any more than enjoyment itself. Even if the concept of libido were clear, it would make sense only in terms of something like stamina or vital energy. There cannot be units of measurement. Love and money are not really comparable. Money is the measure of our love only isomorphically, and love is not the measure of anything. Love creates a circuit of feeling, which doubles back upon itself when love is reciprocal. Each participant then bestows value upon someone who satisfies needs or desires. But this does not mean that people are exchanging anything (other than love itself) or that each will get from the other the same as what is given. It merely means that each will delight in the other, care about the other, derive relevant satisfactions from the other. And though their love be "equal," they may enjoy each other in vastly different, wholly incommensurate, ways. There can be no assignable quantity of love and therefore no economy.

Or perhaps one should say that Freud and Aristotle are using metaphors taken from a *static* economy, one that does not generate wealth creatively. In the closed society we all tend to heed Polonius: "Neither a borrower nor a lender be"; i.e., neither give nor take except through an equalized transaction. That way of life will not issue into love, but it may afford a modest security. Love is always precarious: "For loan oft loses both itself and friend." And yet, how paltry is this ideal of static lovelessness! Like Aristotle, Polonius may say: "to thine own self be true"; but without the openness of love, will it not be a shriveled and a meager self? Libido as a determinate quantity that fills the beloved but leaves the lover depleted Henry James calls "the sacred fount." He speaks ironically, knowing that this source—like the closed society it symbolizes—is stagnant and therefore deceptive about the nature of man. It stands at a great distance from the love of persons and systematically obscures the open possibilities of human enjoyment. For love is not a quid pro quo. Loving another augments, not diminishes, the lover. The more he gives the more he has, precisely because the activity of bestowing is so enjoyable. In wishing to have his love reciprocated, the lover has no need for a like and equal return of anything: the circuit of love itself provides what he most desires.

In a sense, I am suggesting something even more egocentric than what Aristotle says. The love of persons is not reducible to self-love;

nor is it a means of getting the greatest of goods for oneself. Yet the fact that loving other persons involves choosing objects regardless of their deserts can itself be explained as a desire for limitless enjoyment. To one who can do it, loving a worthless man may be more rewarding than loving a paragon of virtue. Who can tell what needs the saint may satisfy in his love for the moral leper? Who can gauge his sense of achievement in delighting in such a person? For most of us the love of unwholesome objects is unattainable, and so we label them "unlovable." But that merely means that their moral worthlessness makes them *harder* to love, not that they are unworthy of it. If love were something given as a reward, only the deserving could merit it. Since love is enjoyment, however, our own self-love encourages us to cultivate it whenever possible. On some occasions an indiscriminate love is highly undesirable, as any moment of enjoyment may be. A love of persons that thwarts the larger interests represented by justice and morality may have to be sacrificed. To the extent that these interests are foundational to the purposive life, all societies are rightly closed in *some* respects. In Utopia each loving gesture will lead to greater happiness, but in the meanwhile the need for justifiable love must always impose limitations.

It is here, in the moral *context* of love, that Aristotle's insight touches deep truths. As James' character Isabel Archer wisely says in rejecting a suitor who offers an immoral love and begs her to run away with him: "The world's very small." And so it must be, alas, for those who live a life of decency and self-respect. Aristotle's mistake occurs when he assumes that virtuous love must be love *directed toward* virtue. Justice then becomes the model of all love, instead of its control. This, however, makes the world unnecessarily small. It shrinks the moral globe when it should be expanding it, closes off the potentialities of love instead of regulating them toward whatever openness reality permits.

What Aristotle calls perfect friendship idealizes unity within a social class. The perfect friends exemplify the class consciousness of a moral and political elite. Their friendship operates within a society of like-minded men (and women) equally dedicated to a code of virtue. Membership in the group is conditional upon success in living up to the code. A loss of virtue automatically ostracizes the offender, disqualifying him from both love and friendship. To this extent, Aristotelian philia idealizes that conformity to reigning ideals which constitutes a sense of social importance. It glorifies the comfort and rectitude that all men feel when they are accepted by their peers and when their virtuous conduct receives the immediate sanction of communal authority. Without this kind of friendship there could be no aristocracies, whether of birth or of excellence, no social distinctions, and probably no society at all. The concept of "honor"—for which men have died from time to time, and women too—expresses the desire for status which philia idealizes as perfect friendship. However limited such a love may be, however narrow its choice of objects, it may nevertheless serve as a first approximation to whatever else man may ultimately achieve.

In using the term *eros* as he does, Aristotle anticipates the modern distinction between love as something sexual and friendship as something less intimate. But even the common usage recognizes the possibility of friendly relations in sexual love as well as emotional ardor in friendship. Freud relies on this linguistic overlap when he reduces both love and friendship to the more elemental concept of libido. In a similar fashion Aristotle's distinction between eros and philia does not affect his adherence to the major tendencies of Platonic love. For all his originality, Aristotle still belongs to what is often called (using Plato's terminology) the eros tradition. He never questions the ultimacy of man's striving for goodness, and many of his ideas about philia come directly from Plato. That perfect friendship can exist only when good men live together, sharing interests and caring about each other's welfare—this is Platonic as well as Aristotelian. The entire sociology of the *Republic* is based upon these ideas. Plato's guardian class, the philosopher-kings, fits almost all of Aristotle's description. It remained for Aristotle to codify Plato's intimations, varying the theme no doubt but only as a way of developing it further. When Christianity appropriated the eros tradition, it often did so through the mediation of Aristotle rather than Plato. Within that tradition ideas about philia—which the Christians took directly from Aristotle—were always considered subsidiary or correlative, never contradictory.

As we shall see, Christian philia is largely fellowship between man and God, a friendship or communion that effects a reciprocal love. To Plato and Aristotle, however, the idea of mutual love between man and God would have been blasphemous. Plato does speak of love as a great mediator between the human and the divine: in one direction it conveys prayers and sacrifices; in the other, commands and rewards. But Plato consistently maintains that the gods do not love. Eros being desire for the perpetual possession of the Good, it can occur only in things that are imperfect, devoid of absolute goodness in however slight a degree. Since everything mortal and material falls short of perfection, love has free reign within the empirical world. But the gods must be perfect; they can have no deficiency of goodness. Consequently, they cannot love.

In the *Symposium* Socrates ridicules the previous speakers for having claimed that love is a great god. Eros is not a god at all, since he exists through desire and desire results from lack. Neither can he be mortal, however, since his transcendental striving takes him into the realm of the divine. He must be a *daemon*, a being partway between mortal and immortal, i.e., like the questing soul of man. The Socratic irony appears when Socrates then describes the power of love. More than any of his predecessors, he sees in eros the explanation for the stirrings of all living creatures. Without being a god, Eros is nevertheless godlike. He is not beautiful, as Agathon had suggested, but possibly ugly like Socrates himself, and he is to be revered precisely because his lack of beauty forces him to search endlessly for the Beautiful.

To all intents and purposes, Socrates seems to worship *only* Eros. Yet on purely doctrinal grounds he denies that love belongs among the immortals. The gods that Socrates believed in were not the anthropomorphic beings of Homeric legend. Neither were they partisan deities worshiped by the Athenians who condemned Socrates on the charge of atheism. To Socrates and Plato, the God or gods (both terms are used) were beings that enjoy the fullness of

achieved ideals, desiring nothing, lacking nothing, at one with absolute goodness and beauty. Magnificent as Eros might be, he could
never attain a condition such as this.

In Aristotle one finds a similar body of thought except that the
idea of God is more thoroughly developed. For Aristotle as for
Plato, everything but the divine is motivated by a search for its own
good. Parallel to Plato's order of salvation, Aristotle's ladder of
being starts with *pure matter* and culminates in *pure form*. Insofar as
these are opposite termini, Aristotle's metaphysics is dualistic. But
between the poles of pure matter and pure form, Aristotle undermines Platonic dualism by showing how all things are linked
together by form and matter, every form being matter for a higher
form. Things in nature drive themselves up the ladder of existence
by their movement from potentiality to an actuality in which they
realize the perfection of their being. At the top of the ladder, pure
form—the form of perfection itself, as in Plato—draws everything
toward it. All things strive for their completion in pure form. But in
itself pure form is uncaused and unchanging. It is the ultimate
phenomenon, the *unmoved mover*, which moves all else and does so
by the force of love: "it moves by being loved." In the *Metaphysics*
Aristotle identifies this final cause, the primal goal of being, as God,
of whom he says: "God is a living being, eternal, most good, so that
life and duration continuous and eternal belong to God; for this *is*
God." But this God, the highest form, the culminating perfection,
loves nothing in return. In his discussion of friendship in the *Nicomachean Ethics*, Aristotle uses God's remoteness from the human
condition to illustrate the fact that philia cannot exist where the
participants are wholly unequal: "When one party is removed to a
great distance, as God is, the possibility of friendship ceases." Between man and the gods there can be no reciprocal love. We love the
divine. It does not love us back.

The idea that love makes the world go round had already been
stated in one of the earlier speeches in the *Symposium* and somewhat
developed in Plato's *Timaeus*. Aristotle systematically shows the
workings of this principle in a purposive universe, and the recipient
of cosmic love he names God. This much of the metaphysics could
easily be amalgamated into Christianity. But the absence of a loving

God was, of course, an impediment. Even in Plato and Aristotle the doctrine engenders internal difficulties. For the remoteness of the gods results from their total sufficiency: they need nothing because they are perfectly good. But the same would be true, at least in principle, of the ideal man whom Plato and Aristotle envisage. Does this mean that for them a perfect man would thrive without love or friendship? In the *Lysis* Plato has Socrates reason as follows:

> "Will not the good man, in so far as he is good, be sufficient for himself? Certainly he will. And he who is sufficient wants nothing—that is implied in the word 'sufficient.'"
>
> "Of course not."
>
> "And he who wants nothing will desire nothing."
>
> "He will not."
>
> "Neither can he love that which he does not desire?"
>
> "He cannot."
>
> "And he who loves not is not a lover or friend?"
>
> "Clearly not."
>
> "What place then is there for friendship, if, when absent, good men have no need of one another (for even when alone they are sufficient for themselves), and when present have no use of one another? How can such persons ever be induced to value one another?"
>
> "They cannot."
>
> "And friends they cannot be, unless they value one another?"
>
> "Very true."

But if this is the condition of good men, how can Plato attain that ideal republic where his philosopher-kings are to live together in perfect unity and familial love? In the *Nicomachean Ethics* Aristotle confronts the problem directly. It is argued, he says, that the supremely happy man needs no friends, since he has the things that are good and needs nothing further. To this Aristotle replies: "But it seems strange, when one assigns all good things to the happy man, not to assign friends, who are thought the greatest of external goods." Furthermore, man being a social animal by nature, the good man must achieve his goodness through action with other men. Where these others are also good, each will fulfill his nature most perfectly. In a sense, this repeats what Plato had said in various places: namely, that no individual can be really good (not even Socrates) unless he belongs to a good society. But unlike Plato, Aristotle concludes from this that love and friendship *themselves* contribute to the perfection of the good man.

The difficulties in this conclusion are tantalizing. Fully explored, they would reveal all the problems of the eros tradition. For if love is in itself a good, it cannot be defined as the *search* for goodness. On Platonic principles one can search only for a good that one desires but does not have. Either love belongs to the good life or else it is but a means of striving for the good life. It cannot be both, unless we admit an infinite regress in which love becomes the search for that good life which in part consists of love itself. This move may be acceptable to Romantic philosophers who openly espouse the love of love, but for Plato and Aristotle it would be ruinous. They think of love as a response to an objective goodness which is prior to that response and independent of it. How, then, can love or friendship constitute the goodness of a good man? And if they do, as Aristotle insists, why not say the same of that perfect being he calls God?

6

Plotinus and Merging

In His "Life Of Plotinus," Por-
phyry, the disciple of the great man, begins by saying: "Plotinus, the
philosopher our contemporary, seemed ashamed of being in the
body." The oracle of Apollo, so Porphyry tells us, described Plotinus
as follows: "Good and kindly, singularly gentle and engaging . . .
pure of soul, ever striving towards the divine which he loved with all
his being, he laboured strenuously to free himself and rise above the
bitter waves of this blood-drenched life: and this is why to Plotinus—
God-like and lifting himself often, by the ways of meditation and by
the methods Plato teaches in the Banquet [*Symposium*], to the first
and all-transcendent God—that God appeared." And on his death-
bed Plotinus utters these last words: "I am striving to give back the
Divine in myself to the Divine in the All." In these glimpses of the
man, we may see the essentials of his philosophy: disdain toward
material being, hunger for spiritual purity, belief in a divinity that
transcends the world and yet appears to it, identification between
man and God by penetrating into the ultimate recesses of oneself.
For Plotinus philosophic love becomes a kind of introspection. It
culminates in a sense of oneness that reveals the oneness of everything. By learning how to "cut away," the philosopher attains that
small still center of himself in which the alone merges with the
Alone. As arranged by Porphyry, Plotinus' *Enneads* ends with a
description of the final merging: "This is the life of gods and of the
godlike and blessed among men, liberation from the alien that

besets us here, a life taking no pleasure in the things of earth, the passing of solitary to solitary."

How neat the history of ideas would be if only Plotinus had lived two or three hundred years earlier! He is one of the great links between Greek philosophy and Christian mysticism. Had he not overlapped with the beginnings of Christianity, the concept of love could march forward in time step by step. But then, it is in the nature of a link to overlap. Writing in the third century A.D., Plotinus completes the Platonistic philosophy in the ancient world and simultaneously renders it amenable to the reinterpretations of Catholic theology. As it became the reigning spiritual institution, Christianity incorporated more and more pagan thought into its dogma. To a large extent, Greek ideas about love were transmitted through Plotinus. And although the Middle Ages particularly revered Aristotle, Neoplatonists such as Plotinus exerted at least an equal influence. In the words of Dean Inge: "To me at least it is clear that St. Thomas is nearer to Plotinus than to the *real* Aristotle."

In some respects Plotinus is himself nearer to Aristotle than to Plato. In other respects he carries the Platonic argument even further than Plato did. The cosmos of Plotinus is more dualistic than Plato's and more unified than Aristotle's. Where Plato had ambiguously suggested a cleavage between the world of sense and the world of reason, Plotinus sharply emphasizes the differences. The world of sense he assigns to a realm of illusion, nonbeing, unreality. Its values are fleeting and insubstantial, as remote from true goodness as a shadowy image from its original. On the other hand, the world of reason consists of that transempirical realm which Plato had mentioned but hardly described. Plotinus writes of it at length, graphically, ardently, with all the poetic imagination later mysticism was to emulate. It is the abode of the Good, the Divine, the Ground of all life, which he now clearly calls God. But at the same time that Plotinus insists upon the utter and awful contrast between the two realms, he also continues Aristotle's effort to establish a unity between them. Aristotle had sought a unified metaphysics by showing the continuities between matter and form, body and soul, sense and reason. For Plotinus the oneness of all things appears in the universal striving for salvation. Between the antithetical worlds he posits emanations from the divine which serve as intermediaries, spiritual steps by which the soul can mount the ladder of its salvation. The dualistic cosmos is one in burning with the same mystical fervor.

Modifying Plato and Aristotle, Plotinus creates a new synthesis. From Plato he takes the notion of eros as a liberating attitude. Where Aristotle idealized friendship as a circumscribed relation between special individuals, Plotinus reverts to the Platonic search for infinite goodness. For him even more than for Plato, eros is open to the universe. It cannot be closed by anything human, not even the ideal republic. Since man must be alone with the Alone, Plotinus rarely concerns himself with the needs of action or morality. Love does not seek a virtuous object as for Aristotle, but one that is endlessly beautiful. In attaining oneness with God, the soul sees how all things make a harmony: love enables us to appreciate the beauty in every object. This sounds like Plato again, but it is Plato seen through Aristotle. For the beauty that Plotinus seeks is not an abstract form. It is the beautiful aspect of all things *in* the world, beauty immanent not merely transcendent. Reality being one, the Plotinian mystic seeks to achieve oneness with the beauty in everything. If he succeeds, he transforms himself into the Good or Beautiful. Through love he loses his old identity and totally merges with God.

Into this synthesis Plotinus fits the ideas of philosophers such as Philo, Ammonius, and the Stoics. But through it all, the *spirit* of Plato dominates. Thus Longinus on Plotinus: "[He] set the principles of Pythagoras and of Plato in a clearer light than anyone before him." It was in the name of Plato that Plotinus attacked the Christian philosophers of his age. He little realized the historical role his thought was soon to play.

The notion of an *ordo salutis* we have already encountered in Plato. In Plotinus the idea is not only enriched by detailed and vivid images of the soul in progress but also linked with the religious origins of Plato himself. Plotinus often refers to initiations into the *mysteries*, religious cults devoted to the purification of the sinning soul. Although scholars have discovered relatively little about these cults, they generally associate them with the Orphic religion of early Greek society. Orphism already contained the idea of man's double nature, his division into body and soul, the former a prison or charnel house into which the latter has fallen. The soul being immortal, it is in essence something divine, a spark out of the heavenly incandescence, and it can never rest within its mortal bonds. Like an actual spark it struggles upward, seeking through ritual purification to reunite with its source. As fire mingles with fire, souls that love the god burst their material casing and merge with divinity.

Ideas of this sort Plotinus takes from Plato and the Orphic mysteries, but he adds a brilliance of conception which is all his own:

> Therefore we must ascend again towards the Good, the desired of every Soul. Anyone that has seen This knows what I intend when I say that it is beautiful. Even the desire of it is to be desired as a Good. To attain it is for those that will take the upward path, who will set all their forces toward it, who will divest themselves of all that we have put on in our descent . . . until, passing, on the upward way, all that is other than the God, each in the solitude of himself shall behold that solitary-dwelling Existence, the Apart, the Unmingled, the Pure, that from Which all things depend, for Which all look and live and act and know, the Source of Life and of Intellection and of Being.

If this were all that Plotinus said, his influence on Christianity might not have been less than it actually was, but it would certainly have been simpler. For thus far we have only traced the upward aspiration of the soul—eros, the typical Greek striving for perfection. In Plotinus, however, there is also a downward path, which he interprets in accordance with the Aristotelian doctrine of unification. Since the cosmos is bound into a unity of emanations from the world of reason, the over-all pattern requires a descent as well as an upward movement. As early as 500 B.C., Heraclitus had said: "The way up and down is one and the same." In the Orphic mysteries descent is symbolized by man's origin in a higher source and the soul's falling into material imprisonment. But more than any of his predecessors, Plotinus emphasizes the unifying *circuit* made by the downward and the upward paths. Throughout the universe he sees a reciprocity of interest, a harmony and a mutual purpose within the continuous movement. Degeneration is no doubt involuntary, he says, but when it has been "brought about by an inherent tendency," it serves some function. What can this inherent tendency be? Plotinus replies that something in the nature of the higher makes it want to "bring order" to its next lower. Otherwise the circuit could not exist and the cosmos would not be unified. From this point of view, one may even deny that descent must be wholly involuntary. In ways that suggest the new religion of his times, Plotinus speaks of "a voluntary descent aiming at the completion of the universe." In one extremely interesting passage he adds: "these experiences and actions are determined by an eternal law of nature, and they are due to the movement of a being which in abandoning its superior is running out to serve the needs of another: hence there is no inconsistency or untruth in saying that the Soul is sent down by God."

How remote from Plato we now seem to be, and how close to Christian dogma! The Soul of Man sent down by God, the descent being a voluntary choice in accordance with an eternal law—these are ideas Christianity will develop and magnify in its own manner. Nevertheless, in their context they are really far removed from the use to which they will eventually be put. In Christianity it is *God's* descent which explains all else and makes salvation possible. In Plotinus, God does not descend, even though he participates in the cosmic circuit by virtue of his emanations. The God of Plotinus, like the gods of Plato, is infinitely perfect and totally self-sufficient. He does not share in man's destiny. Neither does he assume or wash away the sins of the world. Plotinus' God is the unmoving goal of aspiration, like the God in Aristotle's *Metaphysics*. Only man's soul descends in order to rise again, and salvation comes only through man's unaided efforts to slough off his impurities.

So far is this from being Christian that one might well argue that Plotinus' remarks about the downward path add little to what Plato had said. Not only does Plato speak of the soul falling into the body, but also the very existence of the ideal republic assumes a rationale for man's descent. After the philosopher has had his vision of the Good, is he to remain transfixed in loving contemplation or is he to resume the practical duties of mundane life? Plato definitely opts for the latter. The philosopher must be king. Relinquishing the glories of contemplation means descending into the material world. Yet the philosopher must do so—willingly and with a kind of charity. As in the allegory of the cave, the escapee must return to help free those who are still underground. Plato even argues that, given man's double nature, no one can really fulfill himself without descending. Like Plotinus, Plato could have said that there is an eternal law which governs the upward and the downward paths, and that both contribute to salvation. Plotinus presents these ideas more emphatically than Plato, more poetically and more mystically; but they are not essentially different ideas; nor are they yet the ideas of Christianity.

When Plotinus talks specifically about love, his relations to past and future are likewise ambivalent. As the vision of the Good marks the completion of Platonic love, there too Plotinus finds the goal of man's desiring:

> And one that shall know this vision—with what passion of love shall he not be seized, with what pang of desire, what longing to be molten into one with This, what wondering delight! If he that has never seen this Being must hunger for It as for all his welfare, he that has known must love and reverence It as the very Beauty; he will be flooded with awe and gladness, stricken by a salutary terror; he loves with a veritable love, with sharp desire; all other loves than this he must despise, and disdain all that once seemed fair.

Except for the verbal splendor, this seems to follow the normal pattern of Platonic love. Even the emotional tone can be matched by Plato's descriptions of the divine madness in the *Phaedrus*. But then Plotinus says other things. Not only does he speak of higher emanations *caring* for the lower (the downward path), but also he describes God as himself being love: "He is worthy to be loved, and is Himself love, namely, love of Himself, as He is beautiful only from Himself and in Himself." Now a Platonist may surely say that God, or the Divine One, as Plotinus often calls him, is worthy to be loved. But what can he mean if he says that God *is* love? Plato consistently maintained that love merely mediates between man and the gods. It could not itself be divine because it involved desire, which results from deficiency. For similar reasons the divine, being perfect in itself, could never love anything whatsoever. In Platonism, God must always be *beyond* love. Yet here is Plotinus identifying love with the Divine One, even claiming that God loves himself. Surely this is not Platonism pure and simple.

But neither is it Christianity. When the church fathers speak of God as Love and say that God loves himself, they mean something quite different from Plotinus. The language may seem to be identical, and in some ways Plotinus does anticipate the orthodox theology, but the doctrine is clearly not equivalent. Plotinus is merely developing Aristotle's idea that nothing as fine as love can be excluded from the nature of a perfect being. Aristotle had said this about the ideally good man; Plotinus extends it to God. Since God is perfect, however, he cannot love anything outside himself. He is therefore said to love himself, though not in the way that a finite being might. How then does he love? Plotinus does not tell us. And even if he did, his would not be the Christian concept of God's love. His God must love himself as the exemplar of that sheer goodness which elicits love from everything else. The same may be true of the Christian God; but *his* love also seeks out things that are neither good nor beautiful. For the Christian, such freely bestowed love is the *essence* of God's perfection. Plotinus would not say that any more than Plato or Aristotle.

Though Plotinus is far from being Christian, he awakens problems that Christianity would also have to face. His descriptions of mystical experience filter into the writings of many Christians, where they baffle the imagination as much in their new setting as in the old. Like the Christian mystics, Plotinus refers to God as an unfailing *presence*: "Thus the Supreme as containing no otherness is ever present with us; we with it when we put otherness away. It is not that the Supreme reaches out to us seeking our communion: we reach towards the

Supreme; it is we that become present. . . . We are ever before the Supreme—cut off is utter dissolution; we can no longer be—but we do not always attend." In describing the state of love in which we *attend* to God, Plotinus likewise resembles Christians who say that mystical union exceeds mere rationality. Plotinus distrusts the emotions, much as Plato and Aristotle had, but he claims that intellect has a power to transcend itself. As a recent scholar puts it: "There are, according to Plotinus, two capacities of the intellect: *to noein*—the ability to act as intellect, by which in 'possession of its faculties' it beholds what is within it; and *to me noein*—the ability not to act as intellect, by which 'inebriated' and outside itself it attains to what is beyond it." The inebriated condition is one of rapture, of ravishment, of mystical ecstasy. The soul feels drunk with love. Ordinary interests are suspended in what David Hume, speaking of Plotinus, calls "a certain mysterious self-annihilation or total extinction of all our faculties." The very being of the mystic is absorbed into the plenitude of the One. This way of describing the ultimate union will recur throughout the Christian dispensation.

In speaking of absorption as he does, Plotinus explicitly treats the final oneness as a merging and not a wedding. He thereby goes beyond Plato, asserting that the absorbed state is a kind of passivity, a *pathema*. At the top of the ladder of salvation, once the soul has purified itself of sins accumulated on the downward path, it overcomes all separateness from the divine. It sacrifices desire as a whole, surrenders its will to live, loses the capacity for self-love, and becomes totally fused into the One that is God. Reunited with its divine source, the soul destroys its earthly nature. It submits to "a going forth from the self, a simplifying, a renunciation, a reach towards contact and at the same time a repose." The mystic becomes nothing, and yet he is one with the All: he merges with the beauty in everything. This is the consummation of love.

Particularly in its pantheistic implications, the concept of merging in Plotinus must surely have derived from Hinduism as well as from the Orphic mysteries. But the ecstasy that he portrays could easily be detached from these religions. The following lines occur in the *Enneads*, but they might well have been taken from the notebook of many a Christian mystic:

The man is changed, no longer himself nor self-belonging; he is merged with the Supreme, sunken into it, one with it: centre coincides with centre, for centres of circles, even here below, are one when they unite, and two when they separate; and it is in this sense that we now (after the vision) speak of the Supreme as separate. . . . There are not two; beholder was one with beheld; it was not a vision compassed but a unity apprehended. The man formed by this mingling with the Supreme must—if he only remember—carry its image impressed upon him: he is become the Unity, nothing within him or without inducing any diversity; no movement now, no passion, no outlooking desire, once this ascent is achieved; reasoning is in abeyance and Intellection, and even, to dare the word, the very self: caught away, filled with God, he has in perfect stillness attained isolation; all the being calmed, he turns neither to this side nor to that, not even inwards to himself; utterly resting he has become very rest.

What do these words mean? I find them very difficult. They are words the Christian church condemns whenever they reappear in later centuries. For the orthodox believer, mystical union must always be a wedding and not a merging, a spiritual marriage not a pantheistic fusion. Weddings are public and subject to ecclesiastical control. Mergings are private and possibly psychotic, combining self-negation with deification. To fuse with something else is to lose all rationality and all sense of responsibility: the church had no desire to encourage this. Its deity is a person who loves the world but keeps his distance. His eternal substance is holy: he cannot be sullied by merging with his own creations.

The God of Plotinus is not a person, though he resembles one in ways that inspire later mysticism. Plotinus calls him the One and the All; and we may possibly think of him as the oneness *in* all. Plotinus' God is absolute beauty unknowable by any ordinary process but present in every aspect of the cosmos. Thus interpreted, the doctrine may be easier to understand. In moments of aesthetic excitement the heart leaps up and feels itself at one with what it enjoys. Plotinus idealizes the human desire to be *attuned*, to be in tune, to sense a harmony between ourselves and the infinities that surround us. Such ecstasy may come to men in states of self-forgetfulness, in passion and unbearable pleasure. To Plotinus, however, that would be the earthly eros. It must therefore be cleansed and spiritualized. It must be freed of individual relations, directed toward a universal object, reconstituted as the love of a perfect and eternal God. In laying down these Platonistic requirements, Plotinus idealizes the fact of unity in love. All love establishes a oneness, if only in the bond of caring and bestowing value. But—regardless of what Plotinus says—such oneness is an interpenetration, *not* a coalescence. It unifies persons; it does not fuse them. Gases may be fused, but a human being is not ethereal.

Plotinus seeks a unity of infinite dimension, a binding circuit from which nothing can escape, an intimacy so pervasive that everything must lose identity within it. But this, at least in part, is what we mean by death. In striving for spiritual merging, is the Plotinian mystic idealizing the negation of life? I think he is. That natural and universal dissolution which all animate creatures dread, that nothingness of death, Plotinus glorifies as if it were a thing of beauty. In the order of nature, all moments of individuation pass. The body crumbles and turns to dust; the spirit endures only through its creations; the person does not remain. All this Plotinus tries to overcome through a philosophic ritual. To conquer the absurdity of losing the self in time, he symbolically gives it away. In wishing to be absorbed, the mystic freely yields what must eventually be taken anyhow. He becomes nothing, but a *joyful* nothing. For in submitting, he has acted out of love—albeit a love of death. He feels himself transformed into the beauty of everything. Plotinus and the mystics who emulate him make a bargain with the universe. They exchange the goods of ordinary life for a special kind of feeling: a *sense* of immortality, not in oneself or as a personal being, but in the everlasting recurrence of good and beautiful things worthy of their love. Annihilation is a fact of life. Through the concept of merging, the imagination renders it meaningful and much less terrifying. That self-love which is basic to all Greek philosophy dissolves as the self melts away. But really nothing is lost. Self-love has merely been idealized. The soul is one with God, and God eternally loves himself. How then can death have dominion?

In making his bargain, the mystic prevents the imagination from overcoming death in any other way. The church had doctrinal reasons for condemning the notion of merging. To one who loves life in nature, the concept may be equally unpalatable. Ovid and Lucretius antedate Plotinus by the three hundred years I wished to rearrange. But their critique of love might well have had him in mind. It is a critique of all mystical attempts to conquer death and of all idealistic approaches to the nature of eros. In varying ways, Ovid and Lucretius resort to the biological "facts of life." Perhaps this alone contributed to the rhapsodic and rarefied remoteness of Plotinus' antithetical writings about love.

7

Sex in Ovid and Lucretius

SINCE THIS BOOK IS MORE IN-
terpretive than scholarly, I have taken the luxury of limiting myself
to Plato, Aristotle, and Plotinus as the exemplars of idealism in the
ancient world. This may do violence to history, but it facilitates our
major interest in the varieties of idealization. In Ovid and Lucretius
we find an equally partial representation of the reaction against
idealism. Living several generations apart, these poets could be
studied as the brief chronicle of early Roman civilization. That,
however, is not the use to which I shall put them. They interest me as
men who idealize in the very process of trying to free themselves of
idealization. In principle at least, Ovid and Lucretius define love as
basically a shudder in the loins, a meaningless physiological disposition within a nonpurposive universe. All creatures being subject to
the merciless dictates of mechanical laws, human love could not
greatly differ from what happens in lower organisms. Ovid and
Lucretius analyze love as neither a search for transcendental goodness nor an encounter with virtue nor a mystical adventure beyond
the ordinary world. For them it mainly reduces to sexuality, as it
would for any other animal, plus a few oddities that human nature
contributes in deluding itself about its own uniqueness. Rarely do
they portray love as something inherently noble. That it should
unite man with a spiritual order of things, they consider absurd. Nor
would they admit that their perspective itself creates new ideals of

love. They see themselves as the poets of science and common sense. How then can they be idealizing anything?

In citing laws of nature to prove that love is really tamed or humanized sexuality, Ovid and Lucretius anticipate much in Freud. And possibly Freud had them in mind when he said: "The most striking distinction between the erotic life of antiquity and our own no doubt lies in the fact that the ancients laid the stress upon the instinct itself whereas we emphasize its object. The ancients glorified the instinct and were prepared on its account to honour even an inferior object; while we despise the instinctual activity in itself, and find excuses for it only in the merits of the object." If by the ancients Freud meant thinkers like Plato, Aristotle, and Plotinus, he could not easily have said anything further from the truth. For them it was precisely the merits of the object that both elicited and justified love: the better the one, the truer the other; so that inferior objects could be honored *only* to the extent that they were meritorious. In a sense, the idealists did glorify erotic instincts. For in idealizing the category of desire and using the concept of eros to explain the dynamism of everything that exists, they dignify the instinctual (as well as all other) strivings of man. But what they mean by eros is far from being sexuality.

If, however, the ancients to whom Freud refers are Ovid and Lucretius, his generalization seems more plausible. Like Freud himself, these poets are "realists" in approaching love as an effect of sexual instinct in its natural environment. All three condemn the idealists for believing that objective goodness structures the universe and thereby elicits love. They find the possibility of human happiness not in spiritual discipline but in the satisfying of ordinary, observable instincts and desires. And yet they also idealize, making new ideals about love in accordance with what matters most to them as realists.

For that reason I find it very hard to credit the usual descriptions of love in the Roman poets. Speaking of Latin literature in general, one critic says: "'The animal instinct between the sexes and its gratification'—at last an explanation of what the Romans usually meant by 'amor.' Of Platonic love, spiritual love, 'le flirt,' romantic love, they knew very little: love was for them almost entirely physical, a thing of the senses." Yes and no. Ovid and Lucretius do tend to reduce love to sexuality, but (to quote Freud again, adding my own emphasis): they *"glorified* the instinct." They speak poetically and philosophically, not in the manner of actual scientists. They bestow importance upon various aspects of their own experience, interpreting both the attitude and the ideal of love accordingly. This is evident once we place them side by side; for they do not idealize in exactly the same way. Bestowing value differently, Ovid and Lucretius create quite dissimilar ideals. They both glorify the sexual instinct; but their glorifications are often not alike. How could they be, since even sexuality means something different to each of the poets? Is that the cause of their varying idealizations? Or is it possibly the result?

In an earlier chapter I spoke of Greek and Christian ideas as a source of courtly love, which applied them to a human context. In certain respects Ovid and Lucretius do something comparable. Where the Greek idealists had distinguished between heavenly and earthly Aphrodite, the Roman poets try to show that all we know of heaven is here on earth. Ovid in particular humanizes Greek ideas about eros, describing it as a search for satisfaction, as an empirical power that leads to consummation, and sometimes quite successfully. Lucretius is somewhat different, as we shall see, but Ovid inhabits the medieval world of courtly love almost as much as his own.

As in the ancient world eros soared upward with the idealists and then returned to earth with the realists, so too were there two traditions of courtly love in twelfth-century France. The earlier one, represented by the troubadour poets of Provence, reveals the unmistakable influence of Moorish and Mediterranean Neoplatonism. Though erotic in various ways, this tradition condemned adultery and emphasized the ideal benefits that accrue from the frustration of normal desires. The later version, mainly in Northern France, believed in sexual completion as a part of courtly love, even at the expense of adultery, and sometimes for the sake of it. In this northern tradition Ovid was widely read and quoted. What he had done with the idealism of his own age inspired the realists of the Middle Ages. Their problems were similar; and though Ovid lived in the first and not the twelfth century, he takes on greater stature if one sees him as the forerunner of medieval humanism.

However much the two traditions of courtly love overlapped, they differed in one important respect that is relevant to the study of Ovid: the roles assigned to lover and beloved are not at all alike. The southern troubadours generally (though not invariably) treat the beloved as something static—like the Good in Plato, the Unmoved Mover in Aristotle, the Alone in Plotinus. The lady on her pedestal is alive, but she is a living statue. Nor is it the poet's love that gives her life. On the contrary, the troubadour typically chooses an animate woman and then freezes her in the mold of perfection, making a monument of his lady by using her to embody his changeless ideals. Nevertheless, the beloved is not wholly passive. Like the God in Aristotle, she moves by being loved and remaining available for love. She arouses the poet's interest with a glance, she accords or with-holds the solace of her presence, she retains the power to reward, to satisfy, to give salvation.

Yet the beloved does not love reciprocally. The poet begs her to love him and ostensibly this is the goal of troubadour aspiration. But it is a goal that was not usually achieved, just as the Platonic gods did not return man's love. Between the lady and the troubadour there exists a mutual community, but normally it is not a love that moves back and forth. The Christian mystic may believe in reciprocal love; in principle he attains it merely by loving God, since God has loved him from all eternity. The troubadour can hardly hope for anything of the sort. Compared to the religious lover, he is at once more worldly and more idealistic. His beloved is a woman who lives in nature like any other woman; but she is also the incarnation of absolute value, and to that extent she lowers herself by seeking the gratification of desires. Imploring his lady to have mercy, Bernard de Ventadour says: "With clasped hands, with bowed neck, I deliver and commit myself to you." Despite the power and the glory this bestows upon her, the beloved—however merciful—would lose her dignity as a goddess if she underwent an experience similar to the poet's.

In order for the woman to share her lover's ecstasy, it was necessary for him to help her off the pedestal. She would have to descend just far enough to be moved erotically, that is, to feel the universal longing for goodness, and thus to seek the very ideals that she herself embodied. If she descended too far, she would return to the status of a sexual prey or else demean herself by female lust, in either event making it impossible for a man to love her. For love to be ennobling and reciprocal, a delicate adjustment was required. An equalized love between man and woman became the ideal of the courtly tradition that developed in Northern France and England, though traces of it may be found among the troubadours themselves. In this version, the poetic innovations of southern Neoplatonism were freely combined with popular romances devoted to the delights and difficulties of sexual mating. No people, no period in human history, has existed without such romances. But the Mediterranean civilization of the ancient world had uniquely profited from access to the wealth of Greek mythology. And that found its way into medieval Europe very largely through Ovid.

What Ovid particularly contributes is the element of sexual realism the northern tradition required. The myth of Pygmalion and the statue, which Ovid recounts in *Metamorphoses*, may even be taken to symbolize the transformation of courtly love. At the outset Pygmalion (like some medieval anchorite) "lived alone without a mate and took no woman to his bed." One day "with wondrous skill" (for he is an artist like the troubadours, not a mystic who has renounced the world) he creates a figure of ivory. It is the image of a woman, but "of a form more perfect than ever nature could bestow." So too is polished ivory more perfect, less blemished, than any material in nature. If the Platonic forms existed, they would all be made of ivory. When Pygmalion falls in love with his creation, he adores it in the manner of the troubadours: "He addresses and embraces it. . . . He even fears that bruises may appear on the limbs that he has fondled." The southern tradition of courtly love permitted fondling, but with ivory one could not hope for more than that. Eventually Pygmalion prays to Venus for a beloved who can love him back, and it is this that adumbrates the northern tradition of courtly love. Pygmalion does not dare to ask that his ivory maid be rendered human; he only begs for a living woman who would resemble her. With the graciousness of a love deity, Venus bestows more than has been requested. She gives life to the statue; and we may imagine it stepping down from its pedestal to assume the reciprocal sexuality of a human being:

> She was indeed a living body; he felt
> The veins pulse beneath his thumb; and then
> Pygmalion lavished praise to Venus; and real lips
> Pressed his at last, while the maiden felt his kisses
> And blushed, raising her timid eyes at once
> Toward the light and toward her lover. . . .

How fine a touch to have the newborn woman raise her vision to the skies, the abode of Venus perhaps but also the symbol of expansive possibilities in nature. And how different is this embrace from that other one which ends the story of Salmacis and Hermaphroditus. There the female is vile and the male a beautiful, innocent boy she covets. The nymph literally drags Hermaphroditus down, pulling him beneath the waves, into the depths of carnal intimacy where all is fluid. Like Circe in the *Odyssey*, who uses her sexual powers to change men into alien shapes, Salmacis violates Hermaphroditus by merging her body with his:

> . . . their two entwining bodies seemed to merge
> And their forms assumed a single body, even as
> When twigs are grafted from the parent stock. . . .

Here the myth of Aristophanes has been used against itself, for the merged condition is clearly a degradation. Descending, the woman has gone too far. A nice balance is demanded by Ovid, as it was by the medieval writers who learned from him, and most of his investigations into love are devoted to detecting it. To say that Ovid is a mere sensualist, just a "clever dandy" as one critic puts it, is to misconstrue the art he teaches. When he begins *The Art of Love* by saying that his book is for the man who needs instruction and that love must be guided by art, he speaks as a moralist. In accordance with his own teachings, he is also speaking lightly and with humor;

but he is not feigning moral discourse while really doing something else, tickling our inclinations to pornography or giving us hints about indiscriminate seduction. I take it as highly relevant that after giving detailed advice to men in pursuit of women he offers similar, apparently treasonous, counsel to the women themselves. Roman that he is, Ovid sees warfare as the ruling theme in love: Cupid wounds the heart with burning arrows, women are described as birds to be snared, game to be hunted down, booty to be carried off in a general Sabine rape. With supreme impartiality, however, he freely arms the Amazons as well. He delights in the conquest of Venus over Mars, the masculine aggressor, the supreme warrior and now a captive of love. Alluding to the same myth, Lucretius treats Venus as the peacefulness of nature into which war and conflict must eventually issue, an ally and a source of strength to be used against some future enemy. But for Ovid, Venus is herself the antagonist of Mars, woman warring against the male and frequently triumphant. At the same time, Venus is also love; and Ovid equips the opposing sexes with the assurance that she would have it thus: "To arms then, stalwart ladies, and victory under Venus!" Apparently, the struggle must be equal, as in a game or sport in which the participants profit most from a balancing of forces. It is as if Ovid were anticipating the essay by William James entitled "The Moral Equivalent of War." To express human aggression in beneficial ways, James advocates the battles of football. Ovid recommends sexual love.

In befriending women and realistically accepting them as they are, Ovid brings us closer to the northern courtly tradition than almost anyone else in antiquity. Together with his concern about reciprocity, there goes an obvious fondness for the female sex, even a playful and gallant submissiveness, as if he were a comic Tristan. In one of the poems collected as *The Loves* he says:

> If any man deems it base to be the slave of woman,
>   Before that man's judgment I stand convicted base.
> I'll accept that court's indictment, if only I did not burn
>   so!

Furthermore, he insists upon excellence of character in the lover, even to the detriment of physical charms: "*Ut ameris, amabilis esto*: to be loved, be lovable. . . . Though you have all the looks that graced the sea nymphs / Or charmed the Homeric heroes, still you'll find / It always helps to add some grace of mind. . . ." The virtues of tactfulness and tolerance he stoutly commends. They largely interest him as equipment of the hunt, but at least he perceives that such traits are eminently desirable in a lover. It is because he sees love as a delicate thing that lives on courtesy and gentle feelings that Ovid puts marriage in a wholly different category. These are lines that would also influence a type of courtly love:

> Under their contract, husbands and wives may lacerate
>   each other;
> This is their natural privilege and right to rail.
> So be it for wives: the dowry of your spouse is strife.
>   But let your mistress hear only what she desires;
> You are not bound in one bed by legal ties, but entered
>   More freely: love is your bond and deed; love lays
>   down the law.
> Heap up the loving words, the praise, the courteous
>   phrases;
> Words are the honey the lover gathers for her ear.

In everything he writes Ovid reveals an interest in the artfulness of love. Though he presupposes the sexual mores of Augustan Rome, he shows how they may be enacted with style. His men learn to mingle poetic and libidinal impulse, and his women are freed from the necessity of being either a matron or a slut. He *civilizes* the earthly eros, adjusting it to individual needs and temperaments, refining it to the point of elegance and human dignity. This is quite remote from love as "the animal instinct between the sexes and its gratification."

The courtliness of Ovid shows through more clearly when contrasted with the rough and primitive naturalism of Lucretius. Ovid's poem in praise of Venus is said to have been inspired by the dedicatory prayer to the goddess with which Lucretius begins *De Rerum*

Natura. But how the two differ! Both poets worship Venus as the generative power within the universe; but they portray her in vastly different terms. For Lucretius she is an energy through which all living things come into being, a natural force more elemental than the wind or the rain, a ruthless mechanism that instills fierce longing in all species, throbbing passion that leads to wild and infinite growth, to the teeming forth of life in nature. "So throughout seas and uplands, rushing torrents, verdurous meadows and the leafy shelters of the birds, into the breasts of one and all you instill alluring love, so that with passionate longing they reproduce their several breeds." The goddess to whom Ovid addresses himself is much tamer than this. Ovidian Venus instructs all things in the arts of living, as if she were a larger Prometheus. She is the giver of intelligence and imagination, a deity of civilization, humanized to the point of being called a queen:

> Venus reigns as queen; to her alone belongs
> The sovereign law of sky and earth and waves.
> To her the gods can trace their generation,
> As we can count her verdant fertile gifts.
> She it was who filled the woods and fields;
> She it was who taught the world to love. . . .
>
> The ram is fierce in crossing horns with rams,
> But gently courts the amorous brow of his ewe;
> The fearsome bull who ravages the countryside
> Is hardly more than sheepish to the heifer;
> While in tumultuous seas the same rich force
> Drives fish that swim with Venus' tide.
>
> That force first lifted man from savage garb;
> From her he learned to dress and care for self.
> A lover was the first, they say, to sing
> By night to the maid who barred his way.
> Eloquence was born to win that girlish heart:
> Each man then sang his own poetic suit.
>
> This goddess has been the mother of a thousand arts;
> The wish to please has spawned a host of skills.
> Can any man deny the April honor due to Venus:
> Such blasphemy is far from *my* intention.
> Besides, while everywhere the goddess reigns

And worshipers throng her temples, we Romans lead
the way. . . .

Lucretius too had dedicated his lines to Venus in the hope that she
would lend him eloquence. And possibly he merits her support
more than Ovid does. Ovid demonstrates allegiance to Venus by
dallying with all the ladies in her court. But Lucretius loves no one
but the goddess. In him the love of Venus, which is to say, the
generative principle she personifies, is total and exclusive. His devotion is really religious love. It is what Plotinus or Augustine might
have felt if they had been materialists in philosophy rather than
Platonists.

Within his own tradition Lucretius reminds one of Empedocles,
whose cosmic *Love* and *Strife* he translates into Venus and Mars. As
in Empedocles, the two operate in perfect unison: the one creating,
the other destroying, both together in a single, harmonious rhythm.
Empedocles thought that Love combines the like with the unlike,
whereas Strife repels them. Sexuality would, therefore, be Love's
attempt to merge the opposing male and female into a positive
oneness. But this could never succeed: Love must always be coun-
tered by the correlative Strife, which separates the unlike beings and
causes them to hate one another. Love and hatred were thus part of
the same condition, as in the famous lines of Catullus: "I hate and
love, nor can the reason tell: / But that I love and hate I know too
well." In following Empedocles, Lucretius sees no possibility of love
without strife, or creation without destruction. Worshiping Venus,
he worships both principles at once. In their unitary structure they
constitute a single world order and underlie the mechanical nature
of everything. Indeed, they *are* that mechanism. Lucretius would
not worship them otherwise.

Venus being a generative force within a materialistic universe,
Lucretius has little difficulty reducing human love to the mechanics
of sexual impulse. In Book IV of *De Rerum Natura* he describes all
love as an effect of sensation, itself liable to physical analysis. At the
appropriate time in its physiological development, the human
organism manufactures the germs of reproduction. According to
Lucretius, there is only one stimulus capable of evoking a man's

seed; and that is the human form or figure. Nor can the body resist movement in the direction from which it has been stimulated. As if he were explaining a scientific principle, Lucretius compares the ejaculation of seed to the spurting of blood toward the source of a wound:

> So too with a man who takes a blow from the arsenal of
>   Venus,
> Whether the dart be launched by a boy with girlish limbs
> Or by a woman breathing love from all her body,
> The wounded man falls toward the source of his wound
>   and seeks
> Union with it, yearning to spill his fluid from body to
>   body.

A new variation this, though possibly the oldest, on the myth of Aristophanes. In returning to Empedocles, Lucretius may actually be closer to the beginnings of the myth than Plato himself. When he describes the creation of man through the joint functioning of Love and Strife, Empedocles says:

> Many foreheads without necks sprang forth, arms wan-
> dered bereft of shoulders, eyes strayed alone, lacking
> brows. . . . As the two (opposite) divine forces clashed more
> extensively, these things fell together as they came upon
> each other . . . creatures were produced facing both ways,
> with double face and breast. . . .

In Lucretius too love produces double creatures and would seem to desire merely the uniting of body to body. But even the historical (and certainly the Platonized) Aristophanes would have been shocked at the idea that no other kind of union enters into love. To sweeten the absurdity, Lucretius qualifies his analysis. It sometimes happens, he tells us, that the organism has no means of venting its reproductive seed. In that event, erotic images arise and often linger painfully. At length they drive a man into the state of passionate desire. Human love is thus a combination of sexual impulse and erotic imagery, the latter caused by mechanical frustration. Images being mere emanations of matter, Lucretius feels that he has defined love without any idealistic nonsense. Poet though he is, he speaks as if all scientists, all realists, all men of good sense would agree that there is nothing else to the phenomenon. No need to assume a oneness of lovers' souls or a mutual search for the Good. No need to talk about response to another person, or the refinement of sensuous feeling. In his oddly archaic way, Lucretius is too "modern" for all that.

Given this approach to love, it is not surprising that Lucretius extols married life and condemns the "grand passions." The truth is that the pantheon of Lucretius houses more than just the unified deity Venus-Mars. He worships *order in the universe* at least as much as the generative principle. His religious love he extends to both, as Empedocles had also done. They do not conflict, but like the figure of Janus they face in opposite directions: the one toward organized society, the other toward rampant nature. In his devotion to abstract Venus, Lucretius ignores individual human relations because he knows that the reproductive seed can vent itself equally well in any number of bodily objects. All cats being dark in the night of passion, all human bodies being more or less alike, why bother to discriminate? At the same time, sexual activity must be controlled, even systematized—not regulated by an art (as in Ovid) but organized by social practice. Since they result from a thwarting of the generative principle, sexual images must be eliminated as quickly as they arise. But this must be done in an *orderly* fashion. It is a question of administration, and Lucretius discusses different possibilities. He sees the utility in promiscuous attachments and recommends them for those who fall in love with an unattainable object. But promiscuity is haphazard, nowhere as effective as the institution that Lucretius really believes in: matrimony.

Like cynics throughout the ages but without their frivolity, Lucretius advocates marriage as the cure for love.* In married life those harmful erotic images can hardly arise. Marriage is regular and routine, an orderly social method for serving Venus by ejaculating

---

*In *The Devil's Dictionary* Ambrose Bierce defines love as a "temporary insanity curable by marriage. . . . This disease . . . is prevalent only among civilized races living under artificial conditions; barbarous nations breathing pure air and eating simple food enjoy immunity from its ravages."

seed in a fertile direction whenever the need proclaims itself. Indeed, as long as one satisfies both nature and society, Lucretius seems indifferent to all questions about the object of choice. Unlike Ovid he offers no advice to those who seek a suitable mate. Married love depending upon the compatibility of sexual bodies, Lucretius simply reminds men that women enjoy intercourse as much as they do, tells women to keep themselves fresh if they want a man to share his life with them, and briefly concludes that a good marriage is built up by "mere usage"—bit by bit. In a passage that must have amused Ovid, he describes the power and permanence of married love as if it were just an unbreakable habit or a trope in nature:

> For however light the blow, that which is repeatedly
> struck
> In the long run yields to the impact and lies ready to
> succumb.
> Don't you see that even drops of water falling on a stone
> In the long run wear and beat a way through that stone?

In recommending therapeutic marriage, Lucretius condemns all love based on imaginative bestowals. He sees them as an effect of mental disorder, a madness caused by erotic privation. He obviously believes that no lover who was sexually satisfied would assign to his beloved perfections that she does not have. Freud was later to say something very similar. For Lucretius it follows that love must be of two sorts. Either the lover aims for the normal and healthy goal of instinctual gratification or else he submits to a senseless passion and wildly deranges himself pursuing illusory images. It is because he worships order as well as Venus that Lucretius finds the mad type of love so revolting. It does not lead to a transferal of seed, and it always causes irrationality in the lover. The orderly mind perceives things as they are and takes its pleasures sensibly; but the passionate lover, corrupted by his own frustrations, deludes himself into seeing a woman not as she is but as he would like her to be. In depicting the falsifications of love, Lucretius takes them as virtually an insult to the rational principles that his philosophy deifies:

> A swarthy girl is hailed a "nut-brown maid"; and even
> A slattern ranks as "sweet disorder"; a cat-eyed wench

Is a "latter-day Pallas," while if she's all sinew and bone,
Call her a "gazelle"; a sawed-off runt, "my little Grace,"
"Wit's tiny looking-glass"; a lumbering virago, "a miracle
Of nature divinely cast"; if she's tongue-tied, "a charming
    lisp";
Struck dumb, it's "modesty"; scolding and vicious chatter-
    ing
Become "the torch of eloquence"; a girl too skinny
To live is, of course, "fashionably svelte"; half-dead
With consumption? She's "delicate." Bloated, with cow-like
Udders? She's "Ceres herself, nursing the infant Bacchus."
The pug-nosed girl is "faun-like" or "child of the Satyrs";
And a blubber-lipped floosie is "an embodied kiss."

Enough! Enough! we say. But Lucretius informs us, coolly and
with scorn, that he could go on much longer. He ends the catalogue
only because it would be too tiresome to give all the terrible details.
How different is Molière's version of this paragraph. Molière, who
had studied Lucretius under Gassendi and even translated him,
gives the following lines to the rational Éliante in *The Misanthrope*:

Love, as a rule, affects men otherwise,
And lovers rarely love to criticize.
They see their lady as a charming blur.
And find all things commendable in her.
If she has any blemish, fault, or shame,
They will redeem it by a pleasing name.
The pale-faced lady's lily-white, perforce;
The swarthy one's a sweet brunette, of course;
The spindly lady has a slender grace;
The fat one has a most majestic pace;
The plain one, with her dress in disarray,
They classify as *beauté negligée*;
The hulking one's a goddess in their eyes,
The dwarf, a concentrate of Paradise;
The haughty lady has a noble mind;
The mean one's witty and the dull one's kind;
The chatterbox has liveliness and verve;
The mute one has a virtuous reserve.
So lovers manage, in their passion's cause,
To love their ladies even for their flaws.

Molière has softened the attack. Unlike Lucretius he is not condemning love as mental disorder. If anything, he is praising it as a kind of simple courtesy. He does not say that lovers delude themselves, but only that they *speak* as if faults were perfections. The entire passage is designed to support Célimène's complaint against Alceste's offensive honesty. If he truly loved her, both she and Éliante are saying, he would accept her shortcomings and even find a way of glorifying them. To Alceste as well as Lucretius, this may sound like a plea for madness; but Molière does not present it as such. In fact, within the structure of the play, Éliante's speech is reminiscent of Ovid. For he encourages lovers to say the most extraordinary things, anything at all that will give the beloved pleasure. Although in one place he names "Folly, Illusion, and Madness" as the camp followers of Cupid, Ovid hardly worries about the falsifications of love. He sees the utility in distorting facts and feels no scruples about doing so:

> Do not blame a girl for defects of mind or body:
>   Who's to gain by that? Better talk them away. . . .
> Words have a magic power to temper nature's failings:
>   If she is blacker than pitch, "tanned" is the word to
>   invoke.
> Cross-eyed? She has a "Paphian gaze." Albino? "Fair
>   Minerva."
>   Skin and bones? "What willowy grace invests her
>   charm."
> If she's stunted, call her *petite*; if fat, every inch a woman!
> A ready mind can manufacture grace from its opposite.

But all this, which to Ovid and Molière is a laughing matter, Lucretius feels as something deadly serious and simply horrible. According to a legend Tennyson used, Lucretius committed suicide after being driven mad by a love philter. Be that as it may, he appears more sensitive to the penalties of passion than almost anyone else prior to Marcel Proust. Propertius, like any number of ancient poets and philosophers, may have said "Shun this hell"; but Lucretius really knows the domain. All love other than the strictly sexual is, for him, an agony and a deep distress. How else could one experience anything so unreal, unnatural, so disordered and irrational? Like Proust, Lucretius is particularly shocked by the sadism in lovers' passion:

> They clasp the desired object tight enough to hurt,
> And often fasten teeth on lips, crushing mouth on mouth.
> And all because this pleasure is not unmixed; beneath
> It lie secret goads inciting them to hurt the very
> Thing, whatever it may be, from which this frenzy grows.

When he goes on to describe the etiology of passional madness, Lucretius further anticipates Proust. He says that Venus will permit only a single type of reciprocity between the sexes: the sharing of mere sensual pleasure. Once people fall in love, however, they seek a greater reciprocity, a contentment or satisfaction in one another which their relationship itself makes impossible. Lovers delude themselves with "the hope that the flame of passion may be quenched by the same body that kindled it." For Lucretius—as for Proust—this is the worst, the cruelest, of love's deceptions. Though other appetites may be quieted, sexual passion is by its very nature insatiable. Food and drink being material substances actually taken in by the body, one may readily appease hunger or thirst. But not so passion. It is aroused by insubstantial images, and they can never be possessed with any degree of satisfaction. Lovemaking is an "act of physical possession in which, paradoxically, the possessor possesses nothing." Those words were written by Proust, but Lucretius could easily have said the same. He pictures Venus teasing lovers with erotic images that cause them to stare hopelessly at one another or to stroke each other's body, even to entwine their limbs and embrace frantically in sexual intercourse. But all in vain: "No one can devour the body / Of another nor penetrate and be absorbed therein, / Though certainly this is what they sometimes seem to crave. . . ." In other words, the Aristophanic merging is impossible even on the bodily level. Tortured by the painful images of pleasure, lovers can only destroy themselves—both morally and physically—unless they succeed in curing their disease through marriage or promiscuity.

To help free the unfortunates, Lucretius marshals the powers of orderly reason. Instead of deluding oneself about the beloved, one must achieve exact awareness of her imperfections, crediting her with nothing she does not strictly deserve. And even if she were as attractive as anyone could wish, she is just a human being, one among many creatures in nature: "To be sure, there are others; to be sure, we've survived so far without her; / To be sure, she's physically no different, as we know, from the ugliest member of her sex . . ." Even so, we might add, does Shakespeare's Benedick speak before he learns to love: "One woman is fair, yet I am well; another is wise, yet I am well; another virtuous, yet I am well"; or Ferdinand in *The Tempest*, who says: "for several virtues / Have I lik'd several women, never any / With so full soul, but some defect in her / Did quarrel with the noblest grace she ow'd / And put it to the foil. . . ." But Lucretius goes even further. He ends the diatribe with a graphic vignette:

> She drenches herself, poor woman, in clouds of cheap
>   perfume,
> Which moves her maids to give her a wide berth and
>   giggle
> Behind her back. Still her excluded lover, in tears,
> Often covers the threshold with mounds of flowers and
>   wreaths,
> Anointing the haughty doorposts with aromatic herbs;
> And the poor fellow even plants love-sick kisses on the
>   door.
> But were he at last to be let in, one whiff as he entered
> Would drive him to seek some decent excuse to take his
>   leave.
> There would be a prompt end to his oft-rehearsed com-
>   plaint,
> So deeply felt, and he would call himself a fool
> To have endowed her with qualities beyond mortal per-
>   fection.

The scene is familiar to us from the writings of many a modern realist. It is virtually translated (and put to the same use) by Jonathan Swift, who elsewhere defines love as "a ridiculous passion which hath no being but in play-books and romances." All such deflation-ary wit has its literary source in Lucretius.

As with most realists, it is sheer compassion for the sufferings of others that makes Lucretius want to liberate the ensnared lovers. He is like those sympathetic gods who beg Vulcan to remove the net in which he has caught Mars and Venus. In the myth Vulcan is the outraged husband but also the principle of order—dull in comparison to the adventuresome Mars, somewhat ineffectual, yet steady and productive like the law of cause and effect. But if Venus deceives him so readily, how stable can their union be? In referring to the pantheon of Lucretius, I said that its two deities did not conflict. Perhaps that was an overstatement. Lucretius bids us to propitiate Venus as the deepest force in nature, and so as the ultimate goddess in the order of things. In worshiping Venus, we manifest a love of order. And yet, Venus is by nature *dis*orderly. She brings the net upon herself by playing Vulcan false; and then—for no apparent reason—she casts it upon those lovers whom she teases with erotic images. How can the rational man, the realistic philosopher, the quasi-scientific poet, give his undivided heart to her?

He cannot; nor does Lucretius, regardless of what he pretends. He may assiduously devote himself to Venus; but one always detects a shudder of revulsion, as if his adoration contained more fear and awe than love. Within the history of naturalistic philosophy, he reminds one of Schopenhauer saying No to the blind will of nature at the same time that he knows he must submit to it. Lucretius says Yes to Venus, but woefully and with half a heart. In accepting her simply as the mechanical device for propagating a species, he rejects all the wile and artifice of the goddess. He knows it is she who instills the maddening emotions of love—that excitement which is not purely pleasurable and that illusory hope of merging.

This much of Venus, Lucretius will not worship. What he reveres is not even sexual desire: at least, not the experience of sex or the delights of instinctual gratification. It is mere *fertility* that Lucretius idealizes. As if he were a more philosophical Hesiod, he subsumes all life under the aspect of husbandry. The Venus in his pantheon is a category of biology—like natural selection to a Darwinian. Better yet, a superbiology; for the materialism of Lucretius is just as cosmic as the spiritualism of Plotinus. Lucretius idealizes the universal fact of pulsating energy, as if nothing else in nature really mattered. Perhaps that is why he leads into his discussion of love by talking about sexual ejaculations during sleep, just as Proust was later to begin his own investigations with the erotic dreams of a growing boy. According to Lucretius, the data of consciousness are all epiphenomenal. Santayana praises him for writing "the poetry of things themselves." And well Santayana might. For in Lucretius one encounters the clearest idealization of that "realm of matter" on which so much of Santayana's philosophy is based.

But even Santayana recognizes that a love of matter is not the same as a love of life. Discussing Lucretius' arguments against fearing death, he rightly points out their futility: "What is dreaded is the defeat of a present will directed upon life and its various undertakings. Such a present will cannot be argued away, but it may be weakened by contradictions arising within it, by the irony of experience, or by ascetic discipline." Santayana concludes that Lucretius helps us to overcome the fear of death by weakening the will and so leading it into a surrender of life.

But possibly one can go further. Lucretius considers the fear of death irrational because he does not know what it is to love *life*. He idealizes matter as a way of *escaping* those individual and social experiences that make up the life of human beings. In this too he may resemble Plotinus more than one originally suspects. Lovers cannot fuse their bodies, but Lucretius seems to crave a merging with all of matter. And what is that but a wish for self-annihilation? Having started with the fact of vital sexuality, does Lucretius end up with an antithetical love of death? Is this the import of his legendary suicide?

How different are the idealizations of Ovid! How facile are those scholars who classify him with Lucretius because both think of love as sexuality. For Ovid sex is always a gratuitous pleasure, a consummation cultivated by art and based on principles of taste or refinement. Without denying the biological function and material meaning of sexual desire, Ovid bestows importance on the sport itself. He idealizes a highly ceremonial, and even pompous, game: an empire has arisen where once there was only a republic. All men and women participate in the regal sport, though only an aficionado like Ovid understands the rules, the prizes, and the subtle maneuvers of the expert players. Surely this is but a meager part of love; but at least Ovid removes sexuality from the brutish realm of matter. The game he idealizes is an aesthetic activity: it is the dance of life, a merry-go-round in which the gods and goddesses pursue each other with mindless abandon, a gay titillation of hide-and-seek, a shifting kaleidoscope in which the partners change places from episode to episode (hence the theme of transformation, metamorphosis).

Nor is it all delectation in this game of musical couches and antic hay. The sport can be as deadly as a bullfight; at any moment Venus may turn into Diana, the arrows of Cupid drawing fatal blood, the pursuit becoming a murderous hunt, and even the hunter shot down as prey (as in the myth of Actaeon). But the sadness is delicate, lightly etched, almost saccharine, and usually nothing painful lasts for very long in the world of Ovid's idealization. Everything is on the move, like those nymphs and satyrs endlessly tripping round a Grecian vase, or the skipping figures in Botticelli's *Primavera*, or all the pastel countryfolk stealing kisses from one another in paintings by Watteau or Boucher. What Ovid idealizes is not the instinct but the innocent merriment of sex, the sylvan loveliness of pursuit and sweet surrender.

Not all is beautiful in Ovid; but in his verse Venus rises from a half shell and graciously floats into a sunlit atmosphere. We seem to have drifted above the world of Lucretius—that mineral earth where only matter exists, where the stones of Deucalion have not yet become men and women. Were there ever two poets more *unlike*? Ovid and Lucretius both discuss the comparative merits of different positions in sexual intercourse; but, characteristically, Lucretius cares only about facilitating procreation, and Ovid only about the pleasures of sight and touch. Even the sadism that horrifies Lucretius is for Ovid just the rough-and-tumble of a physical sport. His humane art, designed to minimize the pain and maximize the pleasure, encourages lovers to accept the ground rules of Venus: "It's a convention, no more, that man is cast in the role of pursuer; / Women don't chase us; mousetraps don't run after mice."

That this should be a convention, rather than a frightening deception, as Lucretius would say, transforms the entire character of Venus. Ovid can call her "queen" because she establishes a benign harmony between the warring sexes. Far from needing to be checked by some external order, she is herself the inner equilibrium of successful lovemaking. In this sense, Ovid is more fully devoted to her than is Lucretius. Even when he warns against the dangers of love and proposes remedies for those who have been deranged by it, Ovid remains true to Venus after his fashion. We are not to stop playing the game; we are to learn how to play it better. Ovid directs his therapeutic advice toward lovers who suffer needlessly or in a particular relationship that has lost its hedonic potential. He does not try to cure love through marriage or sheer promiscuity, as Lucretius does, but only through a new encounter with a new beloved under new and more promising circumstances. Although Ovid does prescribe measures that reverse the progress of love in the old relationship, his treatment is really homeopathic. A fresh affair replaces the weary one, as in the words of Cicero "one nail drives out another"; but the need to cultivate the art of love remains constant.

These differences between Ovid and Lucretius appear most sharply in the question of self-delusion. To undo the damages of love, both poets create what may be called a counter-idealization. For *his* method of disintoxicating lovers, Lucretius invokes nothing but cold, hard reason. We are to free ourselves of passion by learning how to see the woman as she really is. We must realize that no mortal is perfect, that virtues are not unique to any one person, and that every female is just another human being in a world of material objects.

Ovid's counter-idealization is less rationalistic, and deeper in its psychological awareness. Like Lucretius, Ovid advises us to concentrate upon the woman's faults, to remind ourselves of her wanton behavior, to itemize what she has cost us. But also he calls upon the imagination in ways that parallel the original bestowals. And as these were formerly used to delude the beloved (for the sake of pleasing and to get what the lover wants), their contraries now help us to deceive *ourselves*:

So wherever you can, fool yourself, her attractions mis-
   prize;
Just tip the scales a little and criticize.
If generously plump, call her fat; if dark, black as pitch;
If slender, of course, a skinny old bitch;
If she's clever, she's brazen and sharp;
If she's simple and good, she has the mind of a carp.

And so on, as Ovid fights fire with fire. Unlike Lucretius he has no
doctrinal bias against erotic images and would never think of blam-
ing them for the ravages of love. By quickly propitiating Venus in
the mechanical transferal of seed, Lucretius destroys the amorous
imagination. But Ovid, like any other theorist in the arts, finds it
indispensable. In turning it against a particular woman, he merely
frees it to act more constructively with someone else. One could
hardly think of Lucretius as contributing to courtly love. Ovid does
so not only in studying the intricacies of human relations and advocating equal rights for all contestants, but also in recognizing the
agency of imagination—whether one is in love trying to get out or
out trying to get in.

At the same time, most of Ovid is foreign to the courtly tradition,
the northern version as well as the troubadour. Where their ideals
are noble and aspiring, his are modest, limited in scope. Chaucer
says that "love is a serious enterprise"; but for Ovid seriousness is apt
to be a cause of embarrassment. Though life would not be worth
living without the flame of love, he generally wishes to moderate the
heat, to turn the burner quite low, as low in fact as sexual excitement
will permit. From the very outset, Ovid declares that the theme of his
art is just "a little pleasant indulgence," and elsewhere that what he
sings is merely "good sense." Nowhere do we find that claim to
metaphysical justification which courtly love shares with the rest of
the idealist tradition. If Ovid belongs to that tradition, as I have been
suggesting that in part he does, it is on the periphery and as an
antidote to the hostile influence of a critic like Lucretius. And if by
passion we mean that fever in the blood associated with the self-
hypnosis of "falling in love," then Ovid fears it as much as Lucretius
and almost everyone else in the ancient world. In the nineteenth

century, Romantic love fuses the idealist tradition with a realistic acceptance of sexual passion, making passionate experience itself the source, the vehicle, and even the goal of ideality in love. Courtly love resembles romanticism in giving a quasi-religious value to human intimacy. Ovid differs from both. The sexuality that he idealizes is neither cosmic nor deeply inspiring; for the most part, it is little more than playfulness in the contact between two epidermises.

In Ovid's defense one can point to works like the *Heroides* and sections of *Metamorphoses* that show commiseration for the sufferings of lovers—for instance, Dido abandoned by Aeneas, or Alcyone bemoaning the death of her husband. Some critics have even argued that Ovid was really two poets, that he spoke with two voices: one as a specialist in the cultivation of sexual pleasure, the other as a poet who sympathetically portrayed true love and even blissful marriage. But while some of the stories in *Metamorphoses* indicate that Ovid realized how people can love each other in ways that are constant and beneficial, albeit tragic, he does not formulate an art of love along these lines. He depicts the poignancy of defeated love with authentic understanding, but he never offers instruction in methods of attaining love that can be both passionate and lasting.

In the works that present his teachings most overtly, it is the voice of dalliance and even cynicism that we hear most frequently. Urbane and cultured as he may be, Ovid continually nudges us in the ribs and admits to some motive he himself considers unworthy. Women being cheats, he condones cheating them as well; he crudely assumes that all appetites are as jaded as his own and that only forbidden fruit is tempting to anyone; he confesses that he himself can love only when some female has wronged him; he even states the premises of an implicit syllogism to the effect that "only base actions please, and every man serves his own pleasure"—from which it logically follows that *all* human actions are base. If such is the art of love, it amounts to little more than amoral seduction: pleasant indulgence and good sense perhaps, but only to a sense that shies away from considering the nature of human values. This complaint could not be made against high-minded Lucretius. It can be made against Ovid.

In its major emphasis, Ovid's art would seem to have two objectives: first, the attaining of complete and harmonious enjoyment; second, the maintaining of supremacy within the relationship by means of deception and erotic trickery. The first objective involves the ideal of reciprocity, which Ovid enunciates in no uncertain terms: "Let the woman feel the act of love to her marrow; / Let both partners enjoy equal delights." But though he believes in the sharing of pleasures, Ovid consistently views participants in love as selfish opponents, both jockeying for power over one another. In his impartial manner he advises each to feign a passion for the other while nevertheless retaining independence. Apparently the goal is to get someone to love you without your having to give love in return. Ovid teaches men how to disarm a woman by arousing in her a passion which is not really reciprocated. And then, with suicidal insistence, he tells women the secret of male psychology: all men want to believe that they are loved, regardless of the truth. Even in physical love-making, where Ovid recognizes the virtues of mutual gratification, he advises both lovers to pretend that they are feeling what the other expects. It never occurs to him that what I have called his first objective is possibly being undermined by the ruses of the second.

Perhaps it is this inner contradiction, this shallowness of moral insight, that makes Ovid's laugh sound hollow. A livelier, more lightfoot poet could hardly be found. Yet even his libidinal verse is sad, indeed pathetic, like a wreath of faded vine leaves. Though he teaches us to play the game of love, one feels that in this sport—as he describes it—there is no winning. Does Ovid realize this himself? Is that what he is telling us in the myth of Narcissus at the fountain? Narcissus is doomed to failure at the start. Not only does he love an insubstantial image—as Lucretius would say—but also he chooses as his object a mere reflection of himself. In doing so, Narcissus creates the smallest of all closed societies and makes it impossible for his love to be reciprocal. But the Ovidian lovers are often in that condition: they use the beloved as a way of loving themselves, and they wish to be loved instead of loving someone else. That is why deluding them is both easy and necessary. Ovid may shrug his shoulders, considering this the common state of man; but in fact it merely distinguishes a certain kind of person: the libertine or sensualist.

What Ovid idealizes is not the same as self-love in Aristotle or primal narcissism in Freud. In Aristotle and Freud the desire to be loved leads one to pursue social ideals. These occur in Ovid but he is too close to sheer eroticism for them to have much effect. In loving themselves, his lovers—with the exception of a few counter-instances in *Metamorphoses*—pursue their own unhappy image, and even hunt it down like Humbert Humbert shooting Quilty in *Lolita*. They are in love with little more than their own sensations, as if at every moment they had to prove that they are feeling *something*. Freud speaks of the sensualist as one who cannot love others because really he does not love himself either. If this is right, as I assume it must be, Ovid's gay veneer is itself a deep deception, hiding perhaps a deeper fear—the fear of love, although it is love that he really wants. And behind this ambivalence there may be another fear. In flitting from sensation to sensation, what is Ovid ultimately afraid of? Is it possibly that merging with something else which Lucretius and Plotinus each desires, each in his own way? Ovid is not wrong to fear such merging; for life cannot comprehend it. But instead of conquering his fear, he turns away from its reality and hides his head in the froth of egocentric pleasure, just as Narcissus does.

Some of this Ovid also sees. He *is* two poets. He seems to know that without illusions the kind of love he teaches cannot exist, but that with them comes inevitable disaster. Speaking as the narrator, he says to Narcissus (as if addressing *mon frère, mon semblable*): "What you seek is nowhere; turn your head and you lose what you desire." And as the failure of love is alienation instead of oneness—this myth being the myth of Aristophanes run backward—Narcissus finally comes to hate himself, to wish that from himself he might escape. He does, as all men do, by dying; but in his death he automatically destroys the object of his love. Thus nothing survives his passion, nothing but the little flower into which he is transformed. And what are we to say of that metamorphosis? Is the flower a symbol of beauty rising from the dunghill of artistic egoism? A final tribute to the generative powers of Venus? Or just the incarnation of man's absurd hope that all the suffering of life will somehow issue into something good?

8

Erotic Idealization

THE PHILOSOPHY OF LOVE ORIG-
inates with erotic idealizations of the sort we have been studying. To
the Platonist all realistic attempts to define eros as the child of
earthly rather than heavenly Aphrodite can only misread its spiritual intent. To the traditional realist all love must be reducible to
some organic condition—e.g., direct or aim-inhibited sexuality. Yet
both extremes idealize the fact of human desire, and with it that
appraisive mode of valuation which detects those objects capable of
satisfying desire. And as appraisal is a branch of empirical science, so
too may all these theorists be taken as links within a growing scientific awareness. Though Freud and Plato inhabit different metaphysical realms, they adhere to a similar faith in reason and analysis
as against all belief (whether primitive or Romantic) in wild emotionality, orgiastic intuition, and willful self-delusion. However
nonscientific Platonic idealism may seem to us, it nevertheless embodies that sense of rational distinction and love of expertise without
which there could have been no science. Throughout the eros tradition the goal is always knowledge: warranted assertions about the
nature of man, what he wants and what will really satisfy.

That is why so much of Western philosophy, which generally
seeks to be scientific (or superscientific), presupposes the eros
approach to love. Thus, St. Thomas Aquinas can readily assert that
"a thing is said to be loved, when the desire of the lover regards it as
his good. . . . Since the good is the object of desire, the perfect good

will consist of that which completely satisfies the will. Hence to desire happiness is nothing else than to seek to satisfy desire. This is what everyone wants." But also Hobbes, implicitly attacking Aquinas, has no difficulty maintaining that happiness is "a continual progress of the desire from one object to another" and that this is all that love implies: "That which men desire they are also said to *love*; and to hate those things for which they have aversion. So that desire and love are the same thing: save that by desire we always signify the absence of the object; by love, most commonly the presence of the same."* Of course, Aquinas would never agree to the Hobbesian notion that ideal love is just one satisfied desire after another. He will insist upon God as the only object that completely satisfies, and Hobbes will retort that "there is no such *finis ultimus*, utmost aim, nor *summum bonum*." Still, both assume that love pertains to desire, and therefore both construct types of erotic idealization. Even Romantic philosophers appropriate some of the eros attitude. For them desire becomes the source of creativity; and they worship it as in itself the Good. They are in love with Eros, much as Socrates said that he was, except that they refuse to consider the independent value of those objects that Eros himself desires.

None of my criticism should be taken as a rejection of the eros tradition. Within its limitations, that tradition speaks with the voice of sanity. There is no love without desire, and no love is good except as it conduces to someone's satisfaction. When the eros tradition says that love *is* desire for goodness in the object, the copula may be considered ambiguous. Taken one way, it serves as a colon preceding a definition and alerts us to essential attributes. Taken another way, however, it may only introduce a description, preparing us for facts *about* love that never amount to a definition. Because it falsifies the character of bestowal, a definition in terms of desire could not be acceptable. But as a way of *describing* love, putting it into its psychological and moral context, some reference to desire is absolutely indispensable. The eros tradition idealizes desire much as a man who loves a woman might say: "For me she's all there is." Literally,

*Apparently Hobbes did not think that absence makes the heart grow fonder. Out of sight, out of love?

the words are absurd; but reformulated they indicate facts of the greatest importance.

As an illustration of what I mean, consider the following lines from a popular song:

> Not that you are fair, dear,
> Not that you are true,
> Not your golden hair, dear,
> Not your eyes of blue.
> When we ask the reason,
> Words are all too few!
> So I know I love you, dear,
> Because you're you.

There is something supremely right about these lines; and also something ludicrous. If we are sympathetic or sentimental, we may see in the paltry verse all the trappings of true love. If we are analytical or worldly-wise, however, we may just as easily laugh the lines to scorn. Why is this so? I think the song elicits an ambivalent response by its use of the word "because" and the phrase "not that." When the lover tells his sweetheart it is *not that* she is fair or true or has golden hair and eyes of blue, he announces that he loves her as a person. He does not love her *for the sake of* her beauty or goodness. To him she is not just a commodity satisfying a need—even a need for beauty and goodness. Neither has he reasoned himself into loving her, as an aesthetician might give reasons for finding her beautiful, or a moralist for calling her good or noble. His love is an emotional attachment, imaginative bestowal over and beyond appraisal. But all this is quite different from saying that he loves the lady *because* she's she. That makes it sound as if the delicacy of her complexion and the blueness of her eyes had nothing to do with his loving her, which is most unlikely. In the world of human beings, affections are causally related to the search for values—even though they cannot be defined in terms of it. Sometimes the values are objective, sometimes individual; they vary from culture to culture and person to person; but they are all a function of some need or desire and underlie whatever bestowals eventuate in love. A pretty face naturally disposes us toward the person who is lucky enough to have it. If a lover denies its attraction, he is probably deceiving himself. Perhaps he means to play down the beauty of his beloved in order to glorify her good heart and lovely disposition. That makes sense, since these are generally more valuable than the features of a face. But the verse I quoted seems to say something else. It seems to assert that the sheer *identity* of the beloved brings love into being. And this, I think, is highly implausible. If all those endearing young charms were to vanish and fade away, would not the greatest of human loves vanish with them? We have every reason to think so—unless the lover cultivated new needs and desires, interests that could be satisfied by attributes of the beloved other than those that have died in the hourglass.

With its various emphases the eros tradition elucidates that much of love which depends upon desire. In the manner of speculative philosophy, it idealizes while investigating. But also it brackets reality as science does, approximating greater and greater knowledge about purposive motivation in human beings. If we are optimistic about man's future, we may see in contemporary life-sciences—experimental psychology, psychiatry, biology—the beginnings of new insights about instincts, drives, needs, desires. Purposiveness alone cannot explain the attitude of love; and from no empirical data can we *deduce* an ideal of love—biology tells us what life is, but not how to live it. Still, the future philosophies of love will reflect the new scientific discoveries as surely as the adherents to eros always have. Plotinus might sneer at empirical life-science of the twentieth century, but neither Plato nor Aristotle nor Lucretius would. They would want to use it for their own purposes, as philosophers must; but also they would recognize that here at last their ideas about desire and the search for happiness were being tested against the realities of controlled observation. Eventually they would find themselves evolving newer and possibly grander idealizations.

In ancient Eastern philosophy—Hinduism, Buddhism, Confucianism, Taoism, Zen—the eros tradition scarcely existed. Correspondingly, the East did not develop the concept of love in ways that are comparable to those of the West. Nor is this due to what we might imagine about oriental asceticism. On the contrary, most Eastern philosophies accepted the sexuality of man as neither sinful nor corrupting. Radhakrishnan finds a laudable realism in the fact that the Hindu gods, as opposed to those in the West, are married and enjoy all the pleasures of sexual sociability. As Denis de Rougemont points out: "We find no single Christian equivalent—existing or imaginable—of the *Kama Sutra*, of the Tantras, of so many other treatises on eroticism in the Vedas and the Upanishads, relating the sexual to the divine; still less, of the famous sculptures on the façades of the great Hindu temples, illustrating in the most precise manner the unions of the gods and their wives, for didactic and religious purposes. No secret methods nor sexual magic, no physiology of the mystic pilgrimage, such as the one which the treatises of the Hatha Yoga describe without variation in a thousand years." De Rougemont looks in vain for Christian equivalents, but he could also have extended the contrast to all Western philosophy. In its way of accepting sexuality, the East bestows importance upon it but without those philosophical idealizations ingredient in the occidental concept of love. Even when divinized, oriental sex is still a physiological phenomenon. The imagination goes into portraying it delectably or probing new methods for extending pleasure. The Western ideals of love are as different from this as sublimation is from direct enjoyment. The difference consists in creating erotic idealizations that remove one from the reality of desire at the same time as it becomes the basis of philosophical and literary glorification.

In the East those philosophies that remove one from desire generally do so by trying to destroy desire itself. In Hinduism liberation (*moksha*) involves a selflessness that prevents one from desiring anything. The same is true of much of Buddhism. In the "Fire Sermon" the Buddha says: "The fire of life must be put out. For everything in the world is on fire with the fire of desire, the fire of hate, and the fire of illusion. Care, lamentation, sorrow, and despair are so many flames." And by "care" the Buddha would seem to mean even caring *about*, desiring the welfare of others. Out of compassion (*karunā*) or love (*mettā*) the Buddhist saint will strive to alleviate suffering, but not because of any *desire* or because the beneficiaries matter to him.

As one scholar remarks: "*Mettā* . . . is not so much ordinary human affection, even in sublimated form, as a detached and impersonal benevolence." In Taoism even benevolence seems to fall away. Thus Chuang-tzu: "He who needs others is forever shackled, and he who is needed by others is forever sad. Drop these shackles, put away your sadness, and wander alone with Tao in the kingdom of the Great Void." In Plato and Plotinus (to say nothing of later Christian mystics) we may find a comparable yearning for the end of eros. But for them the culmination of desire is also its *satisfaction*; they find this in a union with an idealized object—the Good or the Alone—which all men are said to *desire*; and prior to the glorious consummation, they envisage a ladder that progressively refines and spiritualizes desires instead of eliminating them. Like Chuang-tzu, Plato's contemplative philosopher wanders alone through a divine kingdom, but for him it is filled with determinate perfections and is not a Great Void. Plato may agree that he who needs others is forever shackled; yet he rears the ideal republic on the foundation of this basic premise: "A State . . . arises, as I conceive, out of the needs of mankind; no one is self-sufficing, but all of us have many wants. Can any other origin of a State be imagined?"

In defining the ideal in relation to human needs, Plato presupposes two things: first, that *some* needs are worth cultivating; and second, that striving in the world can sometimes bring man closer to what he wants. To think in these terms is to assume that man's attitude toward nature must always be problematic. At each moment an individual must decide what he *really* wants, whether he ought to want it, whether struggling with the environment will further his aspirations, and whether these aspirations are authentic, true to nature both human and external. He must also be prepared to change nature, to master and even to conquer it. In the East nature does not seem to have posed this sort of problem. Even oriental philosophers who advocated a harmony with nature, instead of detachment from desire, thought of harmonization as something to be achieved without striving and without considering what one really wants. In Chinese philosophy—Confucianism as well as Taoism—harmony with nature comes from doing as little to it as possible. Criticizing Confucius, Chuang-tzu praises the "pure men of old," who acted without calculation: "They did not know what it was to love life and hate death. They did not rejoice in birth nor strive to put off dissolution. Quickly come, and quickly go—no more." But even Confucius had no wish either to change or to conquer nature. Though he spoke of universal charity and duty toward one's neighbor, he never recommended them as a means of perfecting the human condition. Like sex in popular Hinduism, these virtues were to come forth naturally, not as the solution to questions about wants or desires. In the discipline of Zen an absence of striving is cultivated ritualistically, and the harmony with nature comes from dropping every attempt to formulate a problem *about* nature: "The fundamental position of Zen is that it has nothing to say, or, again, that nature is not a problem. *The blue hills are simply blue hills; / The white clouds are simply white clouds.*"

For Western man nature has *always* been a problem, and erotic idealizations have often helped him work at it. And where there is a problem, must there not be a problem-solver? In deciding what he really wants and what ideally he wishes to be, Western man creates an idea of himself as a separate and independent entity, as a *person.* In the East, prior to the modern era, this concept of a person seems to have had as little significance as the Western concept of love.* In the West the two have gone together since the Greeks. Through its idealizations of desire the eros tradition transforms the human animal into a creature with a soul, a self that aspires to perfect itself, an eternal being that traces a unique trajectory in time and senses its own dramatic unity. The erotic soul strives for something that will satisfy desire. Therein consists its nature as a person as well as a lover.

Though the eros tradition is the source of our concept of a person, it nevertheless misconstrues the love of persons (as I have been arguing). In idealizing appraisal, the eros tradition creates the ideal

---

*Cf. Walter Pater a hundred years ago: "In oriental thought there is a vague conception of life everywhere, but no true appreciation of itself by the mind, no knowledge of the distinction of man's nature. . . . humanity is still confused with the . . . life of the animal and vegetable world."

of love as a search for goodness. To so great-hearted a lover as Plato, the object must be *absolute* perfection; to Plotinus it cannot be anything less than the infinite All; to Lucretius only an ultimate and universal law of nature is really worth loving. Like extravagant lovers these philosophers bestow a maximum value upon the object of their idealization. An ordinary man might accept the beloved while acting *as if* she were perfect. These philosophical lovers also accept the loved one as it is—the highest principle of rationality, the goal of spiritual aspiration, the final category in analysis—but for *them*, all as-ifs must be eschewed. The objects of their respective devotions must be objectively perfect, and even more. They must be the very basis of perfection itself: all goodness in the world must come from them; the word "good" must even mean what it does only in relation to them. Ovid and Aristotle (also Freud) are more moderate in the bestowals that orient their thinking. These are cooler and more cautious lovers. But in idealizing appraisal, they too neglect the element of bestowal in love, particularly the love of persons, and thereby fail to understand fully what it is to be a person.

Nor are the failings of the eros tradition with respect to these two concepts really separate. It is easier to appraise things than a person, and ideals guide appraisal more readily than bestowal. We speak of treating people as things or treating them as persons, distinguishing between these categories in order to indicate that there is something in personality that eludes precise appraisal. We can establish an objective price for various things; but just how much is a human being worth? Similarly, our ideals can elicit an appropriate appraisal, even the appraisal of bestowals, but nothing can elicit bestowals themselves. Either they come or they don't. That is the spontaneity in love, as it is in persons. Both defy our rational calculations. Both are *inherently* vague. In the love of persons the object must always be somewhat mysterious, if only because the beloved is bestowing value as well as receiving bestowals, and so continuously changing. This openness in love—in both the lover and the beloved—escapes the eros tradition. Erotic idealizations always terminate in self-sufficiency, a state in which all desires will be satisfied, all perfections attained, as if there were an "all" to man, as if he could be filled to the brim. But even desire does not function in so static and hydraulic a way, in either the lover or the beloved. If it did, we would probably refuse to call them *persons.*

In Christianity, the Platonic Good becomes a personal deity. In the Judaeo-Christian idea of God's agapē, bestowal achieves its first great formulation as a philosophical principle. Christian love starts with erotic idealizations but then moves far beyond them. The concept of loving another as a person virtually begins with the Old Testament. It develops through a long literary history, reaching a high level of sophistication in the religious synthesis of the Middle Ages. Whether this synthesis is viable, and whether its religious foundations help or hinder our understanding of the love of persons, we must now determine.

Part III
Religious Love in the Middle Ages

9
Elements of Christian Love

Religious Love Is Mainly A product of the Judaeo-Christian tradition. Although much of Buddhist and Hindu thought deals with noble sentiments not unrelated to love, Eastern religions have scarcely developed the concept as we know it. Only Christianity, with its roots in Judaism, defines itself as *the* religion of love. By this I do not mean to say that members of the Catholic or Protestant churches have been more loving than other people. The history of the Western world, which was largely enacted by believers in Christ, is hardly the story of love triumphant. But what distinguishes Christianity, what gives it a unique place in man's intellectual life, is the fact that it alone has made love the dominant principle in all areas of dogma. Whatever Christians may have done to others or themselves, theirs is the only faith in which God and love are the same. The two thousand years of Christian theology and philosophy consist of one attempt after another to understand, and render amenable to worship, a love that might be God.

Over so long a period one cannot expect to find a single doctrine consistently unfolding. Even Catholicism, which seeks to resist ephemeral changes in the human climate, has encompassed different attitudes toward love. Some of these have been exorcised as heresies; others have been nurtured and promoted as orthodoxy. But even the orthodox views have changed from generation to generation. And the same is true—to a still greater degree—of the

Protestant sects. In all their varieties, however, Christian ideas about love retain a family resemblance, and for good reason: they derive from a similar mixture of classical philosophy and scriptural revelation. What especially interests me is the way in which each blend idealizes aspects of human nature. Rather than trace the full development of Christian love, I shall limit myself to elements within the more monumental mixtures, analyzing them in terms of idealization.

In approaching Christian concepts of love, I respect the differences that separate Catholic from Protestant. But I also think that the Protestant Reformation is best understood as a special, in some ways radical, attempt to resolve problems that had confronted theologians for centuries. These problems largely concern the relationship between different elements of Christian love, conveniently designated by four Greek words: *eros, philia, nomos, agapē*.

Eros and philia we have now studied at some length. Christian concepts of eros closely resemble Platonic and Neoplatonic ideas about the soul's search for its highest good. Since Christianity maintains that the highest good is a personal God, the nature of spiritual aspiration required massive reinterpretation. But the general structure of eros remained the same; as was also the case with philia, which comes directly from Aristotle's conception of perfect friendship. Christian philia interprets this as the brotherhood of man, the community of believers, the bond between Christ and his church, between God and the human soul, and ultimately among the Persons in the Holy Trinity.

These concepts (eros and philia) constitute Christianity's inheritance from the Greeks. From its Jewish origins the new religion received the elements of nomos and agapē. Both occur in the Old Testament, and much of the New Testament deals with the differences between them. Nomos is the idea of love as righteousness, acceptance of God's law, humble submission to his will. Agapē is love as the creator of goodness in the world, God bestowing value in accordance with his own design, divinity giving itself in ways that transcend human understanding. Beginning with the New Testament, Christianity develops the idea of agapē beyond its Jewish sources and in a manner that curtails Greek influence upon Western theology. When the Gospel according to John says that God is Love, the relevant term is *agapē*. When Plotinus, overlapping Christianity but still belonging to the old dispensation, says God is Love, he uses the word *eros*. However deceptive the English translations may be, the two statements are worlds apart.

The conflict beyond eros and agapē in Christian theology has been analyzed brilliantly by a Swedish scholar named Anders Nygren, bishop of Lund. In a book entitled *Agape and Eros*, Nygren argues that the Christian concept of agapē contradicts ideas of eros inherited by the medieval church. In general, Nygren's view is the position of Luther, who held that Christian concepts such as those of love could not be reconciled with pagan philosophy. Catholic thinkers deny that eros and agapē are irreconcilable. Much of Augustine and Aquinas is devoted to effecting a viable synthesis between these ideas, and contemporary Catholics like Martin C. D'Arcy try to answer Nygren's criticism by modest reformulations of the traditional doctrine. Throughout this controversy, nomos and philia tend to be neglected. In what follows, I shall consider the four concepts as parts of a unified system, examining the problems that they engender both in themselves and in their combination. Theologians will never cease to argue about such problems:

> Myself when young did eagerly frequent
> Doctor and Saint, and heard great argument
>   About it and about: but evermore
> Came out by the same Door wherein I went.

But as the embodiment of religious idealizations, these great disputes may take on a new significance—for those who believe as well as for those who do not.

10
Eros: The Mystical Ascent

I_N PLATONISM AND THE NEO-
platonism of Plotinus, love is primarily an attribute of man. All
things in the empirical world are said to exist through love; but only
in man does love reach fruition. Man approaches the divine through
his ability to love. Of nothing can this be said, not even the divine. In
this respect the typical Greek attitude is supremely anthropocentric.
In other ways, however, it is obviously limited as a human projection. Aphrodite was a goddess, and aspiring Eros a daemon of some
importance, but neither can compare with the Judaeo-Christian
God who both loves and is love itself. If we think of that God as an
infinite extension of man's creativity and then relate creativity to the
act of loving, we begin to appreciate the revolution that Christianity
effected. Greek philosophers had idealized the purposive search for
goodness; it remained for the Christians to idealize the *object* of that
search as being purposive in itself. This they did by making God not
only the destination but also the primal source of love. Upon Aristotle's unmoved mover they bestowed the precious ability to *care about*
all things, which then becomes its principal attribute. The Christian
God, like the Aristotelian God, draws everything to himself by being
loved. But also he is a lover; indeed, all love originates with him,
inasmuch as nothing could love unless he loved it first. Through this
kind of idealization the Christians could see in the cosmos a meaning
and a purposefulness that no one else had ever found. Their God
takes a personal interest in whatever nature produces. He himself

contains the highest Platonic form, the very essence of goodness or beauty. At the same time, he is infinitely powerful, authoritative, wise. He is a great benefactor who always arranges for the best. And, finally, none of the love he generates is ever wasted: eventually it all comes back to him. However circuitously, God always loves himself. In being love, he constantly descends into his creatures; yet they too have ultimately no object but the Godhead. He is therefore both alpha and omega, the beginning and the end, the apotheosis of eros, the perfection of purposive self-love.

In being a divinized eros, the Christian God becomes the model for new types of erotic idealization. As God loves all things for his own sake, so too is man to love whatever conduces to *his* beatitude. Man's love for God can never be identical with God's love for man or even God's love for himself; but all three belong to a circuit of love that reinforces the eros tradition, encasing it within a larger network of loving relations and employing it for religious purposes. The "good news" of Christ gave assurance that the Good all men loved not only welcomed their devotion but also loved them reciprocally. Hebrew culture had been groping toward this idea for centuries. Its acceptance by the Western world marked the conversion of Greek philosophy into the new theological hegemony. The universe could now be seen as a mutual love of love, at every moment receiving sustenance from a love both purposive and holy. What formerly resulted from the imperfections of man became the living manifestation of divinity. Never before had the human capacity for idealization soared as high.

Although Aristotle had to wait some time, the Christianization of Plato and Plotinus occurs in the writings of St. Augustine. In the *Confessions* he describes his progress away from the ideals of the ancient world. Pagan life had lost its spiritual promise, and primitive Christianity seemed to offer a way of making a new start, of being reborn through love. From this autobiography it is evident that Augustine had needs that could not be satisfied by Greek philosophy. He required a heavenly father who would liberate him from the dominance of the one he had on earth. In being the true source of one's being, the Christian God served this function perfectly. Augustine also needed a radical method for eliminating his sense of guilt, an absolute assurance that even one as worthless as himself could actually be saved. Here too Christianity seemed better able to satisfy his requirements. It proclaimed that man's creation, in fact the creation of everything, originates from an infinite source of love; and it offered the commandment to return love for love as the single but thoroughly sufficient means of attaining salvation. Some of this came to Augustine from the Old Testament, some from the Gospels, some from the writings of St. Paul. He appropriated it all with the fervor of one who rebels against a hated parent. Like most rebels, however, Augustine made his peace with the past by incorporating it into the grand design. He voiced assent to the Christian message, but he perceived it with the eyes and ears of the eros tradition that his father represented. Platonic love was thus converted to Christianity while the Christian love of God assumed the configurations of Platonistic philosophy. Thereafter neither would ever be the same.

For St. Augustine the fundamental fact about the empirical world is its restless, unending search for goodness. This uneasiness of the human condition, its weary treadmill tragedy, is even more apparent in Augustine than it had been in Plato. True, Plato had lived in a time of troubles following the Peloponnesian War; his master had been sacrificed to the moral corruption of Athens; and he himself was to be sold into slavery after fruitless efforts to reform another state. Yet even so, one feels that Plato's aristocratic birth could always sustain him, that the sense of city-state identity and his natural place within the ruling class could effectively bear him from one trying period to another. By the time of Augustine, all this gilt has been tarnished: little remains but the mechanical routine of a demoralized Roman empire. Nor was it a world that Augustine could easily escape, or even feel he wanted to. Somehow it all had to make sense in accordance with God's plan. It was natural for things to seek after their welfare, man no less than the amoeba. In whatever they did, all men desired happiness. To deny this would be to negate the fact of universal striving—which was not Augustine's intention any more than Plato's or Aristotle's. Like his Greek antecedents he wished to affirm the erotic dynamism in everything. But for him it had to occur within a theological cosmos that directed all the stirrings of life toward the Christian God.

It is, therefore, Greek philosophy that enables St. Augustine to describe love as the motive force within the world, to define it as the inescapable striving for the greatest good of which one is capable. In one place he says, "there is no one who does not love," and elsewhere he speaks of love as that which pertains to the fact of desire or appetite: *Amor appetitus quidam est.* Man's appetite being a part of his endless search for happiness, which in turn implies a yearning for goodness, it can be satisfied only by the possession of man's *summum bonum,* or greatest good. "Love eager to possess its object is desire; possessing and enjoying it, is gladness; shrinking from what opposes it, is fear; aware of effective opposition, is sorrow."

From here St. Augustine has no difficulty concluding that really all men love God, just as Plato had said that they all love the Good. For God is perfect goodness; he is by his very nature the essence of what is good. In the everyday world things change incessantly; no valued object lasts for very long; final satisfaction, and therefore true happiness, forever eludes us. Even if some earthly good remained constant, we could not fully appreciate it. For our appetites keep changing; our sensory and intellectual taste, our feelings and predilections, alter day by day. "Man is a giddy thing," as Shakespeare's Benedick says, laughing at the variability of human inclinations. But for Augustine—as for Pascal and many other Christians—the vanity (by which they mean the inconstancy) of mortal desires is no light matter. For them it occasions excruciating anxiety and must be supplanted by a kind of desiring that culminates in total, changeless fulfillment. The Greeks had sought this too, but they had not heard the word of Christ. Only God, eternal and absolutely perfect, could provide a goodness which satisfies fully and constantly without any conceivable change. If not on earth, at least in heaven, human striving could cease. The troubled, self-warring soul might then find peace. Man's love of God having been perfected, the sanctified Christian could finally enjoy what he had sought all along: "unchanging love of a good attained."

From this aspect of St. Augustine's thinking, Christianity acquires its emphasis upon man's *longing* for God. All devout believers are pilgrims, their lives oriented toward the journey of faith, the yearning for "Jesu, joy of man's desiring." As a journey upward toward the divine, the quest is otherworldly, even ascetic. The world of appearance must be left behind, its pleasures renounced, as one moves on to ultimate reality. Like all journeys this one involves a dislocation of oneself, a change in one's condition justified by the hope of future goods. No such attitude toward life as a journey, as movement for the sake of self-perfection, existed in the Eastern world. It is part of the dynamism of the West, caught up by Christianity and fitted into a militant theology, but eventually spilling over into other things: geographical exploration, the growth of science, technological development, and now the flight into cosmic spaces that men as late as Dante thought to be inhabited by the celestial choirs. Twentieth-century man seeks a realm beyond the earth, just as his Christian forebears had. Except in the object of its aspiration, our journeying has come full circle.

For St. Augustine this object, this goal of man's endeavor, was a Being immanent in this world and yet transcendent, present in all places and at all times in the sense that everything exists by virtue of its continuing love, but itself remaining undiminished by the limitations of space, time, or anything else. As a substitute for the Good in Plato, this ultimate category of explanation is often called "the Highest Good." Following Augustine, St. Thomas Aquinas speaks of the Supreme Being as "the common good of the whole universe," which explains why all things love it: "Love is something which appertains to desire, since the object of both is what is good. . . . The attitude or disposing of the appetite to anything so as to make it its good is called love. We love each thing in as much as it is our good." God being the common good, all things exist by loving him. He is, therefore, the principle of goodness, the source and objective essence of good, and so in himself the highest good.

But goodness is only one of God's attributes. Unlike the highest form of Plato, the Christian God exists and wields final power in the universe. He is not the unmoved mover of Aristotle. For he has a personality that speaks to the soul of man. He is a person, and even a trinity of persons in one. How God can be three persons need not concern us here, except to note that Protestants and Jews who find this mystery unbearable should search their souls to see whether their own ideas about the supernatural are less mysterious. Indeed, is there anything one can say about God without talking nonsense? If an entity transcends nature, how can we have *any* idea of what it is? How can we know what a supernatural being would be like or even that this order of language makes sense? To avoid such difficulties, the negative theology of the Middle Ages refers to the deity only by listing attributes that do *not* apply. But surely the negative terms have no meaning except in relation to terms that are positive. One says what God *is* if one can say what he is *not*. What then does it mean to speak of God as a supernatural person? The language is extraordinary, and confusingly metaphoric. In part, however, the Christian talks this way in order to treat the highest good as something more than just a philosophical category. Regardless of the cost in logic, he must conceive of the ultimate form as itself a living spirit. Through introspection we know the life of spirit in ourselves; and by extrapolating beyond himself, the Christian assumes that his Supreme Being must be something similar, though infinitely superior in all respects.

The Christian concept of a personal God is thus an imaginative projection. It begins with ideas about nature and then uses them to speak analogously about an entity *outside* of nature. Like eros itself, the language is a journeying beyond the ordinary world. But also it indicates a universal need to create a God in the believer's own image. In its attempt to become a popular religion, Christianity realized that only philosophers could worship the form of abstract goodness. Most people respond lovingly to what they are and what they know directly: persons, not ideals. Their creative capacities are sentimental, not moral or intellectual. If God was to idealize the power of love in the universe, he would have to be an anthropomorphic spirit, a benign and even friendly personality, a father with whom one could communicate, a sustaining presence who acts in ways that passeth understanding but wonderfully fortify the human heart. In this fashion the love of ideals would fuse into the love of at least one person.

At the same time, Augustine and his followers knew that they must retain as much of Greek philosophy as possible. Otherwise, the Christian God would become anthropomorphic in the way that pagan deities were. These came into existence, flourished in one remarkable episode or another, then departed, often slain by a more powerful god. The Christian God is *in principle* beyond all that, just as Plato's highest form is. By definition God is "that than which no greater can be conceived," to use the words of Anselm's ontological argument. Against the immediacy of calling the Supreme Being a person, even capitalizing words such as "God" as if they were proper names, the church fathers had to balance the advantages of worshiping a deity whose ultimacy *could* not be doubted. God had to be the highest good but also a demiurge who lives and thinks and constantly concerns himself with the world he has created for reasons of love.

In recognizing this double necessity but giving precedence to loving God as a person, Augustine changes the entire eros tradition. From having been the final category of analysis, the Good becomes one among other attributes of a personal deity. Augustine even makes it subordinate to God's will in ways that would surely have distressed Plato. In an early dialogue, the *Euthyphro*, Plato raises the question whether piety is good because the gods like it or the gods like it because it is good. This is one of the negative dialogues and Plato does not give a definitive answer. But he does suggest that the first alternative is unacceptable: it treats the value of piety as something arbitrary—what the gods happen to like—rather than something objective, built into the order of things, discernible by reason. Plato clearly prefers the second alternative, though he is not in a position to defend it until he works out the doctrine of forms. Now it seems to me that Augustine wanted to retain *both* alternatives. It is entirely through God's will that value comes into being, he says, yet by his very nature God is necessarily good. In making goodness depend upon the will of a divine person, Augustine accepts the primacy of God's liking; in asserting that God *must* be good, however, he removes the possibility of value being arbitrary. Like Plato, Augustine maintains that all valuable things derive their goodness from participating in the form of absolute good. But for Augustine the form of absolute good is itself derivative from God's total personality as a living spirit. To say this is to idealize the love of persons beyond the love of ideals. And as there can be only one highest form for Plato, so too Augustine admits only one person who is *truly* worthy of love. Since that "person" is a supernatural God, loving him must always differ from loving other persons. Nevertheless, a great step has been taken: for now the goal of eros is not merely the Good but also, and predominantly, a person.

In redirecting the eros tradition toward a love of persons, Augustine effects a basic reorientation in Western thought. But his doctrine is confused, and it leads Christianity into logical difficulties that have never been fully surmounted. Just *how* can the love of ideals be fused with the love of persons? Goods, and possibly the highest good, can be possessed; but the same is not true of a person. We may desire things, and even people, for the sake of what is good in them; but to love another *as* a person is to establish a different kind of relationship. Insofar as God is our highest good, we use him as something to be sought because it makes us better. We treat him as a thing or an ideal, not as a person. Is this what the Christian would like to say about religious eros?

At times, it would seem so. Following Augustine, Hugh of St. Victor describes the love of God in unmistakable terms: "What is love but to desire and to long to have and to possess and to enjoy? If not possessed then to long to possess, and if possessed then to long to keep . . . for what is love save the very desire to possess?" But since God must also be loved as a person, none of this would seem to be possible. We cannot possess persons; and if they can be enjoyed, it is only in the sense that we delight in *them*. That occurs when the lover bestows importance upon the other person's interests, attends to him, accepts him as the separate individual he happens to be. Some, though not all, of this St. Augustine includes within the love of God. But he does not show how loving God as a person can really be compatible with loving him as the highest good. As if to pose the problem most blatantly, St. Thomas even says: "Assuming what is impossible that God were not man's good, then there would be no reason for man to love God." One could not speak this way if man's love for God were truly the love of a person.

I shall return to this difficulty in various guises, for it is central to all religious love in the Western world. Here I need only point out that the problem would not arise if God were a natural, rather than a supernatural, person. In our relations with human beings, for instance, desiring them for the sake of goods they provide is wholly compatible with loving them as persons. The love of human persons is normally the bestowing of value upon someone who satisfies the lover's needs or desires. But this cannot be if the other person is the Christian God. By his nature, God is infinite perfection, the essence of goodness. How then could one bestow value upon him? How could one enjoy God as just the person he is? The Christian speaks of delighting in the deity, but really he is *admiring* God's absolute goodness, enjoying the fact that he is the highest good. It is not God as a person that he enjoys, only God's attributes. Would he delight in God if God were *not* perfect—if God made mistakes, did bad things occasionally, created evil as well as good? No, for that would not be the Christian God. But then why call the devout response love for a person? At best it is love of objective goodness, comparable to the Platonic love of ideals, and so an idealization of appraisal. At worst it is not love at all, but simply an egocentric desire to possess the benefits of perfection. The Christian may *speak* of God as a person, but does he love him as such?

From St. Augustine's variations upon the eros theme springs all of Christian mysticism. In general, mysticism of the West is an effort to achieve oneness with a divinity more or less conceived to be a person. Some scholars deny that mystical experience requires any object whatsoever; they emphasize the sense of oneness not with a person or even a God, but with ultimate being as a whole. For them the Buddhist saint undergoing *satori* is a mystic, though possibly an atheistic one. But this issue is largely verbal, and it in no way alters the fact that *Western* mystics have generally sought oneness with a personal deity. Even Plotinus, sometimes called the first mystic, spoke about the One as if it had a cosmic personality. In the imaginative thinking of folk tales and primitive superstition, even sticks and stones can be treated like persons. Then why not the universe itself, suddenly, for a shattering moment, compressed into a looming unity and confronting the stricken spirit with more immediacy than may be found in any actual person? The mystic peoples this awesome presence with a consciousness, a will, a purpose. He thereby denotes it as a kindred spirit within an order of supreme spirituality. By analogy to more familiar human relations, it may then be called Father, Lord, the King of Kings. It will be as if one has found a great and marvelous Friend.

At times the magnitude of the infinite and eternal Being turns mystical wonder into fright, much as an ordinary man—even a Pascal—will fear the great spaces within the astronomical universe. To the Spanish mystics of the sixteenth century, particularly St. John of the Cross, the entire experience is a dark night of the soul. In her definitive study of mysticism, Evelyn Underhill shows how the sense of cosmic terror marks a stage in the development of many saints and mystics. Some of them take the dryness and loss of all interest, both spiritual and sensory, as proof of their sinfulness. Others consider this part of the mystical experience to be the work of the devil. Still others merely find it strange and incomprehensible, as well as painful. It is as if God were playing a "game of love" with man. Several mystics use that phrase to refer to the way in which the Divine Presence alternately appears in their lives and then horribly seems to abandon them. For these mystics the oscillations between joyfulness and despair (or to use the clinical terms, mania and depression) become more violent as they move closer to their spiritual destination. In St. John of the Cross the mystical ascent is like an oncoming ocean wave with greater and greater crests and troughs, each more fearful than the last even though the trend is always upward. For some mystics the dark night lasts through many years. In others, e.g., Rulman Merswin who suffered a paralytic stroke, it occasions physical as well as psychological agony. St. John of the Cross, like St. Catherine of Siena, seems to glory in the authenticity of devastating pain: it both symbolizes and effects the transfiguration of the human soul. In no other way could the final blessing of oneness with God be attained. Every day is preceded by a night; we go through death to be reborn; and even life must be a continual dying to our natural interests if we are to achieve perfection. Philosophers and theologians had been saying the same for centuries. The Christian mystics *applied* these ideas, underwent them in the actual suffering of painful experience.

But this dark side of Christian mysticism, so prominent in the sixteenth century, is not characteristic of the twelfth or thirteenth centuries. Since the beginnings of Christendom, ascetics have mortified the flesh, feared God, and often hated themselves. In the Middle Ages, however, these bitter sentiments are often domesticated, modified, cleansed by a spiritual discipline that leads to love. In the mysticism that immediately devolves from St. Augustine one senses a great and terrible fear of the world, but not of God. Where the mystical experience looks like a series of up-and-down curves in St. John of the Cross, in St. Bernard it is a straight line moving quietly and steadily upward toward the greatest love. Four hundred years separate St. Bernard from St. John of the Cross; and during this period Christianity changed the tenor, if not the doctrine, of its ideas about religious love. The sequel to this book will concern itself with the basis for this change. Here I need only note that in the Middle Ages at least, Christian mysticism speaks with a gladness and a confidence it was never to have again. The medieval mystics, more than any other, seem to be at home in God's universe. However much they may have renounced this world in their search for a better one, they sound like men who lived joyful lives (though hardly complete ones). One feels they may very well have achieved oneness with some sustaining power. Theirs is a simplicity of spirit, as in the paintings of Simone Martini or Fra Angelico, that itself fulfills the religious promise. They have the purity of trusting and uncorrupted children. When St. Francis of Assisi wanted to liberate himself from his earthly father, he had only to cast aside the cloak of mundane goods in order to commune with a paternal being who would never fail him. The way was clear and always open. To this day, the God these mystics worshiped remains the closest approximation to that infinitely tender, kind, and affectionate parent which all Western religion seeks.

To the Freudians this aspect of religious love is nothing but regression. And certainly, these gentle mystics do wish to return home and be united with an all-loving father, to be accepted as a child within a holy family, even to feel the oceanic peace of an infant at the mother's breast. In *The Future of an Illusion* Freud claims that religion is simply an obsessional neurosis shared by whole communities but in principle no different from other pathological conditions that arise out of the Oedipus complex. Having lost the protection of his real father, the mystic imagines a spiritual parent who serves in fantasy as a perfect wish-fulfillment. Religious doctrines, and also mystical aspirations, Freud calls illusional in the sense that they are merely devices for pretending that certain unrealistic wishes can actually be fulfilled. How much better it would be, Freud says, if man could learn the facts of life and death, surmount the childish need to have an ever-present parent, and so grow up.

To this the mystic need only reply that he has grown up; and that having seen how trivial are the pleasures of this world, he now chooses a greater joy. Since pleasures are valuable only as they are valued, I see no reason to assume that the mystic necessarily makes the wrong choice. We need not doubt that in loving God he is looking for a father: most mystics say the same themselves. But why call it an illusion? Why think that in God the mystic seeks nothing but a *substitute* for his own father? The mystic is not a child, and he may or may not be neurotic. The father he looks for may resemble his parent in some respects, but not entirely. The mystic turns to God because he needs reassurance about his *spiritual* origin. No earthly father can satisfy this need, however wise, however powerful, however protective he may be. The mystic requires a greater love than any human being can offer. If fathers were perfect and could guarantee eternal life, no mystics would exist. Their parents would be gods, and children would worship them as the Chinese once revered all ancestors. Since fathers lack perfection, the mystic tries to perfect himself in the hope of reaching another kind of father: one who gives him a sense of reigning spirituality in the universe, one who protects against the physical world by showing how little it is worth. Religious beliefs are often unverifiable, but I do not think they are necessarily regressive. The infantile personality is very rudimentary. The mystic's is highly developed, rich with the human experience of a sensitive adult, veined with ideological tradition, capable of idealized projections upon an enormous scale and within a world of highly creative, highly articulate imagination. If this be regression, perhaps we should say of it what George Bernard Shaw said of youth: it is too valuable to waste on children.

In cultivating the love of a Supreme Father, medieval mysticism partly rectifies the rationalism of Platonic eros. Since the Augustinian God must be worshiped as a person as well as the highest good, Christian love seeks for something other than oneness with a metaphysical category. Categories can be thought about, dialectically approximated, their truthfulness possibly known by intellect. But persons are not of this sort. A person must be appreciated, respected in his mysterious identity, approached but not approximated, touched to his living core, not known as abstract truth is known. Oneness with a person pertains to feeling more than reason, to affection (*affectus*) as opposed to cognition. Where Plato's lover attains the Good by possessing it through knowledge of reality, the mystic seeks a conjunction of spirits, a felt communion that unites two personalities. In the state of ecstasy the mystic possesses God and participates in his beatitude, as if he were indeed a Platonic entity; but also the mystical union is described as a mutual embrace, a spiritual marriage, a personal confrontation between the soul of man and the soul-like being of God. The mystic feels the closeness of the Lord much as a bride senses the proximity of her spouse. For this no act of reason can suffice, and ordinary intellect must always be a hindrance.

By asserting the primacy of feeling, mysticism denies that the philosopher (whether Socrates or another) is worthy of being considered the true lover. The love of God does not require superior training in analysis or dialectics. It is not speculative insight or any other refinement of the intellect. It depends in part on faith, in part on the purification of erotic feeling. The medieval mystics are Platonistic in seeking a discipline of progressive spiritualization through which the dedicated soul must pass in its yearning for the beloved. And in both cases the goal is union so complete and overwhelming as to satisfy all the demands of one's nature. But now a different faculty of man is being idealized—feeling which does the work of reason and does it better. Since oneness with God perfects all human interests, the mystical experience includes a vision of truth as well as a sense of communion. This epiphany is itself, however, a consummation of feeling. Aristotle thought that rational contemplation was the highest reach of spirit, and so the Aristotelian God does nothing but contemplate his own essence. For the Christian, contemplation belongs to one of the lower stages of the mystical union. It is a seeing that prepares for the final embrace, and even in itself it involves spiritual feeling more than rationality: "For silence is not God, nor speaking is not God; fasting is not God nor eating is not God; loneliness is not God nor company is not God; nor yet any of all the other two such quantities. He is hid between them, and may not be found by any work of thy soul, but all only by love of thine heart. He may not be known by reason, he may not be gotten by thought, nor concluded by understanding; but he may be loved and chosen with the true lovely will of thine heart."

Christian mysticism is the religious underground rising and asserting its essential dignity. Before there was a Socrates or a Plato, devotees of this or that god sought oneness with him. Their rites or mysteries (and what could be more mysterious than feeling doing the work of intellect?) are even present in the myths that Plato uses. Where else could he have got the paradoxical notion of a "divine madness"? For centuries Greek philosophy had tried to civilize, to stifle if necessary, the Dionysian exuberance of its antecedent mysticism. In the name of order and harmony, of a good and beautiful life woven by the golden mean, reason had to be dominant. But even reason and moderation can be immoderate: their apotheosis in Plato and Aristotle became an act of *hybris*, to be chastened by the *nemesis* of Christianity. Unlike its pagan predecessors, however, Christian mysticism could enjoy the best of both worlds: both public theology and private ecstasy, reason as a way of proving the Christian truth and spiritual feeling as the perfect means of attaining it. Through concentrated devotion, osmotically and by an act of will, the mystic could now know all the truths for which the philosophers had struggled. The Christians would thus have direct access to a God that all men sought, but who was knowable only through a love such as theirs.

In making knowledge of God depend upon devotional feeling, Christianity was not merely putting rationalism in its place. It was also attacking the cynical position which Baudelaire was later to enunciate: "It is more difficult to love God than to believe in Him." For that was to be the difference between the Christian God and all others. To know him was to love him, in the sense that one could neither know nor believe unless one did love. Pushed to its extreme, as eventually happened in nineteenth-century romanticism, the reliance on feeling tended to undermine all ideas of God's separate existence. Throughout the Middle Ages, however, the independent and prior being of God was assumed with the same assurance that Plato felt about his realm of transcendental forms. And though adequately knowing God came from loving him, it was generally agreed that reason could at least prove his existence. The twelfth- and thirteenth-century renaissance, culminating in the work of St. Thomas Aquinas, consisted in one turn of the screw after another, effort after effort to harmonize intellect and feeling in such a way that love would remain supreme but always congruent to the dictates of reasoned orthodoxy. All the elements in the final synthesis are present in St. Bernard's description of the mystical union: "And then between God and the soul shall be nought but a mutual dilection chaste and consummated, a full mutual recognition, a manifest vision, a firm conjunction, a society undivided, and a perfect likeness. Then shall the soul know God even as she is known (1 Cor. 13:10); then shall she love as she is loved; and over his Bride shall rejoice the Bridegroom, knowing and known, loving and beloved, Jesus Christ our Lord, Who is over all things, God blessed for ever."

In this ambiguous triumph over Greek philosophy, Christian mysticism was also ambiguous in its return to more primitive mysteries. The post-Augustine mystic resembled his Eleusinian or Orphic brethren in seeking to love God by incandescent means, by making himself a flame of feeling. But the nature of Christian feeling had itself been filtered by reason. A Greek orgiast could reach unity with the god through emotions of frank sexuality and violent hatred, one for effecting communion, the other for destroying everything that might impede it. This kind of feeling was no longer available to the Christian. The God he loved was pure spirit, and all mystical love attenuated by a long tradition of theology. Not that emotionalism disappeared: the pages of the church fathers are filled with it, no less than the writings of both heretical and orthodox mystics. As time went on, sentimentality became more prominent— as we know from the paintings of Murillo (just to choose one extreme case among many possible examples), or Bernini's statue of St. Teresa with her mouth open, her head tilted back, and her eyeballs rolling. But emotionalism characterizes only a minor part of Christian ecstasy. More significant are the conformity of wills and the oneness in spirit. Between the mystic and his God reciprocal feelings of union are neither sexual nor even carnal in the ordinary sense. That is what St. John of the Cross means when he asserts that "love consists not in feeling great things, but in having great detachment" (from everything other than God). And though his language is more confusing, St. Augustine presumably means the same when he says: "With an incredible fervour of the heart, I yearned for the immortal wisdom, and I began to arise in order to return to Thee."

So here too the mystic speaks in richly metaphoric language, thoroughly baffling to the nonbeliever. The mystic wishes to know God through feeling, but feeling of a sort that others may scarcely recognize. Clearly, Platonistic idealism has had its effect. However much he would like to free himself of earlier rationalism, the Christian mystic continually reverts to it. His feelings have been spiritualized in the manner of Greek philosophy. Nor would it be too difficult to imagine St. Jerome, or many another holy man of the Middle Ages, as a Stoic rather than a Christian, resisting bodily temptations and purifying himself for the sake of sheer rationality rather than the love of God. Since the Christian deity is a father, he must be loved with feelings appropriate to persons. But since he is also the highest good and like no father on earth, these feelings must be purely transcendental, abstract, disembodied. What then are these "feelings"? And are they actually compatible with the human condition? Are they relevant to an authentic love of persons? Once again we return to this question.

The mystics give no literal answer. Their writings are poetical and vague. Hundreds of years before the Symbolist movement, they were the first great symbolist poets in Europe. They differ from the nineteenth-century Symbolists, however, in rising out of the foundations of an explicit orthodoxy. One thinks of Christian mysticism as a constant threat to ecclesiastical doctrine, but in fact few of the medieval mystics had any desire to contradict the church fathers. As thinkers, they begin where St. Augustine does: with the belief that all things are in love with God. From St. Augustine they also learn to distinguish between two types of love, *caritas* (charity) and *cupiditas* (cupidity). Augustine speaks of caritas as the means by which the soul returns to its spiritual source in God. Through cupiditas the body draws man back to the material world, leaving him *curbatus* (bent) until the love of God can straighten him out and allow his soul to move upward. Since all things exist by loving something, cupiditas is love just as much as caritas is. But it is an inferior type. Only caritas is true love: for only then does man desire an object worthy of devotion. In effect this is the distinction between the heavenly and the earthly Aphrodite, inherited from Plato by the eros tradition. Through Augustine it becomes orthodox dogma. For the mystics these ideas serve as the framework of Christian experience, the doctrinal basis for describing the love of God in symbolic language.

In Gregory of Nyssa, one of the early church fathers and a contemporary of Augustine's, we already find many of the mystical symbols. Perhaps the most common is the image of a heavenly ladder. As Nygren points out, the ladder as a symbol of spiritual ascent occurs in various mystery religions of the ancient world but enters into Christianity via Plato's *Symposium*. It is the order of salvation, the *ordo salutis*, by which the mystic rises toward God through self-purification. For the medievals the ladder signified a methodical advance, step by step, toward a preexistent elevation. At the outset all men are on the same low level. In order to reach even the first rung of the ladder, they must turn away from that natural cupidity into which original sin has cast them. The mystic begins to love truly when he feels a spiritual awakening. This enables him to practice humility, and the further reaches of caritas occur only as the soul becomes more humble.

At first the mystic tries to overcome his sins through fasting and doing penance; he spends his time in meditation, prayer, and reflection about the nature of God. These activities are delightful but still at the level of sense experience. They belong to man's fallen condition. Once the mystic realizes that even the consolations of religion must be renounced, he is ready for the next stage. That occurs when God admits the soul to a vision of divinity. The mystic then receives "illumination" or "infused contemplation." God shows himself; and the soul, sensing its proximity to the primal Being, kindles with ardent love. God communicates directly, allowing the soul to undergo a spiritual betrothal with him. By this time the soul has begun to retrieve its original likeness to God; and at this level there is instituted a first "union" between the two lovers. It is followed by further purification, eradicating the last vestiges of pride and preparing the soul for spiritual marriage. The mystic then unites with God to the greatest extent possible for earthbound man. In the spiritual marriage, God and the purified soul become "one spirit." In a moment of ecstasy the mystic is finally drawn out of himself by the divine love. He has reached the top of the ladder. Above and beyond the ladder of love, another stage awaits in heaven. But not until he dies can man savor this final goal. It eternally beckons, or rather radiates: the state of blessedness and ultimate glory, the consummation of God's work, the spiritual completion for which all creatures yearn but only the sanctified can ever reach.

In addition to the ladder of mystical experience, there is also a ladder of merit and a ladder of speculation. Aquinas describes the ladder of merit as the way to rise by doing virtuous acts. In the writings of St. Bonaventura, on the other hand, one finds a clearly articulated ladder of theological speculation—six stages by which the mind journeys toward God. Nevertheless, for Aquinas, who was a Dominican, and Bonaventura, who was a Franciscan, and indeed for virtually all Catholic thinkers, every ladder culminates in the mystical ascent. For as God is love and man perfects himself by loving God, all Christian aspiration leads into the ladder of love. In Dante's *Paradiso* the various ladders unite like candles, making a single flame. The ladder image itself comes from Jacob's ladder in the Old Testament, symbolizing the patriarch's vision of the divine order. Gregory of Nyssa speaks of Jacob seeing God "enthroned upon a ladder"—reminiscent of drawings that show monks climbing up, and sometimes falling off, a ladder that reaches to a winged figure of divinity. In the writings of Richard of St. Victor there occurs a still lovelier image of "angels ascending and descending and God leaning on the ladder." In signifying the *circuit* of love, the ladder expresses the deepest inspiration of medieval Christianity.

Equally interesting, however, are other symbols used to characterize the mystic's love of God. For instance, the wings of the soul, an image from Plato's *Phaedrus* (where the soul flies back to its spiritual source), originates also in biblical references to the wings of the dove. These appear in the Song of Solomon and in the Sixty-seventh Psalm: "Though ye shall sleep between two landmarks, or places, or inheritances, ye shall be as a dove with wings of silver, and her wings shall be as if she is a silver dove, and the back of the dove shall be as finely polished gold." For many mystics the wings of the dove become the "wings of love," a symbol perfectly Platonic, perfectly Christian, and later in another dispensation, perfectly Romantic.

Perhaps from Plotinus, certainly from the Alexandrian world view, Gregory of Nyssa acquires the symbol of the great chain of love binding heaven and earth, God and man, and all existence in a rising-falling unitary order. Possibly the image of a chain evolves from the ladder. Likewise, the medieval Jewish mystic Eleazor of Worms speaks of man as a twisted rope with God pulling at one end and the devil at the other. Also of Greco-Roman origin, the symbol of the arrow was frequently used both for God's love of man and for man's love of God. "Love's arrow" sometimes symbolized the soul being wounded by Christ the Archer, and sometimes the soul itself striving to attain its divine target. Cupid's darts are familiar to us from Vergil and Ovid; but to the mystics the arrows of religious love are equally sharp, equally painful, equally deadly, and equally joyful—though now in a radically different sense.

Finally, the mystical literature abounds in images of the mountain and the flame. As a bodiless force rising upward, the flame beautifully symbolizes the restless fervor of the entire eros tradition. What strikes us most in the Christian mystics, however, is their emphasis upon the holy destructiveness of fire. It is the agency by which matter is both consumed and purified, destroyed and also transmuted into a finer element. The burning bush in the Old Testament burns but undergoes no change, being an epiphany of God. For man with all his imperfections, the burning of fire signifies something else, something both punitive and redemptive. In *The Fire of Love* Richard Rolle speaks for many mystics when he says that either in this life love will "consume the rest of our sins . . . or after this life the fire of purgatory shall torture our souls, if it happen to us to escape the fires of hell, for if there be not in us a strength of love sufficient to purify us, we must be cleansed by tribulations, sicknesses, and suffering."

Like all the other symbols I have been discussing, the image of a mountain recurs throughout the Middle Ages and reaches its fullest representation in Dante's *Divine Comedy*. Not only is purgatory described as a mountain, but even the spheres of paradise take the form of a cone, and hell is divided by inverse ledges as if it were a mountain upside down. Whether it be Mount Sion or Mount Carmel up which they struggle, in imitation of Christ on Calvary, the image is vivid to all Christian mystics. Their mountains are always terraced, the ascent being marked by successive way stations. The medieval mountain is not a wild and unknown Everest, but rather an artifact of spiritual society—like the aspiring cathedrals in Western Europe. The landscape in a painter such as Giotto looks unrealistic to us because we think in terms of physical nature. To him, however, no mountain is visually interesting except as the symbol of a man's orderly ascension toward God. These are not rocks, but building stones for the universal church. The questing souls march up the mountain of mysticism with faith in its solidity and with assurance that every step has been charted in advance. The symbol of the mountain amplifies those of the ladder and the chain, except that it is more obviously hierarchical. Medieval mountains, like the pyramids of Egypt, rise into a single summit, joining the one goal to its many approaches through a number of gradations. As a general presupposition about reality, the concept of hierarchy is to the Middle Ages what the concept of harmony is to the Grecian world. All medieval ideas about love are based upon it.

Through symbols such as these, the mystics reveal the inherent feelings of their faith. It was Freud who first taught us to look at symbols as the expression of a man's deepest feelings. So certain was Freud that man continually deludes himself, however, that he refused to take *any* symbol at face value. For him all symbols revealed the truth by trying to hide it. And if the truth was always the same, as Freud believed, then the diversity of symbols could only be a variety in the methods of concealment. It would follow that, in this reductivistic sense, all symbols must mean the same kind of thing: and for Freud that comes down to libido, or sexual eros. In his dream analysis Freud specifically states that "steps, ladders or staircases, or, as the case may be, walking up or down them, are representations of the sexual act." He justifies this interpretation as follows: "We come to the top in a series of rhythmical movements and with increasing breathlessness and then, with a few rapid leaps, we can get to the bottom again. Thus the rhythmical pattern of copulation is reproduced in going upstairs. Nor must we omit to bring in the evidence of linguistic usage. It shows us that 'mounting' is used as a direct equivalent for the sexual act." However much the mystic wants to sublimate his carnal impulses, they would seem to endure as the underlying import of his symbolism.

But possibly Freud, a one-eyed Polyphemus like all the giants of the nineteenth century, mistakes the nature of his great discovery. That symbols reveal the truth about human feelings we may well agree, but that the truth is hidden or of a single sort sounds like just another dogmatism. The mountain or the ladder symbolizes sexual intercourse? Possibly; indeed, very likely. But what does sexual intercourse symbolize? What does sexuality signify? In calling sex an instinct, Freud thinks he has reached a physiological category beyond which analysis cannot go. But no one lives at the level of instinct. We are of imagination all compact, and instinct itself merely signifies mysterious forces that enable an organism to continue in its environment. As usual, Freud neglects the creativity of imagination, its freedom to symbolize in ways that cannot be reduced to any single pattern of explanation.

Once we recognize this, we may accept symbols at their face value. When the mystic speaks of ascending to God via a ladder of love, he means what he says and his feelings are simply those that the symbolism expresses. In part these feelings are undeniably sexual: why else would anyone refer to brides and bridegrooms, the spiritual betrothal, the spiritual marriage? But for the mystic, sexual desire makes sense as a way of yearning for God; coitus symbolizes a perfect union that earth does not afford; and, in general, everything physical represents something nonphysical, transcendent, spiritual. From within his religious commitment, the mystic interprets all things to suit his peculiar symbolism. We who are not mystics may well refuse to see the world that simplemindedly. But there is nothing in the nature of symbolism to authorize a Freudian *re*interpretation. To read the symbols of mysticism as Freud does is not to translate the mystics into another language, but rather to use the same terms to say something extraordinarily different. The procedure is quite justifiable as a projection of the Freudian ideology. It is not justifiable as an explication of the religious symbols themselves.

I also find it misleading to suggest, as Ortega y Gasset does, that the mystical process is analogous to falling in love. Limiting himself to mysticism as a psychological phenomenon, Ortega sees in it the same "paralysis of attention," the same fixation upon a totally absorbing object, as characterizes the violent state of falling in love. But though this may be true, for both conditions belong to the same family of sentiments, the differences are equally striking. In the Middle Ages at least, mystical experience is based upon a search for *order*, whereas falling in love generally consists of a flight into welcome chaos and disorder. The mystical symbols express a need for an organized universe. They issue from a sense of homelessness in the purely natural world, and a fear that without supernatural support the human personality cannot govern itself. The mystic yearns for a meaningful cosmos, one in which everything has its appointed place, its individual significance, its purposive mission. Within this moral order all things assume a status and a function, each rank leading upward to a final authority. That is why the concept of hierarchy underlies all the mystical symbols. The feelings they express are as much political as sexual. Throughout his system of idealizations the mystic projects a need for an infinite community in which the higher takes care of the lower, the lower aspires to the perfection of the higher, and each accords the other a reciprocal warmth that constitutes an ideal family. To one who does not believe in the existence of such benign administration, these feelings will not be worth cultivating. Nevertheless, they are profoundly *human* feelings, and no one has the right to reduce them to something else.

With the notion of hierarchy as a fundamental theme, medieval writers about love often enumerate discrete stages in the soul's journey toward God. Sometimes these stages are but conventional means of duplicating the stations of the cross; in his "ladder of divine ascent" St. John Climacus even lists thirty steps, one for each of the unknown years in the life of Christ. Frequently, however, the concept of rising levels provides a vehicle for philosophical and psychological analysis. For different mystics the "steep stairway of love" has different turns and different landings, but similar patterns seem to underlie most of their approaches to God. The general form appears most clearly in the writings of Richard of St. Victor and of St. Bernard of Clairvaux, particularly when the two are placed side by side. These great men of the twelfth century, only one of whom was canonized, bear a stereoscopic relation to each other: alike but not the same, similar but significantly divergent.

With the very first words of his major work on love, "Of the Four Degrees of Passionate Charity," Richard of St. Victor strikes a rhapsodic resonance that sounds through all mystical literature: "I am wounded by love. Love urges me to speak of love. Gladly do I give myself up to the service of love and it is sweet and altogether lovely to speak of love. This is a joyful subject and very fruitful." These lines are interesting for more than one reason. In the ambiguity between pain and pleasure, love both wounding and being joyful, the mystic shows himself happy to die in the flesh for the sake of the more blissful life that follows. But the lines could also apply to human love.

The phrase "I am wounded by love" comes from the Song of Solomon, a very common source for mystical writings. In the Song of Solomon the love is both human and sensuous, but the medievals took it as an allegory of the love between God and the soul and between Christ and his church. In Richard the imaginative play between human and mystical love becomes the pivot for his entire discussion. Both types he characterizes in terms of the four stages or degrees. Each helps to explain the other; and merely by describing the two together, Richard hopes to show that a purely human relationship is just a hideous parody of the religious love all men really want.

In the first degree, each lover undergoes what later centuries would call "the bolt out of the blue"—the *coup de foudre*. The lover is astonished by the beauty of his beloved. His desires are aroused, his affections touched. He is "shot through the heart." In passion between human beings, Richard tells us, the wounding is a matter of the body: the desires are then carnal, ultimately sexual. In the love of God, however, the relevant feeling is wholly spiritual. The mystic thirsts for God in the sense that he "desires to experience what that inward sweetness is that inebriates the mind of man, when he begins to taste and see how sweet the Lord is."

When love reaches the second stage, it overwhelms the senses and the imagination. It binds the lover to the object of his devotion. The lover thinks and dreams of the beloved constantly. He cannot free his mind of the exquisite image. In human love this stage marks the beginning of painful anxiety, the lover fixing obsessively upon the object to which he is bound. In the love of God, however, the soul becomes enraptured by the divine. It feels itself caught from above and begins to ascend. In this degree the lover undergoes the grace of contemplation, sees God in all his beauty. As in human love, the mystic cannot put the beloved out of his mind, but only because the supernatural vision satisfies so thoroughly. In the love of God, as Richard of St. Victor describes it, there can be no room for obsessive anxieties.

In the third stage the soul is captivated, all other interests driven out, its subjugation complete. The mind exerts itself only as the beloved demands; the body does not act under its own impulse; the lover loses all autonomy. At this point, human love becomes a veritable disease: "Excess of love makes hands and feet nerveless as in illness." In mystical love, however, the third degree occasions ecstasy. Fully subdued, the soul "passes over" into God. For now "the host of carnal desires are deeply asleep." At one with God, intuitively desiring what God desires, the human personality conforms itself to perfect virtue. Joyfully, ecstatically, it changes into whatever God's good will requires.

This stage of ecstasy is the state of spiritual jubilation, but it is not the end of love. There remains one further step. In the fourth degree the lover goes beyond love itself. The beloved who has held him captive is now found to be insufficient. In human love this happens when the lover realizes that his affections have become diseased. In his great distress, he rejects the obsessive object as best he can. "In this state," Richard says, "love often turns into a kind of madness unless its impetus is restrained by great prudence and an equally great steadiness. There are often outbursts of temper between lovers in this state, they work up quarrels and when there are no causes for enmity they seek false and often quite unlikely ones. In this state, love often turns into hatred since nothing can satisfy the lovers' mutual desire."

In mystical love the soul also separates from its beloved: not because of ambivalent hatred, but in the desire to do God's will on earth. Having joyfully risen above itself, the soul now descends below the scene of ecstasy. Where formerly it was magnified by being "ravished into the abyss of divine light," the soul now demeans itself in order to serve the Lord. It resumes the lowly condition of a human being, but with a difference. In descending "below itself," the soul imitates Christ. Resplendent in the grace that God has given him, the mystic feels love for all mankind. He loves all things for the sake of God. In everything he does and feels and thinks, there issues forth a likeness to the divinity with whom he has been united.

In discussing the four stages of love, Richard does not present them as I have. He first describes human love, and then, by way of contrast, the degrees that pertain to the love of God. The difference between these loves is more than just the difference in the nature of the beloved, or even between carnal and spiritual experience. For Richard explicitly argues that the progression of human love *must* move from evil to ever-increasing evil. The fourth degree of human love leads into infinite suffering, while the final stages in mystical love approximate eternal bliss. In describing human love as a disease, Richard repeats what may be found in every one of the early church fathers. They all assume that there can be only two kinds of love: the love of God and carnal passion. The latter they consider in its most extreme forms and then assert that it typifies human love as a whole, which therefore must be evil. Plato and Lucretius had already seen the elements of madness or disease in passional excesses. The church fathers had only to insist that there was no other alternative to the love of God. Not that loving God prevented one from loving other persons. On the contrary. But loving another *for the sake of God* was more than just a human love; and without the love of God, no love could keep from slipping lower and lower. That there might be a kind of human love which is neither diseased nor derivative from the love of God—an authentic love of persons different from loving others for the sake of God—this is not allowed. To a medieval mystic, it is unthinkable.

The total picture of love, as Richard presents it, resembles a painting by Fra Angelico—neatly divided in half, the upper part showing the celestial choirs hierarchically ordered in a harmony of golds and limpid blues, the lower part revealing horrible monsters enveloped by the blackness of their own fearful sins. For Richard as for Fra Angelico, the dualistic vision doubtless originates with St. Augustine's distinction between caritas and cupiditas. The world could move only up or down. Carnal love bent man into the ground; only the love of God enabled him to ascend. The two series of gradations mirror one another because all things human are alike in stemming from an ultimate love. But in themselves caritas and cupiditas differ as much as spirit and matter, salvation and perdition, heaven and hell.

In the writings of St. Bernard, the dualism tends to lose its sharpness, but only superficially. For though Bernard takes great pains to show how man can gradually move from his natural condition into a more spiritual one, he never admits to any justifiable love other than the love of God. His doctrinal beliefs derive from St. Augustine, though they are more specifically related to problems about the will. Like St. Benedict before him, Bernard emphasizes humility as a principal avenue to God. When the will succeeds in effacing itself, it makes possible that blessed union which is the goal of life. But when the will becomes assertive, it reinforces man's original sin. The human likeness to God is then distorted; man comes to resemble the fallen angel; and pride inimical to true love dominates the soul. Using the traditional symbol, St. Bernard articulates a Jacob's ladder with twelve rungs of humility. The sides of the ladder are the body and the soul. Its highest reach is pure caritas, perfect love of God. In the opposite direction there is another ladder. For pride consists of a downward path, leading us step by step away from the deity. On this ladder the last rung is hatred of God, which in turn means rejecting his love and refusing to emulate it.

In somewhat different, though related, terms St. Bernard divides the love of God into four degrees. In its origin, love is a human disposition within the state of nature. As such, it resembles ordinary emotions like fear, joy, and sorrow. In the first degree, man loves selfishly, seeking to gratify his appetites, to acquire goods that the natural world affords. Although it is basic to his being that he should love God, he cannot do so as yet. Man's estate having been corrupted by original sin resulting from the Fall, his initial, spontaneous love is directed not toward goodness but toward the satisfaction of desires. With this in mind, Bernard quotes St. Paul's dictum: "First . . . that which is natural; afterwards that which is spiritual."

Since it belongs to man in his natural condition, the first degree of love is unbridled and must be rendered harmless to the rest of society. At its best, such love may eventually include a concern about the general welfare, preventing selfishness from turning into oppression or tyranny. But even so, it is hardly worth cultivating. However moral, however humanitarian in its adjustment to the natural loves that others also have, the first degree must always be carnal. If man were limited to it, he would forever remain in the realm of cupiditas. For that reason, this kind of love *must* be deluded about the real object of human desire—God the Highest Good; and thus, it can never provide complete satisfaction.

Over and above these Augustinian ideas, however, St. Bernard introduces others that contribute to orthodox Catholicism. He is very careful not to condemn the life of the body at this stage. The carnality of the first degree results from the *will* of natural man, its giving bodily desires an unwarranted importance. Unlike the Neoplatonists, St. Bernard maintains that everything in God's creation is good—the body as well as the soul. Quoting Scripture, he asks "who ever hated his own flesh?" with the assurance that no one could deny loving every part of himself. The first degree must be transcended not because it involves love of the body, but because it is man loving something *for his own sake*. It is man seeking to be self-sufficient within his own desires. Far from satisfying, that merely arrests man's search for goodness.

Although he himself does not organize the argument in this fashion, St. Bernard clearly moves on to the second degree of love by virtue of a pagan maxim he discusses in another place. I am referring to the motto inscribed in the temple at Delos: *Nosce teipsum*, Know Thyself. Christian theology takes this as prophetic, and St. Bernard makes the injunction central to his reasoning about humility. For once man knows himself, he realizes his pitiful mortality, his constant dependence upon a God who created him for reasons that exceed human comprehension. In the second degree of love, man begins to love God—but only for benefits he thinks he can thereby derive. As a way of helping man to understand himself, God has contrived that in his natural state he shall undergo difficulties which God will then help him resolve. Eventually, man learns from experience that with God's help "he can do all things—those, to be sure, which it is good to be able to do—and without Him he can do nothing." At this level, however, man is merely using God for his own advantage; he does not love God himself. The second type of love is just prudence, and so it still belongs to the natural man. Yet it also puts the soul in contact with God, and that alone gradually purifies it. The man who continually turns to God for help will do so at first for reasons of self-interest or self-knowledge. But by the subtle chemistry of spiritual discipline the second degree of love changes into the third. Love then stops being a love of God for one's own sake and becomes a veritable love of God himself.

To love God himself, as a divine person rather than a source of human benefits, is not yet to love him in the spiritual manner Bernard wishes to achieve. For beyond the third level he discerns a fourth and more nearly perfect love. The ultimate goal of man, that which defines his being, that which liberates him from *cupiditas* and enables him to love truly, is a state so remote that only in heaven can it be attained. In the fourth degree man loves nothing, neither himself nor God, except *for the sake of God*, i.e., in reference and relation *to* God. Loving God himself, as in the third degree, is not enough. Since God loves all creation, he who reaches the fourth degree will love *everything* for the sake of God. At times St. Bernard speaks of this as loving things and persons *in* God; but the same idea is expressed by saying that one loves all being *as* God's creation, and so the manifestation *of* his love. The world is not worthy of love, only the loving presence of God *in* the world. In this sense, beatitude would consist of the ability to love the love in everything. I use this expression, which is Romantic and not to be found in St. Bernard, because once the medieval God loses his independent existence, the fourth degree of Christian love becomes the ideal of all Romantic religion.

In St. Bernard the fourth degree is not at all Romantic. It functions as it would in any transcendental religion and must be understood in the way we interpreted Platonic love. To love something for the sake of God is to love it in its authentic relations with the source of being. For the Christian this means loving it as a creature of that divine author who makes all things in accordance with a benevolent design: just as for Plato loving something for the sake of the Good means loving it as a manifestation of that absolute goodness which underlies all existence. Keeping in mind the great differences between Platonism and Christianity, one cannot help feeling the doctrinal bond that links the passage from the *Republic* which I quoted on page 64 to the following from St. Bernard: "Blessed and holy, I would say, is he to whom it has been given to experience such a thing [the fourth degree of love] in this mortal life at rare intervals or even once, and this suddenly and scarcely for the space of a single moment. In a certain manner to lose yourself as though you were not, and to be utterly unconscious of yourself and to be emptied of yourself and, as it were, brought to nothing, this pertains to heavenly intercourse, not to human affection." And finally, St. Bernard seems to approach the Platonic view of matter inasmuch as he blames the body for preventing the fourth degree from becoming frequent or permanent on earth. As long as the soul is subject to "this frail and wretched body," compelled to feed it with sense perceptions and to guide it through the vexatious material world, man cannot hope to love God in a perfect manner.

Instead of relegating ultimate love to a society of immaterial spirits, however, St. Bernard reserves it for the body that appears in the final resurrection: "a spiritual and immortal body, a body perfect, calm and acceptable, and in all things subject to the spirit." This, at least, did not issue from Platonistic sources of the eros tradition. As if to preclude any possibility of misinterpretation, Bernard goes to some length to show why souls after death cannot fully love God until their bodies are actually restored. Burdensome as it may be, the body also contributes to salvation. A "good and faithful companion" to a good spirit, it helps direct the soul (in life, or death, or afterdeath) to its paramount objectives. With the resurrection, human progress from the natural to the divine completes itself. Man begins with a material body and ends with a spiritual one. In his carnal condition the first degree of love starts him on the ladder that leads to God. At the top, no longer in a state of nature, he enjoys a heightened version of the goods he formerly sought: they could not be fully possessed until he learned how to transcend them. Having first loved things for his own sake, he finally loves them for the sake of God, in their derivation from God: "When it has reached its fulfillment by grace, the body will be loved and all bodily good things for God's sake alone. But God will be loved directly for his sake." Man then loves all things with perfection, and so achieves spiritually what he could never have attained through nature. Indeed, this lovely idealization would *seem* to promise him absolutely everything that anyone could hope for.

In the *Pensées*, Pascal says the following: "If he exalt himself, I humble him; if he humble himself, I exalt him; and I always contradict him, till he understands that he is an incomprehensible monster." Is this God speaking, or Pascal himself? No matter. If we allow for the fact that man in the Middle Ages is a sky-blue monster, a brute capable of becoming an angel, Pascal speaks for all Christian mysticism. In its religious employment, eros embodies a paradox of the will. As with Plato, the true lover seeks the highest good; but he tries to possess it by possessing nothing. The mystic humbles himself in order to be exalted. His greatest exaltation is humility itself. The experience of this paradox must always be dramatic, which explains why mysticism is a state of emotional crisis. Two forces native to the human soul conflict with a violence that sometimes approaches madness, and not always the divine madness. The mystic wants to be perfect, but he also wants to debase himself before the source of perfection. He wants to ascend the ladder of salvation, but he also knows that this glorious ambition must be exercised without ambition: *non nobis*. It may be too much to say that the mystic harmonizes these opposing demands, but at least he puts them into a contrapuntal unity. His is the music of Bach's Magnificat, with its alternations between swelling ascendancy and self-diminishing lowliness. The text comes from the Gospel according to Luke. At the moment of annunciation, the Virgin Mary's ambiguous condition expresses itself in the archetype of all mystical poetry:

> My soul doth magnify the Lord,
> And my spirit hath rejoiced in God my Saviour.
> For he hath regarded the low estate of his handmaiden:
> For, behold, from henceforth all generations shall call
>   me blessed. . . .
> He hath put down the mighty from their seats,
> And exalted them of low degree. . . .

Nor is it coincidental that the speaker is a woman, the purest of women. Love in ancient philosophy was always the prerogative of men. But in the pagan mysteries both sexes participated, and the figures that symbolized divine possession were often feminine—sibyls, priestesses, bacchantes, maenads. In Christianity the three Persons of the God who is love are all masculine, as are the medieval theologians who tirelessly condemn woman as the origin of sinfulness. As if to compensate, Christianity chooses for its savior the very opposite of a predatory male. Its priests are to be as sexless as an unmarried girl within some primitive clan. Though most of the Christian mystics were men, they aspire to a spiritual marriage in which they will be the ardent, yearning, but thoroughly submissive bride. From having been an idealization of masculine aggressiveness, eros transmutes itself into something feminine as well. Despite the misogyny of the medieval church, Christianity dignifies those female components of love which romanticism was later to make into a religion of its own. Woman is physically, and in some ways biologically, the weaker sex. Her aggressiveness must therefore be hidden. Reason being public and feeling private in an obvious sense, she may often use the latter to achieve her ends. To get what she wants, she must seem to yield, not attack. By submitting artfully, however, she exalts herself. Long before there were mystics, women had learned the tactics of their paradoxical eros: seeking by not looking, getting by not wanting, ascending by self-effacement. As Juliet says, preparing herself for the love of Romeo: "And learn me how to lose a winning match." Christian mysticism idealizes this aspect of human nature, extends it to men as well as women, develops it into an organized discipline by which all natural losses may be regained through the realm of spirit.

In cultivating this contrapuntal unity of feeling, mysticism approaches a truth about love in general, and particularly the love of persons. Its recurrent paradox idealizes the give-and-take in all loving intercourse. Nevertheless, Christian eros creates systematic difficulties that must not be ignored. In the Middle Ages these problems were formulated in various ways. For instance, was humility really compatible with a desire for the highest good? Could one really love God if the soul was always motivated by a search for personal salvation? If the love of God required total renunciation, could this possibly include the state of blessedness itself, the very condition to which love aspired? As the only object worthy of love, God had to be loved more than one loved oneself: but how was that possible? Did the love of God preclude the love of self? If not, what were the legitimate demands of self-love?

To questions such as these, Augustine, Bernard, and Thomas give substantially the same answers. Augustine argues that all love, even the love of God, is self-love inasmuch as the lover seeks his own good. But man can love himself well or badly. He loves properly as long as the *object* of love is God. When man seeks his good in himself, his self-love belongs to cupiditas. In caritas man loves himself by loving God: his self-love is then blessed as well as inevitable. To this Bernard adds the idea that pure love of God transcends any selfish interest in recompense, but nevertheless enjoys the greatest of all rewards. To love God for his own sake is itself the state of blessedness; and, therefore, one cannot love God without also desiring that ultimate good which comes from loving God. Finally, Thomas argues that man always loves God more than himself because he is in essence the likeness of God and can truly love himself only by achieving oneness with his source.

In general, this line of reasoning duplicates much of what Plato and Aristotle had said. Without the striving for goodness, there could be neither man nor the universe as we know them; one seeks the highest good in order to perfect oneself; all love is based upon self-love; yet one loves oneself best by loving what is truly good— which Christianity takes to be a love of God for his own sake. In saying this, however, the medievals wished to avoid those two other conclusions that Aristotle had reached: namely, that loving another was *merely* a way of loving oneself, and that loving oneself best meant wanting the greatest good for oneself most of all. God being a supernatural person in whose image man had been created, the Christians felt no inclination to reduce the love of God to human self-love, or anything else. And since loving oneself best meant loving all things (including oneself) only for the sake of God, it made no sense to speak of wanting goods for oneself most of all. On the contrary, in loving things for the sake of God, one no longer wanted anything for one's own sake. Neither Plato nor Aristotle had much respect for humility as such. For the Christians it was the way of the Lord, the means to self-perfection. One loved oneself best by surrendering one's separate will. One desired nothing but what God desired, whether or not this meant getting the best for oneself.

But here the problems return. The answers given by Augustine, Bernard, and Thomas became the orthodox Catholic position, but there were other Christians—never canonized—who saw difficulties in the official doctrine. Peter Abelard, whose *Introductio ad Theologiam* the Council of Soissons condemned in 1121, began with the usual premises about humility but ended up with unorthodox conclusions. Since loving God for his sake meant loving him regardless of rewards, Abelard argued that to love God properly one had to renounce even the desire for beatitude. Like all his contemporaries, Abelard asserts that the perfect love of God is itself beatitude; yet he insists that God must not be loved *because of any desire* for beatitude. Loving God should enable us to renounce *everything* for his sake— including the search for goodness. Regardless of how God treats us, whether he rewards us with goods or punishes us for reasons of his own, he must be loved as the perfect Being that he is in himself.

To someone like St. Bernard, Abelard's argument was nothing but self-contradiction; and Etienne Gilson, in his book on St. Bernard, claims that Abelard spoke of loving God in terms more appropriate to Heloise's love for Abelard. Human beings may be loved despite the consequences; but since the pure love of God *is* beatitude, how can one renounce beatitude and still love God? So Bernard reasons, and Gilson agrees with him. But this solution is too easy: it ignores the conflict between striving and humility within Christian eros. Abelard demands the renunciation of every desire for beatitude in order to make it impossible for anything but God to be an object of love. He emphasizes humility to the exclusion of aspiration as a way of loving God *regardless* of where that love might lead. What Abelard says is not self-contradictory, but it takes us very far from St. Thomas' belief that if God were not man's good there would be no reason for man to love him.

And yet, both attitudes are equally Christian. The statement from St. Thomas applies to God as the highest good, whereas Abelard is thinking of him as that Supreme Person to whom the will completely submits. In most mystical writers final submission occurs as the last stage in the love of God; and Abelard has merely spelled out its fullest implications. In Richard of St. Victor, for instance, the fourth degree culminates in so radical a renunciation of self that one even gives up the hope of beatitude. Like the Buddha or the Bodhisattva who refuses to enter into Nirvana as long as suffering remains, the purified soul sacrifices the blessings of heaven, descends like Christ, and even chooses to be anathema (as St. Paul said) if that will help to save one's fellow man. In describing *this* as the ultimate imitation of Christ, Richard says: "And such a man then desires to be made anathema from Christ for his brethren's sake. What shall we say then? In this degree of love the soul of man might seem to be mad. . . . Is it not complete madness to reject true life, to accuse the highest wisdom, to resist omnipotence? And if a man desires to be separated from Christ for his brethren's sake, is that not a rejection of true life? as one who says: 'Either forgive them their sin or blot me out of the book that thou hast written!'"

Quite so! Richard, like Abelard, has seen the paradox. What he calls madness is but the internal tension within Christian eros. He stands in awe before it and speaks with greater honesty than all the fathers of the church: "Consider to what boldness of presumption the perfection of charity can raise up the mind of man: behold how it induces him to presume beyond the power of a man! That which he hopes of God, what he does for God and in God and effects with God, is more than merely human. How utterly wondrous and amazing! The more he hopes from God the more he abases himself for God. The more he rises up in boldness, the more he descends in humility. Just as the goal to which he ascends by confidence is above man, so is the point to which he descends by patience, beyond man." How close this is to Luther, who also sees the presumption in caritas. And if, in imitation of Christ, one is willing to be anathema from Christ and renounce all goods, then why not surrender the love of God itself?

In effect this is what the Lutheran doctrine does do, as we shall see. Protestants such as Luther would have felt no need to reform the medieval religion if the paradox of Christian eros had been less agonizing. In making their reform, the Protestants rely upon the elements of philia, nomos, and agapē. These belong to medieval Catholicism as well, but there they are synthesized with eros.

Through philia the Christian achieves a fellowship with both God and other men. Insofar as mysticism exalts the soul, it makes possible the highest type of loving union. Insofar as it enjoins humility, it institutes that submissiveness to authority which I call nomos. And through it all, agapē sets the perfect example: God's love descending in a free bestowal and sanctifying everything it touches.

11

Philia: Fellowship and Union

In His Writings On Group psychology, Freud mentions an interesting similarity between a church and an army. He says that both are "artificial," i.e., nonbiological, groups held together by the same illusion: the belief in a leader who loves all the members of the group with an equal love. Though Freud does not avail himself of the analogy, one may easily add that the "equal love" is that of a mother for all her children. Christ or the commanding officer is the loving leader, but they operate through an all-embracing Mother Church or an army that provides for every soldier's needs. The belief in equal love Freud considers an illusion because it is nonverifiable and based upon wish-fulfillment. Without this belief, however, church and army would both dissolve; and Freud emphasizes the importance to Christian solidarity of Christ's having said: "Inasmuch as ye have done it unto one of the least of these my brethren, ye have done it unto me." Christ thus represents a benevolent elder brother or father surrogate. Before him the faithful are all equal: they share in his love and are equally bound to one another through the efficacy of his devotion.

Within the artificial groups Freud discovers two kinds of libidinal ties: one toward the leader, the other toward fellow members. The Christian loves Christ, Freud says, as the personification and embodiment of the individual's ego ideal (in this case, love itself). Among themselves, the faithful enjoy a different kind of relationship. Each Christian identifies with the rest, a sense of oneness binding them into a unity. Over and above this, however, they are also encouraged to identify with Christ. Christians would then love one another with the love that Christ bestows upon them all. No one is *required* to achieve the identification with Christ; but Freud shrewdly remarks that "this further development in the distribution of libido in the group is probably the factor upon which Christianity bases its claim to have reached a higher ethical level."

Nor does Freud doubt that this claim is partly justified. He recognizes that the Christian churches contribute to that shift from egoism to altruism without which civilization would be impossible. He says that only the love for others can limit the selfish love for oneself, and that such love must be sexually aim-inhibited in order for an artificial group to carry out its civilizing function. With this in mind, he even states that the Catholic church had "the best of motives" for demanding celibacy among its priests. At the same time, Freud obviously distrusts any love that derives from religious groupings. By its very nature, he thinks, a religion must be hard and *unloving*, cruel and intolerant, toward anyone who does not belong to it. The stronger the religious bond, the greater the libidinal ties among the insiders; the greater the libidinal ties, the more violent the hatred toward outsiders. To Freud this is merely a natural consequence of those psychological insecurities that create religious illusions in the first place. Likewise, the internal love shared by members of a church may seem to offer cures for various neuroses, but Freud considers them "distorted cures." As long as the group fails to understand the relationship between sexual instincts and aim-inhibited interests, the love it engenders can never provide the kind of healthy-mindedness that Freud wishes to promote. Christian groups in particular misconstrue the bond of love that keeps them together, believing it to be spiritual whereas really (Freud assures us) it is libidinal.

How much of Freud's brilliant analysis would be persuasive without the concept of libido? I cannot say. But here, as elsewhere, his attempt to treat all love as either directly or indirectly sexual, aim-oriented or aim-inhibited but always with the same instinctual goal, seems indefensible. To prove that every emotional interest must have a sexual basis, Freud claims that "even an affectionate devotee, even a friend or an admirer, desires the physical proximity and the sight of the person who is now loved only in the 'Pauline' sense." But why believe that sight or physical proximity is necessarily sexual, in however sublimated a degree? Freud argues in a circle, a fairly small and rather unrewarding one. What he says about the facility with which apparently nonsexual emotions turn into sexual ones, and vice versa, need not be denied. But I reject the idea that love is *always and inevitably* libidinal in the sense that Freud intends. If I am right, the entire psychology of religious groups needs to be reexamined. We make a beginning in this direction by studying the concept of Christian philia more systematically than Freud and by means of an analysis that does not reduce all emotional ties to sexuality. The concept of philia is hardly sufficient for the scientist; but in its proper context, it can serve as one among various philosophical tools that group psychology may profitably employ.

As we have seen, philia originates with Aristotle. Medieval Christianity blends it with Platonic ideas about eros, revising both in accordance with the needs of dogma. Since caritas joins man to a Person who reciprocates his love, what could be more natural than to establish a religious philia roughly patterned after the model in the *Nicomachean Ethics*? That work was well known in the Middle Ages, which Christianized Aristotle even more obviously than Plato. Aquinas frequently cites the leading ideas of the *Ethics*, and they were most effectively propagated by Cicero's essay on friendship. Gilson has noted the influence of Cicero on both courtly and Christian ideas of love in the twelfth century. But he fails to mention that Cicero's major themes duplicate Aristotle's. The idea that perfect friendship involves a desire for the other's welfare, that it is reciprocal and disinterested (rather than practical or selfish), a mutual association between truly virtuous equals—all this comes directly from Aristotle. Writing in Latin, Cicero had a linguistic advantage; but he is a conveyor, not the principal source, of these components within Christian love.

From its pagan origins Christianity also received the idea that all men are brothers and therefore in familial relation to one another. This notion may have derived from some of the later prophets in the Old Testament, but it is hardly compatible with the thinking of a people specially chosen as the testing ground for righteousness. Neither does the implied social laxity, this indiscriminate familiarity among men, come from the virtuous Aristotle. He thought of friendship as something highly circumscribed, a day-by-day association that like-minded and mutually stimulating men might enjoy within the confines of a small city-state. How could there be any basis for opening the closed corporation, for extending it to every human being? The Stoics (though not Cicero, who is sometimes counted among them) revised all this. They managed to throw wide the gate. Like Aristotle they held that perfect friendship is the community of likes, not unlikes. But they also insisted, as Aristotle had taught them, that all men are similar in being rational by nature. It followed that mankind as a whole was one large fraternity bound by a common rationality, in principle benevolent and disinterested. A different kind of fraternity must also have arisen in the orgiastic rituals of primitive mysticism. The frenzied devotee of Dionysus or Aphrodite must have felt that all intimate humanity was brother or sister to oneself, that being washed in the blood of the holy bull automatically created fellowship which no city-state could contain. Through rites such as baptism and communion, Christianity retained the office of these miraculous bonds. But in its wonderfully synthesizing way, it meshed them with its own version of Stoic rationalism. All men being alike, and in a sense the same with respect to reason, they could all, without exception, belong to the same community of love.

In another way too Christianity considered all men alike. They inhabited a common realm of spirit. Created by a Supreme Spirit in his own likeness, human beings belonged to the society of God. That man could be friends with the divine, Aristotle had denied: they were in essence too dissimilar, too remote. But through the mediation of Christ, who was both man and God, Christianity linked the two in a single spirituality. Aristotle insisted that true friends must be equal, even identical in some respects. His choice community is limited to the virtuous because only they can appreciate the company of others who are similar to themselves. Between God and man, however, there could be no significant equality. Even the Christians, who believed that God reciprocates man's love, realized that the two loves could not be the same either in quantity or in quality: God's love for man far exceeded man's love for God. And yet, if God becomes a man, as in the person of Jesus, something resembling equality occurs. Born of a woman, practicing the ministry of life, dying the death that all men face, being the scapegoat for human sins, Christ effects an idealized equalization between God and man. The highest puts itself on the same footing as the lowest, as symbolized by Christ's eagerness to associate with moral outcasts. Jesus is a kind of alter ego for every human being: a bright epiphany revealing the image of God in whose likeness mankind was created. In the degenerate state of nature, man had lost this likeness; but the coming of Christ showed him how to restore it through love.

In all these ways the idea of Christ introduces a kind of equality without which religious philia would not be possible. Love thus becomes an idealized intimacy, a benevolent friendship with everything and everyone that matters in the universe. What a handful of Greeks might have shared, every Christian could now enjoy in the company of an infinite and eternal deity. In magnifying the Lord, the faithful achieved a state of soul that magnified themselves. That the love of God should be what the medievals called an *amor amicitiae* (love based on friendship) was later to scandalize the Protestants as a subtle form of human arrogance. Christ descended to save man, they said, not to make him equal God. Without equality there could be no friendship; and sinner that he was, man could never hope to equal the divine. But if friendship was impossible, how else could man raise himself into the love of God? To which Luther replies: he cannot.

In following the Stoics and establishing a church universal, the Christian fathers were also carrying Platonistic thinking to its logical conclusion. If all men love the same inexhaustible object, the Good for which they need not compete but might rather cooperate, are they not a fellowship by nature? And if this object is a person as well as the creative source of all being, does not the fraternity of man imply the paternity of God? The Stoics had said that all men are brothers. Christianity made them into a family: in fact, two families. The "holy family"—Mary, Joseph, and the Christ Child—symbolized the social dimension of man on earth: the mother pure and unspotted, serenely aware of her function as the vessel of divinity; the father pious, industrious, wisely tolerant and permissive, no longer the absolute ruler of his clan; the child of mysterious origin, growing toward the childlike dream of saving the adult world from its self-inflicted catastrophes, and so becoming the father of the man. On the higher level, of course, human society emanated from the divine family of the triune God: the Creator, who fathered all things forth and ordered their being with the authority of a supreme legislator; the Son, who redeemed the world from its inevitable waywardness by making himself a bleeding ladder on which all men could return to their origin; the Holy Spirit, who bound the Father to the Son by that love eternally issuing from the very essence of God. The cosmos was thus tightly knit into three kinds of overlapping unity: one within the divine family, another among men, and a third joining the two levels of reality.

Love as the Holy Spirit is perhaps the hardest to understand; but for medieval Christianity it serves as the primal unity. In the *Summa Theologica* St. Thomas argues that the word "love" can be taken in two ways with respect to God. It can refer to the divine essence as such, in which case it applies to all three Persons of the Trinity; or it can signify that which proceeds from God's (loving) essence. In the latter event, Love is the proper name of the Holy Spirit, just as Word is the proper name of the Son. There are said to be two "processions" in God: "one by way of the intellect, which is the procession of the Word, and another by way of the will, which is the procession of Love." The procession of the Word is presumably God expressing his intellect, revealing his holy truths, by means of his self-begotten Son—much as an author shows his creative thinking by the words that spontaneously arise in him. The procession of Love would then be God attaching his will, binding himself to his being as Father and as Son, and to each in relation to the other. The love as a something divine that results from this process is the Holy Spirit.

As supernatural insight, Trinitarian doctrine exceeds the competence of one who is not previously committed to it. But its human relevance, which does not preclude its truthfulness in other respects, should not be minimized. For with this dogma, Catholicism succeeded in stabilizing the chaotic polity of the primitive gods. As we know from Homer, these had also begotten one another, but for diverse reasons: for lust and ambition as often as for love. Little wonder then that the sons should plot against the fathers, dethroning and even castrating them as Zeus had done with Cronus. The world was ruled by gods who seemed to fluctuate between Empedoclean Strife and Love (*Philotēs*). Christianity reformed all this. In one stroke it settled the conflict between generations and assured the present deities of immortal tenure. From all eternity the Father had begotten the Son (though the latter's trip to earth occurred at a particular time); they were indissolubly united as the First and Second Persons of the one and only God; not only was strife between them unthinkable, but also love belonged to their essence as divinities. In reality, i.e., in the order of things apart from human aberrations, strife had no dominion. There could be no conflict within God, and therefore no possibility of its real existence elsewhere. For a patriarchal culture, torn by questions of obedience and authority, this was no mean achievement.

Still, God remained in heaven. He no longer walked the earth as once he had. Even for theologians, the oneness of the Trinity is an extremely abstract idea. Another kind of philia was needed to make the Christian model of love effective, thereby establishing the glorious kingdom within us all. This need was met by the concept of spiritual marriage, to which I previously referred. Introduced by Origen in the third century, it was mentioned by Augustine, but most fully elaborated by St. Bernard. As the relevant text he takes the Canticle of Canticles, the sensuous Song of Solomon in the Old Testament. Like others in the Middle Ages, he treats it as an allegorical anticipation of Christian love. In his *Sermons on the Canticle of Canticles*, a work sadly neglected nowadays but surely one of the masterpieces of Western literature, St. Bernard interprets the Hebrew poem as an expression of man's ardent search for union with the Lord. Though the community within the triune God was primarily filial, and though on earth man was to love his neighbor as a brother, nevertheless, the fellowship between the soul and God could only be described as marital. The bridegroom is Christ, either in his humanity or as the Second Person of the Trinity; the bride is sometimes the church, sometimes the individual soul. No detail of the erotic imagery is missed; nor is any the occasion for embarrassment. In some of the later commentators on the Canticle, a kind of puritanism seems to intrude, but never in St. Bernard. He is too pure-minded to be frightened by the fact that human marriage is partly carnal. He knows that literally the Canticle is a wedding idyll, as he also knows that some people find sexual imagery too exciting to be able to take it allegorically. Bernard simply enjoins us to bring "chaste ears" to this discourse on love, to remember that what he describes is a *spiritual* marriage.

Bernard's point could have been made more sharply. The sexual aspects of the Hebrew poem are not fixed quantities to be taken literally or else hidden in some transparent sublimation. The original text is thoroughly sensuous, obviously and admittedly so; but its significance depends upon the way in which the human imagination interprets. As a humanist may read the Canticle for its erotic suggestiveness, so may St. Bernard use it to portray an intimacy that goes *beyond* sexual relations. Notice how he treats the first line of the poem, to which he devotes sermon after sermon: *Let him kiss me with the kisses of his mouth.* Could anyone doubt what this literally signifies? Of course not. But St. Bernard wishes to give it symbolic meaning. He says that the bride is speaking, the soul thirsting for salvation. And how could one show this best? To be a servant, Bernard answers, is to fear one's master. That is not the relationship. Nor is it that of an employee, who strives for recompense; nor of a disciple, who wishes to learn from his teacher; nor even of a son, who dutifully honors his father. The bond is closer than these. It is the union of persons who have all things in common—"one inheritance, one home, one table, even one flesh." This kind of oneness we find on earth in the tie between man and wife. Bernard quotes Genesis: "A man shall leave father and mother, and cleave to his wife: and they shall be two in one flesh"; also the Psalm that commands a wife "to forget (her) people and (her) father's house." This is the unity— though of course more sublime—that the soul wishes to experience with God. Why not express these ideas by having the church or some devout individual assume the posture of a lovesick bride begging for a kiss? The imagery is sensuous, but its employment is not. What interests St. Bernard is the character of the relationship, its particular *type* of unity. This inherent form he illustrates by means of graphic images, much as a logician shows us the nature of mathematical truth by talking about "2 plus 2 equals 4."

Indeed, one feels that St. Bernard could have gone much further. In a kiss there occurs a direct confrontation between two persons, face to face in an immediacy of presence transmitted through the sensitive tissue. As the God of the Sistine Chapel imparts consciousness to Adam by the touching of fingers, so too may the faithful hope for salvation through contact with the lips of Christ. (Think of the ending to Flaubert's story about St. Julien l'Hospitalier—"mouth to mouth, breast to breast . . . with Our Lord Jesus Christ, who bore him up to heaven.") Through our lips we receive, from an abundant world, the food and drink that sustain us; and in a kiss, the very breath of life itself. How wise of the Gospel according to Mark to have Judas betray Jesus by means of a kiss, the kiss of death! In the painting by Giotto we see Judas' protruding, grasping lips affix themselves to those of the all-enduring savior as a testament to the ironic confusion between life and death. Finally, a kiss, though sexually intimate, is not reproductive. So too Christ is not a goat or a bull—like Pan or Zeus—but an innocent lamb. In his humanity, as portrayed by all the Gospels, he is never man in nature but only a distillation from which genital interests have been removed. The kiss within a spiritual marriage is simply the play of love. If it leads to something else, that can only be one's own rebirth in another world, not the perpetuation of this one.

For St. Bernard these details were probably too obvious to need recounting. Instead, he distinguishes among three kinds of kisses, one for each stage of the spiritual life. At the outset of conversion, the soul goes through a purgative period in which, repenting of its sins, it prostrates itself before the offended deity. Bernard refers to this as the kissing of Christ's feet, and one thinks of the Mary who dried Jesus' feet with her hair. One also senses an attitude of primitive obeisance before the fact of power, as if Christ were some oriental potentate. But this is the lowest stage, to be succeeded by the kissing of Christ's hand. Even so do Catholics kiss the ring of the pope, and gentlemen, for courtly reasons, kiss the hands of ladies. Now the soul has been rendered upright, graciously raised by God, lifted into a state of piety, continence, good works, and penance. Only after much purification of this sort is the soul ready for spiritual marriage and the kisses of the mouth. These occur in the unitive stage. Only then, as St. Bernard says, may we "perhaps venture to lift our eyes to that Countenance full of glory, for the purpose not only to gaze upon it, but (I say it with fear and trembling) to kiss."

For all his fear and trembling, however, Bernard must have realized that his interpretation is orthodox. The Arians had been condemned as heretics for denying that Christ was *literally* both human and divine, the actual bearer of two different substances. The idea of Christ in the Gospels is, as Santayana has said, the idea of God in man. By his very nature Christ represents a vertical fellowship. In himself he is a spiritual marriage, a miraculous philia. Even his sign, the crucifix, combines the figure of a man with arms outstretched (as he would be on the cross) with the radiant spokes of the sun, which primitive peoples took to be a god because it was the source of our being. So far does St. Bernard recognize the literal humanity of Christ that he even speaks of religious love that is carnal. This occurs whenever the heart is moved by the thought of what Christ did or said while in the flesh: "the sacred image of the God-Man, either being born or suckled or teaching or dying or rising again." Because this side of Christ is mainly human, Bernard relegates it to a lesser love: a gift of God, but not as great as the love which directs itself toward Christ the Second Person of the Trinity. Nevertheless, it counts as a way of loving the divine; and Bernard commends its utility for prayer or virtue. Doubtless, he knows that popular Christianity rarely rises above it.

For us to consider whether Christ can literally be both God and man would be wholly fruitless. Theologians can always find arguments to suit a desired conclusion, but I am more interested in their desires than their reasoning. Consequently, what I find most significant in the idea of Christ's humanity is the way in which it idealizes reciprocity. Without reciprocity there is no community. Christian philia idealizes the fact that love unites different persons, creates a society in which each bestows value upon the others. For this community to include the divine as well as the human, man must have an access to God more direct than the Greek philosophers envisaged. The personage of Christ provides such access, and in a way that even Aristotle might admire. For if the love of others is merely an extension of one's love for oneself, as Aristotle thought, why not treat the God that man wishes to love as himself partly human? To some extent, one does so by conceiving of God as a loving father. But fathers live in a world of their own, and one can reciprocate more easily with an older brother. To allow one of the Persons in the Trinity to become human without losing his divinity is to make God immediately accessible to man's love. As Freud would say, believing in a Christ who is man as well as God increases the likelihood of identification. The Christian does not identify with God the Father, but by identifying with Christ he reciprocates God's love. And having loved a deity who is also human, he may find less difficulty in identifying with human beings on his own level. Such is the promise of Christian philia. If that promise can be fulfilled, any amount of anthropomorphism may be justified.

Men have always found ways of conversing with their gods; earlier religions were crowded with the visits into nature of these celestial beings. Much of the Old Testament is diplomatic history recording the embassies of angels who had been sent to earth on one mission or another. Not infrequently, men are permitted to appear before the king himself, to make requests on the part of the chosen people, even to haggle for human life as in the trial of Sodom and Gomorrah. The prophets in particular considered themselves as go-betweens, their moments of inspiration serving the same function as eros in Platonism. Indeed, the image of Elijah rising in a fiery chariot (presumably toward the sun) is worthy of the *Phaedrus*. But there was something in the personality of Christ that no previous mediator, whether Jewish or Greek, embodied. It was an unprecedented combination of familiarity with authority, each present to a supreme degree, the one providing a warm and personal relationship, the other assuring the power of divine sanction. In Catholicism the vertical community continually augments itself by additional mediators—the Church, the Virgin Mary, the saints, the popes—each increasing the familiarity of Christ by making him more visible. The sentimental pictures, the painted dolls, even the crucifix, mediate in a similar fashion. This world of mediators contributes to a sense of infinite access, but always at the risk of diminishing divine authority. When the Reformation sought to eliminate many of the lesser mediators, it did not get any closer to Christ. It merely changed the nature of the communion: from one in which God could be approached through devious channels of a familiar and personal sort to one in which the authority of his presence would be felt immediately by each individual in moments of special holiness.

Unless Christ were at least quasi-human, Christianity could not have effected its characteristic shift from reason to feeling. The deficiency in Platonic love ran deeper than the fact that the gods, being perfect, had no interest in returning man's eros. It affected the nature of eros itself, making it abstract, detached, inhuman— and so quite different from a love of persons. If the object of one's love could not reciprocate, if the true lover enacted a self-contradiction merely by hoping to be loved in return, his devotion could hardly take on the personal warmth that Judaism and Christianity both valued. Spinoza, who was understandably banished from the Dutch synagogue in the seventeenth century, maintained that no one who really loved God would want him to sully his perfection by reciprocating. This was the intellectual love of God, appropriate to Spinoza as to Socrates, and in general to all philosophers who want reality to hold still while they dispassionately analyze it. Such love belongs to the life of rationality, if not the life of reason. But one-way love establishes no community. It is deadly to the heart, which cannot function unless something responds to its emotional signals, someone human or divine, or both, who hears and understands its secret murmurs.

Plato held that all men loved the Good but only the philosopher loved it properly. For this to be so, one must exclude from successful love that demand for reciprocity which motivates everyone other than the philosopher. Far from making this exclusion, Christianity found its way to a benevolent deity whose sheer humanity is based upon his eagerness to reciprocate. This eagerness itself creates a circuit of tender feelings. Christian dogma idealizes the mutuality of love, but also something deeper in the human soul: the need to be at home in a kindly environment. In their rationalistic way, and on a smaller scale, Aristotle's perfect friends achieved something comparable. They limited the environment to a society human virtue could easily control. The Christian is more ambitious. The outer spaces frighten him, and so he humanizes them as well. Nothing less than a cosmic community will satisfy him, nothing less than a God of infinite love perfectly receptive to every heart's desire.

At the same time, Christianity had to protect itself against the extremes of anthropomorphism. In his relations with divinity there were some feelings that man could not share. St. Bernard insists that only through love can a human being reciprocate with God. If God were to be angry with him, a man could not grow angry in return. He would quake with fear and pray for mercy. If God were to rebuke him, he could not defend himself by rebuking God. Only in love can the attitudes be identical. "It is love alone in which the creature can make a return to the Creator. . . . For when God loves, He desires nothing else than to be loved. In fact, He loves for no other reason except that He may be loved, knowing that those who love Him have attained happiness by that very love itself."

For some Christians, philia was principally of the vertical sort we have been discussing. The ascetics, the anchorites, the solitary saints seemed to have found in the company of Christ the only community they required. But though these men are revered as instances of holiness, they really serve as museum pieces—works of religious art that one might inspect for Sunday edification, like the skeleton of a saint on view within some crypt, in contrast to art that one lives with day by day. For most Christians, philia had to be horizontal as well as vertical, and horizontal on the lower level of man's existence rather than the higher one of God's. Moreover, the system had to be unified—one vast community of the entire cosmos—and the distinction between levels a matter of appearance not reality.

Christian theology satisfies these requirements with the idea of the Mystical Body of Christ. Following St. Paul, Christ is sometimes referred to as the head of the body (i.e., society) that consists of those who have faith; at other times, he is taken to be the entire body, including all its members within himself. "And I live, now not I, but Christ liveth in me," St. Paul had said to the Galatians; and to the Roman congregation he asserted: "You are the body of Christ." In the Gospels, Christ himself says: "You shall know, that I am in my Father, and you in me, and I in you." Finally, the doctrine receives its definitive formulation by St. Augustine: "No one can love the Father unless he love the Son and he who loves the Son . . . loves also the members of the Son. And by loving he too becomes a member; through love he enters into the unity of the Body of Christ—and there shall be one Christ loving Himself—for when the members love one another, the body loves itself."

The derivation from Greek philosophy, with its emphasis upon self-love, is obvious; but the passage raises questions. Does it mean that one becomes a member of Christ merely by loving—regardless of whom or how one loves? That idea belongs to Romantic religion, but not to the Christianity of St. Augustine. When Christ forgives the woman taken in adultery "because she has loved much," he means she has loved *him*. At least, that was the interpretation of everyone in the Middle Ages. As Augustine has told us elsewhere, all things love in some fashion or other. But salvation required love of Christ, and love of other men only because they too are capable of loving Christ. This in turn sanctified the temporal institution of the church. For one could not become a member of the body of Christ without being baptized—as one cannot join other fraternities without an initiation. Nor could one remain a member without participating in holy rituals, such as the Eucharist, which miraculously enabled men to take the body and blood of Christ into themselves. Human beings were thus transformed (by another miracle) into that of which they partook. It was not love alone, not even the love of humanity, that made one a member of Christ. There had to be adherence to a system of corporate rules, established by the church. Likewise, the spiritual marriage described by St. Bernard is not really union between *either* Christ and the soul *or* Christ and the church, but only between Christ and the Christian congregation—to which (by definition) all devoted souls belong. "But although no one of us would dare to presume to such a degree that he would make bold to call his soul the Spouse of the Lord, nevertheless, because we are members of the Church which rightly glories in this title and in this reality, not unjustly we appropriate to ourselves a share in this glory." In other words, man can love God only en masse, as an ecclesiastical flock.

Within Protestantism the church as such loses much of its efficacy for working the miracle of love. The human soul may still hope for oneness with God, and in his *Commentary on Galatians* Luther explicates the verse from St. Paul by saying: "Faith connects you so intimately with Christ, that He and you become as it were one person." But note that *faith* connects, not the love of God or a spiritual marriage. To the Protestant the church is not a mystical body, and neither may it glory in being the primordial spouse of the Lord. At most, it is a vehicle that must not be allowed to separate the individual soul from God. To the Catholic this attitude undermines Christianity; and certainly it destroys all mystical ladders of the traditional sort. For though the Protestant aspires to oneness with God, he renounces human or institutional means of ascending toward the divine. Faith provides him with a kind of vertical philia; but otherwise he awaits God's condescension.

Consequently, the philia in Protestantism often seems to be more horizontal than vertical, and generally horizontal on the human level. If devout believers are not the members of a mystical body, they nevertheless constitute a self-conscious fellowship united to one another in varying degrees. Whether by singing together or just sitting silently in a meeting place until the spirit moves one to social intercourse, individuals effect a community among themselves by virtue of their similar beliefs. In some Protestant sects, Christ mainly symbolizes the love of one's fellow man: so much so that the transition to sheer humanitarianism requires little more than a change of images. From this side of Protestantism there issues an allegiance to moral, but nonreligious, communities that is often absent in Catholic countries. Within the Protestant world one finds the typically

Anglo-Saxon concept of a profession—the teaching profession, the legal or medical profession, etc. These semi-autonomous societies, dedicated to a sense of responsibility and governed by various ideals relevant to practical goals, operate as a kind of secular Protestantism. In a deeply ironic way, they reintroduce much of the corporate authority that the Reformation sought to destroy. The professions not only mediate between the individual and the state—thereby making even the democratic absolutism of a country like France unnecessary—but also between man and God. Concretely, through hard decisions about human relations, they indicate how God's will may be done. The nearest equivalent in Catholicism would be the clerical orders, particularly those in monasteries or convents. Even the mystical theology of St. Bernard makes sense, as Gilson has suggested, only in the context of the Benedictine rules to which he subscribed as a clergyman. But of course, the rules stem from life in the church; not, as for the Anglo-Saxon professions, from its elimination.

These remarks need further development, and I shall return to them in another place. Nevertheless, Protestant ideas about philia are useful as a way of seeing the difficulties within the medieval doctrine. Is it really possible for friendship to exist between man and the Christian God? When St. Bernard denies that man can reciprocate with any emotion other than love, when he says that man cannot return anger for anger or rebuke for rebuke, is he not precluding the possibility of friendship—and, in general, the love of persons? If bride and bridegroom were so related that only one could be angry or critical, would it not be a relationship of enslavement? Surely, theirs could not be marriage of a friendly and loving sort, or one based on equality. Moreover, the love between God and man must always be incommensurate, disproportionate. St. Bernard, who is sensitive to this problem, argues that "although a creature loves less because he is less, yet if he loves with his whole being, there can be nothing wanting." So too does the widow's mite equal the great man's legacy in being all she has. The idea is that man resembles God in loving without measure, and of love there can be no excess—as Aquinas remarks in the *Summa Theologica*, pointing out that here at least Aristotle's golden mean does not apply.

Actually, Aristotle also says that when each party gives his utmost a kind of equality is established, even if the quantity must be disproportionate. But in what he calls perfect friendship this would not be the case: there each would give something similar and comparable. As I have already suggested, this provision contributes to the closed and narcissistic character of Aristotelian friendship. Christian philia refuses to measure the benefits exactly. It thereby makes possible open friendships that Aristotle would never have condoned, and to that extent it is closer to the love of persons than what Aristotle recommends. In the relationship between man and God, however, one still has difficulty imagining the configuration of love. If it is really friendship, each person must wish well to the other. But how does man wish well to God? Is there any goodness God does not already have? At times, Christian (and Jewish) writers have spoken of God *needing* man's love. But how can this be if God is infinitely perfect? The Greeks may have been wrong to assume that a perfect God cannot love. But certainly they were right to think that he cannot stand in need of man's good will. How then can the saint or mystic enact the reciprocity that friendship requires?

There are two answers worth considering. The first is offered by Aristotle when he refers to the equalization of goods. God gives man salvation, and in return man gives God honor, respect, gratitude. In the *Euthyphro* Plato had said more or less the same. But this way out, with all its anthropomorphic overtones, St. Bernard explicitly rejects: "Nor believe that the inequality of persons here renders halting the accord of wills, for love has no respect of persons. It is from loving that love is named, and not from honor. Let him honor who is struck with awe, with astonishment, with fear, with admiration; all these are nothing to him who loves." And further on: "God then requires that He should be feared as Lord, that He should be honored as Father; but as Bridegroom He would be loved. Which of all these outweighs the rest? Surely love." Still, just how can the bride respond? How does the soul of man love God in a manner that makes friendship possible? St. Bernard mentions "the accord of wills," which is basic to the concept of nomos; but this both exceeds and falls short of that concern for the other's welfare in which friendship largely consists. Is man *benefiting* God by yielding to his will? And how can there be friendship if one person's will must always dominate, man conforming to God's will but not expecting God to conform to his?

The second answer is suggested to me by the opening line in the Magnificat: My soul doth magnify the Lord. If love glorifies its object by bestowing value, even treating it as perfect in relation to the lover, then perhaps the sanctified soul *can* give God something equal and comparable to what it receives. For in loving me, the Lord doth magnify my soul just as I magnify his. He is perfect and man is not, but God bestows value in loving man despite his imperfections. Man bestows value in recognizing the infinite goodness of God and delighting in it. They reciprocate within a community of bestowals. But is it really friendship, or even a love of persons? Does God take pleasure in magnifying me? It is a good for me, but is it a good for him? He desires me to love him, but is his desire like the desire other persons have? When my soul doth magnify the Lord, does it affect his value? For Christian philia to be a love of persons, the replies must all be affirmative—in *some* sense. Mere reciprocity is not enough. Much depends upon the nature of the union, the specific character of oneness. Let us then consider how various mystics have described this high fulcrum of religious ecstasy, this total embrace by the God who both loves and is love itself.

The end of Christian love is union with God. According to orthodox dogma, this means a wedding and not a merging. In the Middle Ages, the church condemned the concept of merging as a pantheistic heresy. The spiritual marriage between God and man allowed each to retain his separate substance. Still, something there is that hates a wall. However intimate the orthodox wedding, it always seems to keep the lovers apart. To men who seek absolute unity, the merging of souls inevitably suggests a more ultimate oneness. Theologians may establish an orthodox position, but how are they going to control what a mystic feels and says? In the Middle Ages even the greatest Christian saints and mystics deviate freely from ecclesiastical doctrine, though they usually return to it in their more official declarations. Since the language of mysticism is generally metaphoric, certainly unconcerned about the dubious rigors of logic, it would be useless to present one mystical utterance as the contradictory of another. Nevertheless, descriptions of spiritual union arrange themselves in a spreading continuum, statements at one extreme being vastly different from those at the other. At one end of the continuum we find mystics who characterize the union as a total and complete destruction of their individuality. In ways that are reminiscent of Plotinus, they speak of merging with the highest good, of becoming one in every sense with the One, of being taken out of themselves (which is, after all, the meaning of "ecstasy") and being transformed into the deity. At the opposite extreme are those mystics who consider total merging with God to be either impossible or undesirable. For them the consummation of religious love preserves the identity of the lovers. It is contact infinitely close, but not absorption, God and man eternally belonging to different dimensions of being.

Although the Plotinian extreme often occurs in Christianity, we may illustrate it most graphically by statements of Hindu and Muslim mystics—who also influenced the Christians. In the case of Hinduism the "undifferentiated unity" of mystical experience is not identified with the love of God. Far from describing a mysticism of love, the Upanishads and the Sāṁkya-Yoga treat sheer liberation as the end of man. Plotinus employs the Hindu concept of liberation, but he revises it in accordance with Platonic ideas about love. In the early Hindu texts, however, the saint merely strives to free his soul from the debasing lure of the sensory, empirical world. He effects a return to the *Atman*, the ground or purified essence of his selfhood. Each self being identical with *Brahman*, ultimate reality, he thereby merges with the metaphysical totality of everything. Where Brahman is called God, the saint speaks of losing his identity in God. He may then say: "I am He" or "I am this All" or "I am Brahman." As in Platonism, the soul returns to its origins in the divine. A spark struck off from the eternal fire, it again ignites.

In Hinduism the concept of merging is explicitly pantheistic. Since God pervades all being, the mystic merges with him simply by purifying his soul of inessential accretions. Spiritual exercises enable the mystic to apprehend God's sustaining presence, but they do not change anything in reality. Whatever man does, God is in his soul as in everything else. Pantheism of this sort leads to what the Christian calls "quietism": instead of changing his condition, man sinks more deeply into it. Without its pantheism, however, the Hindu notion of mystical union resembles the goal that many a Christian has sought. The following passage, which comes from the Upanishads, could very well have been written by a nonpantheistic Christian:

> As a lump of salt when thrown into water melts away and the lump cannot be taken out, but wherever we taste the water it is salty, even so, O Maitreyi, the individual self, dissolved, is the Eternal—pure consciousness, infinite and transcendent. Individuality arises by identification of the Self, through ignorance, with the elements [i.e., empirical content]; and with the disappearance of consciousness of the many, in divine illumination, it disappears. Where there is consciousness of the Self, individuality is no more.

In another Upanishad there appears an even more Christian-sounding description of mystical union:

> As pure water poured into pure becomes like unto it,
> So does the soul of the discerning sage become like unto Brahman.

In the Upanishads, at least, the "discerning sage" is not the lover of God. He is merely the prisoner liberating himself from the charnel house of body. In the *Bhagavad-Gita*, a much later work though still several centuries older than the New Testament, the love of God as a person who transcends Brahman enters into Hinduism for the first time. But religious love of this sort receives very little attention, either in the *Gita* or in the religion emanating from it. Moreover, the love of God is not described as union in the sense of merging. It involves a separation between the human and the divine, and this we can illustrate better elsewhere. In general, merging is what Hinduism emphasizes, but with an impersonal Brahman, not with God.

In Muslim mysticism the situation is quite different. Here the mystic devotes himself to the love of God, and yet his union is a total identification, unmistakable merging. This conception of unity may have resulted from direct Hindu influences, as some scholars believe; but the rest of Muslim mysticism belongs to the same medieval world as Christian mysticism. In some ways the Christian problems are more evident in the Muslim variety. At least, the conflict between mysticism and orthodoxy appears to have been more strident. Like the Catholic church the Islamic authorities banned as heretical the notion of undifferentiated unity. They insisted upon an even greater separation between man and God than Christianity had required. At the same time, however, Muslim mystics took greater liberties than their Christian colleagues in describing union as a merging. Whether or not the Christian mystics really differed from the Islamic, they obviously felt less need to run the risks of actually contradicting the orthodox position. In any event, the two extremes are more sharply accentuated in Islam than in Christianity. On the one hand, the Muslim authorities were vigorous in attacking the very idea of undifferentiated unity, even executing the Sufi mystic Al Hallaj for saying he was God; on the other hand, poets like Jalal al-Din Rumi were able to write rhapsodies of merging hardly to be equaled anywhere else:

> With Thy Sweet Soul, this soul of mine
> Hath mixed as Water doth with Wine.
> Who can the Wine and Water part,
> Or me and Thee when we combine?
> Thou art become my greater self;
> Small bounds no more can me confine.
> Thou hast my being taken on,
> And shall not I now take on Thine? . . .
> Thy Love has pierced me through and through,
> Its thrill with Bone and Nerve entwine.
> I rest a Flute laid on Thy lips;
> A lute, I on Thy breast recline.
> Breathe deep in me that I may sigh;
> Yet strike my strings, and tears shall shine.

In this poem all is not undifferentiated unity. But that Rumi believed in merging as the highest mystical state is evident from his description of "deification":

> The man who says *Ana 'l-'abd* "I am the slave of God" affirms two existences, his own and God's, but he that says *Ana 'l-Haqq* "I am God" has made himself non-existent and has given himself up and says "I am God," i.e. "I am naught, He is all: there is no being but God's." This is the extreme of humility and self-abasement.

At the opposite extreme from deification of this sort stands the belief that God and man can never be transformed into one another, that even in mystical experience they remain separate and distinct. This end of the continuum is best represented by Judaism. To the Jews, as to the orthodox Muslims, the principle of a strict monotheism forbids anything even resembling merging. Neither man nor any other creature can share God's ineffable divinity. Although Hasidic mystics occasionally seem to go against the Jewish current, the mainstream of this tradition denies the possibility of undifferentiated unity. For the mystics of Judaism, ecstasy generally implied admission to the throne of God, contemplation in the sense of seeing and hearing the magnificence of the Lord, but nothing like absorption or undifferentiated unity. As one scholar says: "Throughout there remained an almost exaggerated consciousness of God's *otherness*, nor does the identity and individuality of the mystic become blurred even at the height of ecstatic passion." Even the word "passion" here needs modification since the mystical relationship is filial rather than erotic or marital. Again with certain exceptions in Hasidism, which was atypically influenced by medieval Christianity, Jewish mystics generally characterize the love of God as the devotion of child to parent, not the search for union between lover and beloved.

If we now return to Christian mysticism, we find a spectrum that includes every aspect of the continuum. Even the orthodox mystics describe the state of union in widely differing ways. Perhaps this results from the long history of Christianity, immersed in the crosscurrents of local doctrines that vary from country to country. Perhaps de Rougemont is right in claiming that latter-day mystics appropriated secular language, unaware of its origin in earlier heresies. What seems to be more significant, however, is the fact that Christianity springs from divergent sources. From Hellenism it gets the tendency toward merging, suggested by Plato and enunciated by Plotinus, they themselves having possibly received it from Hinduism via the Orphic mysteries. From Judaism, Christianity takes the belief in separateness between finite man and the infinitely awesome God whose nature transcends everything tinged with mortality. As the offspring of such contrary parents, Christianity turns into a series of syntheses, each mixing more or less the same elements but in a different composition.

The orthodox view, maintained as dogma by the established churches of Christendom, St. Augustine states with great emphasis. Himself highly conscious of his Hellenistic paternity, Augustine nevertheless insists upon the insuperable distance between man and God. With the concept of merging clearly before him as a possible interpretation of mystical union, he rejects it as Satanic pride:

> There was danger lest the human mind, from being reckoned among invisible and immaterial things, should be thought to be of *the same* nature with Him who created it, and so should fall away by pride from Him to whom it should be united by love. For the mind becomes like God, to the extent vouchsafed by its subjection of itself to Him for information and enlightenment. . . . So by love it returns to God—a love which places it not along with God, but under Him.

If this position was to be enforced, however, there were various statements in the Gospels and St. Paul that required extensive interpretation. For instance, the First Letter to the Corinthians asserts that "he who is joined to God is one spirit." St. Bernard devotes much space to showing that this does not mean identification between God and man:

> For how can there be unity where there is plurality of natures and difference of substances? The union of God

and man is brought about not by confusion of natures, but by agreement of wills. Man and God, because they are not of one substance or nature, cannot be called "one thing" ("unum," like Father and Son); but they are with strict truth called "one spirit," if they adhere to one another by the glue of love. But this unity is effected not by coherence of essences, but by concurrence of wills. God and man, because they exist and are separate with their own wills and substances, abide in one another not blended in substance but consentaneous in will.

Notice "the glue of love," signifying here the adhesion at their surfaces of two different substances. To the Christian mystic Gerlac Petersen, however, glue means something else, something much closer to the position St. Bernard is attacking:

> Thou givest me Thy whole Self to be mine whole and undivided if at least I shall be Thine whole and undivided. . . . For this means nothing more than that Thou enjoyest Thyself in me, and that I by Thy grace enjoy Thee in myself and myself in Thee. And when in Thee I shall love myself, nothing else but Thee do I love, because *Thou art in me and I in Thee, glued together as one and the selfsame thing*, which henceforth and forever cannot be divided.

Doubtless this would be considered heretical by the Catholic church. Indeed in 1329 Pope John XXII condemned propositions of Meister Eckhart, the German mystic who maintained: "We are completely transformed into God and changed into Him. As, in the Sacrament, bread is changed into the Body of Christ, so I am changed into him." In the writings of St. Teresa, however, we find similar statements which have never been condemned. In one place she distinguishes between spiritual betrothal and spiritual marriage in a way that sounds like the distinction between orthodox wedding and heretical merging. But of the two, it is merging that appears as the ultimate consummation. Thus, of spiritual betrothal she says:

> Here the two persons are frequently separated, as is the case with union, for, although by union is meant the joining of two things into one, each of the two, as is a matter of

common observation, can be separated and remain a thing by itself. . . . We might say that union is as if the ends of two wax candles were joined so that the light they give is one: the wicks and the wax and the light are all one; yet afterwards the one candle can be perfectly well separated from the other and the candles become two again, or the wick may be withdrawn from the wax.

This sounds quite orthodox, except that spiritual betrothal is not the final union. In the spiritual marriage a closer relationship is achieved. As St. Teresa describes it, the mystical ascent would seem to culminate in a merging of substances:

But here it is like rain falling from the heavens into a river or a spring; there is nothing but water there and it is impossible to divide or separate the water belonging to the river from that which fell from the heavens. Or it is as if a tiny streamlet enters the sea, from which it will find no way of separating itself, or as if in a room there were two large windows through which the light streamed in: it enters in different places but it all becomes one.

Even in St. John of the Cross one finds statements that seem to be at variance with the orthodox position he usually defends. In one place he compares spiritual marriage to a ray of sunlight striking a window: "If the window were entirely clean and pure, the ray would transform and illumine it in such a way that it would become almost undistinguishable from the brightness of the ray and would diffuse the same light as the ray. And yet, however much the window may resemble the ray of sunlight, it actually retains its own distinct nature." Though this is already a step from St. Bernard, the soul being "transformed and transfigured in God," the image can certainly be called orthodox. But notice how the language of St. John of the Cross differs from St. Bernard's when he reaches his interpretation of the line from First Corinthians:

As by natural marriage there are *two in one flesh* (Genesis II, 24) so also in the spiritual marriage between God and the soul, there are two natures in one spirit and love. . . . He who

is joined to the Lord is one spirit. So when the light of a star,
or of a burning candle, is united to that of the sun, the light
is not that of a star or of a burning candle, but of the sun
itself, which absorbs all other light in its own.

Elsewhere too St. John of the Cross insists upon the separateness
of God and the soul, but also says that God "in the omnipotence of
His unfathomable love, absorbs the soul with greater violence and
efficacy than a torrent of fire a single drop of the morning dew."
Possibly such utterances can be rendered wholly consistent with
orthodoxy. This is for others to debate. I only wish to show that even
Catholic saints describe the mystical union in language that *seems* to
employ the concept of merging.

St. Teresa and St. John of the Cross lived in the sixteenth century,
but similar examples could have been drawn from the twelfth or
thirteenth. Richard of St. Victor describes the soul as "rising above
itself" (or as St. Gregory would have said, being "ravished" above
itself) with the suggestion that in a state of ecstasy one loses one's
former nature. Richard compares mystical union with the chemical
behavior of aromatic powder of spices thrown into a fire: "In so far
as it is not consumed by the devouring flame, [it] is transmuted by
the violence of the heat into a thin and smoking exhalation, rising
upward." The same idea is more forcefully expressed in a summary
statement about ecstasy in general:

> The human mind is raised above itself by the greatness of
> its devotion, when it is kindled with such fire of heavenly
> desire that the flame of inner love flares up beyond human
> bearing. And the soul melted like wax is released from its
> former state, and vapourized as smoke, ascends upwards
> and is breathed forth to the heavens.

In Richard of St. Victor one does not sense any conflict in allowing
religious love to vaporize the nature of man. But in many other
writers one constantly feels that their mystical inclinations run counter to the dictates of orthodoxy. In Luis de León, for instance, one is
rudely jolted by statements such as the following apparent self-
contradiction about Christ's love of man: "So intimately does He

take possession of them that, though His Nature in no way destroys or mars their own, there will be nothing seen in them at the Last Day, nor will any nature be found in them other than His Nature. There will be that one Nature in all, and both He and they will be one and the same in Himself."

In view of this ambivalence within Christian thinking, it is almost predictable that some mystics should try to accommodate both the merging and the wedding interpretations. In the fourteenth century Jan van Ruysbroeck and Meister Eckhart do so by distinguishing between spiritual marriage with the Persons of the Trinity and spiritual marriage with the Godhead. The latter they refer to as the "Essential Unity" whereby the three Persons make up one divinity. In his love for the Persons of the Trinity, the mystic is still separate from the one God: "the creature does not become God, for the union takes place in God through grace and our homeward-turning love: and therefore the creature in its inward contemplation feels a distinction and an otherness between itself and God." In this condition union is likened to sunlight mingling with air or heat penetrating iron. However intimate the relationship, substances remain distinct—just as the orthodox position required. But when Ruysbroeck and Eckhart speak of union with the Godhead, their language changes radically. Since the Trinity is merely a revelation of the Godhead, Eckhart claims that final blessedness comes from union with the Godhead and not the Trinity. When that happens to the soul, "its identity is destroyed." It may then say: "God is the same One that I am" and "With Him we are one, not only as united, but in an absolute At-one-ment." Of this final fruition Ruysbroeck states: "All uplifted spirits are melted and noughted in the Essence of God . . . so onefold that no distinction can enter into it. And this was prayed for by Christ when He besought His Father in heaven that all His Beloved might be made perfect in one, even as He is one with the Father through the Holy Ghost. . . ."

In *Mysticism East and West* Rudolph Otto documents the ways in which Christian mystics like Eckhart seem to rely upon the concept of merging. Nevertheless, Otto insists that even for Eckhart mystical union with the Godhead is not really a merging such as Plotinus or the Hindus sought. Where Plotinian mysticism yearns for passionate enjoyment "of a sensual and supersensual beauty," Eckhart's depends upon humility, faith, surrender of the will. Though Eckhart may sound like Plotinus, Otto says he is formulating a totally different, thoroughly Christian, type of mysticism. He illustrates this by quoting the following:

> Ours to know all and deify ourselves with all. Ours to be God by grace as God is God by nature; but ours also to resign all that to God and to be as poor as when we were not.

But is the problem so easily resolved? I do not think so. Certainly, the Christian mystics used concepts of love—nomos and agapē—which hardly appear in Plotinus or the Hindus. Certainly, these concepts tend to make Christian love significantly different. In this sense Otto is right and even the heretical Eckhart must be taken as describing a mysticism not reducible to anything non-Christian. But these considerations do not pertain to philia or indicate the type of union that mysticism idealizes. I have quoted from Christian writers at such great length because I think the texts themselves reveal a general confusion about the possibility of merging. Orthodox Christian mystics, even the nonorthodox like Eckhart, insist upon a separateness between God and man; but they speak also of a final union in which the soul is transformed, transmuted, absorbed, and raised above itself. At times they describe the ecstasy—in terms indistinguishable from those of Plotinus—as an enjoyment of supersensuous beauty. Though Eckhart may not, Dante and many others do. In its major import, Christianity clearly wishes to synthesize a kind of merging with a kind of wedding. Christian philia unites men to a God who preserves their identity and also destroys it. Herein resides, perhaps, a great mystery of consummated love. But just how are we to make sense of it?

Let us begin with an elementary distinction. When the mystics talk about oneness, are they referring to the nature of their relationship with God; or merely to the condition within themselves—e.g., a sense of harmony or peace—that they experience as a result of that relationship? Religious philia puts man into a loving fellowship with God, enabling them to commune. The reciprocity of love binds each to the other, not remotely as in Aristotelian friendship but more intimately, much more. But is it this intimacy that the mystics mean by oneness or is that a state within the human soul that undergoes such intimacy? Obviously the Christians seek both types of oneness and assume that the latter depends upon the former; but it will help us to distinguish between them.

Now if oneness is taken to characterize the mystical relationship, we ask whether it implies the existence of a new and homogeneous entity. This would involve merging, analogous to the fusion of gases: hydrogen and oxygen making the unity we call water. Orthodox Christianity denies that oneness between God and man can be such a merging. For it would entail the creation of a new substance mixing the divine and the human; and that means either a pantheistic violation of God's transcendence or else a blasphemous deification of man, and possibly both. If, however, the oneness in the relationship is just an identity of interest or even the closest agreement between two spiritual substances, we end up with something *less* than Christianity desires. Even where the union consists of perfect unanimity between the disparate wills, it would not yet be a spiritual marriage. In communing with God, the Christian hopes for more than just a wedding of souls. Though the substance of man cannot mingle with the substance of God, still God and man are to become one spirit in a way that magically (or miraculously) changes human nature. For this to happen, there must be unanimity in the sense that man conforms his will to God's—as we shall see when we discuss the concept of nomos. But unanimity is only a necessary condition: the oneness in the relationship also involves a *transformation* of man, and so the making of a new entity. To this extent at least, merging would seem to be an inescapable element in Christian dogma.

As against what I have said, Gilson argues that mystical oneness merely eliminates original sin and restores the essential likeness of man to God. The relationship does not *change* human nature, he says, but rather liberates it of impurities that have accrued since the Fall. But surely Gilson is being disingenuous. Surely he neglects all those statements in St. Paul, St. Augustine, St. Bernard, even St. Thomas, which describe the Holy Spirit descending into the soul of man and forming a special oneness with it. When St. Paul says that Christ lives in him, he refers to much more than *just* the restoration of likeness; when St. Augustine exhorts the members of the church to love one another for that will be Christ loving himself, he is speaking of a union that transforms and transfigures—in the words of Dante's *Paradiso*: "as it were, fused together in such a way that what I tell of is a simple light." God is the object of Christian love, but also love itself. Consequently, the mystic must love God by means of God, by incorporating the deity within himself. Since love is the essence of God, the mystic shares God's nature in loving him at all. The Christian may deny that this means that the human and the divine become a single substance; but in some respect the two would have to merge, in part if not entirely. How else can they be joined as *one spirit?**

To the extent that Christianity describes the mystical union as a kind of merging, it defies reason. It aligns itself with any number of primitive religions, wrapping its moral message within the orgiastic mystery of self-contradiction. If God and man are separate spirits, they may conceivably love one another. Their union may even be a fellowship based on reciprocity. Assuming that it is purified of carnal ingredients, the relationship may poetically be called a spiritual marriage. But God would not be in us literally, or we in God. By analogy to human intercourse we may say that spirits enter into one another insofar as they communicate. I know your idea because there is something of you that has become a part of me. This

---

*In his *History of Medieval Philosophy*, Maurice de Wulf says the following about St. Bernard's concept of ecstasy: "Bernard gives us celebrated comparisons, such as the drop of water lost in a great amount of wine, incandescent coal which can no longer be distinguished from the central fire, air which becomes transparent when the sun's rays pass through it. Bernard has recourse to these to explain that this state of intimate union leaves nothing human in man save his substance as a finite being. The latter indeed remains distinct from God and inalienable. This reservation is of fundamental importance and separates Bernard's theory from any suspicion of monism." What I am suggesting is that the "suspicion of monism" cannot be so easily eradicated—at least, not by a few doctrinal words inserted ad hoc.

language is figurative, however, and needs to be interpreted. Strictly speaking, we do not communicate *because* we become a part of one another—but vice versa. The idea that you articulate and I understand is not really a part of you that becomes a part of me. If anything, it is part of a system of communication to which we already belong. Otherwise, I could never decipher the words or signs by which the idea expresses itself and so exists. Similarly, the love between spirits (persons, if you wish) creates a union in which each participates. But they do not participate in *one another*. They share their love in the sense that both experience it. Neither can love from the other's point of view. If man loves God with God's own love, he is no longer man. He is God, or nothing. Plotinus triumphs after all.

These dire difficulties may be eliminated, but perhaps at too high a price. What if oneness were taken to describe a condition in the mystic's soul, and not the relationship with God? It is this interpretation, and only this, that Santayana will admit: "the union that mystics speak of seems to be emphatically a state into which they pass, internal, certain and overwhelmingly actual. It has the surprising and all-solving character of a datum: and the character of a datum, by definition, is exactly the same whether it happens to be true or merely imaginary. Therefore the only spiritual union that can be certain, obvious, and intrinsically blissful, must be not a union between two spirits but the unity of a spirit within itself." To the Romantics, whose influence Santayana partly reflects, the "all-solving character" of the mystical datum will always suffice: no need to introduce an external spirit. To the medieval mystics, however, and to all Christians, this solution is ruinous. The union they are seeking can only occur in relation to that Supreme Spirit whose very existence serves as the source of love. And if they cannot prove that their experience originates with God, they will nevertheless posit it as the foundation of all belief. Nothing shall be allowed to question this assumption.

For my part, I have no desire to pry into the ontological bases of mystical union. It is religious attitudes that interest me, and the play of imagination within them. Given the categories of his superior science, the same is true of Freud. In one place he discusses mystical experience as an effect of "oceanic feeling": it is "a sensation of 'eternity,' a feeling as of something limitless, unbounded . . . a feeling of an indissoluble bond, of being one with the external world as a whole." The wording suggests some kind of pantheism, but let that pass. What matters here is the nature of the experience, not the object to which the mystic feels himself related. In his usual manner, Freud analyzes the feeling genetically, tracing it to the infant's sense of omnipotence. As long as the newborn child encounters no resistance from its environment, it does not separate itself from the world. Indeed, it has no feeling of itself *as* a self until reality frustrates its various demands. In losing the sense of omnipotence, the individual achieves self-consciousness: he comes to recognize an otherness between himself and the world in which he lives. Ordinarily, the adult ego maintains what Freud calls "clear and sharp lines of demarcation." In one exceptional case, however, he finds a counterinstance that seems to resemble the infant's oceanic feeling: "At the height of being in love the boundary between ego and object threatens to melt away. Against all the evidence of his senses, a man who is in love declares that 'I' and 'you' are one, and is prepared to behave as if it were a fact." This state of mind Freud considers unusual but not pathological. Would he say the same of mystical experience? He does not tell us. And yet he obviously believes that oceanic feeling reverts to an infantile condition. It is a form of regression. It exists in adults as a counterpart to the "more sharply demarcated ego-feeling of maturity." At least in the use of pejorative terms like "infantile" (as against "mature"), Freud implies that all oceanic experiences are psychologically undesirable. Whether or not they are actually pathological, they turn back the adult processes of ego development that Freud considers healthy and realistic.

Unfortunately, Freud gives us no case histories to illustrate the nature of "oceanic feeling." Had he wished to do so, he might have found a remarkable diversity among the mystics themselves. In their unitive experiences some of them do seem to regress. These are the mystics who find the pressures of adulthood unbearable (e.g., Henry Suso, at least as William James depicts him in *The Varieties of Religious Experience*). The world is too much with them, and the littleness of soul they pathologically feign is surely a device for gaining infantile omnipotence. But there are other kinds of mystics. Are we even certain that all oceanic feelings are alike? Is the "feeling as of something limitless, unbounded" the same as "a feeling of an indissoluble bond"? A St. Francis or a St. Bernard might well deny that his is an experience of something limitless in which the ego seems to melt. Each of them could well insist that he feels only an indissoluble bond between himself and God. To the extent that this is so, mystical language need not be taken as an indication of regression. For it expresses a universal, and possibly instinctive, need to be *at home*, a need that begins in childhood but is not especially infantile. As the individual develops, his conception of "home" changes from the family to the group and sometimes to the cosmos. Its reference being variable, different persons can satisfy the need in different ways. The mystic hungers for a metaphysical home to which he can bind himself with the strongest of ties. His need is peculiar, and possibly more intense than it would be in others. But as King Lear says to one of his grasping daughters: "Reason not the need." In seeking oneness with God, the mystic feels at home with everything. So great a sense of belonging may not be necessary for mental health, but in itself it is neither regressive nor psychologically harmful. The mature adult whom Freud idealizes must always be alone and afraid—though very courageous—in a world that no one made. He runs the constant risk of sensing his painful alienation from a universe without meaning. He is heroic if he can surmount the anxiety of being a purposive creature in a purposeless cosmos. Most men can live with such anxiety, but the mystic is possibly one who fears the sense of alienation more than anything else. This does not make him less of an adult, only a different type.

In one way or another we are all indissolubly bound to the universe. Through space exploration one can leave *this* world, the planet Earth, but one cannot leave *the* world. We are linked to the reality of things through chains that are infinite in number. In that sense, everything we do *must* be in harmony with the cosmos and no one can be alien to it. But in our experience the harmony need hardly register. The mystic, however, orders his life for the sake of *feeling* the inescapable unity. He bestows upon it the value of conscious admiration, thus making it suitable for love. What the man of reason might well consider trivial or even tautologous, the world being one, the mystic takes as a basis for enjoyment. His attitude is appreciative, not scientific. To experience the oneness of the world *as a harmony* is itself an act of aesthetic bestowal. The sense of union is thus an idealization, oneness assuming a felt importance that need not have been elicited. In the Christian tradition a further idealization intervenes. The oneness of mystical experience comes to be dignified, idealized as union with a transcendental God. Otherwise, the sense of harmony could be interpreted pantheistically. That might satisfy mystics who wish to feel at home in nature, but not those who require a cosmic father.

The sense of harmony belongs to all the consummations of love. In their moments of greatest passion men and women feel this oneness with each other, if not with anything else. A single rhythm— what to the mystics might seem to be God's foot upon the pedal of the universe—creates a unity between their bodies, their senses, their instincts, and their emotions. If this rhythm brings simultaneous enjoyment, it may well reach a climax in something resembling the oceanic feeling. Possibly this is what Freud means when he says that at the height of being in love the boundary between ego and object threatens to melt away. Even so, erotic ecstasy may happen only rarely to those who are in love. The condition known as "falling in love" makes it the governing model for love in general. To *fall* in love is to lose all sense of separateness, to fuse in one ecstatic harmony after another with whatever sexual object that happens to be available. Consequently, when Freud draws his parallel between mystical experience and being in love, one should possibly take him to mean the special case of falling in love. In effect, that is what Ortega y Gasset does. He compares mystical union with falling in love, making it very clear that love itself is something quite different. As a result, however, Freud and Ortega seem to limit mystical experience to an extreme form of merging. Ortega insists that all mystics are alike in undergoing an act of hypnotic attentiveness which excludes everything but the object, causes the mystic to lose the sense of selfhood, and culminates in a feeling of total and ecstatic absorption: "God filters into the soul and merges with it or, inversely, the soul dilutes into God and no longer feels that He is a different being from itself. This is the *unio* (union) to which the mystic aspires." With no difficulty at all, Ortega then shows how persons who fall in love undergo a similar experience, seeking to be saturated with one another in the same ecstatic fashion.

That Ortega's analogy is faithful to *some* types of mystical union,

Christian and non-Christian alike, one may readily admit. But many mystics do not fit the pattern. As falling in love receives its greatest idealization in romanticism, so too is the analogous mystical union prevalent only in certain eras of religious love. All mystical experience seeks a cosmic harmony, but not in the same way. To assume that the ecstasy must always be a fusion as in Romantic love is to miscontrue the fellowship in philia. We often feel a oneness with those with whom we share nonsexual experiences, exchange ideas and impressions, cooperate for mutual benefit; those who agree with us about important matters of will or belief; those who support our ideals and whom we admit into the privacy of our dreams, our hopes, our secret fears. This is the aspect of union that Freud considers when he talks about the growth of civilization through aim-inhibited affection. By eradicating the sense of separateness, falling in love subverts society to that extent. For it melts away the interpersonal barriers without which there could be no social order. And often the mystics, with their hatred of "the world," are equally destructive—as when St. John of the Cross says of his earthly associations: "Move them aside, my beloved, / For I am in flight." At the same time, the mystic desires a new and superior society. His idealizations may seem fantastic, but they help him create a sense of community with God and other spirits. Insofar as oneness bears an "all-solving character," it may resemble a sense of merging. As Santayana says, the feeling will then belong to the unity of a spirit within itself. But insofar as the mystic loves an external and necessarily separate deity, the harmony within his experience can also allow differentiation of the sort that exists in all societies.

The nature of this harmony reveals itself in the concept of nomos. Every society presupposes submission to law and authority. For Christianity this means obedience to God, which is then idealized as an act of love. Without humility there can be no mystical union. Without the total renunciation that nomos requires there can be no philial sense of harmony. These religious concepts lean on one another: they stand or fall together.

12

Nomos: Submission to God's Will

A Christian or a Jew must believe that man is created in the likeness of God. But a likeness is always inferior to the original. Even in the consummations of loving union, the religious soul submits to God's supremacy. Indeed, Christian love *consists* of a proper self-abnegation. Spiritual marriage is not only unanimity but also *conformity*, man's will succumbing to the will of God. In the marital imagery of the medieval church, the human spirit is always feminine while God is always supremely masculine. Through mystic oneness the bride may be elevated toward the Bridegroom's supernatural realm, but her eyes remain lowered. Although the Lord's countenance will shine down upon her and she may even see it face to face, the bride can never presume to any real equality. This unity of love resembles a Victorian wedding photograph: the husband sitting in a solid chair while his dutiful wife stands at his side ready to be of service. Pride, the major sin, is willfulness. It is man refusing to conform, and so hating God. The aspect of Judaeo-Christian love which predicates submissiveness I call nomos. In some respects it is fundamental to all religious love.

As we shall see, Christian nomos implies renunciation of the world. In this Santayana perceives a great spiritual truth. For the world, he says, is always capable of violating God's will; and, potentially at least, its crimes are rooted in every human soul. "Therefore the true saint unaffectedly thinks himself the greatest of sinners, because he finds in himself, in so far as he is himself and not pure spirit, the potentiality of all sins." As one might expect, Freud's account is somewhat different: "When saints call themselves sinners, they are not so wrong, considering the temptations to instinctual satisfaction to which they are exposed in a specially high degree—since, as is well known, temptations are merely increased by constant frustration, whereas an occasional satisfaction of them causes them to diminish, at least for the time being."

In general, Freud thinks of renunciation as a mechanism by which civilization controls the individual's antisocial impulses. It originates with the universal fear of some external authority. In order to neutralize this fear and retain parental love, the child renounces various instinctual satisfactions that the parent has condemned. Eventually the child internalizes the authority and forms a conscience or superego within himself. Thus, the sense of guilt or sinfulness (these being much the same for Freud) arises from two related sources. A man will feel guilty if he refuses to renounce a forbidden gratification; but also he may have a sense of guilt for even wanting it. Though he gives up the satisfaction, he will continue to have desires; and they cannot be hidden from his superego. The more the saints frustrate their instincts by renouncing the world, the more they increase temptations; the more they are tempted, the greater their sense of sinfulness. Since the superego takes over the child's original hatred of the restraining parent, its punitive power may exceed anything that could have been expected from the external authority itself. In his fear of losing love, the child identifies with the aggressor demanding renunciation; the superego represents this aggressor but punishes with a violence that comes from the child's own resentment; this violence turns inward and sometimes leads to self-destruction.

If Freud's analysis is right, and in its major outlines it seems to be, the sinfulness of saints may also be explained in a way that Freud does not mention. What he calls initial resentment the saint interprets as something deeper than hostility toward a parent. For him it is the rejection of God's will, and so hatred toward the greatest of all possible authorities. This is the original sin, which the saint—in his desperate need to love and be loved—feels more keenly than other people. Willfulness being the worst of sins, his superego must take the most radical means of eliminating it. Thus, the Christian renounces the world in the hope of conforming perfectly with the divine authority. If he succeeds, his self-denial leads to identification—not with an aggressor, but with a loving deity in whose likeness he was created. From the Christian point of view, Freudian analysis explains the psychological workings of sinfulness, but not its underlying import.

For his part, Freud can never admit the idea of a supernatural being. He assumes that the figure of God must have come from prehistoric legends about social authorities. The primal father, so Freud speculates, must have been slain by sons who then repented of their patricide. In the primitive imagination the primal father changed into a deity who would eternally stand as the ultimate will: "For men knew that they had disposed of their father by violence, and in their reaction to that impious deed, they determined to respect his will thenceforward." Unless men had renounced some of their aggressive instincts, society could never have existed. The fiction of a heavenly father made it easier for the superego to operate in ways that civilization required. But all too often, Freud reminds us, religion and the superego make impossible demands upon the individual. When that happens, the religious concepts are not only illusional, but also psychologically harmful.

In one place Freud talks about the "impoverishment of the ego" as a consequence of love. Everyone is exalted by *being* loved, he says, but loving another involves deprivation and lowers self-esteem. Though Freud is not here referring to the love of God, that would seem to be an extreme case of what he has in mind. Elsewhere he distinguishes between identification and infatuation in a way that is also relevant: "In the former case the ego has enriched itself with the properties of the object, it has 'introjected' the object into itself, as [Sandor] Ferenczi expresses it. In the second case it is impoverished, it has surrendered itself to the object . . . there is a hypercathexis of it by the ego and at the ego's expense." Now if we put together identification and infatuation, as Freud describes them, we have the paradox of Christian love. Through eros and philia the mystic soul enriches itself with God, introjects the divine object into itself.

Through nomos, however, it renounces all enrichment, empties itself of self, yields up its separate will, and surrenders with love to God's lawful authority. After making his distinction, Freud relates the state of being in love to hypnosis: "There is the same humble subjection, the same compliance, the same absence of criticism towards the hypnotist just as towards the loved object. There is the same absorption of one's own initiative; no one can doubt that the hypnotist has stepped into the place of the ego ideal." All this fits mystical aspiration perfectly, except that for the mystic God does not step into the place of the ego ideal: He *is* the ego ideal.

The concept of nomos belongs to the Jewish side of Christianity. That the Christian is a fusion of Greek and Jew everyone recognizes; but scholars concerned with love have traditionally neglected that major element in Christian love which comes directly from the Old Testament. Jesus himself proclaims that his God is "the God of Abraham, Isaac, and Jacob." Moreover, the two "Great Commandments"—to love God and to love one's neighbor—appear in the Gospels as quotations from the Old Testament, mandates of the religious life which Jesus is reaffirming rather than initiating. The Gospels take these commandments from different places in the Old Testament, put them together, and declare emphatically that there are none greater, As we shall see, there is reason to think that this codification had already been effected by the Jews. But even as an innovation, it was hardly cataclysmic. Hanging the law and the prophets upon the Great Commandments might have made primitive Christianity a new sect within Judaism: it could not make it into a separate religion.

What enabled Christianity to become a new religion was its way of *applying* the two commandments. In allowing the possibility that *anyone* could love God, and that all human beings might *equally* qualify as neighbors to be loved, Christians like St. Paul undermined Jewish philia. For that depended on the sense of community as a nation of chosen people. The Jews defined themselves in terms of their history and the historical destiny it revealed: the covenant their forefathers had made with God, his having sanctified them as a vessel of holiness, his promising to reward this little clan with a homeland on earth and a time of political greatness. In earlier periods the nation had been victorious, the dream of dominion partly realized by David and Solomon. By the time that Jesus and Paul arrived, the Jewish state was overrun, the people demoralized, and the glories of the past receding rapidly. In many ways Christianity was to the Jewish nation what Platonism had been to Athens disoriented by the ruinous Peloponnesian War; or Stoicism to *all* the Greek city-states, by then submerged in the Roman Empire. In each case a system of local, traditional, indigenous beliefs was rejected at a moment when—in the most obvious and materialistic sense—they had failed to prove themselves. In each case the old beliefs were replaced by an idealistic doctrine offering goals in principle unattainable on earth, and therefore absolutely secure within their self-appointed limits. What Plato did with the Athenian myths, Christianity did with the Old Testament. The ancient legends were refined and reinterpreted. They were not to be taken as proof of God's special interest in a single people. They had universal reference and symbolized God's love for mankind as a whole. Salvation was achieved not through national success, but through individual commitment. And it was available to anyone who saw the light and worshiped God in Jesus Christ.

Except for belief in Christ, much of this tranformation was also taking place within orthodox Judaism. The possibility of an individual relationship between man and God had already been suggested in the writings of the prophets, who even said that loving one's neighbor could include non-Jews. In the Old Testament these intimations occur within a context that emphasizes the uniqueness of Israel as a nation. But in the first century A.D., many Jews were denying the nationalistic aspects of their religion in ways that at least run parallel to the revisions of Christianity. Were the Jews being influenced by Christian thinkers? Their later history would show a great deal of that. Or were the Christians merely disseminating the latest development in Jewish thought? I leave it to the scholars to determine the exact boundaries between Christian and Jewish ideas about love. I am primarily interested in analyzing the concepts themselves.

Whatever the historical relationship, the fact remains that Jews and Christians belong to the same religious tradition. In one place Nietzsche argues that Christian ideas about love are really the Jewish will to power taking a new and subtle turn in the struggle for survival. Having lost their national identity, Nietzsche says, the Jews created Christianity as a more effective means of ruling the world. Presumably they were motivated by unconscious desires: at least, Nietzsche does not claim that the Jews knew what they were doing. An overt will to power he always admires, in the Jews as much as in the Greeks; but its sublimation in Christian love he finds particularly obnoxious and deceitful. Obviously Nietzsche is too extreme. Christianity fascinates him to the point where he feels the need to condemn it wholesale. This impairs his comprehension and leads him to sheer absurdities: e.g., identifying all Christian love with the special phenomenon of asceticism. Nevertheless, one feels that Nietzsche's basic insight may be right. To a considerable degree Christianity is indeed Judaism enlarged and extended, spiritualized and reconstructed by Greek philosophy, modified by various dogmas at different stages of history, but through it all the God of Israel asserting his dominance over the minds of men. And possibly this explains the persecution of the Jews. As if they could escape history by virtue of personal innocence, the Jewish people have always been astounded by the senseless cruelties that have chronicled their life in the Western world. But to certain Christians the Jews are primal parents, ideological fathers who refuse to recognize their own children, and therefore suitable objects for infantile aggression. (Perhaps that is why, until very recently, the stock image of the Jew was a bearded old man dressed in black gabardine.) To the sadist, persecution may always serve an ad hoc moral purpose: in this case, punishing the Jews for having offended God, for having lost his protection, for having betrayed their integrity by creating the very Christianity in whose name they can now be persecuted.

But despite the truth in Nietzsche's insight, it is misleading to speak of Christianity as the continuation of Judaism. For one thing, this neglects the importance of Hellenic ideas in Christianity. For another, it seems to imply that there was a single Jewish doctrine (about love, for example) which the Christians propagated more subtly than the Jews. As a matter of fact, the concept of love undergoes a complex evolution throughout the Old Testament. It starts as

a fairly simple notion and ends up highly interpreted. In drawing
upon this tradition, Christianity chose what it needed and discarded
the rest—as later Jews have also done. There are Jewish elements in
Christian love, and most of the ideas about love in the New Testament are already present in the Old; but within its own dimension,
Christian love is not reducible to either its Jewish or its Greek
origins.

The Jewish elements in Christian love I identify as nomos and
agapē. The word *nomos* literally means justice, righteousness, adherence to the law. In the Old Testament as well as the New, these are
only partial indications of love; but within the Judaeo-Christian
development they provide the basis for subsequent idealization. To
many scholars, however, the ideals of nomos embody ethical values
(or what I would call appraisive attitudes) that the New Testament
completely rejects. According to Nygren, Christian love "is the
opposite of 'Nomos,' and therefore a denial of the foundation on
which the entire Jewish scale of values rested." Like many theologians before him, Nygren sees in Christianity the transcending of
what he calls Jewish legalism, the substituting of mercy for retribu-
tion and charity for equity—in other words, Portia for Shylock. But
this is just the black gabardine again, the child pretending it had no
parent. The American philosopher Douglas Morgan comes closer to
the truth when he says: "Love defines the meaning of the Torah,
exactly as it defines the meaning of the Sermon on the Mount"; and
elsewhere, "What distinguishes Christianity from Judaism . . . is
Jesus Christ, nothing more and nothing less." No religion could be
as new and original as theologians like Nygren would like Christianity to appear. On the one hand, the relation between love and mercy
had already been established at great length in the Old Testament;
on the other, righteousness in the sense of legalism *never* was the
Jewish attitude toward love. Let us leave the theologians and return
to the texts.

The key to nomos resides in the characterization of God. In Genesis
we first encounter him in the process of making a world. The
opening pages of the Bible are devoted to creativity much as the

Greek poets begin their works by invoking the inspirational powers of the Muses. It is the artist's way of acknowledging the mysterious and inventive forces within himself. But he does more than just acknowledge: he glorifies, idealizes, that without which his life would have no meaning. And so, in the beginning God makes all reality, just as the authors of the Bible are making an objective testament to what is deepest and most real in themselves. As a grand artificer, what in Plato would be the demiurge, God enjoys his work. Like any other artist, he is a little surprised and somewhat impressed by what he has created. "And God saw everything that he had made, and, behold, it was very good." It is as if heaven and earth might not have turned out quite that way, as if the production could have been less successful. We are not told that the creation was perfect. How could it be? It is only a work of art. The outcome is said to be "very good"; and even that is not a precise appraisal but only an indication that God is satisfied with his work and can now allow himself a day of rest.

Implied in these artistic metaphors is the possibility that the product may always be recalcitrant. A work of art can defeat the artist's intentions. And indeed, throughout the Bible one senses that God's creation keeps moving away from him in ways he had not foreseen. I can imagine the Lord returning—in the days of the prophets, let us say—inspecting anew this world he had created some time back and sadly admitting to himself: "No, it was not as good as I thought." David Hume wondered whether the universe might not have been botched several times before the present draft. His idea is implicit in the Bible. Not only does God make a fresh beginning after the Flood, but also he constantly complains about the failure of his art. This imperfection is most apparent in the case of man. As the climax of his labors, with a magnificently joyous "let us make," God created man after his own image, in his own likeness. He gave man dominion over all living things on earth, just as God has dominion over everything everywhere. He enjoined man to be fruitful and multiply, just as God himself was doing. The supreme artist was creating a lesser one, as a master will train an assistant to help him in his work. The rest of the Bible recounts, in painful detail, man's waywardness, rebellion, and alienation from his source.

The Old Testament is a very sad book, possibly tragic in its mixture of terror and pathos. Compared to it, the New Testament is sweetly simple and benign. Even the crucifixion of Christ will chill the body but not the soul: we know it is preordained and for the best. At most the New Testament is cathartic, cleansing emotions *after* the tragedies of the Old Testament. These result from a conflict of wills, without which there can be no tragedy. Like Lear with his daughters, God distributes powers to an offspring who cannot control them and will not give them back. The "sorcerer's apprentice" is man. His ultimate power issues from the free will that God shares with him thoughtlessly, in an act of unthinking and possibly unpremeditated generosity.

That God himself has a free will is a matter of consequence. The demiurge in Plato had a will, which human artists could approximate, but its freedom was subject to metaphysical hedges. *Could* the demiurge have refused to pattern the world after the eternal forms? One is inclined to say No, and that the very idea of a Platonic universe not governed by the forms is self-contradictory. But then one cannot be sure. The demiurge in Plato is really just an abstraction, a figure of speech, a poetic symbol for the fact of creation. The God of the Old Testament, however, is a *person*. He has a character, and his will can be described in graphic imagery. His cosmos is more or less purposive, perhaps as much as that of the Greeks. But he rules it from above, as an absolute monarch, subservient to no constitution of logical entities such as the Platonic forms. As a result, his universe is not wholly rational. It is often mysterious, his will operating inscrutably and through secret agents. One cannot be certain that God, the Jewish God at least, acts providentially. Does he create in accordance with a prior plan? Does he intervene in history to reestablish an original design? It all seems to be a matter of momentary impulse, like the Negro legend in which God creates the world because he has made too much custard and needs a place to drain off the excess. While Jehovah is imparting the law to Moses on Mount Sinai, he almost changes his mind about everything. Noticing that the Israelites below have begun to worship the calf of gold, he suddenly flares up in anger and decides to destroy them. He has already destroyed other offending subjects, in fact, most of mankind at the time of the Flood. Like a Jewish Odysseus, Moses reasons with the Lord, arguing that God would lose face in Egypt if he slaughtered the people he has brought forth. This, together with reminders about the patriarchal ancestors (for whom God bears a special love), has its effect. The anger subsides; a new decision is made.

Despite such frightening unpredictability on God's part, his attitude is generally benevolent. He shows the care and concern of any dedicated craftsman. He takes responsibility for his work. He realizes that creation is not enough: the product must also be preserved. For Adam and Eve he makes the Garden of Eden as a kind of reservation. He puts them into it much as an artist hangs his painting in the best museum he can find. Once this fails, God tries something else. Men are not yet ready for the abundancy of leisure; life will mean more to them if they have to work for it. When new difficulties arise, God occasionally helps man out. His experiment seems to bring further responsibilities, which he accepts. In the multiplicity of their wills, men need a touchstone for virtue, and so God arbitrarily chooses a nation, one of the smallest—as if to prove how great his own powers are. He makes this people the exemplar, the bearer of truth, the light moving through the darkness. He promises them eventual goodness, gives them laws to regulate their lives, annihilates their enemies. Step by step the nature of God's creativity becomes more socialized. From having been a supercraftsman, he turns into a father with all that this word implies about the creation and sustenance of communal life. As a devoted patriarch, he institutes the laws of his people, setting them out in the firm, explicit way that children require. His punishments are severe but well-intentioned. To his offspring he is a familiar figure, yet not an intimate one. His name cannot be spoken; no one may look upon his face, only a unique favorite like Moses being able to see him at all. Though he admits to jealousy and other emotions that signify love, he is also remote: a distant king, an untouchable monarch. Men may speak to him in a special language, but they must keep their spiritual distance. As time passes, he suffers the abuses of aging parenthood. Finally, he withdraws his personality, though not his presence, from the surface of history. His children, remembering past kindnesses and still suffering unresolved guilt in their misuse of freedom, lament his absence, fear that he has forsaken them. As in these lines by the Deutero-Isaiah, they glorify his loving character, recapitulate the good old days, and beg him to return:

I will mention the lovingkindness of the Lord,
And the praises of the Lord,
According to all that the Lord hath bestowed on us,
And the great goodness toward the house of Israel,
Which he hath bestowed on them according to his
    mercies,
And according to the multitude of his lovingkindnesses.
For he said, "Surely they are my people,
Children that will not lie":
So he was their Saviour.
In all their affliction he was afflicted,
And the angel of his presence saved them:
In his love and in his pity he redeemed them;
And he bore them, and carried them all the days of old.

But they rebelled, and vexed his holy Spirit:
Therefore he was turned to be their enemy,
And he fought against them.
Then he remembered the days of old,
Moses, and his people, saying,
"Where is he that brought them up out of the sea with
    the shepherd of his flock?
Where is he that put his holy Spirit within him?
That led them by the right hand of Moses
With his glorious arm,
Dividing the water before them,
To make himself an everlasting name?
That led them through the deep,
As a horse in the wilderness,
That they should not stumble?
As a beast goeth down into the valley,
The Spirit of the Lord caused him to rest":
So didst thou lead thy people,
To make thyself a glorious name.

Look down from heaven,
And behold from the habitation of thy holiness and of thy
    glory:

Where is thy zeal and thy strength,
The sounding of thy bowels and of thy mercies toward
    me?
Are they restrained?
Doubtless thou art our father,
Though Abraham be ignorant of us,
And Israel acknowledge us not:
Thou, O Lord, art our father, our redeemer;
Thy name is from everlasting.

O Lord, why hast thou made us to err from thy ways,
And hardened our hearts from thy fear?
Return for thy servants' sake,
The tribes of thine inheritance.
The people of thy holiness have possessed it but a little
    while:
Our adversaries have trodden down thy sanctuary.
We are thine:
Thou never borest rule over them;
They were not called by thy name.

What emerges from this idealized portrait of the masterful father, this image of God in the Old Testament, is the conception of a deity who loves and is loved as a person. Plotinus refers to the One as "the Father," but only in the sense (quite Platonic) that divinity is the source of being. Not so the biblical God. He has the explicit and familiar personality of a loving parent, albeit in heaven. Despite his distance Jehovah *cares* about human welfare. He performs acts of love as well as loving-kindness. He takes a particular interest in the Hebrew patriarchs and favors their descendants as the continuance of a love to which he remains loyal. In the Book of Exodus he describes himself as "showing mercy unto thousands of them that love me, and keep my commandments." The Psalmist extols him as follows: "The Lord is gracious, and full of compassion; / Slow to anger, and of great mercy. / The Lord is good to all, / And his tender mercies are over all his works." The prophets repeatedly speak of his fatherly attachment to Israel. Isaiah says that he comforts like a mother; and Hosea compares God's love to his own love for a whoring wife. Through the force of his devotion alone, God promises to redeem the faithless people: "And I will betroth thee unto me for ever; yea, I will betroth thee unto me in righteousness, and in judgment, and in lovingkindness, and in mercies. I will even betroth thee unto me in faithfulness; and thou shalt know the Lord." Unto the righteous the Deutero-Isaiah prophesies: "And as the bridegroom rejoiceth over the bride, / So shall thy God rejoice over thee."

The Christian idea of a spiritual marriage takes root in these descriptions of God's betrothal to Israel. But in the Old Testament they are mainly allegorical. The mystical implications are not developed. As time went on, God's love for Israel was interpreted as a personal concern for each and every Jew, eventually for all men. But the idea of *union* hardly occurs; there is virtually no suggestion that love itself could be a marriage between God and a human soul striving for oneness with him. In the Old Testament, God's paternal love is more characteristic. Men are his sons, and he loves them as such. Unlike other gods he shows no signs of sexual interest. He wants mankind to obey, to be at one with him, but not united in the way that a bride might unite with a bridegroom. It is only after a long history of alienation that the Judaeo-Christian faith envisages a return through a spiritualized sexual embrace.

For all its prominence in the Old Testament, God's love remains mysterious and ill-defined. Like God himself, it amounts to a presence that Jews might feel but hardly investigate. At the same time, it serves an important moral function: it authorizes a specific type of religious love. Nomos (to revert to the Greek word) is man's adequate response to his parental God. It is man, in his likeness to the heavenly father, assuming a comparable sense of responsibility. What may have been obscure in the deity becomes definite and concrete in the course of human action. Nomos manifests itself in various ways, themselves a mirror image of God's loving attitude. God being the creator, all men must revere him as their source. The human race could then return love for love, responding to God with the authenticity of creatures who recognize their derivative condition. Is this love? Possibly not, but reverence often turns into love; and in romanticism, love itself eventuates in a kind of reverence.

Actually, at this point nomos is neither more nor less than native piety: fidelity to one's beginnings, whatever they may be. And much of this certainly belongs to love. The pious man bestows upon his origin a value that appraisal could never have discovered in it. The free spirit will always see something arbitrary about the source of his being. Why limit one's identity to just this parent, this religion, this people, this country, this world, or even this God? Are any of them objectively perfect? The Jews had no reason to think so. The Christians, who say that God is perfect, believe that his being the creator gives a sufficient reason for man to love him. But creativity is no more reason than anything else. If the pious man loves God, he does so by bestowing a gratuitous value—as love always does. Instead of turning away from his beginnings, he accepts them with loyalty and spontaneous devotion. It is this element of love that the Christians learned from the Jews, via the concept I am calling nomos.

The feeling of piety has objective values that the Jews, like the followers of Confucius, were quick to recognize. Like the ancient Chinese, the Hebrews realized that no man attains integrity within himself if he denies his origins. Having come to where we are, from a source we never chose, may seem absurd: indeed it is. But the events can never be escaped, and anyhow history is nothing but the succession of these random occurrences. Until he accepts the factuality of the past, no one can live securely in the present or the future. This idea of Judaism underlies so much in Freud that I cannot believe his being born a Jew is wholly irrelevant. For the ancient Jews, piety was a social as well as a psychological necessity. Their life as a primitive people forced it upon them at every moment in their history. A nomadic tribe in a hostile land, they could not have survived otherwise. There cannot be national cohesiveness without patriotism; and patriotism always presupposes reverence for a common past. The actual events may not be glorious, but they will seem so once they symbolize the irrevocable unity of a single origin. The mute, routine, successive moments take on a retroactive importance; for now they represent the dynamics of time, without which the present community would not have come to be. The Bible itself performs this unifying function. In its mythic way, it transforms the disparate lives of scattered generations into the oneness of a chosen people. In their threatened condition the Jews obviously felt the need for some extraordinary means of tying children to their parents, parents to their tribe, freethinkers to the established but wholly fictional destiny of their nation. These bonds were not exclusive to the Jews: the daily necessities of family and social life forge something comparable in all men. But the Jews were especially imaginative in making durable links. And what could be more cohesive than pious love toward a God who jealously exacts the same total devotion from every member of the group?

Over and above the sentiment of piety, however, nomos is also a paying-back. Having received various gifts from God, the sensitive soul feels a need to express gratitude. Men have often thought that life itself was a debt they owed to their creators. The idea is odd, but very intriguing. Is nonexistence a peril from which the God or gods have rescued us? Is that the basis of our gratitude? "I thank whatever gods there be for my indomitable soul." (And are they to say: "You're welcome"?) The Muslim philosophers believed that God graciously created the world in order to save all things from the metaphysical evil of nonexisting. On the other hand, Plato thought that existence itself engendered evil. His attitude survives in the joke about two men discussing the good life. One man says he has enjoyed living, but if he had it to do over again he would prefer never to have been born. To which the other replies: "Ah, but who can be so lucky?"

But even if we do not agree with Plato, shall we give thanks to a God who created us in his own image (O, supreme narcissism!) without our being consulted and for reasons of his own? Beneath the gratitude for having been saved from nonexistence, perhaps there lurks a plea about the future, a hope that someday God will save us from the nonexistence of death. What looks like a paying back is thus a payment in advance. In either event, the response remains identical, and it is not the same as love. Loving another person must always be more than feeling gratitude. For what have we bestowed if we but give measure for measure? At the same time, the attitude may always turn into love. Paying to an inscrutable deity, paying in advance for we know not what, our gratitude may be a way of affirming the goodness of our benefactor. Our payment then expresses trust and confidence in the order of things and may even be a dedication typical of love in general.

Like the other concepts, nomos manifests itself in action. The pious Jew loves God by giving up the goods of life. How can this be done? One way is through rites of sacrifice—burning animals on an altar, for instance. This was a normal practice in Canaan, and the ancient Jews adopted it. By sacrificing something, one returns benefits the creator has magnanimously given. The act duplicates God's original gesture, indicating a comparable sense of love toward the recipient. In Genesis, God empowers man to take the life of nature and to use it for his own, as he sees fit. This murderous dominion the Jews exercised by killing animals for the sake of God. They would thus affirm that man has no final right to any of the benefits he enjoys. The goods of life come and go. Like the slaughtered beast, they are holy: but only in their relationship to divinity. And yet, the sacrificing of animals was not sufficiently radical for the Jews. If it had been, they might have suffered the historical fate of all their neighbors—themselves sacrificed to the march of other peoples. Instead, the Jews banished the practice of giving God material goods and required a more difficult expression of pious love. As the prophet Samuel says: "To obey is better than sacrifice, and to hearken than the fat of rams." Throughout their writings the prophets insist that God despises burnt offerings. He will accept nothing but adherence to his will, a spiritual submission that cannot be symbolized by the killing of animals.

Obedience to God's will is itself a kind of sacrifice. Instead of giving the choicest goods, one yields a part of one's natural freedom. Man's willfulness had propelled his tragic history from the very beginning. In their pristine state Adam and Eve were disobedient in the way that children are: through innocent love of what seems good. The sinfulness of disobedience is the first thing that they learn—it is *itself* the fruit of the tree of good and evil; and they learn it, as children do, by suffering a loss of goodness. In less innocent fashion Cain repeats the parental experience. He violates the forbidden tree by letting his own will decide who shall live and who shall die. That Abel was his brother hardly matters. If Cain had killed him at God's command, there would have been no sin. On the contrary, Abraham proves himself by refusing to believe that his preferences determine what is good or evil. He passes the test of piety by stifling a lesser love and obediently agreeing to slaughter his own son. But even Abraham is sacrificing only flesh and blood. Though dearer than any burnt offering, Isaac is still an animal on the altar. The upraised knife of Abraham may symbolize the painful necessity to obey; but in itself it effects a material rather than a spiritual privation. The latter involves more than just the willingness to slay a beloved child. It requires a death in the slaughterer's soul, a drying up of his God-given will. Only through absolute trust and total submission can willfulness be overcome. Only by the giving of *oneself* can God be properly loved.

Sacrificing the will may seem to be a crude way of expressing devotion, but it is not surprising in a people so powerfully motivated to survive. Though it strikes at brute tenacity, it also fortifies. Like the sacred fire, it cleanses without destroying. God himself had called the Jews "a stiff-necked people"; and yet he makes them a peculiar treasure to himself by teaching them how to obey. This he does by giving them the law. Obedience to God will henceforth mean obedience to his commandments. For in them the divine will has revealed itself. Loving God now becomes indistinguishable from living in accordance with his explicit rules of conduct. The pious man thereby accepts God as the source of his being and properly repays his many gifts. To a nation seeking harmony within and security without, the establishment of legal mandates emanating from an absolute authority is itself the greatest gift.

The idea that nomos means justice, righteousness, adherence to the laws is thus partly correct. Throughout the Old Testament—in Exodus, Leviticus, Deuteronomy, the Psalms, the Prophets—there pervades a sentiment not unlike the one that Socrates articulates in Plato's *Crito*. Given the chance to escape execution after having been tried and found guilty, Socrates refuses to leave prison. He argues that though he is innocent, his trial conformed to the laws of the state; and it is to them that his deepest allegiance goes. Personifying the Athenian laws and calling them his true parents, Socrates says it is they who really gave him life. If he were now to withhold total obedience, he would indeed be guilty of impiety as originally charged. Conservative as this may sound, in Socrates it was profoundly subversive. For obviously Socrates would not have accepted the laws unless his reason assured him of their goodness, the little voice inside always being free to say No. In the Old Testament, however, the attitude is really conservative. The commandments are *holy*. Their authority cannot be questioned by *anyone's* reason. They issued from the mouth of God, who with his finger inscribed them on the tables of stone. Was God advising man about the good life? Not at all. He was telling him how he *must* live. What sanction could be more ultimate? Reason cannot upset the commandments any more than it can change the laws of nature. Sheer, unmitigated obedience—this is what God requires of the loving soul.

How secure this Old Testament morality must have made the Jews feel! How little they must have known of any other security! Their devotion to the laws inoculates against the bitter doubts that reason always fosters. Certitude is a great human value, but one that questioning inevitably corrodes. The certainty through reason that Plato sought could satisfy only a Platonic philosopher. For ordinary mortals, thought is threatening in its uncontrollable freedom, and divisive in its contrary implications. Even a mathematical sum, so absolute in its inner form, is always liable to recount. By subordinating reason to obedience, the Bible offers the kind of peace that Greek philosophy continually shatters.

In other ways, too, Jewish nomos provides advantages not to be found in either Plato or Christianity. It renders justice as familiar as the image of God himself. It makes the sense of righteousness immediate, direct, visceral: as emotional perhaps as one's feelings toward mother or father or any other human authority. In Plato's moral philosophy, justice is the major concept, but it is rarely vital or concrete. The cardinal virtue, a grand principle discovered by dialectical reasoning, Platonic justice is merely the basis for valid arguments in ethics. It is not something to be felt. It does not live in the hearts of men. However Socrates may poeticize about the laws being his parents, he talks as a philosopher spinning out the cobwebs of reason. The abstract and purely discursive burden of his myth is always evident, as in Plato the goals of conduct are always utopian. But the Jews believed in the goodness of *this* world, and they fully expected to establish the kingdom of God on earth in a literal and palpable fashion. Their dream lives on in men like Karl Marx, that flame of moral indignation, that homeless wanderer seeking to change history by submitting to its changeless laws, forever guided by the ancient faith in a promised land within the confines of a temporal existence.

To the Jews, justice was not a blindfolded woman holding balanced scales—a fitting image of reason closing its eyes to the material world and aspiring toward nothing but abstract equity. To them justice was a means of responding to the presence of a personal lawgiver. God would not neglect what he had created, and neither would he refuse to administer its complex machinery. His voice was heard in every plea for righteousness. Nothing this direct and intimate can be found even in the Christian attitude toward justice. The major inspiration of Christianity is geared to God as a redeemer, not a legislator. Despite the Jewish overlay, Christianity remains utopian like Plato in reserving the Day of Judgment for another world, a world the Jews had scarcely believed in. In some respects the Anglo-Saxon love of professional life to which I have alluded owes more to Judaism than to anything else. For it is based on that sense of *immediate responsibility*, powerfully felt in practical circumstances, which Protestantism assimilated in its return to the spirit of the Old Testament.

Because it bears this emotional immediacy, nomos is always more than just obedience to laws. It is devotion to God *by means of* laws. If one thinks of nomos only as an interest in justice, one misconstrues the concept. It then belongs to an ethical code at best, and at worst to legalism. In either event one might call it a variety of love, but only as a linguistic courtesy—to show our own good will. What makes nomos an authentic element in love is something else: its being a total consecration, a commitment of the will, a dedication of oneself. Nowhere in the Old Testament is love *identified* with justice or righteousness. Unless one lived righteously, one could not love God: this is implied on every page, but it does not constitute a definition.

For nomos is not obedience itself so much as the *acquiescence* in obedience. It is man adhering so thoroughly to the will of God that breaking the enunciated commandments becomes a moral impossibility. Acting justly was not enough, and even the Pharisees would have denied that it was. The essential thing was to be just through a conformity of will, a loss of inclination to rebel, a bestowed acceptance of God's authority—complete, spontaneous, irrational trust.

"Hear, O Israel: the Lord our God, the Lord is one; and you shall love your God with all your heart, and with all your soul, and with all your mind, and with all your strength." This is the first of the Great Commandments above love. In it nomos articulates its kind of attitude. Discussing the occurrence of this commandment in Exodus and Deuteronomy, Santayana doubts that the word "love" is really appropriate. He sees nothing but an appeal to legal and tribal unity: "There is no suggestion of any inward or mystical love, of any consuming fire or transforming insight." And yet how forceful, how devastating is the nature of the appeal! Mystical it is not, at least not in the sense of promising absorption into the divine being or anything like the union between husband and wife. Nor is there anything sentimental about the first commandment. Loving the remote and awful God who created all things does not mean having warm feelings toward him. The attitude is closer to respect, a sense of deference before a prior being, just as another commandment enjoins us to honor our father and mother. The religious fellowship may be tenuous, but it is based upon the fear and trembling of men who confront their mortal fate. It is the will yielding to the authority of ultimate power and the legitimacy of unquestionable morality. The commandment humanizes these realities by demanding self-instituted submission, the giving of heart, soul, mind, and strength, the commitment of total allegiance which itself means unity with God. Certainly this is an inward, consuming, transforming love. Possibly it is the purest love, since it puts man into the hand of God without the assurance of any future beatitude. Having little or no conception of life after death, the Jews believed that God would dispose of all things in his own way and for the best. Man had only to rely on God's goodness of being. Indeed, what else *could* men rely on, since nothing was good or evil except by the Lord's inscrutable fiat? As they feebly marched into the huge moving vans the Nazis had fitted out as gas chambers, the old Jews chanted the "Hear, O Israel" to one another—triumphantly and almost joyously, overwhelmed perhaps to find themselves capable of accepting the divine order even in the face of *this*.

Possibly those who doubt that nomos is an element in religious love have been misled by its lack of sentiment. But feelings of the most diverse sort cluster about it: the fear of God, which helps man to make the painful sacrifice of his rebellious will; pride in God's achievements, as when the Psalms depict the beauties of the world, not that beauty matters in itself (as for the Greeks) but only because it manifests the creative powers of the Lord; adoration—even adulation—of God himself, these being verbal means of bestowing importance and disclaiming one's own willfulness. Obedience, acquiescence, trust, submission of the will provide the root meaning of nomos, but within a fluid context of feelings that enable man to acknowledge and reciprocate God's loving-kindness.

Though God was to be the principal object of love, he was not the only object. The prophets, who were social reformers as well as religious leaders, emphasized the commandment that later became the second of the two great ones: "Thou shalt love thy neighbor as thyself." This commandment does not supersede the first or in any way conflict with it. Both devolve from total obedience to God's intention and both presuppose the priority of nomos. Despite their moral enthusiasm, the prophets do not proclaim a nonreligious love of humanity—loving one's neighbor simply because he is another human being. The prophets offer themselves as men so thoroughly seized by the will of the Lord that they can transmit his word with something like its original authority. They speak in their own voices, but with God's message. Not having chosen their vocation, they can talk in ways that enunciate the divine will and not their own. Through the agency of nomos their very words are henceforth holy.

Inspired as the prophets may have been, their teaching led to philosophical questioning of the sort that appears in the Book of Job. The prophets had generally assumed that God, being a responsible monarch, would punish those who broke his laws and reward everyone who piously lived up to them. If Israel suffered, it could only mean that the nation no longer hearkened to God's will. The same would hold for individuals. But Job, a pious and a righteous man, is made to suffer terribly. From this most critics have concluded that the drama must be a *testing* of the prophetic assumptions. And to some extent this interpretation is right. The question of punishment recurs throughout the work, and the three friends of Job are obviously convinced that he is paying for some hidden sin. At the same time, however, we know from the very outset that God considers Job to be "a perfect and an upright man," that he is wreaking miseries upon him "without cause" and merely to prove to Satan that under no circumstances would Job lose faith. Moreover, Job wins the wager for God. When he loses his children, Job says: "The Lord gave, and the Lord hath taken away; / Blessed be the name of the Lord." When Job's body is covered with boils, he exclaims: "What! shall we receive good at the hand of God, / And shall we not receive evil?" Even in his final plea of innocence, Job does not renounce God. He only expresses painful confusion. And well he might, if—as the prophets said—God is too good to make any but the wicked suffer.

The drama ends by vindicating the prophets. Having passed through his trials, Job is fully reinstated. God gives him "twice as much as he had before"—with the suggestion that this latter bounty erases all the miseries he had undergone. What brings about this reversal of fortune? Is God rewarding Job for having won his wager, like a gambler paying off a victorious prize fighter? Possibly. But this is never indicated. And in any event, Job was not consulted about the sport in which he was to participate. He had expected rewards for living up to the covenant, for being righteous before the laws. Instead he was punished; and when his goods are finally restored, he is rewarded for something else. For what then? What indeed but sheer submissiveness! God takes care of the godly, just as the prophets had said, but now the requirements of godliness have been made more stringent. To be a *truly* pious man, one must be as patient as Job. Job earns God's favor by attaining a level of self-abnegation beyond anything he had previously experienced. In his closing speech he makes himself as abject as man can be. He accepts God's will *not* as a man who freely obeys but as a nonentity that suddenly realizes its nothingness. Having just heard the awful words of the voice out of the whirlwind, Job drops all pretense to an independent will. His obedience turns into subservience, and his acquiescence into self-hatred: "I had heard of thee by the hearing of the ear; / But now mine eye seeth thee./ Wherefore I abhor myself, and repent / In dust and ashes."

In other words, the Book of Job dramatizes nomos. The concept appears within the structure of the narrative, which finally presents it in an extreme formulation quite different from the one presupposed at the beginning. To love God one must obey his commandments, as Job did throughout his life. But now obedience to the laws is shown to be a mere preliminary. As I have suggested, nomos always involved an acquiescence that exceeded mere legalism. It was assumed, however, that obedience manifested the required acquiescence. This is what the Book of Job denies. It reinterprets nomos as a consecration *beyond* obedience. Conforming to God's will as expressed in the laws is not enough. One must undergo a self-abasement that virtually welcomes the visitation of evil as well as good. All conceivable prerogatives must be yielded. Not only must the will of man dry up: it must also turn to ashes. Before the august power of God, all things human are merely dust. The Deutero-Isaiah had said something similar: "All nations before him are as nothing; / And they are counted to him less than nothing, and vanity." But this prophet, unlike the others, believed in vicarious righteousness. He thought that it pleased the Lord to make the innocent suffer for the guilty, and therefore that his chosen few would be the righteous ones who bore the sins of others: "And the Lord hath laid on him / The iniquity of us all." However loving this God might be, his ways were not the ways of man and there was no searching of his understanding. One could only submit to his mysterious being, to that indefeasible "I AM THAT I AM" by which God had originally identified himself to Moses. It is from this aspect of Judaism that Christian nomos arises.

In a scene in the Gospel according to Mark, a doctor of the law interrogates Jesus. The scribe asks him which commandment stands first. Jesus answers by reciting the commandments to love God and to love one's neighbor. The scribe, now addressing Jesus as Master, replies that he has spoken truly. Jesus ends the discussion by telling the man: "You are not far from the Kingdom of God." From this exchange one may well infer that the Christian codification of the two Great Commandments was already a part of Judaism. When Jesus says, as in Matthew's version of the same incident, that on these commandments hang "all the law and the prophets," he is un- doubtedly preaching what his audience expected of a rabbi.*

In other ways, too, Jesus indicates that he has come to fulfill the Jewish tradition and that for him as for the prophets, love means submission to the dictates of a jealous (though benevolent) deity. Telling his people to forgive others, he warns that if they do not, "neither will your Father which is in heaven forgive your tres- passes." He even suggests that punishment and reward are to be meted out by some precise calculation. Presumably there is an actual code of divine legality, perhaps of the sort imagined by Dante: "For as you give, so you shall receive, measure for measure." The Chris- tian dogma of assigning heaven to those who love God properly, and hell to everyone else, is largely an extension into afterlife of what the Jews had all along expected on earth. Details such as a day of judgment and the resurrection of the body merely complete the symmetry. In Christianity, no less than in Judaism, are we admon- ished to fear God. Even the Jewish idea of love as a paying back

*In "The Testaments of the Twelve Patriarchs," written by a Pharisee about 108 B.C., the following precepts occur: "Love the Lord and your neighbor"; "Love the Lord through all your life, and one another with a true heart"; "Love ye one another from the heart; and if a man sin against thee, speak peaceably to him, and in thy soul hold not guile."

occurs in statements by St. Augustine, St. Bernard, and many other Christians who say that the most obvious reason to love God lies in the fact that he loved us first.

With all these continuities, however, Christian nomos belongs to its own stage of development. In its interpretation of the two Great Commandments, Christianity changes the concept of righteousness and so alters the conditions for obedience. Requirements of the law, such as dietary scruples or the minutiae of keeping the Sabbath, are now treated like other sacrifices that had already been superseded. These modifications serve two functions: they adjust the religion to the diverse customs of foreign peoples, and they simplify the attainment of salvation. That done, faith in Christ could easily be extended to the Gentiles. Since God created all men, there was no reason why only Jews should be able to love him.

Of even greater importance is the way in which Christianity reconstituted the notion of conformity. If obedience was not enough, as Job had learned, possibly this was due to something in the nature of obedience itself. Strictly speaking, the ability to obey depends upon a *repository* of will: some may be given up, but much is retained as the surety of one's moral involvement. For the early Hebrews, obedience to the deity was a means of establishing a man's identity as well as God's supremacy. In obeying God, man assumed responsibilities that strengthened his will in the very process of subjugating it. Job's self-abasement, however, is the annihilation of will. Perhaps it should no longer be called obedience, though it certainly eliminates the possibility of *dis*obedience. Nomos was being transformed, and in Christianity the change continues. Obedience in the earlier sense is often stated, but always subordinated to a selflessness even more devastating than Job's. For Job had merely bowed his head and ceased to wrestle with the spirit of the Lord. He was not expected to renounce his material interests. Without them he would never have suffered in the first place, but that is not the moral of the drama. Job must repent in dust and ashes. Once he has done so, the world is restored to him and his earlier attitude fortified not diminished.

As opposed to this, Christianity bids us to renounce the world entirely—as Jesus does in submitting to the passion of his death. The dying of the will must be complete and permanent, not partial or

momentary as in the case of Job. We are to "despise" nature and all
its works, putting it behind us like Satan. The Jewish God was jealous
lest other gods be placed ahead of him; but the Christian God is
jealous even of his own creation. He demands more than just allegiance, much more than just scrupulous obedience. Nothing on
earth must *really* matter to man. Human beings must care deeply
only for God. All else leads to treason. One cannot serve two mas-
ters, and the flesh is always weak. It is as if the soul of man were in a
state of siege. Martial law has been declared, all former freedoms
revoked. Primitive Christianity did believe that the day of judgment
was at hand. In the face of cosmic death how could anyone worry
about this transient world? In that glorious and catastrophic moment of history the universe would be destroyed, a new celestial
order established, and salvation awarded on a highly competitive
basis. Belief in the extinction of nature may only have been a wish-
fulfillment; but it obviously had the effect that approaching death
has on many people: the will shrivels up as if to lessen the imminent
blow, turning necessity into virtue, yielding man's involvement in
the physical world as a way of being reborn in the better one of spirit.

Total renunciation of the world is not humanly possible. However
far it may contract, the will remains until something external destroys it. Even the saints admit that perfect conformity to God
cannot be attained in this life. Are we to conclude then that the
Christian attitude is logically untenable? Possibly so. But not if we
see it as an idealization. As such, it glorifies a spiritual need: the need
to withhold final and ultimate love from anything as insubstantial as
physical or psychological reality. Words like "final" and "ultimate"
may be hard to define in this context, but in part they are designed to
render renunciation compatible with most of the vital attachments
man must have in order to exist. These natural interests are to
operate as instrumental devices, proximate and immediate but always subsidiary to the eventual love of God. The double nature of
Christian man is such that he must support two attitudes at once:
one, the major concern, despising the world, renouncing the will,
even hating oneself, insofar as this is required by absolute conformity; the other, a minor and temporary disposition, caring about the
world to a minimal degree, doing what is barely essential for sur-

vival, living in nature if only for the sake of having something to transcend. Though experience then takes on a piebald coloring, it need not be pathological. Even in asceticism, as most Christians have practiced it, renunciation is not necessarily a *revulsion* from life. Christianity, like Judaism, has characteristically maintained that all creation is good. How could it be otherwise, having come from a perfectly good creator? The world becomes abhorrent to the Christian only when it is loved for itself, apart from its source. For then the lesser interest pretends to be the greater. Only God is worthy of being loved for his own sake. Once that love has been achieved, the saint may return to the world, accepting it like himself and everything else, as an effect of God's creativity.

To the extent that a soul renounces the world, it opens its hand, unclenches the fist, allows all vestige of power to escape. In submitting to God, the soul automatically commits its fortunes to the material dictates of the very world it has renounced. The saint cannot buffet for his own. Can he even assert a moral authority? Morality tries to change the haphazard character of things, but the saint wishes to replace them altogether. Whatever good works he may do, he must ultimately prefer martyrdom. He must turn the other cheek, as a sign of indifference.

To the early Hebrews this attitude would have been unthinkable, even vile in its suicidal implications. For them the Garden of Eden, that *earthly* paradise, was still the goal of human endeavor. As in the myth of Aristophanes, they longed for the day when man would be restored to his primal unity within the benefice of nature. Originally Adam and Eve had been each other's alter ego, but once they fell it became necessary for men and women to labor in a hostile soil. This was for their own good, however, and by the proper use of religious influence they might someday be reinstated. That Christ would be a messiah announcing God's intervention, which would occur like the arrival of government troops during an Indian attack, the Jews could easily understand. Likewise the Second Coming, when the efficacy of the righteous and the futility of the sinners would finally reveal itself. What the Jews could not accept was the preliminary stage of self-transcendence through renunciation. Had not God made man in his own powerful image, giving him dominion over all the earth, enjoining him to be fruitful and to multiply? To turn away from nature, even partially, would seem to border on ingratitude and so *preclude* conformity of will. The Jews have rarely been ascetic. Their great men have dedicated themselves to a rational, responsible use of power, based upon a loving fidelity to the material world. Very little of the Jewish genius has gone into activities that detach themselves from nature. At least in the Western world, the sense of spiritual disintoxication (with all its varieties of idealization and aesthetic innovation) comes from the Greek side of Christianity, not from Judaism.

The Christian symbol of will repudiating its own power is, of course, Christ himself. What counts is not merely his nonviolence, or the fact that he renders unto Caesar what is Caesar's, or even that he refuses to invoke the hordes of angels who would readily free him from the cross. Equally important is the way he teaches his followers to pray. Preparing for the final agony, Jesus asks that the cup of imminent death pass from him, "nevertheless not as I will, but as thou wilt." In the suggestion that the two wills can possibly differ, the text seems to have reverted to the older notion of obedience. But Jesus is also the Christ, the Son of God, divinity engaged upon a mission wholly predestined in every detail. Surely we are not to believe that he is now requesting that the painful part be eliminated. Since Jesus is human as well as divine, it is natural for him to recoil from death. The prayer expresses this, but the preeminence of God's will shows that no petition is being made. Jesus is *not* saying that he wishes to go on living but is prepared to yield if God insists. He and God are one: their wills cannot diverge. In his capacity as a man he is free to vent an all-too-human preference; this, however, does not diminish his total renunciation of a separate will. The same applies to the Lord's Prayer, in which Jesus illustrates the correct manner of speaking to God. The second line reads "Hallowed be thy name," much as the Psalms might say "Be thou exalted." The words are a tribute to greatness and a bestowal of value. They illuminate what follows: "Thy kingdom come. Thy will be done in earth, as it is heaven." As an exhortation, all this would be ridiculous. There is no need to ask God to extend his dominion, and no one thinks that a human request is likely to encourage him. The prayer makes sense only as we realize that the speaker is himself "in earth," frightened by the possibility of having a will at variance with God's, and therefore eager to renounce it.

In its dependence upon renunciation, nomos also explains the Christian idea of forgiveness. The Old Testament was not lacking in references to mercy. The prophet Micah makes it a central part of the religious life: "And what doth the Lord require of thee, / But to do justly, and to love mercy, / And to walk humbly with God?" But "mercy" here scarcely means forgiveness: it is more like kindness, leniency, or sympathy with the downtrodden. In earlier books of the Bible, Exodus for instance, God cautions his people about driving too hard a bargain or coldly neglecting the poor. The Jews are to be merciful in *this* sense, but they have no authority to forgive those who have acted unrighteously. That kind of mercy could only come from God, which seems logical since he had given the law and only he could be in a position to vary its sanction. The Jews felt that God was not ruthless, that he would surely forgive them if they atoned sincerely, and possibly they comforted one another with this belief. But the actual stay of condemnation always lay in God's hands, not in theirs. They could not forgive one another any more than they could forgive themselves. For the Christians, however, this now becomes possible. The law itself is relegated to the world that one renounces. Why not forgive the sinner, since otherwise we magnify his erring will by giving it undue importance? I do not mean that the law was to be destroyed or neglected. When Christ addresses himself to its contents, he refuses to modify them by a jot or a tittle. In fact, he interprets several of the commandments more strictly than the scribes and Pharisees, whose righteousness he says must now be exceeded. At the same time, righteousness is treated as merely the operation of a human will; and, as such, it must be subordinated, transcended, spiritually renounced. When that happens, one is merciful toward the unrighteous in the sense of minimizing the importance of righteousness itself. Even the man who is pure enough to throw the first stone acts by virtue of his will. Ex hypothesi, we are all sinners—though some of us are righteous and some are not. Better then to recognize our joint condition, align ourselves with the unrighteous, and so forgive them.

In effect, this concept of forgiveness idealizes humility. When Christ tells us to forgive men their trespasses, he does not mean that prison terms should all be commuted and penal institutions razed. He means that we who are fortunate enough to live on the outside must not pretend to any ultimate superiority. Similarly, when he exhorts us to love our enemies, he does not expect us to stop annihilating them. If they are the enemies of God, they must be dispatched to the safekeeping of hell, and as rapidly as possible. In performing this service, however, we are not to assume that the love of God has thereby been achieved. For the soul to be one with God, it must elevate itself to so great a height of detachment that all earthly distinctions lose their magnitude. This height is the lowliness of humility in which Christian nomos consists. In Leviticus the commandment to love one's neighbor as oneself is obviously designed to *strengthen* the body politic by getting people to share their interests harmoniously; and it follows hard upon the commandment about equity, requiring judges to favor neither the mighty nor the poor. In the New Testament the same commandment is used to serve a totally different function. It now encourages men to *efface* themselves by mutual aid, to recognize their equal pettiness before God, to crawl into the spiritual kingdom side by side.

Throughout this revision in the concept of nomos, one senses increasing alienation from God the Father. He hardly appears in the New Testament, though Jesus speaks to him on many occasions. As a dramatic personage in human history, divinity takes the form of a wandering Son, who suffers and dies as we all do, rather than a powerful or supremely patriarchal Father. Through Christ, identification with the deity (hence, mystical union) becomes possible in a way that it never was for the Jews. The remote creator is still present to the religious consciousness, but worshiped less immediately than the Man-God who has come to earth. Even the practice of addressing God as "our Father" is now primarily a way of imitating and approximating the Son. The Jews had recognized that men accede more readily to the will of a divine person than to law alone. Christianity goes further. As if to compensate for its more radical renunciation, it imagines the highest love as identification with a humanoid aspect of the deity. As Christ submits to the law of nature in freely assuming the yoke of mortality, so may the saint aspire toward the final submission of holiness. It is as if men had outlived a stage of infantile dependence and now demanded participation in the God-head through an idealized embodiment of themselves. If they succeeded, that much of man which responds to spirituality would be godlike and immortal. This was more than the Jews had ever hoped for. They were satisfied with the kind of sanctity that comes from accepting one's inferior status and making the most of it. Giving more through humility, the Christians demanded a greater salvation. By means of love they might change their status and achieve something like equality with the Father. In being the symbol of submission, Christ became the ladder into divinity.

By teaching man to rise through self-abasement, Christian nomos augments human opportunity. It adds a subtler technique to the earlier forms of eros. But in its desire to crush the will and liberate the soul, perhaps the method is self-defeating. Has the spirit really advanced? Or merely experimented with a more drastic type of infantile delusion?

In trying to answer these questions, it will do no good to assume a priori that renunciation is simply impoverishment of the ego. Even Freud admits that some people find happiness by giving up the ordinary pleasures of sexuality in the name of religious love. He cites St. Francis of Assisi as one who "went furthest in thus exploiting love for the benefit of an inner feeling of happiness." Explaining how this is possible, Freud says that by "displacing what they mainly value from being loved on to loving," such people protect themselves against the disappointments of losing a beloved object. To avoid the frustrations of genital love, they inhibit their instinctual desires and prevent them from focusing on any human being. "What they bring about in themselves in this way is a state of evenly suspended, steadfast, affectionate feeling, which has little external resemblance any more to the stormy agitations of genital love, from which it is nevertheless derived." Leaving aside the question of derivation, what follows if we accept Freud's account? Certainly not that St. Francis of Assisi suffered from an impoverishment of the ego. On the contrary, Freud may be interpreted as showing how renunciation provides its own kind of happiness. Freud may be able to justify his condemnation of Christian love on other grounds, but his description of what a saint actually feels makes nomos sound like a rather fortunate type of sublimation.

Of course, Freud also uses health as a criterion of happiness. And he never suggests that St. Francis is healthy-minded. Since inhibited aims cannot be eradicated, genital interests remain: they join the unconscious. The happy feeling of the saint may therefore cover a cauldron of disabling frustrations. When these bubble over, the inherently neurotic condition becomes manifest. But if the cauldron never does come to a boil, how can we be sure that what goes on under the benign covering is undesirable? People vary greatly, saints as well as sinners. Unless we study the diversity of religious experience, as William James does, we have little basis for generalizing about the psychology of renunciation.

The work that James did was largely a sifting of empirical data. James thought that biographical and autobiographical descriptions of religious experience would reveal its inner constitution. At the time that he wrote, however, virtually no one had tried to analyze the concepts that govern the aspirations of a saint. As a result, the profound insights of James seem to flutter in a vacuum. By analyzing religious love as a cluster of idealizations, studying concepts such as nomos for the sake of their human import, we may eventually be able to further the research of the empirical psychologist. Once he knows how the relevant concepts structure a saint's world outlook, the psychiatric theorist can better determine who is really happy and who is not. Thus far, philosophy and the life sciences have barely begun to collaborate. When they do, their joint enterprise will be the making of a new world.

In relation to nomos, what strikes me as most significant is the way the concept reflects a need for order. The Greek word (which neither the Jews nor the Christians happened to use) signifies a purposive regularity. Heraclitus took nomos to mean a rational, lawlike ordering of all being. In a similar vein Plato assumed that the universe conformed to *laws* of reality: so much so that justice in the individual or the state had only to pattern itself after the essential orderliness of the cosmos at large. For the Jews and the Christians the presence of a fatherly God proved that the world was purposive. In legislating for the Jews, God revealed the metaphysical objectivity of moral goodness; in descending as Christ, he showed how love itself explained the being of everything. To the medieval mystics in particular, awareness of God's love meant recognition of an ultimate and irreducible design within the universe. Unless one conformed to it, one could never be authentically oneself or in tune with the nature of things.

The concept of nomos projects, therefore, an idealized demand for allegiance to reality. One can align oneself *with* the order of being or one can rebel *against* it. Satan burns and freezes in his own hatred because he refuses to conform. In him total rebellion is the same as absolute pride. Human beings face a similar choice, though the drama may be less grandiose. Ivan Karamazov rebels merely in offering "to give back the ticket to the universe." In being a nay-sayer, saying No to the way things are, he rejects the authority of the cosmic status quo. He becomes a rebel without a cause, for no cause can include the universe as a whole, and in the end he goes mad. By the nature of his commitment, the mystic is a yea-sayer. Whether it comes hard or easy, whether he has a sick soul or what James called a sky-blue temperament, he accepts all destinies. He sees in every-thing the systematic working of God and refuses to question it. He need not be a quietist: he may alleviate suffering and seek to change the world. But for him the world is not ultimate reality. What he changes he also renounces. The unchangeable, which is God, he loves with fervor and self-abnegation. This, I think, is what Margaret Fuller meant when she said: "I accept the universe." Carlyle replied: "She'd better!" But the joke is on him. For though we cannot fall out of the universe, we need never accept the way of things or see an order in them. To a mystic like Margaret Fuller, it is not enough to live in reality: one must also conform to it, agree wholeheartedly to what there is, say Yes despite all mysteries.

In articulating this need, nomos enables man to feel that he is duplicating the grand design within his own soul. The mystic emulates Christ by sacrificing himself. Through an act of will he destroys his own willfulness. In this there is much pain, but the suffering creates a sense of oneness with God. In making such conformity possible, nomos idealizes the element of submissiveness in all love. To love another person is to give ourselves, if only in the act of bestowing value upon him. We submit to the other in the sense that we no longer use him for wholly selfish purposes. In caring about the beloved, the lover subjugates his impulse to dominate; in valuing her separate identity, he curtails the inclination to aggress and destroy; in being concerned about *her* welfare, he denies that much of the purposive life which thinks only about advantages to oneself. Even in making his attitude predominantly a bestowal, the lover renounces the exclusiveness of appraisal. He gives up a significant portion of the will: the part that leads to cruelty, to egoism, to self-assertion, to the madness of enslaving people as one would master things.

The willful man is incapable of loving persons. For he wishes to use them in a way that defeats their autonomy. He treats them as merely a means, and so he will not submit to their individuality. In bidding us to renounce, nomos idealizes that nay-saying to ourselves which is essential if we are to say Yes to anyone else. But then the Christian magnifies this attitude into a cosmic response. The loved one is now a person with infinite authority. He establishes an order in all things, and we express our love by yielding to it. We are even to die in our independent will as a means of eliminating willfulness. Nothing less will satisfy the mystic. He requires a *total* renunciation, much more than love itself involves, a limitless devotion directed toward a limitless person. And yet, there may be no such person—either in or out of the universe; and certainly the life of man makes the desired renunciation a contradiction in terms.

Nevertheless, the mystical attitude may survive its own paradoxes. For regardless of what he says, the mystic continues to will the loss of will. And though there be none outside, he may then create a loving order within himself. He may thereby lose his sense of willfulness and feel a union with divine authority. In loving as he does, the mystic will experience his own love as the reflection of one unutterably superior. This love he may call agapē, love radiating from God and in some sense being God.

Is the mystic living in delusion? Perhaps. But in considering that possibility, let us first examine the idealizations built into the concept of agapē.

13
Agapē: The Divine Bestowal

IN THE FAMOUS COURTROOM
scene in *The Merchant of Venice*, Shakespeare counterpoints love and
justice. Shylock the Jew wants justice done against Antonio his
debtor. Portia, defending Antonio, begs Shylock to be merciful.
When Shylock replies, "On what compulsion must I? Tell me that,"
she recites her speech about mercy. Her lines augment our revulsion
toward the creditor who keeps demanding a pound of flesh, but
actually they may serve as condemnation of the Christians in that
scene as well as the Jew. For though Shylock is odious, so too are
those who use the law to deprive him of his wealth. Shyster that she
is, Portia does not act mercifully toward Shylock. It is in the name of
justice, not love, that she finally crushes the old man: measure for
measure. By the end of the scene Portia has long since forgotten her
famous speech, and (despite some minor leniencies) so have the
other characters. But the audience does not forget it. The speech
lingers as a commentary upon the action. It reminds us that what
people say is not what they do and that cruel persons often speak of
love. Even we, though we pity Shylock, cannot help but enjoy seeing
him hoist with his own petard. As a result, only the speech remains
untrammeled by the experience. And well it might. For if we substitute the word "love" for "mercy," it expresses the Judaeo-Christian
ideal of agapē with uncanny precision. The remainder of this chapter may be taken as a gloss upon the following:

The quality of mercy is not strain'd;
It droppeth as the gentle rain from heaven
Upon the place beneath. It is twice blest:
It blesseth him that gives and him that takes.
'Tis mightiest in the mightiest; it becomes
The throned monarch better than his crown;
His sceptre shows the force of temporal power,
The attribute to awe and majesty,
Wherein doth sit the dread and fear of kings;
But mercy is above this sceptred sway,
It is enthroned in the hearts of kings,
It is an attribute to God himself;
And earthly power doth then show likest God's
When mercy seasons justice. Therefore, Jew,
Though justice be thy plea, consider this—
That in the course of justice none of us
Should see salvation;* we do pray for mercy,
And that same prayer doth teach us all to render
The deeds of mercy.

The concept of agapē does not occur in isolation. It makes no sense apart from nomos and philia, and it serves as a response to the entire attitude of eros. In its own way, agapē is the reverse of nomos. Through nomos man loves God in a total commitment of the self. Through agapē God loves man (and everything else) in a free bestowal of unlimited goodness. Agapē precedes man's love and excels it in every respect. Agapē is God giving himself, descending as the gentle rain from heaven, in acts of love that man reciprocates by renouncing the will. As the bond that establishes a fellowship between divine and human, agapē creates philia. As the ultimate fact about the universe, agapē makes eros possible. Unless God had loved him first, man could never ascend toward that perfect good-

---

*Cf. Psalm 130: "If thou, Lord, shouldest mark iniquities, / O Lord, who shall stand?"

ness which defines the end of desiring. Eros belongs to nature, particularly human nature: it is man loving God by striving for him. Agapē is God suffusing all things with spontaneous, unbounded love. It may possess a man, but it cannot be possessed by him. In varying degrees, agapē sustains the being of everything. Without it, nothing could have existed at all.

The concept of agapē idealizes bestowal, and in Christianity it divinizes love. Therein lies the philosophical greatness of the New Testament, which proclaims—not uniquely, but with singular force—that love is the supreme virtue encompassing all others. So marvelous indeed that it *must* be holy, supernatural, the essence of the deity. Galileo said that with a lever long enough he could move the earth from the moon. To the Christian, love is itself an infinite lever, moving the universe from all eternity, making everything to be as it is. Eros was merely the spirit of movement within the world. But agapē is the Holy Spirit, the spirit of God himself, active in the world and yet belonging to another realm. No greater monument to the fact of bestowal has ever been created. And though this type of valuation requires subtler analysis than any supernatural religion allows, its presence in the Judaeo-Christian tradition first makes the love of persons into a philosophical concept. Without the notion of agapē, Western thinking about love would not have advanced beyond Aristotle's modifications of Plato.

Nevertheless, nothing is ever wholly new in the history of ideas. Everything has been anticipated by something earlier in human thought. The concept of agapē is no exception. The idea that God's love comes first, that it is fortuitous and unmerited, occurs early in the Old Testament. God chooses Israel as the bearer of his covenant for no reason discernible to man. In Deuteronomy, God reminds the Jews that he has not singled them out because of any original excellence on their part. What he does for them he could as easily have done for any other people. In short, they are to serve as an example of free bestowal as well as the proof of God's continuing love. In his definitive study of Judaism, George Foot Moore discusses Jewish agapē as follows:

> Not only does [God] freely forgive, but he gives [the Israelites] merit that they have not earned. When he showed

Moses all the treasuries of merit prepared for the righteous, one for those who give alms, one for those who provide for orphans, and so on, Moses saw one large treasury and asked whose it was. God replied: To the man who has (merit), I give of his own; and on him who has none I bestow gratis, as it is written, "And I will show favor to whom I will show favor" (Exodus 33, 19).

It should be remarked, further, that "a lot in the World to Come," which is the nearest approximation in rabbinical Judaism to the Pauline and Christian idea of salvation, or eternal life, is ultimately assured to every Israelite on the ground of the original election of the people by the free grace of God, prompted not by its merits, collective or individual, but solely by God's love, a love that began with the Fathers. For this national election Paul and the church substituted an individual election to eternal life, without regard to race or station.

These facts are ignored when Judaism is set in antithesis to Christianity, a "Lohnordnung" [a system based on rewards] over against a "Gnadenordnung" [a system based on grace.] "A lot in the World to Come" is not wages earned by works, but is bestowed by God in pure goodness upon the members of his chosen people, as "eternal life" in Christianity is bestowed on the individuals whom he has chosen, or on the members of the church. If the one is grace, so is the other.

Though conceiving of God's love as a sheer bestowal, the Jews also insisted that man earned salvation through righteousness. As Moore points out: "All the good things God promised in this world or the world to come were conditioned upon conformity to his righteous will as revealed in the Law." By maintaining that salvation, too, is a product of God's inscrutable love, the Christians revised the concept of agapē. The divine bestowal could now show itself in the sacrificial descent of Christ. This event not only cleansed the world of sin, but also revealed that God and love were one. The Jews had idealized bestowal; the Christians divinized it. The Jewish God was a loving person. He showered goodness upon man and glorified himself in Israel. The Christian God was love itself. This idea could not have come from the Old Testament, but it permeates the Hellenistic world and belongs to Neoplatonism as well as the Greek mystery religions. That God's bestowal was an outpouring of divine energy the Hindus had already suggested in the concept of *lilla*—the cosmic dance, the play of God shimmering through all the movements of the world. And in the *Bhagavad-Gita* God identifies himself as the source of all bestowed value: "Whatsoever is glorious, good, beautiful and mighty, understand that it goes forth from out of a fragment of my splendor."

Similarly, the idea of man possessed by divine love could have come from any number of predecessors. The mysteries of Dionysus and Orpheus, which Herodotus traces to the Egyptians, culminated in a state of ecstasy as the god entered into the supine soul. As Erwin Rohde has remarked, the Orphic sect believed that salvation came to persons possessed by Dionysus, that this could happen only through the revelation and mediation of the man-god Orpheus, and that mortals could facilitate the process by means of total submission: "Not his own power, but the grace of the 'releasing gods' is to be the cause of man's liberation." So too among the Jews, the Spirit of the Lord fell upon certain individuals, possessing them wholly and investing them with wonderful powers. Samson possessed could act with the virtuous anger of a god, and Isaiah wrote the words of divinity through direct inspiration. The prophets in general were thought to be possessed by sudden visitations of the Lord. They differed from the neighboring priests of Canaan, who also underwent ecstatic trances, in denying that they could *initiate* God's condescension. Unlike their pagan colleagues, the prophets also denied that possession assured personal salvation. It was for them God's way of using a man as the vehicle for his design. As if at random, God would choose some hapless mortal, enter his soul miraculously, transform him into a trumpet of indignation or a battering ram of action.

Even the idea that God descends for reasons of *love* was fully prepared for. In many primitive religions the masculine divinity (God the Father) is the sky or the sun. At appropriate times—such as the rainy season—he comes down to possess Mother Earth in sexual intercourse. Ceremonies that occur on such occasions are described by one anthropological writer in ways that richly suggest various elements of Christian dogma: "During the ceremonies the sun is

supposed to come down into the holy fig tree to fertilize the earth.*
To facilitate his descent, a ladder with seven rungs is considerately
placed at his disposal. It is set up under a tree and adorned with
carved figures of the birds whose shrill clarion heralds the approach
of the sun in the east."

From Greek mythology we are all familiar with stories about gods
and demigods descending to earth on some amorous mission. In the
form of a swan Zeus takes possession of Leda; as an eagle he swoops
down on the boy Ganymede; as a holy bull he carries off Europa; as a
column of sunbeams he immaculately fertilizes Danaë. In a slightly
varied context, more useful for the practices of the Eleusinian
mysteries, Aidoneus seizes Persephone, daughter of Demeter the
earth goddess, and drags her underground to the Halls of the Dead.
In these myths love is mainly masculine sexuality, and it generally
expresses itself in a rape of the helpless female. Nevertheless, the
stories are not just erotic fantasies. As in more sophisticated religions, the recipient of love prefigures nature, including human
nature, dependent upon external visitation for its fruitfulness and
indeed for its very being. Nor is the rape simply brutal. Ravished by
the god, a woman becomes holy and her offspring partly divine. To
be touched by ultimate powers was frightening, awesome, to the
Greeks as much as the Hebrews. But it was also a condescension that
raised man and promised immortality.

With all this anticipation, and more, the Christian concept of
agapē is nevertheless original. Through it the New Testament introduces a philosophy of love that would eventually become a profound and comprehensive ideology. We may see the transition by
comparing the story of Christ with that of Prometheus, whom he
resembles in some respects. Like Christ the Man-God, Prometheus
is an intermediary, a Titan who associates with the Olympian deities
without really being one of them. For no reason other than obscure

---

*Because of its shape and softness the fig was often used by primitive
peoples to symbolize the female sex organs. (In Italian the word *fica* still
serves that function.) Does this bit of primitive symbolism throw any light on
the strange incident in the New Testament where Jesus curses the green but
as yet barren fig tree?

love, he bestows fire and "the gift of understanding" upon mankind. In bringing the spark of divinity to earth, Prometheus takes upon himself sufferings he could easily have avoided. He willingly undergoes them for the salvation of man and is finally chained to a rock, much as Christ is nailed to a cross. In Aeschylus' *Prometheus Bound*, the Chorus, who themselves benefit (as human beings) from his self-sacrifice, condemn Prometheus for having honored mortals excessively, and out of pride or sheer willfulness—just the sentiments of the mob on Calvary toward the man who, though mortal, spoke and acted as if he were God. As a leitmotif within the ruling theme, Aeschylus introduces the character of Io. She has refused the nocturnal visits of Zeus, has somehow remained a virgin, and now suffers punishment for having rejected the god's love. Like the Wandering Jew, she must forever be homeless—as all people are once they alienate themselves from sustaining powers.

These points of resemblance between Aeschylus and the New Testament must not be magnified. They should interest us precisely because Christ and Prometheus are so very different. Prometheus acts out of love, giving men the greatest goods of life. But he is not God or the Son of God, and his love for man is motivated by his hatred of Zeus. Moreover, he belongs to hero myths rather than cosmological ones: his behavior explains the origins of man, but it does not account for the nature of the universe. In Christianity, however, the love that issues through Christ reveals the meaning of everything. Within the aesthetic dimensions of a moving narrative, agapē provides a complete doctrine of love triumphant—in reality, if not in appearance. Father and Son are one; they are bound by a progression of love; divinity descends to earth for no aggressive or personal reason, but solely to create further goodness. Through the mystery of his passion, the Son takes away the sins of mankind. He teaches others how to love by undergoing self-sacrifice. Even to immerse himself unnecessarily in this world of bitterness and mortality is to reveal the nature of true devotion. In general, the only abiding reality is the permanent love flowing from a purely nonmaterial God. His agapē belongs to a deeper dimension than physical being. It is a constant outpouring of perfection, a spiritual energy, a transcendental field of force active through all eternity. In divinizing bestowal, Christian agapē eliminates the carnal crudities of primitive thinking. Could it have done so without the example of Platonic idealization? There, too, the nature myths of earlier generations are transformed and given a spiritual message. In both cases the universe that emerges from the idealization is one of peace, order, perfection, and manifest beauty. In both cases love—whether eros or agapē—creates a blissful harmony within the otherwise chaotic soul of man.

In his great scholarly work on agapē, Anders Nygren describes its content in terms of four points basic to Christianity.

First, agapē is spontaneous and unmotivated. By this, Nygren means that love arises for no reason external to the nature of God. Love is not generated by any *desire* for an object, regardless of how good that object may be. In the eros tradition love was always the striving for goodness, and therefore limited to beings who are deficient in some respect. The gods, complete within their total perfection, loved nothing because they desired nothing. With the Christian God all this changes. He too is perfect and presumably beyond desire, but *his* perfection consists in love itself. *Because* he is infinitely good, indeed the principle of goodness, God loves without motivation. His love issues spontaneously from his very nature as a perfect being. Even nomos and philia are motivated by man's need to respond to God's prior goodness. Only agapē is unmotivated and spontaneous. It simply radiates, like the glorious sun or the universe at large, giving forth energy for no apparent reason. Such love transcends the powers of any finite creature—particularly man, so painfully bound to the wheel of causation.

Second, in Nygren's enumeration, agapē is indifferent to value. Not only is God's love uncaused, but also it bloweth where it listeth. As it does not involve a search for goodness, neither does agapē direct itself exclusively toward goodness. It is indiscriminate, unconcerned about the prior value of what it chooses as its object. The worthless, the sinful, the evil may receive God's love as readily as the holy and the upright. The quality of mercy is not strained. "He maketh his sun to rise on the evil and on the good, and sendeth rain on the just and on the unjust." In saying this, Jesus refers to more than God's infinite mercy: he is also describing a love that excludes appraisiveness. To agapē, considerations of objective value, inherent goodness or badness, are no longer relevant. Whence the images of sunshine and rain. For they originate at a great height, are not elicited by the objects upon which they fall, and do not withhold themselves from anything. It is as if God's perfection so tremendously exceeded the goodness of even the best human beings that a nice discrimination between the just and the unjust was hardly worth making. This, in turn, can be taken two ways. One could say that all men are sinners to some extent, but also that all sinners are men made in the image of God and so equal recipients of divine love. In either event, the concept of agapē shows a side of God that transcends the difference between good and evil. Though the sinners reject *him*, God does not withdraw his love. And though the righteous will be rewarded, God's love is not motivated by their righteousness.

Third, agapē is creative. Judaism consistently maintained that God created all things with a good intent—with the benevolence of loving-kindness, and with something like paternal love. In giving the commandments, God also created justice. Did he create good and evil as well? This might seem to be implied, but the Old Testament speaks ambiguously about the source of values. In the Garden of Eden the serpent claims that God forbids the tree of knowledge to Adam and Eve because it will open their eyes: "And ye shall be as gods, knowing good and evil." Possibly, then, God did not create values, but only recognized their eternal character. Such was the view of the Greeks. In Plato the demiurge creates the world with an eye to the prior perfections laid out in the realm of forms. Since the Good was dialectically the highest of these, the eventual product would be the best the demiurge could manage, given the recalcitrance of matter. Of course, the demiurge was a limited being. By the time of Christianity, however, Western man was ready to believe in an omnipotent creator. The Christians combined this idea with the Greek belief in goodness as the highest form. The Good became one of God's infinite attributes, and its being henceforth depended upon the uniqueness of his personality. It then followed that God created values, along with everything else. And since God made everything through love, his innate agapē would be the ultimate source of goodness. To the extent that God's love radiated the universe, all things were good. Without his love, nothing would have any value.

The Greeks had thought that the human soul was a divine spark cast off from the realm of forms, temporarily imprisoned in matter but inherently good and godlike. In later Jewish sects, e.g., Hasidism, the same idea recurs as a way of explaining man's likeness to God. It also appears in the Platonistic aspects of Christianity. But more characteristically, Christian doctrine holds that nothing in the world, not even the human soul, is intrinsically valuable. Only God's loving fiat creates goodness. The Jewish sense of power and the Greek sense of value are thus united. Agapē can be indifferent to any apparent value of an object because in itself no object really has any value. Things are objectively good only as they are touched and transformed by God. His love makes them to be good as well as to exist. Consequently, the righteous man is not *truly* worthy except as agapē wills it; and even sinners *become* worthy once agapē has descended upon them. Love literally washes their sins away. As Luther puts it: "Rather than seeking its own good, God's love flows forth and bestows goods. Therefore, sinners are attractive because they are loved; they are not loved because they are attractive." In all this, great mysteries remain; but now they are the mysteries of creative love.

Fourth, agapē is the initiator of fellowship with God. Here too Christianity resembles its Jewish antecedents, but also differs. In the Old Testament, God often takes the initiative toward establishing relations with human beings. He puts Adam and Eve into a lovely garden, walking there in the cool of the evening as much to assure them of his presence as to enjoy the paradise himself. Later he appears on earth in various forms and takes men like Moses into his confidence. He even raises the prophets toward his celestial throne. But despite the graciousness of these acts, they do not provide salvation or the kind of fellowship Christianity was seeking. For the Jews, as for the Buddhists, man had to work out his own salvation: in diligence, through works of righteousness and the self-purification that comes from a contrite heart. When God made the covenant and gave the commandments, he but set the stage. The drama consisted of man's struggle with his rebellious will, man's problematic effort to live up to God's expectation. In this respect the Jewish conception was similar to the Greek. The Platonic gods have no eros because they are not in need of salvation. Though the demiurge created the world, human beings did the work of saving it.

These views are deeply humanistic; but Christianity arose because men had begun to despair. The Christian doctrine is theocentric in a way that neither Judaism nor Greek philosophy was. It maintains that only agapē can bring salvation, for that depends upon the fellowship which only infinite power makes possible. As a divine force, Christian agapē operates through all history and all eternity. It descends to all men at all times: it is not limited to moments in the past or the lives of chosen individuals. It constantly saturates, drawing souls toward God by infusing them with his essential goodness. In creating fellowship, however, agapē acts with varying intensity. When the soul is summoned to the first heaven, St. Bernard speaks of its being "led up." But when it mounts into the third heaven—as in the case of St. Paul—the soul is *raptus*, "seized" or "caught up." Of course, agapē does not have this effect for most people. The sun is always shining, but clouds often intervene. Nevertheless, agapē reaches in every direction, offering that union with God which all men desire but none—not even the best—can initiate.

Throughout this unfailing shower of God's love, several occasions take on special importance. As through agapē the world was created and all things in it, so too for each man's existence: his birth, his growth, his sustenance in being. The newborn child is baptized, dipped in holy water (the gentle rain), to symbolize his immersion in God's love. That a man should be what he is, living when and how he does, issuing out of the nothingness that precedes birth—what could be more baffling to the human mind? To *realize* that the something of one's being is surrounded by an infinite nothing is to sense the greatest of wonders. Christianity expresses this gratuitousness of all existence by seeing everything as a gift, a spontaneous and unmerited bestowal, God's mysterious way of loving. Once man has lived in the world, once he has sinned and suffered and felt the need for salvation, he further recognizes his dependence upon agapē. Without God's miraculous aid, no man could ever achieve his mystical aspiration—or even embark upon it. St. Augustine's ideas about divine grace are addressed to these occasions of agapē, and I shall return to them in the next chapter. But most significant for Christianity is the Passion. For then agapē shows forth vividly to human eyes, occurring as the climax of terrestrial history, so greatly charged with supernatural glory that mere faith in its semihuman embodiment assures salvation.

As the epiphany in time of God's eternal love, agapē descending through Christ establishes the final category of Christian belief. I associate it with that line from Thomas Nash's poem: "Brightness falls from the air." In their splendid ambiguity these words can refer to a loss of godliness, as when Lucifer was cast headlong out of heaven, or else to its manifestation in the coming of Christ. That divinity should incarnate itself as a man, that he should be born to woman ("between urine and faeces," as St. Augustine said of birth in general), that he should demean himself still further by an attitude of lowliness, that he should submit to painful crucifixion between two thieves—to non-Christians, this could only sound like the *loss* of godliness and not its manifestation. Christ crucified could only be, as St. Paul says, "unto Jews a stumbling-block, and unto Gentiles foolishness."

For those who believed, however, the Passion revealed once and for all the nature of agapē: "Hereby know we love, because he laid down his life for us." The Passion is also God's final effort to cleanse the world of sin. Originally the Jews had sought redemption by sacrificing burnt offerings. Then they were to sacrifice their willfulness through obedience. This much could be achieved by man alone. But when the Christians went further, changing nomos into total self-sacrifice, man required new miracles from above. Christian nomos inherently exceeds human capacity: and so God's great love must lead to a sacrifice of *himself*. Like the king or the priest who incarnates the vegetation god and dies in rituals that renew the life of nature, Christ becomes his own holy scapegoat. But as self-sacrifice is now a means of expressing divinity instead of losing it, the

Passion seeks to remind us of a life that transcends nature: "For God so loved the world that he gave his only begotten Son, that whosoever believeth in him should not perish, but have everlasting life." Is that life a resurrected continuation of what we already know through nature? Yes, in part, but also spiritually revised. Once Christ has cleared the air, nothing can intervene between man and God's agapē. The everlasting life is brightness itself.

The word *agapē* appears only a few times in the Synoptic Gospels (Matthew, Mark, and Luke). The concept is not made explicit in these writings, but at least two of the parables suggest it.

In one parable the Kingdom of Heaven is likened to a landowner who hires laborers for his vineyard. Some he hires early in the morning, but then as the hours pass he finds others who are unemployed and eager to work for the remainder of the day. In the evening the employer arranges the men *inversely* to the number of hours they have worked. He pays first those who came last, and last those who came first. All of them receive the fixed wage originally offered in the morning. When those who have worked long hours and borne the heat of the day argue that they should be rewarded more than the newcomers, the landowner replies: "My friend, I am doing you no wrong. . . . Take your due and go. It is my pleasure to pay this man who came last the same as you. May I not do what I like with my own people? Or are you jealous because I am good?"

The other parable recounts the story of the prodigal son. A man who has two sons agrees to divide his property between them. The elder stays at home and works by his father's side. As in many folk tales, the younger goes away, squanders his fortune recklessly, and then faces starvation unless he comes back. He says to himself: "I will set out and go to my father and say, Father, I have sinned against Heaven and yourself. I am no longer worthy to be called your son. Treat me as one of your hired men." The son returns home and utters the words he has prepared. Instead of being castigated, he is treated with extreme hospitality. The father clothes him with the best robe in the house, puts a ring on his finger and sandals on his feet, orders the fatted calf to be killed, declares a general feast. The elder son, working in the fields, hears the sounds of merriment but refuses to join the celebration. When his father pleads with him, he retorts: "All these years I have slaved for you and never disobeyed you once. Yet you never gave *me* a kid so that I could enjoy myself with my friends. But here comes that son of yours, when he and his harlots have got through your estate, and for him you kill the fatted calf!" His father replies, "My boy, you are always with me, and all I have is yours. But we *had* to make merry and rejoice, because your brother here was dead and came to life, he was lost and he is found."

Both parables are odd and intentionally paradoxical. They violate common sense; they seem to make a point of flouting elemental morality. Above all, they go against the appraisive attitude toward values and contradict the habits of purposive life. Is it not right and fitting that those who work harder should benefit more? How can the landowner expect to recruit workers in the morning if those who arrive toward evening are sure to receive equal pay? And how can the father hope to chasten the prodigal son by virtually rewarding his waywardness? Indeed, how can he know that the elder will not be corrupted by the example of his younger brother's success? Surely no society could be organized along these lines. Of course, with a bit of casuistry we *could* tidy up the human relationships: the landowner does not *guarantee* that he will be generous each time; the father can always discipline the prodigal son *after* celebrating his homecoming, etc. These details are omitted from the Gospels, and for good reason. The parables are not interested in the principles of political economy, which must be renounced like the world as a whole. Instead, they serve to illustrate the loving attitude which constitutes the kingdom of heaven.

In the first parable we see the superabundant goodness of agapē. Though some of the workmen are dissatisfied, the landowner has actually paid out more than anyone expected. He has not cheated those who came early; he has merely bestowed an unforeseen generosity upon those who came late. He does this because he enjoys being generous; it is in his nature and anyhow his resources are obviously endless. But then why not give *still* more to those who grumble and to whom extra payment seems to matter so much? Would this not have been *truly* bountiful? Possibly, but it is essential to the story that even those who get more than they deserve get only as much as the others. For in being indiscriminate, God's love must be uniform, as well as free and unmotivated. It falls equally upon those who have labored hard (the righteous) and those who have not. To all who remain his children and do his work as best they can, God graciously extends a like reward.

When we consider that in the parable (as in life) money symbolizes love, further intricacies appear. In complaining about their payment, the men are really saying that God has not loved them enough. And that is what the parable wishes to rebut. For God gives all of the men an equal opportunity to work, i.e., to live profitably. In this he has already loved them and assured the possibility of their salvation. Moreover, questions about payment are largely extraneous. The landowner's generosity is internal to *his* nature, since it defines his character, but external to the workmen *as* workmen. To benefit from their lives, they need only concentrate upon the inner demands of the job itself. That one kind of work or one period of labor should yield the goods that come with money more easily than another, is purely fortuitous. We may rationalize such discrepancies by citing facts about the economy. But this will always seem ad hoc: for in a different system of values, or another world, the facts would not be the same. To the dedicated workman it will always be a matter of humorous luck that payment should be as it is. He will shrug his shoulders and try to get more out of the labor itself. If the grumblers had truly loved their work, would they have felt an injustice in not receiving more money? They might even have thought themselves amply rewarded by the opportunity to put in extra hours. Their complaints prove that the Lord's work was merely a burden to them and that they have not realized the love he was affording them all day long.

In its context, the parable serves as a warning to the faithful: they are not to expect payment in proportion to either their godliness or their righteousness before the law. To a man who acts out of love, the inherent goodness of his life will always seem sufficient; he will not begrudge the benefits God freely bestows on others. The parable occurs immediately after the disciples ask what they shall get in heaven for having renounced the world and followed Christ. They learn that the first shall be last and the last shall be first, which is how the workmen in the story receive their wages. If we assume from this that those who are humble on earth will be elevated in heaven, so that renunciation pays off in the long run, we cheapen the Christian message. The valleys are raised and the mountains lowered, and all that results is either a meaningless substitution or a vulgar leveling. Since the parable is addressed to the disciples—who have just been proclaiming their own righteousness—I think it means that though they are among the first in humility, they must not expect to be the first in heaven. Indeed, how humble can they be, if they are calculating advantages or questioning God's eventual dispensation? Thus, within a story about agapē, the teaching comes as a gentle reproof. It reminds the faithful that no one has a prior right to salvation and that God's love depends on him alone.

In the second parable the situation is quite different. We can make only rough parallels between the older son and the workmen who come early, the younger son and those who come late, and the father and the landowner. For in the parable of the vineyard, everyone is righteous. The laborers all do their work from the moment they happen to be hired, and the landowner is simply a generous man. In the other parable, however, everyone is suspect. The younger son is obviously a sinner, possibly a rogue and a cheat. He seems to be wily and unrepentant, mechanically reciting the speech he has memorized because he knows it is what his father would like to hear. The older son may not be a sinner, but neither is he beyond reproach. Far from rejoicing at his brother's safe return, he will not attend the celebration even as a matter of form. He disassociates himself from the father's attitude of love and forgiveness. He clearly hates his younger brother.

And what about the father? He does not seem wholly spotless either. Unlike the landowner, he does not give equal payment. One senses an unfair predilection for the younger son—"that son of yours," as the elder calls him. One feels that in the past as in the present the father spoiled the boy with lavish preferment, and even that his great tenderness in seeing the prodigal return arises from a secret sense of guilt for having reared him badly. The parable leaves all this unstated. But the fact remains that the father is now affording the younger son pleasures he would never have allowed the older. Nor should we forget that the celebration comes out of the estate of the elder brother, who has not even been consulted. The father had already divided his property; the younger having dissipated his share, everything that remains must belong to the older. How chilling to hear the father tell him, "All I have is yours." We know that, strictly speaking, the father has nothing; he has given it all away but apparently retains control. By comparison, how noble the older son now appears if, as he says, he has continued to slave for the father and not once disobeyed him.

But if this reading is correct, how does the parable illustrate agapē? I think it does so by virtue of the father's attitude toward each of the brothers. Upon the prodigal he lavishes goods beyond all expectation. His loving gesture arises spontaneously, unmindful of what the younger son may or may not be worth. His love gushes forth, as if to celebrate the mere existence of his child: "dead and come to life." How glorious are those words! How suggestive of the sun that quickens everything on earth. Just so, agapē shines its countenance upon all men, even sinners, burning harder perhaps because it knows there is greater need. But in this the righteous do not suffer. The father loves the older son as well as the younger. How touching when he says: "My boy, you are always with me." If he has not killed the fatted calf for the older son, it is because he takes him for granted, as one does with members of one's own body. The father dignifies this son by identifying with him. His pleading shows a desire to have the elder recognize their oneness by joining in his gesture toward the younger. I can imagine the old man adding: "I never killed the fatted calf for myself either." This kind of love is delimited by the force of habit. It lacks courtesy and the recognition that all along the older son may have wanted something that does not interest the father. Nevertheless, it bestows upon the son a precious intimacy that he, too, doubtless takes for granted.

From this point of view, how affirmative "All I have is yours" now sounds. For the father gives the son a world in which to work, and the promise of eventual authority. Someday the older son will be "the father," which is more than the younger can hope for. What the father feels toward the prodigal is largely the function of a special occasion. (Notice the emphasis in "But we *had* to make merry and rejoice.") What he feels toward the elder is constant and repetitive, like our daily bread or the daily sunshine. This love symbolizes the eternal *presence* of God's agapē, without which nothing could survive. Whatever the older son has earned through righteousness, the love he receives is ultimately unmerited. Even the best of men could not be righteous unless they were sustained by the goodness of the world about them. Such sustenance may be less spectacular than joyous celebrations, but possibly it more fully represents divinity.

Finally, let us consider the role of the sons. For the prodigal the issue is happy; his welcome exceeds anything he has a right to expect. Still, two things are in his favor: regardless of motivation, he does return home; and when he does, he admits his faults, even though his admission may lack sincerity. These are steps toward repentance. They can hardly count as atonement, but even less would seem to have been required by the Deutero-Isaiah in the Old Testament: "O Israel, thou shalt not be forgotten of me. / I have blotted out, as a thick cloud, thy transgressions, / And, as a cloud, thy sins: / Return unto me; for I have redeemed thee." And in Psalm 133, God acts toward all the children of Israel like the father toward the prodigal son: "He will not always chide, / Neither will he keep his anger for ever. / He hath not dealt with us after our sins, / Nor rewarded us according to our iniquities." The God of the Old Testament continually offers redemption to his erring children, affording them one opportunity after another to accept his freely given love. In the tale of Jonah he even sends the prophet across the seas to the pagan city of Nineveh. Once the city turns from its evil ways he acts mercifully, but his forgiveness does not seem motivated merely by deeds of repentance: "And should I not spare Nineveh, that great city, wherein are more than sixscore thousand persons, that cannot discern between their right and their left hand; and also much cattle?" In the parable, too, God goes out to the sinner, even rewarding him in advance, as if he had already atoned. The dubious efforts of the prodigal have put him in a position to receive assistance. If he can now respond to this outpouring of God's love, he will have been saved. For his part, the older brother will not be saved until he purifies his heart. Working in the fields is not enough: precisely the moral that Jonah learns. The righteous son must acknowledge the source of his fortunate capability. That done, he will see the love that has surrounded him all these years. He will say *non nobis* and realize that his ability to work is itself an infinite good bestowed by God. It will then be a pleasure to participate in the father's love toward the erring brother.

In discussing these parables, Nygren argues that they not only symbolize the mysteries of agapē but also "exclude completely the principle of justice from the religious relationship." Throughout, he says, the allegories assert the claims of justice and then systematically defeat them for reasons of love. He holds that righteousness demands that laborers who work more should be paid more, and that the older brother has every right to charge the father with injustice. On Nygren's interpretation, the parables show the irreconcilable conflict between Jewish justice (nomos) and Christian agapē. If this were true, however, the New Testament would be strangely inconsistent. On many occasions Jesus insists that he comes to fulfill the law, not to destroy it. In the chapter before the parable of the vineyard, a man asks what good deed he can do in order to gain eternal life, and Christ replies, "If you wish to enter Life, keep the commandments." In the same place, he tells the disciples that everyone who has renounced the world for the sake of his name "shall be many times repaid and come into eternal life." In the chapter before the parable of the prodigal, he advises his host at a celebration to invite the poor and lowly: though they cannot reciprocate, they will earn him repayment "at the resurrection of the just." To this extent, Jesus definitely promises measure for measure and a fair reward to those who live righteously. In the parables, agapē does not occur at the *expense* of justice. The landowner has not been unjust, simply generous. Where is it written that those who work more *ought* to be paid more? Nor is the father unjust to the older son. Even the son does not say that. He complains that his father does not *love* him enough, and this is what the father denies.

In general, the Gospels do not put love and justice in conflict, any more than the Old Testament had. Instead they reinterpret these concepts and place them on different levels. Just as the Jews had said, those who wish to be saved must follow the path of righteousness. But now that means *more* than just honoring the commandments or submitting to God's authority. It involves renunciation and the rest of Christian nomos. This is what man can do. But because it exists at the level of man, righteousness alone cannot effect salvation. Beyond our merely human, purposive, appraisive attitudes there remains the free play of God's unmotivated love. It is the source of all goodness, including salvation. Nygren is quite right in saying that for the Christian the concept of agapē must always take precedence over the concept of nomos. But I fail to see that, in the Gospels at least, one excludes the other.

Whether or not he misreads the parables, Nygren rightly sees how they illustrate agapē's indifference to objective value. It is this insight that the philosopher Max Scheler denies. He sees the prodigal as holier and more deserving of the fatted calf than his brother. Scheler claims that in the eyes of Jesus a sinner who confesses is actually better than the man who conforms to the law by merely suppressing his sinful impulses. The sinner cleanses his heart and so prevents his iniquity from poisoning the soul; the other man, however righteous, languishes in treacherous self-deceit.

Now as a matter of psychological fact, what Scheler says may well be true. But I find no reason to believe that it is a truth the Gospels were trying to promulgate. As support for his interpretation, Scheler quotes the text in which Jesus says there is more rejoicing in heaven over one sinner who repents than there is over ninety-nine of the righteous. But this, like his saying that he comes to call not the righteous but the sinners, must be seen in context. These statements are given as answers to those who complain that Jesus associates with the ungodly, that he "makes sinners welcome and sits down with them to eat." In such places Jesus explains the nature of his ministry. He has come for the sinners not because they are better than the righteous but because they need him more. Why else would he say that the healthy do not require a physician, only the sick? The parables of the lost sheep and the lost coin, which show the Saviour leaving the righteous and going in search of the sinners, indicate how far agapē will extend itself for those in greatest need. When the search is ended, there occurs the extravagant rejoicing to which

Scheler refers. But this heavenly outburst does not signify that it is better to have been a sinner. The efficacy of divine love is being celebrated, not the value of the newly minted saint. God's successful ministry occasions special delight, his extraordinary effort culminating in a blare of trumpets. There is always something dramatic about the conversion of a sinner: it adds a touch of excitement to the serenity of paradise. But who is to say that the undramatic are any less holy?

Scheler's way of looking at the parables shows the influence of nineteenth-century Romantic love. In romanticism repentant sinners are generally better people than the dullards who remain natively righteous. Like Christ himself, they follow the maxim of Joseph Conrad: "In the destructive element immerse!" There may be great wisdom in this, but it is not the wisdom of the parables. And, in any event, the prodigal son is not repentant.

Between the Synoptic Gospels and the Gospel according to John much time is thought to have elapsed. Certainly the Fourth Gospel shows doctrinal sophistication beyond anything reached in the earlier ones. In particular, it develops the concept of agapē in ways that make it distinctively Christian. This also happens in John's epistles and those of Paul, which are roughly contemporaneous. The First Letter of John states the Christian approach to love more completely than anything else in the early history of that religion. The entire letter deserves the closest analysis, but I want to concentrate upon the following paragraphs:

> Beloved, let us love one another; for love is of God; and everyone that loveth is born of God, and knoweth God. He that loveth not knoweth not God; for God is love. In this was manifested the love of God toward us, because that God sent his only begotten Son into the world, that we might live through him. Herein is love, not that we loved God, but that he loved us, and sent his Son to be the propitiation for our sins. Beloved, if God so loved us, we ought also to love one another.

No man hath seen God at any time. If we love one another, God dwelleth in us, and his love is perfected in us. Hereby know we that we dwell in him, and he in us, because he hath given us of his spirit. And we have seen and do testify that the Father sent the Son to be the Saviour of the world. Whosoever shall confess that Jesus is the Son of God, God dwelleth in him, and he in God. And we have known and believed the love that God hath in us. God is love; and he that dwelleth in love dwelleth in God, and God in him. Herein is our love made perfect, that we may have boldness in the day of judgment: because as he is, so are we in this world.

There is no fear in love; but perfect love casteth out fear: because fear hath torment. He that feareth is not made perfect in love. We love him, because he first loved us. If a man say, "I love God," and hateth his brother, he is a liar: for he that loveth not his brother whom he hath seen, how can he love God whom he hath not seen? And this commandment have we from him, that he who loveth God love his brother also.

In the opening paragraph we encounter, for virtually the first time in Christianity, the slogan "God is love." In English the words are identical with those of Plotinus, and the phrase often occurs in Hellenistic Neoplatonism. But in Plotinus the word for love is *eros*. In St. John, as in St. Paul, it is *agapē*. Plotinus might also have said that love is *of* God and everyone who loves is *born* of God, but he would merely have meant that love is holy. It would still consist of man's search for the highest good. When St. John uses these phrases, however, he is saying that love comes from God rather than man, that it literally originates with God, that indeed love belongs to what we even mean by God. From this it follows that he who loves not does not know God. For one who loves not has rejected the essence of God. How then can he know what God is?

Of course, one could answer that Satan knew God and yet loved him not. But St. John and all other Christians would seem to assume that Satan did not *really* know God. If he had, he would have been overwhelmed by agapē, found it irresistible, and so loved God in return. Possibly the word "know" is being used in a sense that logically implies love. It would then be true by definition that only those who loved God could know him. In any event, no other sense of "know" is allowed. As John says in the second paragraph, "No man hath seen God at any time." Sight here represents all the senses, and John would undoubtedly include ordinary reasoning as well. In a way that later mysticism was to consider fundamental, he means that *only* by loving do we really know what God is like. And that could not be the case unless God were indistinguishable from love, i.e., agapē.

But how can that be? Our love is not agapē. Only God can have it as an attribute. In the second paragraph St. John tries to answer this kind of question by invoking Christian philia. God being love, union with him comes only in the act of loving. This, however, depends upon the agapē which God himself bestows: "Hereby know we that we dwell in him, and he in us, because he hath given us of his spirit." In this context, the term "spirit" may refer to the essence of God which is given in love, or else to the advent of Christ—God's love descending in mercy upon the world. But also, God's spirit signifies the Third Person of the Trinity, the Holy Spirit. For, as Aquinas puts it hundreds of years later: "Love . . . is the proper name of the Holy Spirit, just as Word is the proper name of the Son." Through the Holy Spirit the Father loves himself, the Son, and all created beings. In the Gospel according to John, John the Baptist reports of Jesus: "I saw the Spirit descend like a dove from heaven—it rested on him." In mysterious moments such as this, agapē infuses all nature. It creates the mystical union of philia by giving man the love which is God, and so enabling him to know God through love. The love remains agapē; yet man miraculously participates in it.

In the third paragraph Christian love reaches its highest point of idealization. St. John fuses the two Great Commandments into a unity and then completely reformulates them in terms of agapē. The first commandment exhorts us to love God, the second to love our neighbor. St. John relates them internally: no man can *truly* say "I love God" unless he also loves his neighbor. The reasoning begins with the idea that there is no fear in love—itself a revolutionary suggestion. In the New Testament as well as the Old, the fear of God had always been considered ancillary to loving him. Man being a willful creature, how could he possibly love God without being frightened into it? So too have parents always assumed that without the stringencies of discipline their children would not be capable of loving them. But here is John separating fear and love completely, as if he were not dealing with human beings at all. The next line makes it clear that, in a sense, he is not. There he speaks of "perfect love" as that which casts out fear. Obviously, he is referring to agapē, since only God can be perfect. God's love can be free of fear; and when it possesses a man as an indwelling spirit, it leaves no room for anything else. Once fear has been banished, hatred likewise disappears. How profound of St. John to see the connection between these two psychological states! He glosses over the point as if it were too banal to need emphasis. Or perhaps he failed to realize how deep his insight was. What he does perceive, and what matters most to him, is the idea that agapē cleanses a man of all emotions other than loving ones. Man loves God only by virtue of God's love for man: "We love him, because he first loved us." This being so, agapē will permeate the being of one who truly loves God. It will make him *incapable* of either fearing God or hating his neighbor. The two Great Commandments are therefore really one.

In receiving this highly developed formulation, the concept of agapē also diverges from the Synoptic Gospels. For who is the brother we must love if we hope to love God? In the earlier Gospels he is every man, sinners as well as the righteous, enemies no less than friends. He is our neighbor, that is, any man with whom we have direct relations. Unlike the Buddha, Jesus does not exhort us to feel compassion for "all sentient beings." Neither does the Bible articulate anything like the following from the Hindu *Bhāgavata:* "I desire not the supreme state [of bliss] with its eight perfections, nor the cessation of rebirth. May I take up the sorrow of all creatures who suffer and enter into them so that they may be made free from grief." Compassion of this sort means taking the suffering of others upon ourselves. Christ does not do that, any more than Jehovah. The Judaeo-Christian tradition seeks the *sharing of love*, and not the sharing of suffering. Christ removes sins in order to extend the dominion of agapē. His Passion does this for all men, and every man may imitate him by loving whomsoever he encounters.

Such at least is implied in the Synoptic Gospels. But in the First

Letter of John and the Gospel according to John, the second commandment seems much narrower. The need to love one's enemy is no longer mentioned, and sinners are admitted to brotherhood only as they belong to the faith. Although the terminology is ambiguous, the word "brother" comes to mean "the brethren"—fellow members in Christ. In a way that will surprise no one who has studied social movements, the radical ideas of earlier days have now been modified by an institutional concept. To change the tribal character of Judaism, primitive Christianity had insisted upon a kind of brotherly love that would include Gentiles as well as Jews. Actually, the Old Testament had repeatedly indicated that "neighbor" in the second commandment could be any human being, not necessarily a Jew. In the first century A.D. the idea was a commonplace in Judaism. Possibly the earliest Christians distinguished themselves by emphasizing it more than some of the (other) Jews. But in order to stabilize itself as a separate community, their religion had to intensify the emotional bond among Christians as opposed to all outsiders. The narrow way of interpreting the second commandment had originally enabled Judaism to survive. It would have been astounding if the new sect, fighting to emancipate itself, had not incorporated the methods of its discarded parent.

Though this move strengthens Christian philia, it raises questions about the nature of agapē. God's love is not spontaneous and unmotivated if it may be guaranteed to "whosoever shall confess that Jesus is the Son of God." And neither can agapē be indiscriminate if it is reserved only for one who thus accepts the Christian faith. The epistle tells us that God dwells in such a man and he in God, just as later on it says that one who dwells in love (meaning love toward the brethren) dwells in God and God in him. As a *condition* for God's love and for brotherly love, faith in Christ would seem to undercut the very concept of agapē on which it is based. Only if faith itself exists as a free, indiscriminate, unmotivated gift of God's love does the text escape inconsistency. Is this the meaning of the line that says agapē is manifested in God's sending the Son "that we might live through him"? In the Gospel according to John, there occurs a similar reference to agapē as operating within sectarian limits. Jesus tells his disciples: "This is my commandment: that ye love one another, as I have loved you. . . . Ye have not chosen me, but I have chosen you, and ordained you, that ye should go and bring forth fruit, and that your fruit should remain: that whatsoever ye shall ask of the Father in my name he may give it to you."

If we take these passages to mean that faith itself comes from God's freely given love, the Christian concept of agapē remains inviolate. But then there seems to be no point in exhorting human beings to *anything*: either to love or to have faith in Jesus Christ. If agapē so elects, they *will* have Christian faith. Love will dwell in them proportionate to God's design. If agapē does not give them faith, the fault is not theirs. In either event, religion would have no function, and man would have no way of approaching God. He can only wait quietly for agapē to descend. Such patience may be admirable, but it hardly counts as love: either toward God or toward one's neighbor. In revising the concept of agapē, Christianity would seem to have eliminated not only Judaism but also itself.

The problem I have just mentioned recurs time and again in the letters of St. Paul. Like St. John, Paul emphasizes the inner bonds of Christian philia, predicated upon a faith in Christ which itself results from God's predestinate love. Just as the Gospel according to John says that God loved Jesus "before the foundation of the world," so too does Paul praise God for having bestowed love upon the faithful prior to creation: "In Christ he chose us before the world was founded, to be dedicated, to be without blemish in his sight, to be full of love." This love, being agapē, cannot be motivated by any act of man. But then why concern oneself with extending Christianity or even creating a new church? Yet Paul defines himself as primarily an evangelist. Brotherly love he reinterprets as willingness to admit all human beings into the Christian community. Having been converted on the road to Damascus despite his sinfulness, he is eager to share his experience with every other sinner. Doing so, he becomes an instrument of God's love; and indeed St. Paul generally thinks of agapē as divine grace mercifully giving men the true faith. Nevertheless, the original problem remains. If agapē creates faith, then *it*

does the choosing; and the idea of man saving himself by loving God no longer holds. Instead of being a *response* to agapē, human love would merely illustrate it. The Great Commandments would not be injunctions so much as descriptions of God's loving immersion in the world. By this circuitous route, Christianity would have returned to a modified pantheism.

It is in the context of this problem, I think, that Paul's Letter to the Romans must be read. As one who had been a Jew persecuting Christians in the name of the old order, St. Paul devotes this letter to the relationship between nomos and agapē. Because he says things like "Now we are delivered from the law," theologians have often assumed that Paul is rejecting Jewish righteousness entirely. As a matter of fact, however, his statements about the law are carefully balanced. Thus, after telling the faithful that they have been delivered from it, he asks: "What will we say then? Is the law sin?" And he answers: "God forbid. . . . Wherefore the law is holy, and the commandment holy, and just, and good." Elsewhere, after asking whether Christian faith makes "void" the law, he replies: "God forbid: yea, we establish the law."

But then what was he saying when he declared that Christians are "delivered" from the law? Clearly Paul does not mean to recommend anything that violates the law. Neither does he wish to glorify sin, even though the miraculous cleansing of it illustrates God's infinite mercy. As against the notions of Scheler to which I have referred, Paul specifically says: "Shall we continue in sin, that grace may abound? God forbid." Instead, St. Paul is trying to incorporate the law into a larger framework of Christian faith. He does not *reject* Judaism: he wishes to *convert* it, as he himself was converted. Righteousness is holy love, but man must be delivered from it in recognizing a love that is holier still. Nomos thus remains an authentic response to God's love; and yet, in being subordinated to agapē, it becomes distinctively Christian.

If I am right in this interpretation, the epistles articulate and develop a conception of Christian nomos. The Jewish law is to be renounced, like everything else, in the sense of being transcended. Righteousness must be encouraged, even revered, but also exceeded. That is why Paul says that all men "have sinned, and come short of the glory of God." He does not mean that those who live up to the law are *no better* than the sinners, but rather that even the most perfect among the righteous cannot attain salvation through the law alone. Salvation requires God's love, which the just men desecrate if they rely on *nothing but* the law. Paul states this clumsily: "Therefore we conclude that a man is justified by faith without the deeds of the law." In context he is arguing that God belongs to the Gentiles as well as the Jews. He does not mean to repudiate deeds of the law; and, in fact, this is the paragraph that ends with the words "we establish the law." He expresses himself better in the Letter to the Galatians: "I do not frustrate the grace of God: for if righteousness come by the law, then Christ is dead in vain." And elsewhere, in the Letter to the Romans, he insists that what the law could not do because it was "weak through the flesh," God does by sending his Son: "that the righteousness of the law might be fulfilled in us, who walk not after the flesh, but after the Spirit." In other words, the Jews did well to seek righteousness. But they were wrong in not subordinating it to faith, which is to say, faith in Christ as the embodiment of agapē.

If Paul does believe in Christian nomos, however, why is it that he rarely speaks of man loving God or Christ? Nygren points out that even St. Augustine "remarks with some surprise that when Paul uses the word 'caritas' he nearly always means love to one's neighbor, and only very seldom love to God." Moreover, Paul compounds the confusion by emphasizing the second commandment to the exclusion of the first. In one place he says: "The *whole* law is fulfilled in one word, even in this: Thou shalt love thy neighbor as thyself." In another letter he declares: "For he that loveth his neighbor hath fulfilled the law. For this, Thou shalt not commit adultery, Thou shalt not kill, Thou shalt not steal, Thou shalt not covet, and if there be any other commandment, it is summed up in this word, namely, Thou shalt love thy neighbor as thyself." But why should St. Paul slight or ignore the love of God? In all the Gospels, even in the First Letter of John, man is exhorted to love God. Why should Paul not do so as well? And why, if he is going to neglect the first commandment, does he make the second so important? For not only does he say that loving one's neighbor fulfills the law, but also he uses the term *agapē* for this relationship as well as for God's inherent love. Are there then two kinds of agapē, one for God and one for men who satisfy the second commandment? But if two, then why not three—adding another for the first commandment?

Nygren answers these questions by suggesting that for Paul there is really only one kind of love: God's love, agapē as the essence of the divine nature. On Nygren's interpretation, Paul believes that love always exceeds human capacity: God loves all things, but man cannot love anything insofar as he is merely human. From this Nygren concludes that sheer consistency leads Paul to drop the first commandment; and that "agapē" is used for neighborly love because that too originates with God. The Christian's love for his neighbor is itself but an instance of God's love. Agapē uses the Christian as its vehicle, establishing through him an ever expanding community of love.

Nygren's reading of St. Paul follows Lutheran theology. It limits Christian love to agapē, explaining all occasions of what is apparently human love as really being manifestations of divinity. I shall return to Luther's ideas about agapē in the following chapter. Here I should like to mention several difficulties in Nygren's interpretation of St. Paul.

To begin with, it is not at all obvious that Paul denies the human capacity to love. He never does so explicitly; and when he says the second commandment sums up the entire law, it certainly sounds as if loving one's neighbor is something men can do on their own. That, presumably, is why he exhorts them to it. Perhaps he is describing how God's love works itself out; but the wording does not *seem* to refer to a love that transcends human nature.

Furthermore, the absence of the first commandment need not be accounted for in Nygren's way. He claims that St. Paul rarely speaks of man loving God because God's love was the only kind he recognized. But then why does Paul speak so often of man loving his neighbor? If the second commandment does not interfere with his conception of agapē, why should the first? Paul probably thought that only those who were saved through Christ would be *able* to love their neighbors. But he could have said the same about the love of God. In both cases the priority of agapē would serve as a *causal* explanation rather than as proof that what looks like human love actually exceeds human powers. And, finally, what are we to say about the places in which St. Paul does speak of man loving God? Is he to be taken as uttering self-contradictions?

It seems more plausible to believe that St. Paul was not denying the human capacity for love, that he had no intention of dropping the first commandment, and that he rarely mentions it because he wishes to reconstruct it. The first commandment orders man to love God with all his heart, with all his soul, with all his mind, and with all his strength. But one did not have to be a Christian to accept this as the basis of religion. If the Pauline churches had given this commandment the importance that Jesus does in the Gospels, they would have remained Jewish sects. In order to become separate and Christian, they had to reinterpret the first commandment, making one's love of God synonymous with faith in Christ. And, of course, it is faith of this sort that Paul takes to be the great advance over Judaism. As a structural element within his theology, Paul's insistence upon faith parallels the use of the first commandment in both the Gospels and the Old Testament. Far from making it impossible for man to love God, as Nygren maintains, Paul would seem to be advocating faith in Christ as that which truly satisfies the first commandment. And for St. Paul faith is Christian nomos: man responding to God's prior love, renouncing all else in the name of Christ, yielding his will for the sake of perfect conformity. If nomos is a type of human love, so too is Pauline faith.

As I say this, I must confess that the ambiguities in St. Paul trouble me. His statements are primitive and exploratory compared to those of later theologians. They may certainly be interpreted in different ways. With some modifications Nygren's thesis may be defensible after all. I have suggested that Paul's references to the first commandment indicate a love of God which is not reducible to God's love. But one can also find passages in which Paul describes Christian nomos as if it were merely a special form of agapē. In the Letter to the Romans he says that "the love of God is shed abroad in our hearts by the Holy Spirit which is given unto us." And to the Galatians, Paul addresses the most tantalizing description of spiritual union to be found in Christian literature: "I am crucified with Christ: nevertheless I live; yet not I, but Christ liveth in me: and the life which I now live in the flesh I live by the faith of the Son of God, who loved me, and gave himself for me."

Similar ambiguities confront us in the famous hymn to agapē in First Corinthians. The King James translation uses the term "charity," but this of course must be understood as love. Whose love is it? God's or man's? And if it is man's love, must it too be reduced to agapē? Ostensibly at least, St. Paul begins by describing human love, almost in the manner of the eros tradition. Discussing the relative importance of different members of the church, he arranges them in hierarchical order: first come apostles, then prophets, then teachers, etc. He tells the congregation to "covet earnestly the best gifts" and offers to show them a more excellent way, which belongs to those who love. So far does love exceed all else that without it even the highest must realize that "though I have the gift of prophecy, and understand all mysteries, and all knowledge . . . and though I bestow all my goods to feed the poor, and though I give my body to be burned . . . it profiteth me nothing." At the end of the passage he again exhorts the congregation to direct their "aim" toward love. This way of speaking makes the relevant love appear to be a human one.

But then other parts of the hymn raise the usual doubts. In one place, love and faith are contrasted: "And though I have all faith, so that I could remove mountains, and have not love, I am nothing." Does this refer to love of neighbor or love of God? And if the latter, does St. Paul really mean to distinguish it from faith in Christ? Or, as Nygren would suggest, is it agapē that he has in mind, God's love transcending faith as well as every other human response? This idea comports with the fact that the hymn discusses "spiritual gifts" throughout. Paul begins by declaring that only through a gift of the Holy Spirit can a man even assert that "Jesus is the Lord." He then leads into the hierarchy of gifts culminating in love as the most excellent by saying: "Now there are diversities of gifts, but the same Spirit. . . . And there are diversities of operations, but it is the same God which worketh all in all. But the manifestation of the Spirit is given to every man to profit withal." Should this not be taken to mean that love, which supremely manifests the Spirit, is itself God's agapē rather than something human? And yet the hymn concludes with the line: "And now abideth faith, hope, love, these three; but the greatest of these is love." This conclusion would *seem* to put love in the same category as faith and hope. Are we not justified in thinking that St. Paul considers them all human responses, with love ranking highest? Or does he mean that all three alike are instances of agapē?

However we resolve the ambiguities of St. Paul, assuming they can be resolved, the hymn to love shows better than anything else how far we have come from the concept of eros. Even in the First Letter of John we find references to a kind of cupiditas or debased eros, as when the author says: "Love not the world, neither the things that are in the world. If any man love the world, the love of the Father is not in him." That this kind of interest could even be designated as "love" would seem to be denied by Paul's entire approach. In naming the qualities of love, the hymn contradicts—almost point by point—Plato's description of eros. To see the enormous differences, we need only put the relevant passages side by side, first from Plato and then from St. Paul:

He [Eros] is always poor, and, far from being sensitive and beautiful, as most people imagine, he is hard and weather-beaten, shoeless and homeless, always sleeping out for want of a bed, on the ground, on doorsteps, and in the street. So far he takes after his mother [Poverty] and lives in want. But, being also his father's son [i.e., the son of Plenty, also translated as Contrivance], he schemes to get for himself whatever is beautiful and good; he is bold and forward and strenuous, always devising tricks like a cunning huntsman; he yearns after knowledge and is full of resource and is a lover of wisdom all his life, a skillful magician, an alchemist, a true sophist. He is neither mortal nor immortal; but on one and the same day he will live and flourish (when things go well with him), and also meet his death; and then come to life again through the vigour that he inherits from his father. What he wins he always loses, and is neither rich nor poor, neither wise nor ignorant.

Love suffereth long, and is kind; love envieth not; love vaunteth not itself, is not puffed up, doth not behave itself unseemly, seeketh not her own, is not easily provoked, thinketh no evil; rejoiceth not in iniquity, but rejoiceth in the truth; beareth all things, believeth all things, hopeth all things, endureth all things. Love never faileth. . . .

In saying that Eros dies and then comes to life "through the vigour that he inherits from his [all-plentiful] father," Plato may be thought to anticipate Christ. Eros and Jesus both are messiahs: mediators, messengers, and agencies of salvation. Through them the gods communicate with man, and vice versa. Moreover, Plato describes Eros as he does in order to refute an earlier speech in which love was said to be beautiful. As an intermediary, Eros can only be the *search* for beauty. His human embodiment is not the handsome Agathon, but rather the ugly Socrates. Like the crucified Jesus, Socrates appears to be the lowliest of men, while really incorporating the highest of human values. But the irony of Christ's condition illustrates the workings of agapē. Can something comparable be said of Socrates? Are the eros and agapē attitudes toward love less different than they seem to be? Do the concepts overlap, or join to make a unitary system? On these questions hinge all the diversity between Catholic and Protestant. Before examining them, however, I feel a need to clarify the concept of agapē somewhat further.

In *The Art of Loving* Erich Fromm distinguishes between two phases in the development of religion. In one the deity is endowed with a loving attitude Fromm considers specifically maternal: "Mother's love is unconditional, it is all-protective, all-enveloping; because it is unconditional it can also not be controlled or acquired. Its presence gives the loved person a sense of bliss; absence produces a sense of lostness and utter despair. Since mother loves her children because they are her children, and not because they are 'good,' obedient, or fulfill her wishes and commands, mother's love is based on equality. All men are equal, because they all are children of a mother, because they all are children of Mother Earth." In the other phase the deity's loving attitude is authoritarian and paternalistic: "The nature of fatherly love is that he makes demands, establishes principles and laws, and that his love for the son depends on the obedience of the latter to these demands. He likes best the son who is most like him, who is most obedient and who is best fitted to become his successor, as the inheritor of his possessions."

Is this the key to agapē? Shall we say, as Fromm implies, that agapē is a religious projection of mother's love as opposed to father's love? The idea is suggestive, but hardly defensible. For at least as Fromm presents it, the distinction between mother's love and father's love cannot be upheld. I do not deny that mothers and fathers love their children in different ways. But I see no reason to believe that their attitudes correspond to Fromm's analysis. A mother's love is not typically unconditional, all-protective, all-enveloping, beyond control or acquisition. On the contrary, it is conditioned by the way in which she needs her children and they need her. If it were beyond acquisition, no child would have to extend himself in order to *get* maternal love. Far from this being the case, children do all they can to increase their mother's love—even learning how to bestow value upon her. The idea of an all-protective, all-enveloping mother itself idealizes what the child would *like* to have. Fromm perpetuates the myth of the bountiful mother-goddess, as if motherhood were simply a state of endless giving. But as a human being who creates other human beings, the actual mother imposes demands and expectations. She is as much an authority as any father could be. During those matriarchal stages of civilization in which Fromm believes, the mothers would have been the *exclusive* authorities. Did this prevent them from having "mother's love"?

And why assume that a father's love is typically directed toward the son who resembles him or is most obedient? Is there anything in the nature of fatherhood to keep a father from loving his children equally? In a patriarchal society the fathers will have a predominant responsibility for law and order. But this pertains to social power, not love. It determines who will succeed the father or inherit his property. It does not create a uniquely paternal type of love. Think of the parable of the prodigal son. The father loves the useless younger child in a way that he does not love the responsible one with whom he identifies. It would be very confusing to think that *either* way of loving is inherently foreign to paternity. Fromm might want to say that the parable illustrates mother's love. But I see nothing atypical in the father's response. His kind of paternal love is very common. Fromm's distinction merely fails to recognize it.

Indeed, I wonder whether Fromm is even distinguishing between two types of love. What he calls father's love belongs to the appraisive attitude. It makes laws and rewards obedience to them. As Fromm describes it, paternal love bestows no special nonpurposive value. But then why call it *love*? It would seem to be an aspect of social morality or parental ambition. On the other hand, the maternal attitude that Fromm mentions does sound like a kind of love. At least, it involves bestowing. Agapē idealizes an infinite bestowal, and possibly that is why Fromm's concept of mother's love resembles it.

Although Freud rarely discusses God's love, his incidental analyses are extremely helpful. Let me first return to that "similar illusion" which holds together both armies and churches: "The same illusion holds good of there being a head—in the Catholic Church, Christ, in an army its commander in chief—who loves all the individuals in the group with an equal love. Everything depends upon this illusion; if it were to be dropped, then both Church and army would dissolve." In each group, Freud points out, the members are bound together by their identical relationship with the loving leader. To illustrate this, he could have cited Christ's explication of the second commandment: "Even as I have loved you, that you also love one another." The fellowship of a Christian community must claim to have its source in God's agapē. It is the equality of this love that makes the faithful equal participants in the church. Freud also recognizes that the idea of divine love serves a further ethical function. Loved equally by Christ, all Christians are able to identify with one another; and yet they may also hope to identify with Christ himself. When that occurs, the saint comes to love in the way that Christ does—indiscriminately, regardless of value in the object. The church could exist as a group without the possibility of such identification, but Freud rightly sees that Christian idealization ultimately depends upon it: "One can be a good Christian and yet be far from the idea of putting oneself in Christ's place and of having like him an all-embracing love of mankind. One need not think oneself capable, weak mortal that one is, of the Saviour's largeness of soul and strength of love. But this further development in the distribution of libido in the group is probably the factor upon which Christianity bases its claim to have reached a higher ethical level."

In *Civilization and Its Discontents* Freud argues that this claim is neither reasonable nor psychologically defensible. For it assumes that all men are worthy of love, and therefore that virtue consists in the ability to extend it universally. As we saw earlier in this book, Freud believes that love must be limited to those who deserve it. His is the attitude, transposed to the psychoanalytic ideology, of the ancient Jews who expected God to love only the righteous. And like those Jews, Freud insists that if Christian love were actually carried out, it would violate the moral demands of one's "own people." For loving indiscriminately means giving to outsiders the love that ought to be reserved for intimates. The unworthy are then treated like the worthy, and the stranger like those who depend upon our love for their very sustenance. To Freud this is not only unjust, but also self-defeating. Were all men loved equally and indiscriminately, merely because they inhabit the earth—"like an insect, an earthworm or a grass-snake"—then Freud suspects that not much love could fall to any one of them. "What is the point of a precept enunciated with so much solemnity if its fulfillment cannot be recommended as reasonable?"

In a sense, Freud answers this question himself: at least, he sees the *motive* for advocating universal love. In a later context he remarks that the commandment to love one's neighbor as oneself curtails instinctive aggressiveness. It thereby does the work of civilization. It belongs to the cultural superego, which socializes man by forcing him to repress destructive instincts. At the same time, Freud insists, such commandments do more harm than good. Not based upon psychological fact, the idea of universal love leads to social neurosis. Far from increasing the quantity of love, the second commandment merely augments human aggressiveness by turning it into an unsatisfiable sense of guilt."The commandment is impossible to fulfil; such an enormous inflation of love can only lower its value, not get rid of the difficulty. . . . What a potent obstacle to civilization aggressiveness must be, if the defence against it can cause as much unhappiness as aggressiveness itself!"

To many readers these words have conveyed a great pessimism

about the human race. Yet Freud had no such intention. He wishes to be realistic about man's capabilities and obviously thinks that the truth shall set us free. He attacks the Judaeo-Christian precept, as he attacks the superego in general, for expecting too much. And certainly he is right about the millions of persons who have been tyrannized by the biblical injunction, feeling themselves inferior because they did not love everyone with an equal love. Freud is right and the precept is indeed unrealistic—if it means that all men are to be loved in the *same* way or *as much as* one another, ideally as much as we love ourselves. This may occasionally happen, as when a parent bestows the same importance upon a child's welfare as upon his own; but no man can hope to treat *everyone*, not even every neighbor, that way. The Christian recognizes this in assigning agapē to divinity. God can do anything. Why should he not be able to give an equal love to all his children? But then the Christian uses agapē *as if* it were human, making it the model for an ideal love between men. At this point the precept becomes harmful as well as magical.

Interpreted differently, however, the second commandment may be defended both psychologically and morally. For we need not take it to require equal quantities of an identical love. In telling us to love others *as* ourselves, the commandment enjoins us to love persons who are *not* ourselves, i.e., who do not resemble us. Whether applied to all neighbors or all Jews or all Christians or all mankind, the precept bids us to open our hearts. It breaks down the walls of a closed society and encourages our love to flow wherever it can. In this there can be no injustice. Loving a stranger does not mean treating him as a member of one's family; for that he is not. We love the stranger by responding to him as one who *is* a stranger, and therefore different from us. We bestow value by accepting his separateness, not by giving him intimate rights to which he has no claim. Neither does our attitude lessen the amount of love that remains for others; for love, unlike the libido, as Freud conceives of it, has no fixed quantity. Similarly, we take nothing from the worthy in loving the unworthy. We love the unworthy by responding to them as persons who struggle and fail. We recognize their unworthiness, but treat them with an indefeasible respect. In following the ideal of universal love, we need not try to love all men in a way that is appropriate only for those who mean the most to us. We merely allow ourselves to love indiscriminately, in whatever way is relevant to the other's reality and our own. Such love will vary from object to object; but it excludes no human being a priori. It is equal not in strength or configuration, but in availability. Judaism and Christianity read much more than this into the second commandment; but even this much Freud would reject as inimical to moral growth. I cannot believe that he is right.

Throughout his analysis Freud assumes that the *real* object of love is always either oneself or one's ideal of oneself. From this it follows that one *cannot* love the stranger, and therefore that the concept of universal love need not be taken at face value. When civilization pushes man in this direction, as in the second commandment, Freud can only interpret the maneuver as an attempt to control antisocial aggressiveness. Since the control represses natural instincts without adequate compensation, he condemns the Judaeo-Christian precept as both dangerous and unrealistic. But none of this holds if, as I have argued, Freud is mistaken about the objects of love. That the second commandment serves society by repressing hostile instincts cannot be doubted. But why think it does nothing else? Why not see in it a means of opening society to new possibilities? As an attitude that does not, *need* not, limit itself to any one preferential object, an indiscriminate love allows the individual to establish new and unforeseeable relationships with new but equally authentic objects of love. By getting us to love our neighbor without specifying who he must be, civilization progresses into greater inclusiveness. As long as this attitude satisfies, the precept remains morally and psychologically viable without being reducible to self-love. Like Freud, Santayana fails to recognize this. Discussing agapē without naming it, he says: "There is therefore no love not directed upon the Good, not directed upon something that makes for the fulfilment of the lover's nature. This good may be the good of others, but doing good to others will to that extent be a good for oneself." But Santayana is equivocating. True, one could not do good for others unless the doing were also (in some respect) a good for oneself. To say this, however, is not to say that love must be *directed* upon that which "makes for the fulfilment of the lover's nature." Only in the closed society of narcissism is that the case.

Agapē takes us out of the closed society. It idealizes that aspect of man which fulfills itself by being unmindful of itself, by directing its love elsewhere. The Christian or the Jew gives importance to this human disposition by considering it God's principal attribute. The harder it is for Western man to bestow value indiscriminately, the more he feels the need to posit a God who does so unto perfection. And often the tactic works. Believing that such a deity exists and rules the universe makes it easier for some people to achieve a sense of oneness with other men. Are they not all equal recipients of an unmerited generosity? The mighty will realize that no amount of power can elicit freely given love; the lowly will feel dignified, uplifted, by the very idea of a loving descent. Appraisive differences will no longer separate the faithful. Inspired by the concept of agapē, devotees will try to imitate Christ; they may even sacrifice themselves for the welfare of others. To them it will seem as if the Holy Spirit had taken possession of their souls. Whether or not it has, their faith will have created in them a special kind of loving attitude. Even we who have no religious faith may call them saints. The term need not denote a superior state, but only the one peculiar to their type of idealization. In all human beings bestowal operates as an element of love. In the saints it becomes something to which they dedicate their hearts, their minds, their conduct, and above all, their amorous imagination. Without being necessarily the best or truest love, such dedication may well succeed in making the saints more loving human beings than *they* could have been otherwise. In any event, it is through this pattern of idealization that mankind first began experimenting with the possibilities of an open society. Judaism and Christianity have often walled themselves up in rigid enclaves; but they did so by retrenching from their own concept of agapē.

Treating agapē as the idealization of bestowal liberates us from Freud's constraining ideas about sublimation. In one place Freud declares that when he uses the term "love" in its wider sense he means the same thing as St. Paul (presumably in First Corinthians). Since Paul was talking about a supernatural power, Freud has been criticized for ignoring the fact that his position is diametrically opposite from the Pauline. For St. Paul love is the showering forth of divinity; for Freud it is human acquisitiveness seeking to satisfy instincts that are ultimately biological. But Freud is not confused about this. When he says that love in the wider sense includes what St. Paul had in mind, he means that Pauline love is just a special type of sublimation. So much does Freud take this for granted that he even allows himself the following statement: "Those instincts which are inhibited in their aims always preserve some few of their original sexual aims; even an affectionate devotee, even a friend or an admirer desires the physical proximity and the sight of the person who is now loved only in the 'Pauline' sense. If we choose, we may recognize in this diversion of aim a beginning of the *sublimation* of the sexual instincts. . . ."

But how weak an argument this is! That friends should desire physical proximity and the sight of one another does not manifest a sublimated sexual interest. At least, not necessarily. How else are the friends to share one another's company? How else can they communicate directly? Can they even be friends if they never want to be together? Freud arrives at this kind of absurdity because he thinks that *all* love must be reducible, directly or indirectly, to love in the "narrower sense" of sexual instinct. He is willing to admit that Christian love pertains to love in the wider sense, but then, he thinks, it must somehow depend upon sublimation. This entire way of thinking becomes unnecessary once we analyze concepts such as agapē in terms of idealization. Love "in the Pauline sense" need not be the sublimation of anything. It belongs to the human practice of making ideals that govern responses—whether sexual or nonsexual. We understand the concept by showing how it idealizes. Idealization *controls* and *modifies* basic instincts: it is not a devious way of satisfying them. Like everything else, idealization may satisfy; but its satisfactions are not reducible to anything like the Freudian ultimates.

At the same time, agapē does more than just idealize bestowal. Agapē is not human love. It is God's love, and for the Christian, God himself. Bestowal is just a category of valuation: a way of responding, an attitude that gives to objects value they would not have apart from the lover. To some extent, agapē does the same. It is God's way of responding, and apart from his response nothing could have value at all. But when the Christian says this, he means that God makes value in the same objective sense that he makes reality. Agapē *creates* goodness. Values exist only in relation to God's will, whether or not human beings recognize them. In this respect, Christian agapē resembles Platonic eros. Both imply an objective goodness that transcends the empirical world while also explaining everything in it. To this the Christian adds the idea that value *comes* from God. And since the ability to love is that in man than which nothing could be more valuable, all love must originate with agapē. Without God man could not bestow anything; nor would anything be worth bestowing. When man does bestow—doing good to his neighbor or sacrificing himself for the greater glory of God—he *exceeds* human nature. Either he is imitating Christ or he is serving as a vehicle for agapē. Plato thought that through love men perfected their nature, and so made themselves godlike. Christianity says something similar. But the love it believes in is ultimately divine, too glorious to belong to the nature of man.

In idealizing bestowal *this* way, the concept of agapē confuses the wonderful with the magical. Even the most prosaic mind will sense a wonder in the fact that the world seems to *give* itself to us. The goodness of life, when life is worth living, comes as a spontaneous and unmerited gift. When the sun shines upon what matters to us, it is as if some unknown lover were showering diamonds at our feet. We all feel this when things go better than we expected. And as "wonderful" is a word with which we bestow value upon others, we may feel that in so bountiful a world we too are something wonderful. All manner of goodness awaits our pleasure. We need only *enjoy*, like children of a loving parent—whether it be Mother Nature or Father Time. To the Christian, however, nature and time are consecrated to the devil. Man must get beyond them; his salvation lies in supernature, in eternity. The sense of wonder thus changes into a yearning for the miraculous. It is this that creates the belief in magic. Through magic one destroys the laws of nature, and that (by definition) is a miracle. Because he thinks that mankind is necessarily corrupt, the Christian despairs of ever loving properly within his human nature. He therefore postulates a love untainted by this world, a transcendental love without which there could be no empirical love, a love that miraculously transforms human nature and gives it the capacity for loving. What was formerly a wonder now seems to issue from the heart of power. The idea is comforting, and I do not wish to minimize its humane intention. But I also feel that it weakens our moral fiber without increasing the gifts of life. Like its critic Freud, Judaeo-Christian love expects too little of men—not too much. The idealizations in agapē seek to change man by magical means instead of exploring the ways in which his sheer humanity may itself augment the wonders of nature.

Agapē—at least Christian agapē—also confuses the joyful giving of oneself with a self-sacrifice that is basically suicidal. As the bestowing of value, love enables one to give to other persons. In loving, we engage our emotions where otherwise we might have withheld them; we run risks for the sake of those we care about; we share our interests and parcel out our goods; we allow the other to touch us to the core of our being; above all, we change our own reality by imparting a new importance upon *his*. In these and other ways, our giving is imaginative, a means of self-expression, an act of power. Through it we become creators, like the Judaeo-Christian God making a world out of the goodness of his loving nature. But in Christianity, God's love is also sacrificial. Since agapē is divine, it must degrade and so diminish itself in descending to human beings. Having begun as a virile artisan giving life to the world, God ends up as a messiah, laying down his own life for the sake of a sinful and well-nigh worthless creation. In Christ's Passion there is also much potency. It is not entirely self-destructive. For we know that Christ is God and God must have eternal life. But it is a life that negates, destroys, the life of man on earth. The Christian can renounce the world because Christ has done so for him. In coming to teach man how to love, Christ also teaches him to die, to die to nature, and to love that death. Would any people have made this idealization if they were really capable of loving life? Is it worth making if the love of life is what we hope to achieve?

Throughout the magical play of agapē, one always senses what D. H. Lawrence called "the greed of giving." What God would give life but not the wisdom to live it well? In Genesis he seems more concerned about his creative power than about the welfare of what he has created. Perhaps the Judaeo-Christian God is *over*abundant, like the sun that burns at noon or like a cancer that kills through a surfeit of energy. In love there must be more than mere giving, even the giving of unmerited goodness; there must be a taking as well, God exchanging goods with man, each being satisfied in the very process of satisfying the other. Even Christ takes nothing from the world other than its sins. What a strange thing to take! How bizarre the very idea that a lover would want to *remove* sins, assuming that he could. To a Supreme Being nothing is impossible; and to the mind of magic what could be more glorious than saving the world through one heroic passion? And yet, the god who miraculously cleanses sin demeans the sinner's reality. Only for the dead can the past be erased. For those who live, it remains as facts to be confronted or ignored by what one does in the present. He is no savior who enables man to ignore these facts or to pretend that they may be washed away. Such purification simplifies the moral life, but only as death does. What seems a love of humanity may thus be a further means of destroying it. What looks like a merciful descent may really be a secret scorn. Speaking of mystical love, though not of God's agapē, Ortega y Gasset says: "The height of disdain consists of not condescending to discover a fellow being's defects but, from our inaccessible height, projecting upon him the favorable light of our own well-being." Is this the truth that inspires the Grand Inquisitor in Dostoyevsky? And in that fable does Christ remain silent because he has learned that even giving may be vicious?

In making bestowal a magical force, Christianity assures us that all is well in reality. Power and value reside together within an infinite and eternal source of love. Though we perish, goodness lives on. This, and more, is what every human being hopes. The concept of agapē transforms these hopes into articulate beliefs, bestowing upon the universe the greatest dignity man has yet conceived. Faith in agapē, like adherence to Platonic metaphysics, is itself an act of love. And like all love it is supremely creative. But if the religious beliefs turn out to be illusory, this kind of love will have created dangerous falsehoods. It will be magical in changing man into *less* than what he really is. Having begun this chapter with Shakespeare on agapē, let me finish it with the speech in *A Midsummer Night's Dream* that explores love's potentiality for delusion. The character

Theseus never mentions the religious imagination, but the metaphysical tenor of his allusions may easily suggest it:

> More strange than true. I never may believe
> These antique fables, nor these fairy toys.
> Lovers and madmen have such seething brains,
> Such shaping fantasies, that apprehend
> More than cool reason ever comprehends.
> The lunatic, the lover, and the poet
> Are of imagination all compact.
> One sees more devils than vast hell can hold;
> That is the madman. The lover, all as frantic,
> Sees Helen's beauty in a brow of Egypt.
> The poet's eye, in a fine frenzy rolling,
> Doth glance from heaven to earth, from earth to heaven;
> And as imagination bodies forth
> The forms of things unknown, the poet's pen
> Turns them to shapes, and gives to airy nothing
> A local habitation and a name.
> Such tricks hath strong imagination,
> That, if it would but apprehend some joy,
> It comprehends some bringer of that joy;
> Or in the night, imagining some fear,
> How easy is a bush suppos'd a bear!

As against this view of the imagination, we may answer that not all love is delusional. In bestowing value, it *need* not tell lies. And even that idealization in which the concept of agapē consists may—for others, if not for me—eventually justify itself as something rich and valid. In the speech that follows the passage quoted above, Hippolyta replies:

> But all the story of the night told over,
> And all their minds transfigur'd so together,
> More witnesseth than fancy's images,
> And grows to something of great constancy,
> But howsoever, strange and admirable.

14

Luther versus Caritas

THUS FAR, I HAVE ANALYZED FOUR
concepts of Christian love: eros, philia, nomos, and agapē. In doing
so, I have abstracted elements within a totality. For the medieval
Christian, religious love made an integrated whole. But, in spite of
Wordsworth, we *need not* murder to dissect. Having begun with
analysis, we may now seek the relevant synthesis. We do this by
putting the elements together again, in their authentic relations to
one another. None of the terms I have used is adequate to describe
the medieval synthesis. Not even agapē indicates the total relationship. And that is why de Rougemont's pages on Christian love in
the Western world strike one as so inaccurate. For de Rougemont
assumes that even in the Middle Ages, Christian love amounted to
nothing but agapē. Not only is that false historically, but also it
prevents de Rougemont from analyzing eros and agapē correctly.
For instance, he claims that eros cannot be Christian because it
involves possession by some divinity. And yet, is not infusion of this
sort precisely what agapē entails? In demarcating the concepts as he
does, de Rougemont neglects the ways in which each *may or may not*
be Christian. This in turn leads him to ignore the actual complexity
of the medieval synthesis; and without that structure, orthodox
Christianity can hardly be understood.*

*Cf. *Love in the Western World.* In the opening chapters of *The Mind and
Heart of Love,* M. C. D'Arcy summarizes de Rougemont's thesis about Christian love and then criticizes it quite properly. Cf. also my review of books by
de Rougemont in *The New York Review of Books,* January 28, 1965.

In Nygren's study of Christian love we find a more satisfying introduction to the medieval synthesis. Nygren tends to minimize nomos and philia, but eros and agapē he analyzes exhaustively. The medieval attempt to harmonize these two concepts he calls the *caritas-synthesis*. Nygren himself believes that the synthesis fails. He argues that concepts of eros and agapē are ultimately inconsistent with one another: they formulate attitudes wholly divergent, necessarily irreconcilable. To summarize the contrasts between the eros attitude and the agapē attitude, Nygren lists their characteristics in parallel columns. If one reads across the columns, the differences seem even more remarkable: "Eros is acquisitive desire and longing—Agape is sacrificial giving. Eros is an upward movement—Agape comes down. Eros is man's way to God—Agape is God's way to man. Eros is man's effort: it assumes that man's salvation is his own work—Agape is God's grace: salvation is the work of Divine love. Eros is egocentric love, a form of self-assertion of the highest, noblest, sublimest kind—Agape is unselfish love, it 'seeketh not its own,' it gives itself away. Eros seeks to gain its life, a life divine, immortalized—Agape lives the life of God, therefore dares to 'lose it.' Eros is the will to get and possess which depends on want and need—Agape is freedom in giving, which depends on wealth and plenty. Eros is primarily *man's* love; God is the *object* of Eros, even when it is attributed to God; Eros is patterned on human love—Agape is primarily *God's* love; 'God *is* Agape,' even when it is attributed to man; Agape is patterned on Divine love. Eros is determined by the quality, the beauty and worth, of its object; it is not spontaneous, but 'evoked,' 'motivated'—Agape is sovereign in relation to its object, and is directed to both 'the evil and the good'; it is spontaneous, 'overflowing,' 'unmotivated.' Eros *recognizes value* in its object, and loves it—Agape loves, and *creates value* in its object."

Before Nygren no one had delineated these two concepts with anything like this sharpness and clarity. On the other hand, no one had ever doubted that eros and agapē articulate different approaches to the nature of love. To this Nygren adds the further idea that eros and agapē are inherently inconsistent and therefore that the medieval synthesis cannot be upheld. Nygren is a little unclear about the form of his argument, but it seems to consist of two major theses: first, that the concepts of eros and agapē—in their ordinary use within Christian theology—logically contradict one another; second, that even if the concepts are not contradictory in a strictly logical sense, they nevertheless belong to irreconcilable attitudes toward life. Of course, Nygren recognizes that many theologians have used the concepts of eros and agapē as if they were not contradictory. How else could the medievals claim to have made a synthesis? But Nygren believes that these men were confused and that analyses such as his reveal the logical incompatibility of crucial statements within the dogma. At the same time, Nygren admits to being more than just an analyst. He argues as he does in order to strengthen the cause of Evangelical Reformation and to weaken the authority of traditional Catholicism. A Christian cannot adhere to eros alone, if he is to remain a Christian; but Protestants can and do believe in nothing but agapē. To prove the attitudes irreconcilable tends therefore to undermine Catholic theology, forcing the devout believer toward an alternative version of Christianity.

As an outsider, not partisan to any variety of religious faith, I may be of service by pushing the analysis wherever it leads. In its own way, the problem assumes the dimensions of man's usual difficulties with his past. For Christianity much of the past consists of the ancient world, classical philosophy, and so the concept of eros. Agapē being more clearly its own, Christianity must decide whether to reject all other concepts or else to assimilate as much of its antecedents as possible. In view of the ambivalence with which all human development regards the past, it is not surprising that Christians should have moved in *both* directions. Nor even that the return to primitive Christianity should have taken fifteen hundred years to begin. If it was even to survive, the new religion had first to make its peace with ancient philosophy. This alone took five hundred years, culminating in the work of St. Augustine. Another thousand years were needed to perfect the synthesis, and to establish it in every corner of the European imagination. Only after this long period of increasing success and security could the religion allow itself to disengage from its antecedents. To Catholics, with their sense of tradition and continuity, the Reformation will always seem patricidal: not only in its rejection of the parental church, but also in its denial of Christianity's classical forebears. To Protestants there will always be something heroic about the self-liberation of the modern sects. And indeed the courage of a Luther does inspire admiration. Whether he was right or wrong, blasphemous or holy, Luther's sense of integrity—at least in the search for purity of belief—cannot be denied. With him the Middle Ages end and the ancient world fades from human consciousness. The past would never be the same again.

Luther's attack upon the caritas-synthesis I find especially interesting in view of the idealizations that govern it. What mattered to previous theologians no longer affects him in the same way. His ideas about love indicate that he is already living in a different emotional world. To see this, however, we must first re-create the medieval synthesis out of which he emerges.

The Christian synthesis of eros and agapē is best seen in the writings of St. Augustine and St. Thomas Aquinas. Himself a child of Neoplatonism, Augustine visibly molds it into Christian dogma. To a large extent, the product of his labors becomes established doctrine for the Catholic church, a touchstone against one heresy after another. By the time of Aquinas, Aristotle as well as the Neoplatonists may be fitted into the pattern. In the meantime, important philosophers (such as Peter Lombard and Peter Abelard) have used Augustine in arguments that run counter to the synthesis; and they need to be answered. With St. Thomas the doctrine finally hardens into a fusion of pagan and Christian thought that becomes definitive for much of the Middle Ages.

The Latin word *caritas* is the one St. Augustine prefers, though he uses it interchangeably with terms such as *amor* and *dilectio*. He clearly states that caritas is neither eros nor agapē, but a combination of the two. Augustine does not analyze these elements of religious love, any more than the elements of Christian nomos or philia. Yet in his writings all four mingle, jostling one another from text to text, receiving variable emphasis as required by the doctrinal needs at hand. So important is love to Augustine that he makes it a principal canon of interpretation, using it to clarify obscurities in the New

Testament and defending ancient philosophers to the extent that they employ it as a central concept. It is Augustine who really establishes Christianity as "the religion of love." "The Devil believes," he says, "but he does not love." And in another place: "Where love is, what can be wanting? Where it is not, what can possibly be profitable?"

In approaching Augustinian caritas, one may use any of its elements as a point of departure. This is true because it is an authentic synthesis rather than mere eclecticism. Agapē comes first in the sense that God's love precedes and sustains everything else. At least as much as Paul, Augustine stresses the primacy of grace and predestination. These evidences of agapē operate in Christ's incarnation as well as God's mercy toward sinners. But now, in addition, they explain man's eros. For although he insists that God's love is freely bestowed, Augustine provides it with a rationale in terms of human love: Agapē reveals itself *in order* to teach man what love is like and so to help him love God properly. Christ descends that even sinners may emulate him, that they too may rise to heaven on the wings of ascending love.

Since agapē gives itself to fortify man's upward striving, one might think of eros as the primary element in caritas. And so it is, from the perspective of a finite creature seeking its highest good, struggling to achieve individual happiness in accordance with its nature. Because man is limited, however, his love may easily be deflected from its ultimate object. Unlike Plato and the Greeks, St. Augustine does not believe that the human soul is inherently divine. It strives toward God as the perfect goal of aspiration, but only in the way a mortal might. Consequently, man always runs the risk of losing himself in cupidity, the carnal eros. Indeed, without the aid of agapē, eros would inevitably curve into the ground instead of rising. Augustine speaks of the two Great Commandments about love as themselves inculcating the proper direction of eros: "Love, but see to it *what* you love. Love to God and love to neighbor is called Caritas; love to the world and love of temporal things is called Cupiditas."

Thus, far from being the only element in Christian love, Augustinian agapē particularly concerns itself with the purification of eros. After the commandments have been given, after Christ has set his miraculous example, after the individual soul has received faith and the ability to strive upward, agapē continues to intercede. Otherwise, man's pitiful efforts could hardly take him out of nature's gravitational field. Even the most perfect of all imaginable saints—the man who has achieved the spiritual peaks of humility, devotion, renunciation—would still fall short of the beatitude for which he yearns. But Augustine does not despair. He sees agapē reaching down once more and finally drawing the saint across the infinite gap. Caritas, as eros or the human love of God, is then transformed into something beyond humanity: it becomes a part of agapē. Only in this manner may spiritual union, Christian philia, be accomplished.

In the sense that oneness with God is the culminating state, the condition all creatures desire, philia is the primary element in caritas. For it denotes the destination of the clarified will. Those who live in ignorance or sin may not realize that they too pursue the universal goal. But nevertheless they do. So Augustine tells us; and if he lived today, he would insist that those who do not admit to this unconscious craving are guilty of what the psychoanalysts call "denial" and the existentialists "bad faith." They commit the lie in the soul. For Augustine, that is the greatest pride of all, and it incurs the worst of all possible punishments: eternal separation from God, and therefore failure to satisfy the need for love. On the other hand, the oneness of philia brings everlasting joy. Through it man resumes his likeness to God and triumphantly fulfills the law. While still on earth, he succeeds in renouncing the world. In blissful acquiescence, through love instead of fear, he subjugates the will to self-aggrandizement. Toward his fellow men he acts virtuously, doing what is right and freely bestowing goods upon them. With a sense of glorious rectitude, he conforms to the divine authority. From this point of view, Christian nomos is the primary element.

The Augustinian synthesis is one of the supreme creations of the human mind. In the unity of its design, the depth of its inspiration, the brilliance of its execution, it is a masterful work of art. But even this golden bowl has cracks. Of the various ways in which they could be traced, I shall emphasize one that is especially relevant to Luther's attack. It deals with the relationship between eros and agapē.

In explaining why eros is insufficient by itself, Augustine argues that striving for the Good inevitably generates pride. Eros alone is thus self-defeating. Through it man can envisage the highest good, but he needs agapē to achieve that humility of spirit without which the desired destination cannot be reached. It is for this reason that Augustine finds Platonism deficient and Christianity superior. If he is right, however, he must show how agapē functions in man's experience as a precondition for aspiring eros. When Augustine criticizes the Pelagian ideas about divine grace, he says that God literally intervenes in human life at every moment in time. God's grace is constant, continuous, always active. Without this ever-present infusion of agapē, man could not even strive for God. Augustine maintains that since the fall of Adam, man's sinful nature prevents him from having caritas in himself. As faith is a gift of God, reserved for those who have been uniquely chosen, so too is caritas. It comes to man in a special act of grace and through no doing of his own. This means that agapē not only sets an example, not only helps human beings in their upward struggle, but also *causes* them to love in the first place. St. Paul had suggested something comparable when he said that the love of God is shed abroad in our hearts through the Holy Spirit. Augustine takes that statement literally. Only through divinely infused love, he says, can caritas be approximated, or even undertaken, in sinful man. He sums up the entire doctrine in a single sentence: "The Grace of God makes a willing man out of an unwilling one."

But if this is what St. Augustine believes, I fail to see how he can still retain the element of eros. For the saint who strives upward would merely be a vehicle for God's love. If caritas must be added to human nature by the external agency of the Holy Spirit, then in himself man does not love God. Only God would be capable of love, and when caritas operates in man, it would really be the working of the Holy Spirit. How else are we to take passages such as the following: "When God gives Himself to us in Christ, He gives us at once the object we are to love and the caritas with which to love it. The object we are to love is Himself, but Caritas is also Himself, who by the Holy Spirit takes up His abode in our hearts. Even the fact that we love God is itself entirely a gift of God."

On this problem the whole of medieval Christianity depends. If man in his own nature does not love God, then Christian eros is simply a device, an instrument, a contrivance of God's love. Since the Fall at least, all religious love would be reducible to agapē. To say this, however, is to give up the original synthesis.

Post-Augustinian philosophers, including St. Thomas Aquinas, fully recognized the seriousness of this problem. In his *Quaestiones Disputatae de Caritate* (recently translated as *On Charity*), St. Thomas analyzes the difficulty with his characteristic thoroughness. The first of the "disputed questions" about love deals exclusively with the relationship between eros and agapē, though neither word is ever used. The question runs as follows: "Whether charity is something created in the soul, or is it the Holy Spirit Itself?" By "caritas" Aquinas means what Augustine meant; for him, too, it covers both the love of God and the love of neighbor. To say that caritas is simply the Holy Spirit is to deny that it belongs to human nature. But then man could have no way of ascending, and therefore nothing like the eros attitude could explain the love of God. On the other hand, to say that caritas is something created in the soul—as opposed to the Holy Spirit, which is a Person of the Trinity and so uncreated— would seem to imply that a finite being immersed in the imperfections of matter can attain the love of God wholly by its own effort. This idea might satisfy the Greek philosophers, but it would be un-Christian. It would make the giving of grace unnecessary and severely limit the functioning of agapē. As a true Aristotelian, Aquinas tries to find the golden mean between these extremes. He criticizes both alternatives, but retains a saving remnant from each. The caritas-synthesis he then reconstructs by weaving together the disparate but doctrinally acceptable pieces.

In beginning with the possibility that Christian love is nothing but agapē (i.e., that caritas in man is just the Holy Spirit), Aquinas summarizes the arguments of Peter Lombard in favor of this view. He criticizes Lombard, but with interesting restraint. For Lombard cites Augustine as his authority and offers many quotations from the epistles of Paul and John. Obviously there is at stake a version of

Christianity which might have become orthodox if certain adjustments in the dogma had been made along the way. Aquinas will not
make these adjustments. As we shall see, Luther does—and in ways
that are very similar to Lombard's interpretation of Augustine. Had
Aquinas read Luther, he would have criticized him for committing
the same errors.

Nevertheless, Aquinas does not condemn Lombard's position as
heretical, although he uses that term for the opposite extreme. He
accepts Lombard as a master, says that it was the "excellence of
charity" which moved him to espouse his view, but concludes that
the argument itself is "ridiculous." In effect, Aquinas reasons as
follows: Caritas, the love of God and our neighbor, is an act of will. It
is therefore voluntary, which means that it proceeds from an "intrinsic principle." The intrinsic principle is that by which something acts
in the way that it naturally does. A stone falls to ground because of its
natural inclination to move downward. This inclination can be
thwarted, as when the stone is thrown upward, but then its movement proceeds from an *extrinsic*—not an intrinsic—principle. In
man voluntary behavior, based upon freedom of the will, is natural
and intrinsic. Human action that is not willed must be extrinsic, even
if it involves divine infusion. Consequently, if the act of caritas
proceeds from the Holy Spirit, it must be extrinsic to man—like
throwing a stone upward. If caritas is extrinsic, however, it cannot be
voluntary. And this is impossible, since loving implies willing
(freely).

Thus, as against Lombard, Aquinas maintains that caritas must
belong to some human disposition. But he also wishes to avoid the
opposite extreme, which considers caritas as something *purely* natural. To Aquinas this is heresy, leading directly into the Pelagian
belief that "natural principles of man are sufficient for meriting
eternal life." To avoid both extremes, Aquinas compromises. He
holds that caritas is indeed created in the soul and so operates by an
intrinsic principle, but that it nevertheless exceeds the capability of
nature. How can this be? Aquinas replies that caritas is a habit of will
created in man *as if* it were a natural inclination, yet specially given
by the Holy Spirit as the means by which God and neighbor are to be
loved. In this way Aquinas can maintain that charity proceeds from

an intrinsic principle while still being "added to human nature . . . perfecting the will." Superficially this solution may not seem to differ greatly from the thesis of Peter Lombard. For he too held that love was a created thing in man. But he thought it was created as an *embodiment* of the Holy Spirit, which moved the will immediately through itself without the institution of a human habit. Aquinas sees the importance of considering love as a habit. Not only does that give caritas an intrinsic principle distinctly human, but also it explains how caritas can be enjoyable and fully satisfying "in the manner of a natural inclination."

In reformulating the Augustinian synthesis, Aquinas does not deny that God is literally present in man's love. At least with respect to the love of neighbor, he says (as Augustine had before him): "That very celestial love by which we love each other is not only from God, but also is God." This love (agapē) is an uncreated love operating on the human level. Far from doubting its existence, Aquinas merely wishes to supplement it with love that is intrinsically human love—eros. Does this mean that in loving his neighbor the Christian combines two kinds of love? Apparently so. But then how does Aquinas distinguish between them in each actual occurrence? Where in neighborly love does he find the evidences of one or another? What should we look for in our attempt to discover eros and agapē cooperating in human caritas?

Unfortunately, Aquinas never answers these questions or any remotely comparable. The truth is that his reasoning is neither empirical nor commonsensical. At best, it consists of deductive arguments designed to reach preestablished conclusions based on preestablished premises. Here, for instance, it never occurs to him that he must show *how* agapē and eros mingle in specifiable occasions of human love, or *how* they may be separated out. He reasons as he does because one or another principle of theology, particularly those the church has canonized with the stamp of orthodoxy, requires him to move in fixed directions. Nor does Aquinas deny this. In criticizing Lombard, he makes it perfectly clear that an acceptable analysis of caritas *must* not challenge its ability to provide merit for the loving individual. For Aquinas as much as for Augustine, "love is the basis of meriting." Since it is only through love that man can *earn* the blessings of eternity, at least part of his caritas must depend upon an agency within himself. The basic motive underlying Aquinas' treatment of this problem reveals itself when he says: "Therefore if the soul does not effect an act of charity through some proper form, but only because it is moved by an extrinsic agent, i.e. by the Holy Spirit, then it will follow that it is considered only as an instrument for this act. There would not be, then, in man the power to act or not to act, and he would not be able to gain merit."

Now we see the forces really at work! It is the notion of human merit that determines the Thomistic argument. Caritas fulfills the law, he wants to say. It constitutes righteousness and leads to salvation. It is joyful in itself, but also it is the means by which men earn the reward of eventual beatitude. Consequently, caritas must—at least in part—pertain to some human disposition. If a Christian is to merit the benefits of heaven, his love must be authentically his own: belonging to an intrinsic form within his being, as Aquinas would put it. To say that love must be the effect of a free will is to restate the same idea. But since there can be no love without divine assistance, the Holy Spirit must also be present in a man, alongside that created caritas which is intrinsic to him. The love of God or neighbor is therefore the joint functioning of eros and agapē.

This much of St. Thomas' argument is wholly sound, at least as far as deductive reasoning is concerned. What seems to be illogical, however, is the further notion that created caritas must have been infused by a special and unique act of the Holy Spirit. Aquinas requires this idea because otherwise he would be treating caritas as a natural effect, which is the Pelagian heresy. But if created caritas comes as something "added to human nature," can it *really* be free or intrinsic to man? This is what Aquinas thinks he has proved. But I wish to question his success. Even if the Holy Spirit acts through a human habit of love, has it not coerced man just in causing the habit itself? Aquinas sees that man's will is not free if the Holy Spirit moves it immediately, directly, to the deeds of love; but he does not consider the possibility that the same holds true if the Holy Spirit acts *mediately*. For human caritas to be truly free of any extrinsic principle, each man must be allowed the opportunity to reject the habit of caritas itself. This, however, would give one the intrinsic ability to resist the Holy Spirit, to accept or spurn its love on the basis of one's independent nature. But that too leads to the Pelagian heresy with its reliance on "natural principles." For accepting God's love is already loving God, and if man can do one without divine infusion, he can also do the other. In his attempt to compromise, Aquinas would seem to be caught between two fires: on the one hand, the Pelagian heresy if man's love is to be truly intrinsic; on the other hand, the admission that human caritas can hardly be free or meritorious if its very character and existence are determined by the Holy Spirit.

In one place, Aquinas restates his position as if to answer this kind of criticism. He says that the Holy Spirit "moves man's soul to the act of love, as God moves all things to their own actions to which they are inclined by their own proper forms. And thus it is that He disposes all things sweetly, because to all things He gives forms and powers inclining them to that which He Himself moves them; so that they tend toward it not by force, but as if it were by their own free accord." But, as Aquinas said of Lombard: This opinion clearly cannot stand. For Aquinas can avoid the Pelagian heresy only by *denying* that God moves man's soul to the act of love in the way that he moves all things to their own actions, etc. If caritas is created in man just like all the other "forms and powers" that incline things to that which God designs, then it is a part of man's natural state and not something special. True, it may occur only at a particular moment in one's life; but the same would hold for all events in nature.

If Aquinas replies that caritas differs from most occurrences in being directly caused by the Holy Spirit, he once again vitiates the concept of merit. With love as the basis of meriting, no man could ever merit anything. Only the Holy Spirit, which instills caritas, would seem to have acted in a free and meritorious way. There is something almost sinister about the final line in the passage above: "so that they tend toward it not by force, but as if it were by their own free accord." One can imagine the universe being wholly determined, every man acting out a prearranged destiny but (because he feels no compulsion) doing so as if he were free. To those who lived *within* this universe merit could be earned in various ways, depending on the internal standards of morality or salvation. But if one stood outside and realized the deterministic situation, as Aquinas does, would it not be *dishonest* to assign merit on the basis of a sheer illusion—an illusory sense of freedom?

To a considerable extent, it was this kind of scruple about love that caused Luther to reject Catholicism. Certainly his return to the New Testament, particularly the letters of Paul, evinces distrust of the medieval synthesis. When Luther says that faith alone justifies us and fulfills the law, that Providence decides who will succeed in having faith, that good works do not make a man righteous but proceed from faith as "purely and simply outward signs"—in all this he is obviously avoiding the difficulties Aquinas tried to resolve. Faced with a choice between a world in which man merits salvation by freely striving upward and one in which God determines all things for reasons of his own, Luther unequivocally opts for the latter. He not only denies that man has a free will (except in minor, material matters—"to milk kine, to build houses, etc.") but also he claims that men who expect to attain anything spiritual by means of free will thereby deny Christ. As Paul had said "if righteousness come by the law, then Christ is dead in vain," so too does Luther condemn as ultimately un-Christian the entire medieval emphasis upon merit.

But the Lutheran attack runs even deeper. The medieval view is founded on more than just a belief in merit resulting from free will. It also, and more fundamentally, expresses faith in the perfectibility of human nature. The medievals took hope from the fact that man was created in the likeness of God. With the fall of Adam the image was sullied, and that was why Christ had to descend. With the help of God's love, however, the medievals thought that man could redeem himself—painful though this might be. Through the proper exercise of will, reason, and faith, human nature might be cleansed. It could even rise into divinity. Caritas, combining all the elements of love, was thus man becoming something more than man, the natural condition transcending itself. For Luther such melioration is impossible: man cannot improve his nature. Born a sinner, he must always remain a sinner—unless something miraculous happens, and that must come from outside of nature. Luther is contemptuous of holy men who claim to have ascended, however slightly, up the ladder of saintliness. "Human nature, through original sin, is wholly spoiled and perverted, outwardly and inwardly, in body and soul." As a result, one who thinks he has earned righteousness must really be guilty of either pride or self-delusion. "No one can exclude himself or boast that he is better than another. All are alike before God, and all must admit that they are guilty and deserving of eternal death and damnation." In his *Table Talk*, Luther honestly admits to his own inability to change for the better: "I have often been re-solved to live uprightly, and to lead a true godly life, and to set everything aside that would hinder this, but it was far from being put in execution." Given this frailty, which Luther considers in-escapable in man rather than a weakness peculiar to himself, one does best to recognize one's sinful being and leave the rest to God: "I will not lie or dissemble before my God, but will freely confess, I am not able to effect that good which I intend, but await the happy hour when God shall be pleased to meet me with his grace."

From this it follows that man cannot hope to approach God via the human will, that Christianized eros is an absurdity, the caritas-synthesis untenable, and the very idea that man can love God a dangerous snare of the devil. In one stroke the governing ideal of medieval religious society is deflated and vilified. What for hun-dreds of years had served as the highest aspiration of man is sud-denly turned inside out, condemned as a demonic ruse by which one is led downward at the very moment one *seems* to be ascending. The heavenly ladders are all deceptive: they are really "the way to the anti-Christ."

It takes a devil to recognize so devilish a plot, and Luther would have been the first to admit that his very sense of worthlessness has enabled him to solve the spiritual enigma of his times. In his book *Young Man Luther* the psychiatrist Erik Erikson assigns great impor-tance to the fear of hellfire and damnation inculcated by the popular religion of the late Middle Ages. But Erikson misses the other half of the ambivalence: the ideal of love as caritas, which was to save the sinner and without which nothing else really mattered. Approached as either religious turmoil or psychological disturbance, Luther's moral crisis results from the conflict between the medieval ideal he had inherited and the personal reality he felt within himself. Being unable to love God as the prior ideal said he *should*, Luther could choose among three alternatives: he could condemn himself but adhere to caritas as a way of life others might hope to achieve; he could reject caritas and substitute other ideals that would enable him to accept his natural inclinations; or else, he could condemn both himself and the ideal of caritas that had been forced upon him.

Of these three, Luther chose the last. The first was rendered impossible by his refusal to believe that others were really more loving than he. Human nature being corrupt and poisoned, the very desire to purify oneself through love could only indicate a secret *praesumptio*. "Thou holy Devil," he says ironically, "thou wilt make me a saint." And clearly with saints in mind, he argues that the search for godliness is always motivated by a false will: "Why are you choosing this way of life, this order, this work? Is it so that God may be placated or that you may be justified? You scoundrel, do you not hear that the son of God was given and that he shed his blood for you?" The conclusion is inescapable: "No one is godly purely for God's sake or solely because it is right and godly. Nature always will and must seek some reason why it should be godly; it cannot and may not be godly for godliness' sake, will not be satisfied with godliness as it should, but seeks to merit or escape something thereby." Where the medievals had considered ascension through caritas a way of imitating the risen Christ, Luther attacks it as self-inflation through a bogus sanctity: "Wherefore, all hypocrites and idolators essay to do those works which properly pertain to divinity and belong to Christ solely and alone. They do not indeed say with their mouth: I am God, I am Christ, yet in fact they arrogate to themselves the divinity and office of Christ."

But if the first alternative was unacceptable, the second was even more so. Had Luther chosen it, he could hardly have remained a Christian. To idealize one's natural inclinations, including carnal love and self-aggrandizement, might alleviate the sense of worthlessness but only by destroying the concept of sin. A God who could tolerate human nature as it is—man loving the world instead of the deity who created it—would have been to Luther no God at all. For him, as for Paul, Christianity showed its superiority over Judaism and the pagan cults by *refusing* to accept nature as it is, by insisting that apart from God's agapē *all* things in the world are evil. This much of the caritas-synthesis Luther had no desire to attack.

In choosing the third alternative, condemning himself and rejecting caritas, Luther emancipates himself from his Catholic origins in the only way that a man can achieve freedom from his source: by satisfying the letter of its ideals while replacing them with a new spirit. Luther fulfills this requirement to the point of absurdity. If the natural world is to be renounced, he says, everything in it must be treated as sinful—*including* the love of God. Love God by admitting your utter and total inability to love God. By these paradoxical means could Luther satisfy his Catholic heritage at the same time that he rejected it. As primitive Christianity considered the Jews halfheartedly religious for wanting to change the world instead of renouncing it, so too does Luther find the Catholics halfheartedly Christian for wanting to perfect man's love instead of sacrificing it with all the rest. So great is Luther's fervor (or supererogation) that it frees him to question the very possibility of loving God. In emphasizing faith, Paul had largely ignored the first commandment; but nowhere does he challenge its feasibility. Luther does, and on purely realistic grounds: "No one is able to love God from his whole heart, etc., and his neighbor as himself." The law in general he accepts as a guide to moral conduct which is nevertheless useless for salvation. Even when it is taken "spiritually" (subsumed under the Great Commandments about love), the law cannot cleanse the soul: "But this understanding of the law spiritually is far more deadly, since it makes the law impossible to fulfill and thereby brings man to despair of his own strength and abases him, for no one is without anger, no one without lust: such are we from birth. But what will a man do, whither will he go, when oppressed by such an impossible law?"

In saying that even the precept of love is "an impossible law," Luther remains a Christian but a Christian with different ideals. His is not a reformation of the old faith: it is a *new creation*. He may appeal to earlier texts, but he is making what is virtually a new religion. In denying that man can love in the manner of caritas, he magnifies human dependence upon God's love. And since agapē most dramatically manifests itself in the descent of Christ or the Holy Spirit, fellowship with divinity occurs at the level of man rather than the level of God: "God's grace and His kingdom with all virtues must come to us, if we are to attain it; we can never come to Him." Not through holiness but only through faith in the midst of natural evil is oneness with God possible. Faith itself being something God instills through love, there could be no element in the process of redemption for which man could claim the slightest credit. For Luther, Christ comes only to sinners in the sense that *no one can be righteous* except through the coming of Christ. Never before—not even in the writings of Paul—had the concept of agapē been given such prominence. The worse a man is, the less one can expect him to be capable of love; but then, Luther argues, the more essential is it for him to rely exclusively on God's love. And if human nature is as rotten as Luther thinks, there may be little else that one *can* turn toward. For him at least, the doctrinal and psychological sustenance of Christianity could not be found elsewhere.

Allowing into his idealization nothing but agapē, Luther describes it in terms as ecstatic as those of any predecessor. He speaks of the divine nature as a "furnace," a fire of love that fills heaven and earth with its burning energy. "If it were possible to paint and picture love," he says, "we should have to make such a picture as would be not of works nor human, yea not of angels nor heavenly, but God Himself." In drawing this picture, Luther sees agapē as a free and overflowing bestowal. Indifferent to the worthlessness of its object, it lavishly makes all things good. It issues forth for no reason other than joy in being able to give itself. It is that in God which "loves sinners, evil persons, fools, and weaklings in order to make them righteous, good, wise, and strong." Luther compares God's love to a brook or fresh streamlet which wells "from within out of the heart . . . which ever flows on and cannot be stopped or dried up or fail, which says: I love thee, not because thou art good or bad, for I draw my love not from thy goodness as from an alien spring, but from mine own well-spring." In one place he describes agapē as a mother's tender solicitude; in another, he shows it quieting the fears that have been rightly aroused by Moses and his "most terrible" law.

In saying that only God is capable of love, and in depicting it as something that sinful man can hardly imagine, Luther does not mean to deny its occurrence among human beings. On the contrary, he sees God's grace continually descending into the community of men. If only we stop *trying* to raise ourselves toward God, he says, we can easily recognize the presence of agapē in our midst. In terms reminiscent of what Aquinas considered to be self-evidently wrong, Luther claims that God uses man as the "instrument" or "medium" of his love. Man himself cannot love, but he can receive God's love and pass it on to his neighbor. Though faith increases and facilitates man's receptivity, God's love does not require it. The Holy Spirit works its will equally on those who resist and those who consent—"as a potter makes a pot out of clay." More precisely, as Luther remarks, the Holy Spirit so molds the will of man that he spontaneously agrees to be God's vehicle. When that happens, agapē flows freely through its appointed circuit. Having originated with God, it establishes a community of love among men by using each of them as a means of conveying the divine love to his neighbor. Indeed, the *entire* Christian message now consists of faith and love, which Luther characterizes as that "by which a man is placed between God and his neighbor as a medium which receives from above and gives out again below, and is like a vessel or tube through which the stream of divine blessings must flow without intermission to other people."

In saying that agapē is the essence of God, Luther hardly deviates from the Christian tradition—whether primitive or medieval. But once he describes loving relations among men as *nothing but* agapē, his new theology becomes radical and subversive. For although Paul had said "I live; yet not I, but Christ liveth in me," neither he nor any other Christian authority had ever denied that love could in some sense be human. The paradox or ambiguity of Paul's statement to the Philippians had been typical of the entire tradition: "Work out your *own* salvation with fear and trembling: for *it is God* which worketh in you both to will and to do of His good pleasure." Luther cuts the knot, resolves the ambiguity. You cannot work out your own salvation, he insists, *because* it is God which worketh in you.

Why did Luther feel the need to make so devastating a change? Nothing in the New Testament or the church fathers *required* him to deny that human nature could be miraculously changed by the Holy Spirit. For Luther no less than Aquinas, the descent of agapē is infinitely creative, an intervention free to alter natural conditions in any way whatsoever. Given this latitude, Aquinas imagines the Holy Spirit creating a new faculty in man and thus perfecting his will by means of the love he now enjoys. Only Luther insists on limiting the miracle: agapē will flow through man, but he himself cannot acquire the capacity to love. Why *should* Luther make this limitation? If he wishes to remind men that they are by nature sinners at the mercy of an inscrutable deity, he makes the point merely in assigning faith and love to the predestination of the Holy Spirit. If he wishes to emphasize that love has a divine source, he does so—as all the Catholics had—by identifying agapē with God's essence. There is nothing in the logic of the Christian dogma which forces Luther to believe in his kind of miracle rather than that of Aquinas.

To some people the solution to such problems must always be found in political considerations. We know that Luther condemned the Catholic church as a temporal as well as a spiritual force; and we know that the church promised salvation on the basis of good works that perpetuated its power as an institution. If man could not ascend to God by merit, good works would have to be subordinated to faith—an attitude inherently noninstitutional. And what better way to undermine the search for merit than to deny that love—"the basis of meriting"—was even available to man? The Lutheran attack on caritas could thus be explained on ecclesiastical grounds alone.

I find this interpretation very hard to accept. It is abstract and artificial: remote from what goes on in the thinking of a man like Luther. For the most part—just how much, it is not for us to say— Luther attacked the power of the church for reasons that were not political, but spiritual or ideological. Since nothing in the dogma of Christianity *obliged* him to reconstitute the accepted theology as he did, his attitude can only be understood as a new moral commitment. It was a creative reorientation that nothing external required, but without which his personal life would have lost all meaning. In other words, it was Luther's way of formulating a new idealization.

Approached in this manner, Luther's rejection of his medieval past takes on greater authenticity. Instead of an institution that thought it could teach men how to love, he needed faith in a God whose own love would make up all human deficiencies. Though caritas was intended as a doctrine for all Christians, its development as a human faculty was largely reserved for those in the church, particularly the monastic orders. It is surely no coincidence that young man Luther entered an Augustinian monastery. Was he not a troubled soul like St. Augustine, and did not Christianity offer him the same opportunity to escape an earthly father he could not love? Through the church, Augustine had found the ability to love a spiritual Father whose love for him was guaranteed. A kind of miracle had happened, and one can imagine Luther at the monastery in Erfurt waiting to see whether it would happen again. It did not happen to him or to anyone around him. These spiritual failures, or what he took as such, convinced him that neither as a monk nor as anything else could a man be trained to love the spiritual Father. At best one might only hope that God would accept a human being with all his imperfections, simply as he was, unable to love but assured of its supreme importance. In living with this hope, one already emancipated oneself from the earthly father. He too was incapable of loving, and above all in the manner of agapē. That could be found only in the bountiful, but unmerited, grace of God.

Because Luther idealizes a fatherly agapē, Fromm sees in his doctrine a peculiar mixture of matriarchal and patriarchal influences. "We can recognize here that the Catholic doctrine of good works is part of the patriarchal picture; I can procure father's love by obedience and by fulfilling his demands. The Lutheran doctrine, on the other hand, in spite of its manifest patriarchal character, carries within it a hidden matriarchal element. Mother's love cannot be acquired; it is there, or it is not there; all I can do is to have faith (as the Psalmist says, 'Thou hadst let me have faith into my mother's breasts') and to transform myself into the helpless, powerless child. But it is the peculiarity of Luther's faith that the figure of the mother has been eliminated from the manifest picture, and replaced by that of the father; instead of the certainty of being loved by mother, intense doubt, hoping against hope for unconditional love by *father*, has become the paramount feature." Of course, this presupposes Fromm's distinction between mother's love and father's love. Once we give that up, there no longer remains the need to characterize Luther's faith as a mixture of manifest and hidden elements such as the ones that Fromm predicates. Instead, the Lutheran doctrine may be seen as an idealization of what children often hope to get from their fathers: not morality with its restrictive laws, but infinite and unconditional love. Having found no such father on earth, Luther posits him in heaven. Obviously, he felt he could not live unless there were some such father *somewhere*.

And yet, this much in Luther hardly explains his rejection of caritas. After all, the medievals believed in agapē just as firmly as he. They too yearned for the infinite love of a spiritual Father. For them God showed this love merely by helping sinful man to merit his own salvation. If the doctrine no longer worked for Luther, it must have been because he needed a *different kind* of father. And that means he must have been a different kind of son. Especially in its medieval setting, there is something innocent and benign about the caritas-synthesis. It provides man with a new Garden of Eden, a new world where mortals may collaborate with God, each in his own way helping humanity to rise toward salvation. And like the Eden story, the medieval picture is a glorious wish-fulfillment, a dream of success, a paradise of love earned through love itself. But for Luther as for Hamlet, the garden of life is poisonous: it is "an unweeded garden, / That grows to seed. Things rank and gross in nature / Possess it merely." The desirability of aspiring love, Luther can easily recognize; but it seems to him unrealistic. In its magnificence caritas exceeds all human capability: "For such love is not a natural art, nor grown in our garden." Luther's attitude is anything but innocent. It is gnarled with the sores of real life, anxious, tormented, possibly pathological. For all his activism, Luther throws himself into a passive role as if even God would despair of this man's ability to serve as anything but an instrument. When he speaks of man as the vessel or tube through which the stream of divine blessings must flow, one is reminded of the way in which primitive religions worshiped the semen. Luther is not referring to sexual matters, but his image is interesting not only because of its physiological suggestiveness but also because Luther so clearly doubts his own potency. For him the stream of love *must* belong to God: it is awful and inhuman but irresistibly holy. Would he have felt this way if he had not magnified his own inadequacies as a human being in nature, if he had not idealized the very failures that convince him man cannot love?

I also detect something defiant in Luther's refusal to believe that caritas is really possible. Though God has infinite power, perhaps Luther does not trust him to use it as the medievals had promised. With the wisdom of a peasant, Luther will not budge from what he knows best: his own worthlessness. It is as if the Lutheran man will meet God only on the human level, where he is at home among the sins of nature. Far from venturing upward, man will dig his heels into the earth, resist and struggle rebelliously, like a sensitive, honest, neurotic child who wants it clearly understood that he is being bad. If then the loving parent can graciously descend, accepting recalcitrance as a human reality yet bearing it away on an infinite stream of love, he will have proved himself a savior and a living God indeed. "I can do no other. Here I stand. God help me." Luther may have uttered these words before the Diet of Worms, but he was speaking to God.

As often happens with single-minded extremes, Luther's position turns into its opposite. Even wayward children grow up to become parents themselves. Luther originally cast out the medieval synthesis as being pretentious, the most insidious of all devilish attempts by which man tries to arrogate divinity to himself. And yet, by the time he has completed his doctrine of love, the wheel has come full circle: Luther too—and more than most theologians—describes the loving man as a kind of god. "But we are gods through love, which makes us beneficent to our neighbor, for Divine nature is nothing else but pure beneficence." In using a man as the instrument of its agapē, the Holy Spirit transforms him even more completely than the caritas view had suggested. For no Catholic saint could hope for ultimate union within this life, partly because his love would still be human. Since Luther denies that love can *ever* be human, he sees its occurrence as the means by which God "produces a divine man, who is one cake with Him." And elsewhere: "Moreover, he that abides in love, abides in God and God in him, so that he and God become one cake." Through love the faithful become "each the other's Christ." Miserable creatures that they would be without God's grace, their love now makes them the saviors of the universe.

In a similar vein, Luther describes the spiritual marriage with all the joyfulness of medieval literature (though none of its purity): "Who then can fully appreciate what this royal marriage means? Who can understand the riches of the glory of this grace? Here this rich and divine bridegroom Christ marries this poor, wicked harlot, redeems her from all her evil, and adorns her with all his goodness. Her sins now cannot destroy her, since they are laid upon Christ and swallowed up by Him. And she has the righteousness in Christ, her husband, of which she may boast as her own and which she can confidently display alongside her sins in the face of death and hell and say: 'If I have sinned, yet my Christ, in whom I believe, has not sinned, and all his is mine and all mine is his!' "

Is Luther inconsistent then? Or is he showing us how human nature *really* changes from the sinful to the loving condition? Is he closer to the caritas-synthesis than either he or his followers realize?

In his biography of Santayana's later years, Daniel Cory records an attempt by Santayana to explicate the concept of caritas:

> Santayana made a sustained effort to explain to Edman after luncheon just what he understands by "charity." Renunciation of self and all the allurements of life are the essential preliminary steps—the indispensable discipline in the ascent to God. The genuine saint must pass through a dark night of the soul in order to be alone with the Alone. (This does not entail that God is "lonely"—he has plenty to think about—but only that he is utterly self-sufficient.) But having reached this pinnacle, or climax in spiritual progress, the mission of the saint has only begun: he has graduated, so to speak, in the school of charity. For the soul must descend again into the world and issue in good deeds. If the initial purification in Divine love—or the Alone—is genuine and complete, however, the soul is never the same, for it henceforth loves *impartially* all creatures, because they are God's creatures, and God is nothing but Love.

In referring to a dark night of the soul, Santayana could be thinking of St. John of the Cross. His type of mysticism belongs to a special development in sixteenth-century Catholicism that goes beyond the scope of this book. Otherwise, Santayana's explication perfectly fits the medieval concept of caritas. The trajectory is cyclical: the saint rises into mystical union and then descends for the sake of fellow man. Up the mountain of love and down again, out of the Platonic cave and back in again. In articulating this trajectory, caritas idealizes the circuit of give-and-take in all reciprocal love. Agapē descends that man may rise through eros; and having purified himself, the saint imitates Christ's self-sacrifice with the knowledge that he too will be resurrected. The underlying pattern—higher and lower caring about each other—derives from Plotinus, as do Santayana's references to the Alone. But in caritas the circuit of love becomes a *personal* transaction. God and man relate to one another as persons. The giving of agapē and the taking of eros are not metaphysical principles so much as the total commitment between lover and beloved. Caritas is thus the idealization of a happy and harmonious love. In a perfect reciprocity that duplicates the rhythm of successful coitus, God and the saintly soul love each other in the only way appropriate to their natures. Having been made creative through caritas, the saint may then bestow himself upon all other creatures. With the certitude that God cares about *him*, he freely and joyously takes care of everything else that God may care about.

As I have suggested, there is something innocent and optimistic about medieval caritas. St. Bernard and St. Thomas were not tortured souls like Luther; and even St. Augustine became less troubled once he found Christianity. The Catholic saints, like Plato himself, retain a serenity of aspiration wholly lacking in Luther. The gravity of the world does not pull as hard on them. Their idealized souls soar upward because they have nothing in their experience to hold them down. They have little sense of material cathexes, the dynamism that makes things to be as they are on earth. Temporal considerations they leave to men who care more about power than about salvation. Not that the medieval church ignored the uses of worldly dominion; but the theological saints show meager awareness of it in their writings about love. They belong to a different type of humanity from Luther and St. Paul. The latter feel their human weight, the drag of being mortal and possibly worthless. The medievals thought only of rising above the realm of matter; Luther thinks only of struggling against it. Learning how to live with his material limitations, he becomes a man of action. Like all doers of the deed, he suspects that those who wish to rise are somehow out of touch, cut off from the realities of this world, insensitive to the coarseness and crudity of human nature. In Marlowe's play, Mephistopheles tells Doctor Faustus: "Why, this is hell, nor am I out of it; / Thinkst that I who saw the face of God / And tasted the eternal joys of heaven / Am not tormented with ten thousand hells / In being deprived of everlasting bliss?" Luther might have said the same, except that he had never seen the face of God—only read the accounts of mystics who *thought* they had, and whom he distrusted.

In eliminating from love all elements except agapē, Luther would seem to be idealizing nothing but bestowal. Yet he does so in a way that also idealizes self-recognition, particularly the recognition of one's sinfulness. He refuses to believe in caritas because he thinks it violates the *integrity* of the human condition. Selfish, carnal, aggressive by nature, man cannot love and neither can he work out his own salvation. But, Luther insists, he can *admit* to being what he is. As if to rub a dog's nose in its own excrement, Luther demands a realistic confession of spiritual failure. From this a new ideal arises: the ideal of what Nietzsche called becoming what one is. As against the medievals, Luther asserts that caritas tries to make man into something else. And so it does. Caritas glorifies change and melioration, human growth issuing from the very search for perfection. It idealizes what Sartre calls "self-transcendence," the aspect of man which prevents him from having an essence because he is always creating a new one. In criticizing the caritas-synthesis, Luther idealizes what Sartre calls "facticity"—man having become a definite something whose reality cannot be denied.

But Luther says more than that: he also claims that man transcends himself only by realizing he cannot transcend himself. How similar to Freud is Luther in all of this! Both come at the end of a great idealistic tradition (for Freud it is the Romantic movement), which they attack as being unrealistic, self-delusory, naive about human goodness. They both fear the *hybris* that comes from trying to be spiritual. They both idealize descent (God communing with man at the lower level, man immersing himself—for therapeutic reasons—into the unconscious); and they both explain everything in terms of metaphysical energy, agapē and the libido being less dissimilar than one might expect. Above all, they both idealize the facing of bitter facts. In Luther this love of seeing and admitting what is hateful in oneself becomes a virtual precondition for salvation. It does not elicit agapē, for nothing can. But it is the only *honest* thing a man can do while waiting for Godot.

Oddly enough, this realistic side of Luther aligns him with precisely those pagan philosophers he wished to expunge from Christian dogma. He rejects caritas because it embodies Greek notions about the ideality of eros. And yet, his argument is based on doubts about reciprocity that resemble, even duplicate, those of the Greeks. As Aristotle had seen that the inequality between men and gods prevented them from enjoying perfect friendship with one another, so too does Luther deny the possibility of mutual love between sinful man and the infinitely good God of Christianity. Also like Aristotle, Luther predicates an ultimate narcissism in all human nature. Of course, Aristotle had argued that loving the ideal *is* the best way to love oneself; and the doctrine of caritas uses this as a major support. But long before Luther, medieval thinkers had begun to wonder whether Aristotelian narcissism was really compatible with the caritas-synthesis. Abelard, for instance, had maintained that "true love goes out directly and solely to the person loved, excluding all consideration of recompense to the person loving." From this he concluded that the love of God must be selfless and gratuitous, that it must not consist in desiring God as the highest good or for the sake of beatitude, but simply because God and only God is infinitely *worthy* of love.

In his book on St. Bernard, Gilson shows how remote is Abelard's position from the orthodox doctrine of the Middle Ages. For if Abelard were right, caritas would not be a proper way of loving God. Caritas assumes, as Aristotle had, that man *must* love himself in the sense of seeking a perfect goodness for himself. For the Christian this meant desiring God as the highest good and for the sake of the beatitude that comes from uniting with him. In effect, Abelard was saying that if the Aristotelian psychology was right, caritas must be wrong; if man loved God on the basis of self-love, then he did not love God properly. As the only way to salvage the love of God, Abelard rejects the narcissistic premises. Like him, Luther claims to have found a flaw in the caritas argument. He, however, accepts the narcissistic premises but rejects the traditional conclusions. Man cannot love either God or the ideal as he should, Luther says, *because* he really loves only himself. Luther presupposes the Aristotelian psychology just as much as the caritas-synthesis had. He merely uses it for a different end.

Possibly it is Luther's belief in narcissism that explains his ideas about deification. Because man loves himself, he cannot love God; but when agapē uses man as an instrument of its love, he *becomes* a kind of god. Overtly, in terms of the Lutheran doctrine, this transformation is not narcissistic. For man himself has no way of effecting his deification. On the contrary, it was belief in caritas that presumed to make man into a god; and for Luther this *praesumptio* was self-love at its worst. Nevertheless, the result is similar. In one way or another, human nature is portrayed as merging with divinity. Whether in caritas or unaccompanied agapē, religious love encourages man to identify with God. The paths may be different, but the goals seem indistinguishable: the spirit of man swells into a cosmic narcissism, first creating God in its own image and then imagining itself as an instance of the divine. From Plotinus to Luther the distance may not be great after all.

As against what I have been saying, Rudolph Otto argues that deification does not mean the same in Luther as in Plotinus. Through the writings of John Tauler and the *Theologia Germanica*, Luther had been deeply influenced by Eckhart; and Otto suggests that neither in Luther nor in Eckhart does one find anything comparable to the state of ecstasy in Plotinus. This may well be true. Plotinus belongs to the eros tradition and does not employ the concept of agapē. For him ecstasy is the culmination of mystical ascent. It precedes the soul's return to worldly duties, as in the doctrine of caritas; but for Plotinus, God himself does not descend. Since Eckhart and Luther believe in deification on the human level,

they readily discard Plotinus' ideas about ecstasy. From this, however, it does not follow that Plotinian merging is wholly foreign to
their thinking. Otto claims that in Plotinus deification means the
annihilating of man, whereas in Eckhart and Luther it is man living
and working in God. But if this is so, why does Eckhart describe
deification in the following terms: "The 'I' is reduced there to utter
nought and nothing is left there but God . . . and with God's own
all-penetrativeness she streams into the eternal Godhead, where in
an eternal stream God is flowing into God." And why does Luther
characterize God's loving descent as "a true 'bestowal of being,' a
sharing of the nature of the divine with the creature"? (my italics) In
holding out the promise of *unio substantialis* (union of substance)
with God, Luther would seem to accept something very like Plotinus'
notion of merging. Given the usual Christian ambiguities, he would
seem to hope for a comparable annihilation of man.

In both Eckhart and Luther deification empties the soul of its
humanity and fills it with the divine spirit. The emptying leads to
total passivity as a special case of Christian nomos; the filling, however, issues into activism and supernatural power. Thus, Eckhart
says: "To be installed in God, this is not hard, seeing that God
Himself must be working in us; for it is Godly work, man may
acquiesce and make no resistance; he may be passive while allowing
God to act in him." And Luther, arguing that good works proceed
from faith, associates faith with a passive receptivity. "To be passive
is to be perfected and consummated." In the perfected state, however, "a man of faith, without being driven, willingly and gladly
seeks to do good to everyone, serve everyone, suffer all kinds of
hardships, for the sake of the love and glory of the God who has
shown him such grace." As if to anticipate Portia's speech about the
quality of mercy, Luther describes the "passive righteousness of
faith" as follows: "Like as the earth engendereth not rain, nor is able
by her own strength, labour, and travail to procure the same, but
receiveth it of the mere gift of God from above, so this heavenly
righteousness is given us of God without our works or deservings."

On the surface, this combination of passivity and activism may
resemble the pattern of caritas; but really it is quite different. The
passivity of Luther and the humility of the medievals are both

renunciation, but not of the same type. Passivity destroys natural processes through a *suspension* of the will. It is religious catatonia, and for Luther it is not especially meritorious except as a preliminary to the divine infusion. As opposed to this, humility is an act of man, indeed a habit. It subjugates nature by conforming the will to its supernatural source. Humility constrains, but does not suspend the human will. It therefore enables man to transcend himself and so to earn the promised beatitude. Likewise, when the caritas-saint returns to earth, he represents a purified human nature acting in accordance with God's original intention. But in Luther it is not man, even perfected man, who really acts: it is God. How can the human soul descend in loving action when it is too sinful to have ascended in the first place? No, the works of love by which agapē binds one creature to another can never belong to mortal nature. They must be a literal epiphany: the march of God on earth.

In saying this, Luther contributes to a revolution far greater than any he could have imagined. Henceforth, the Christian could hold not only that God is Love but also that Love is God. And in that event, should we not revere—equally and indiscriminately—*every* occurrence of love? It was precisely to avoid this conclusion that the medievals distinguished between caritas and cupiditas. And though they idealized the former at the expense of the latter, treating caritas as the one virtue that merited salvation, they never identified it with God. Caritas was either eros rising toward man's highest good or else agapē helping man to work out his salvation. By retaining the human element, the medieval synthesis could always discriminate (in principle, at least) between that in love which is God and that which is not. When Luther denies that natural man can truly love, he makes all such distinctions impossible. In every instance love must be miraculous, a showing forth of God, nothing but agapē working in the world. But then love must always be holy, all love and every occasion of it. How could Luther have known that later generations would lose the faith in a transcendental deity but retain the rest of his doctrine: that for them what Dylan Thomas calls "the force that through the green fuse drives the flower" would *be* divinity? Luther did not suspect that men who consider themselves Christians could worship love in nature as the only God one knows directly. Yet this was the effect of his teaching. The idea that love is the unmerited sanctification of the sinner degenerated into the notion that sinners become sanctified through *any* love whatsoever. God disappeared, but there remained the holiness of indiscriminate love binding one worthless person to another. From the Lutheran source there sprang a new naturalism and a new humanism, and much that we call Romantic love—both within Christianity and without. Even Luther's idea that Christian love is a *lost love*—"a divine, free, unceasing, yea indeed a lost love for people"—led to sentimental romanticism in ways that would have increased his sense of guilt if only he had realized the anti-Christian implications. With Luther religious love of the Middle Ages comes to an end. In its struggle for survival, Christianity would have to contend with forces previously unknown, with idealizations it may have fathered but could no longer control.

If now we return to Nygren's thesis about the caritas-synthesis and its rejection by the Protestant Reformation, we may possibly find the issues easier to clarify. Nygren maintained that the idea of caritas was internally inconsistent and therefore untenable on purely formal grounds. He held that the concepts of eros and agapē were logically incompatible, or at least that they structured irreconcilable attitudes toward love. Luther having been the first theologian to suspect this, Nygren thus argues for the preferability of his position.

From my discussion thus far, it should be obvious that I do not consider the concepts of eros and agapē to be logically incompatible either with themselves or with nomos and philia. There is no logical contradiction in thinking that man's love is the created effect of God's love, which both complements and causes it, leading it to spiritual union after all other inclinations have been renounced. I do fail to see how caritas can be a free and meritorious love; but this difficulty does not result from an incompatibility between eros and agapē. All Christian love would seem to be determined by the Holy Spirit, whether agapē occurs by itself or in the company of eros.

These concepts are all confusing, and on a verifiable theory of meaning, unintelligible. But this too is different from claiming a logical incompatibility.

Neither do I believe that eros and agapē formulate attitudes inherently irreconcilable. The conflict lies elsewhere, between Christian attitudes that *choose to harmonize* these elements, as in the caritas-synthesis, and those that refuse to do so, as in Luther's thinking. Nygren is right to emphasize the vast differences between Catholic and Protestant ideas about love. But these differences are not built into the concepts of eros, agapē, nomos, and philia—at least, not necessarily. What really separates the two versions of Christianity is the way in which they combine the elements or try to lessen their number. It is not eros and agapē that conflict, but rather the caritas-synthesis and the Reformation doctrine as a whole. This divergence is sufficiently great, however, to make us wonder whether Christianity can actually effect a single ecumenical religion. At stake is more than just a formula, or the right word for love. Two antagonistic types of idealization have been constructed, two separate though overlapping clusters, and they differ almost as much as realist and idealist attitudes toward love in the ancient world. One might even say that Luther is to St. Thomas Aquinas as Lucretius was to Plato. Regardless of what they call themselves, men seem to fall into two classes: those who believe that human nature is inherently good, and therefore capable of an ideal love, and those who do not—Hsün Tzu versus Mencius, Hobbes versus Locke, Schopenhauer versus Hegel, Proust versus Stendhal. Such differences may ultimately be temperamental. They are not superficial, or easily resolved. But neither do they preclude great areas of agreement. Luther and the caritas doctrine are alike, if only in idealizing a transcendental love. They are equally, jointly liable to whatever criticism religious idealization may warrant.

15

Religious Idealization

As a Philosophical Concept, the love of persons is the foundation of all Christian religion. At least in principle, Christianity dedicates itself to this above all other attitudes. St. Augustine explicitly argues that the love of persons is the highest virtue, the supreme ideal, the basis for all morality. In the *Symposium* Plato had suggested that love—though not of persons— was the pinnacle of the good life; but he never developed this idea, and in the *Republic* he lists only justice, wisdom, temperance, and courage as cardinal virtues. In formulating the ethics of the Catholic church, Augustine subsumes these four under love. True love would issue into them, he says; and without love, they could not really be virtues. The inspiration of the *Symposium* is thus combined with the religious idealization of First Corinthians, Plato and Paul being synthesized into a new morality of love. Aquinas continues the tradition; and so does Luther. Though he denies that sinful man can reach as high as Christian love, Luther affirms its ideality and believes in a God whose supreme goodness creates the love of persons. In the following pages I shall argue that this type of idealization fails to understand what it is to love another person, indeed that it renders the love of persons impossible. This failure reveals itself in problems about the object of love. It is here that traditional Christianity must make its final defense.

❋

For the caritas-synthesis there can be only one authentic object of love—God. Aquinas says "the proper and essential object of charity is God," much as Augustine had insisted that "God then alone is to be loved; and all this world, that is, all sensible things, are to be despised." If this sounds too extreme, too violent to human nature, too exclusive in its limitations, one need only remember the wording of the first commandment. *Can* the man who loves God with all his heart, and all his soul, and all his mind, and all his strength have room for any other object of love?

Particularly in Augustine, though this is true of many Christian mystics as well, one senses a great spiritual calm that pervades the religious soul once it realizes that only God is worthy of love. Choice has been simplified by eliminating all competition. For those who are sensitive to the infinite and competing allurements of life, as Augustine surely was, the idea of loving only God can bring peace and freedom from distraction. It disciplines one's scattered inclinations, like blinders on a horse, and may even serve as a means of overcoming Satan. For others, however—those who have less reason to fear the devil or maybe less capacity to envisage God—the narrowness of the choice will always seem barbarous and self-destructive. Even within the Judaeo-Christian religions, the commandment to love one's neighbor encourages a more inclusive attitude. Certainly for the Jews the first commandment was never to be taken in isolation. God was the prime, the most exalted, object of love; but not the only one. The Jews had even assumed that one could not love God *properly* unless one also loved every aspect of his creation—one's neighbor as oneself, but also nature and the world at large. Since God was the greatest of all artisans, how could one glorify him without cherishing his handiwork? Nor has this sentiment been lacking in Christianity. It is represented by the idea that somehow all things must be good and therefore lovable, God having no reason to create an imperfect universe. Since Augustine and Aquinas both hold this view, how can they say that only God is worthy of love?

Augustine deals with the problem by distinguishing between two kinds of objects. First, he says, there are things we love *for their own sake*, in themselves, as ends or termini. These we wish to enjoy (*frui* in Latin). But also there are things we love merely as the *means* of attaining what is enjoyable. Such goods are valuable only in their use (*uti*); and though their utility may be great, we do not love them for their own sake. In this way Augustine distinguishes between uti and frui, two different types of love: on the one hand, a love of in-strumentalities that lead to an end beyond themselves; and on the other hand, a love that terminates in that which is purely enjoyable. He gives the example of a man who uses a ship to return home. The ultimate objective is the enjoying of one's native land; the journey on the ship serves an important function but only as a means toward the further interest. Similarly, all Christians must act like voyagers in a foreign country. If they loved the world in the sense of enjoying it for itself, they might forget their essential destination. They must therefore love only God in the manner of frui, and all other objects in the manner of uti. Nothing but God can be the proper object of an ultimate love since he alone is worth enjoying for his own sake. All else must be "detested" as candidates for frui. Things of this world are not good enough to be loved in themselves, even though they may (and indeed must) be loved as the means by which God enables man to journey toward him. The distinction between caritas and cupiditas naturally employs this line of reasoning, as does Augus-tine's distinction between virtue and vice: "Good men use the world in order to enjoy God, whereas bad men want to use God in order to enjoy the world."

I have no desire to minimize the advantages of this formulation. The man who cannot subordinate means to ends can never attain happiness or truly love either the means or the ends. Augustine would have us remember at every moment that different objects require different kinds of love. And he is right: for moral turpitude consists in rendering to one object the love that belongs to another. Moreover, the Augustinian distinction is oddly liberating and may even be taken as a naturalistic sanction not at all foreign to the spirit of Catholicism. For if the world and all things other than God are simply means, they lose their ability to enslave us. They become subject to human employment, man having been given dominion— as Genesis affirms—"over every living thing that moveth upon the earth." All objects may then be used for the sake of salvation;

everything may be loved as an instrument if only it brings us closer to God. Thus, after the passage in which Augustine says that sensible things must be despised, he adds: "while, however, they are to be used as this life requires." He offers the same idea in the famous dictum, quoted by Rabelais and many others who distort or modify its major import: *Dilige, et quod vis fac* ("Love, and do as you wish"). For if one loves *properly*, which is what Augustine means, loving only God as the final object of aspiration and enjoyment, nothing one does can possibly be wrong. The man who truly loves God may freely love himself, the world, and all conceivable things that serve to further his spiritual ends.

But although Augustine succeeds in subordinating lesser loves to the one considered most important, his doctrine falsifies the love of persons. It even commits a disrespect toward the works of God. If everything is but a means to an ultimate object of love, nothing can be *cherished* or *fully appreciated* except that ultimate. As a mere instrumentality, no person, thing, or institution could be loved in itself. But then how can we satisfy the second commandment? Do we love our neighbor as ourselves if we but use him as a vehicle to something else? Can we even love ourselves? According to Augustine, self-love provides a reason for loving God since we thereby attain beatitude; but Augustine also says that man must never love himself in the sense of frui. The self is to be loved only as an instrumentality, never as an object of enjoyment. But then how can self-love be a reason for loving God? Moreover, I fail to see how anyone could love himself *merely* as an instrument. Though the Augustinian saint cares about himself only as a vehicle for enjoying God, still it is *he* who does the enjoying. Would this be possible unless the saint bestowed value upon the activity itself, treating it as an end and not merely as a means? But to that extent he would be loving himself in the sense of frui: himself as well as God. And if these objects of love are compatible with one another, why not say the same about our neighbor—indeed everything else that Augustine relegates to the category of uti? Why should we not be able to love everything as both a means and an end?

Augustine's distinction between uti and frui is designed to strengthen the love of God without weakening the love of neighbor.

But actually it mutilates the spirit of neighborly love. For the second commandment tells us to love our neighbor as ourselves in the assumption that to ourselves we are always more than just a means. Loving another as yourself would make no sense if you were both mere instruments and only God could be loved as an end. The precept does not command us to love ourselves; it takes it for granted that we do so already. And all men do love themselves inasmuch as they could not live without bestowing value upon some aspect of their being. In one way or another, and for better or worse, we all accept ourselves as ends. But it often happens that we treat others as nothing but a means, nothing but instruments for our own advantage. *This* is what the second commandment condemns. It prohibits the exploitation of other persons by demanding that we love our neighbor *in the manner in which* we love ourselves—i.e., as ends. I stress these words because the commandment does not pretend that the neighbor is an alter ego. Nygren argues that Marsilio Ficino, the Renaissance Christian Platonist, interprets the precept in just that way: "In the fellow-man whom we love, we recognize ourselves and love in him nothing other than ourselves." This interpretation, which may or may not be Ficino's, would enable Christianity to answer Freud's criticism by claiming that the second commandment satisfies the requirements of narcissism. But it ignores the actual wording of the injunction. That is "Thou shalt love thy neighbor *as* thyself," not "as if he *were* thyself." We are to love the other as something more than just an instrument, and also more than just an image of ourselves. We are to love him as an end, this being the way in which we love ourselves.

A man may exploit some or all of his faculties; but it is meaningless to say that he exploits himself. Why? Because to ourselves we are always ends, and possibly this is part of what the term "human being" connotes. Even the man who gives his life for a cause beyond himself has chosen that cause to serve his own ends. One might even say that he does not sacrifice *himself*: for though he dies, he asserts his identity as just the person he actually is, as one who chooses to die in this way and under these circumstances. In bidding us to love our neighbor as ourselves, the second commandment enjoins us to treat others as human beings who are ends to themselves and never

347

merely means. In this it enunciates an important component within the love of persons. But when St. Augustine claims that only God can be enjoyed, he makes it impossible to fulfill the second commandment or to respond to any human being as just the person that he is.

Indeed, I wonder whether the Augustinian attitude toward everything other than God may be dignified by the word "love." There are many things we use as instrumentalities without loving them. Should we say that an object which is not enjoyed, in the sense that Augustine intends, may nevertheless be *loved*? I do not think so. To love something is to enjoy it; and that is why Augustine reserves frui for what he really cares about—the love of God. But if, as I am suggesting, all love is a kind of frui, what he calls uti cannot be love at all. At best, it may be something neutral, sheer use without personal significance: beneficial but loveless utilization. At worst, uti could be a distasteful, even repugnant, submission to something that we tolerate solely as the means to a desired end. That Augustinian uti must be limited to this range of possibilities, and so remain very remote from love, is indicated by passages such as the following: "The man who is temperate in mortal and transient things . . . should love none of these things, nor think them desirable for their own sake, but should use them as far as is required for the purposes and duties of life with the moderation of an employer instead of the ardor of a lover."

And if I am right about uti not being love, perhaps we ought to probe further when Augustine tells us to "despise" the world. Although he says that this means using everything (and everyone) as a vehicle to God, Augustine's actual description of uti makes us wonder whether the world is not being despised in a more venomous way. This, of course, is closer to the ordinary meaning of "despise," which suggests a negative appraisal plus personal animosity or contempt. To despise the world, in the sense that now seems applicable, involves hating rather than loving it. Is this what Augustine wishes to say? As a matter of doctrine, certainly not. He would deny that one should hate anything other than sin, and he would never say that everything but God is necessarily sinful. Nevertheless, the idea that only God is worth loving for himself leads one to treat all beings in nature *as if* they were sinful, or at least inherently worthless. Asceticism, which is based upon the desire to love God and nothing else, often contains abhorrence of life, rejection of ordinary experience, distrust toward the neighbor, and above all, hatred of oneself as the greatest of sinners. The ascetic tries to glorify God by minimizing nature. Instead he often glorifies death by minimizing life. Possibly the ascetic impulse begins with love, as a bestowal of all conceivable goods, giving them back en masse in a total sacrifice to the one who first made them. But this gesture may easily turn into the self-indulgence of mere destructiveness, much as a child will smash something he secretly covets but feels he ought not to. To despise the world as many ascetics do is not to love *in any sense*, even as a means to salvation.

The general bearing of these criticisms applies to Aquinas and Luther as much as to Augustine. In Aquinas the distinction between uti and frui hardly appears, but the Augustinian position remains the foundation of Christian dogma. Interpreting the second commandment, Aquinas maintains that "neighbor" means anyone who shares the fellowship of reason with us. From this he concludes that "rational nature is the object of charity." In effect, Aristotle had said the same. Aquinas goes beyond Aristotle, however, by placing this conclusion within the larger framework that derives from the primacy of God. He says that since love means wishing well to someone (as Aristotle suggested) and since the greatest good is eternal beatitude (as Augustine held), true love or caritas must be directed toward one who is capable of enjoying the good of eternal beatitude. This capability being limited to rational beings, Aristotelian ideas about the fellowship of reason are thus fitted into the Augustinian theology. All that now remains is for Aquinas to distinguish among different kinds of objects that can be loved through caritas. God comes first, enjoying eternal beatitude by his very nature, as the ultimate "root of beatitude." Next comes the individual soul of each rational creature, who loves himself as a possible participant in beatitude. Then come other rational beings, as fellow members of the community established by their joint access to beatitude. Finally, one can even love one's own body in the sense of caritas; for the body "is glorified through a redundance of glory from the soul to itself."

But if one can love the body through caritas, why not the rest of nature? And indeed Aquinas argues that *all* things may be loved out of caritas, provided they are first ordered to beatitude. In words reminiscent of Augustine, he remarks: "For all creatures are a means for man to tend towards his beatitude, and, further, all creatures are ordered to the glory of God inasmuch as the divine goodness is manifested in them." It follows from this that all human loves which are not sinful belong to caritas, either directly or in-directly, on a higher or a lower level. Sinful loves, such as adultery, cannot be ordered to beatitude, and therefore (by definition) they are excluded from caritas.

It also follows that the Christian virtue of loving one's enemy can now be explained in a fairly realistic manner. Aquinas rightly points out that having an enemy means hating him to some degree, that conflict itself creates hatred. Between this fact about human beings and the precept of love which Christianity inculcates he finds no inconsistency. For the latter does not require that we love each and every person in what Aquinas calls "a particular way," i.e., with a special regard for his welfare. Not only is this impossible for finite creatures, he says, but also it would prevent us from according an adequate concern to those who are closest to us as a matter of circumstance—one's family, one's friends, one's immediate neigh-bors, even oneself. Specifically, the enemy is one we *cannot* love with that intimacy reserved for those who matter most to us. For that reason Aquinas denies that the precept of caritas makes it sinful to hate those who happen to be our enemies. At the same time, how-ever, he reminds us that all men are related to God as his creation and that all are capable of participating in beatitude through their rationality. Aquinas takes this to signify that even our feelings toward an enemy must be based on caritas. Insofar as we allow hatred to predominate, we consider the enemy in his opposition to ourselves; but once we see him in his relationship with God, it becomes possible to love him *as* ourselves. If the love of God were perfect in us, caritas would banish hatred and enable us to appreciate the way in which everyone is related to God. God himself loves even those he has condemned to perdition. He loves them as creatures who manifest his divine justice. He hates only the vice in them, for that (which is not his doing) puts them *out* of relation with him.

In these ideas of Aquinas there is much psychological sophistication. Even in the saint he senses the ambivalence of human feelings toward an enemy: caritas causing one to see the other man as a fellow creature before God, hatred arising from the mere fact of conflict and being entirely eliminated only in the ideal condition— unattainable in this life—where everything but the love of God finally drops away. In all this Aquinas shows deeper (more realistic) insight than Freud, who associates the second commandment with the precept to "Love thine enemies" but then ridicules both injunctions as foreign to human nature. Freud says: "If this grandiose commandment had run 'Love thy neighbour as thy neighbour loves thee,' I should not take exception to it"; and likewise, he would have us hate our enemy as our enemy hates us—neither more nor less. In this proportioning of love and hatred, there is a native wisdom which Aquinas recognizes as normal to man's estate. But Aquinas also penetrates to human possibilities that Freud ignores, for Aquinas would have us remember that even our enemy is a "child of God," a speck within the infinite as we are too, equally in need of love and equally seeking it, so close to us in hatred as to facilitate the most dramatic of reversals. Despite his great humanitarianism, Freud never attains this wholesome vision of what man may yet achieve through love.

And yet, Aquinas commits the same mistakes as Augustine. For even in the most extensive applications of caritas, nothing is really loved but God. Through caritas we may love the world and all its creatures *as the manifestation of divine goodness,* but not as the infinitely various things they are in themselves. That which is nonrational— lower organisms and inanimate nature, in short the major part of the universe—Aquinas admits into the system of caritas only as the means by which God enables rational beings to achieve beatitude. Rational beings, in turn, are loved through caritas only because they can participate in that eternal goodness which is God himself. As a result, God serves as more than just the prime object of love: he is ultimately the *only* one. Other objects must be loved *solely* in relation to him, derivatively, and therefore not as they are within the tiny being of their own reality. Despite his medieval hierarchy, Aquinas resembles Plato in using nature as merely a vehicle to the divine. Everything other than abstract vice can elicit caritas, but only God is loved as more than just an instrumentality. This, however, makes it impossible to accept another in all his diversity, as the total individual that he happens to be. The doctrine of Aquinas distorts, not clarifies, the love of persons. That attitude cannot be limited to an object as a creature of God or in relation to eternal beatitude. If it were, we could not treat a fellow human being as an end. His importance would merely be a function of his rationality and his ability to participate in goodness. We would be loving not *him* but only attributes in his nature—his derivation or his destiny. A man is more than this. To love him as a child of God is not yet to love him for himself. If we but use him as a corridor to that ultimate object we desire, are we not exploiting and possibly misusing him? Can we really show that our relationship is based upon a good will?

So evident is it that a good will requires us to treat all rational beings as an end, and not as a means merely, that Immanuel Kant makes this one of the fundamental principles of all possible morality. I think Kant is right; and that his maxim reveals why a theologian like Aquinas misconstrues the love of persons. But starting with Kant, perhaps we can push the analysis much further. Why confine ourselves to rational beings, or even persons? Would not a reverential attitude toward life require us to treat all sentient creatures as ends? Indeed, why only things that live? A truly universal love would enable us to respect the sense in which *all* entities are more than means or simple instrumentalities. At this point, we are doubtless beyond the domain of ordinary ethics, which normally deals with relationships between persons or between individuals and society. Furthermore, we must mean something special (and possibly odd) if we say that inanimate things are ends in themselves. We speak that way of other persons because we know how to put ourselves "in their place"; but this hardly makes sense if the other is a material object. Nevertheless, our ability to love the world involves acceptance of the fact that in themselves all things are more than just the uses to which

just how are we to take this article of faith, this belief in the cosmic circuit, this assurance that everything manifests God's all-explaining love for himself? Is it a projection of primal narcissism, an idealization of an ultimate self-love, all reality put to use and nothing wasted within the static confines of the divine libido? Is it Christianity's way of satisfying in God what it prohibits in man? Analyzed in terms of the medieval elements—eros, agapē, nomos, philia—the idea that God loves himself is inherently chaotic, scarcely comprehensible. For eros is a striving based upon deficiencies in the lover. How then can God love himself, either directly or through his creatures? Philia and nomos are the means by which man achieves oneness with God. But God is eternally one within himself, even as the Trinity. Is it this oneness that God's self-love signifies? But then what kind of fellowship can it be? Does one Person in the Godhead conform to the will of another? And is God's essential oneness any different (surely not better) if it includes an infinite union with all his creatures? Or does God love himself in the sense of agapē? But then agapē cannot be a free bestowal of goodness. For that would mean that God is always making himself more valuable. To the Romantic religions of the nineteenth century, this possibility might be attractive. But not to medieval Christianity. Or to any other religion that believes in a perfect deity.

If we cannot make sense of the idea that God loves himself, neither can we make sense of the cosmic circuit—God loving himself through all things, and all things loving one another in God. An episode in Dante's *Divine Comedy* may illustrate this as well as any other text. In paradise the poet encounters Piccarda, a blessed spirit who savors the sweetness of eternal life. As a young girl she had taken religious vows and entered a convent. When her brother Corso decided to marry her off for political purposes, she yielded to his influence, left the convent, broke her vows. Now she inhabits a low estate in heaven, the sphere of the inconstant moon. Piccarda accepts her lot and piously tells Dante that, kindled by the Holy Spirit, her heart joyously espouses whatever delights God most.

Surprised at such contentment, Dante wonders whether Piccarda does not yearn to move higher, to see God more nearly, and to be more dearly loved. She replies: "Brother, the power of charity quiets our will and makes us will what we have and thirst for nothing else. Did we desire to be more exalted, our desire would be in discord with His will who appoints us here, which thou wilt see cannot hold in these circles if to be in charity is here *necesse* [logically necessary] and if thou consider well its nature. Nay, it is the very quality of this blessed state that we keep ourselves within the divine will, so that our wills are themselves made one; therefore our rank from height to height through this kingdom is pleasing to the whole kingdom, as to the King who wills us to His will. And in His will is our peace. It is that sea to which all things move, both what it creates and what nature makes."

In discussing this episode, Santayana detects a conflict between Christian and Platonic elements in Dante's philosophy. Nevertheless, Santayana thinks he finds a rough consistency in the ideas that Dante expresses: "For Piccarda to say that she accepts the will of God means not that she shares it, but that she submits to it. She would fain go higher, for her moral nature demands it, as Dante—incorrigible Platonist—perfectly perceived; but she dare not mention it, for she knows that God, whose thoughts are not her thoughts, has forbidden it. The inconstant sphere of the moon does not afford her a perfect happiness; but, chastened as she is, she says it brings her happiness enough; all that a broken and a contrite heart has the courage to hope for." If Santayana's gloss were accurate, it might possibly eliminate the difficulties he himself recognizes. However, not only does his explication run counter to the ideas of Christian love in the Middle Ages, but also it misreads what Dante says. Piccarda does *not* admit to anything less than perfect happiness. Her heart is not broken. Though residing in a lowly sphere, she is blessed for all eternity. She does not merely submit to God's will: she shares it joyously. So she tells us, and so we must believe. From her, Dante learns that beatitude *consists* in conformity to the divine order, willing only what one has, rejoicing in everything that pleases the Holy Spirit. Piccarda has not been chastened; she has been *converted*, transformed into an exemplar, at her own level, of God's love working throughout. After hearing her speech, Dante remarks: "It was clear to me then that everywhere in heaven is Paradise, although the grace of the Supreme Good does not rain there in one measure."

But if Piccarda is perfectly happy, loving God *because* she has no desire to exalt herself, the conflict within Dante remains. For in the context of paradise, "going higher" means getting closer to God, enjoying a more intimate union, receiving more of love and giving more of it back. This is what the variable downpouring of grace determines. Is it conceivable that Piccarda, or any other creature yearning for the highest good, should not want the greatest proximity possible? In a later canto Beatrice intimates that Piccarda is where she is because on earth she showed too little willpower. In submitting to her brother's authority, she had not striven hard enough to fulfill her spiritual mission. Here in heaven Piccarda seems to compensate for that by conforming to the divine authority with perfect dedication, delighting in her appointed rank and never desiring to rise above it. Even Luther would have to commend her attitude, for in no way does she seek to assert herself. But does she really love God? If she merely wills what she has, is God an object of love to her? Accepting her condition but not striving for anything, is it even love that motivates her? She yields herself, and that resembles love; but *her* self contains nothing but a disposition to yield. And love requires much more than that. Dante has not solved the problem. He has merely presented it dramatically.

The paradox of Piccarda's love is indigenous to medieval Christianity. I see no way in which the traditional dogma can escape it. Even the Lutheran must want to be as close to God as possible, to be "one cake" with him; and yet, such oneness means renouncing every desire for anything other than what God ordains. But then the blessed soul wants nothing on its own. Bathed in universal charity, it has no personal identity. It gives nothing, it takes nothing, it *is* nothing. In the medieval heaven there can be no reciprocity between persons. Piccarda and all the celestial host are just pawns within the game that God eternally plays in the process of loving himself. They do not love themselves, for they no longer have a separate self. They do not love others, for the others have no selves either. They do not love God, for it is he who does all loving. They are merely flickering lights that he illumines at his will. In their timeless state God's love may give them virtual existence, but theirs is the life of an idealized death. It is not love, and certainly not the love of persons.

In worshiping God, the medieval Christian posits an absolute end that can never be instrumental to anything. He identifies it with an infinite being, complete and perfect within its eternal goodness, a friendly influence more marvelous than man can possibly imagine, a living but purely transcendental person whose mere existence explains all mysteries and reinforces all justifiable hopes. No wonder a forthright theologian like Luther admits his inability to love so stupendous an object! Can one even understand what this unique and wonderful entity must be like? Can God be a person if he *is* love? For love is an attitude, or an ideal, or a phenomenon, or a category of analysis. How then can love be a person, or a person be love? Persons may personify love—as do all the Cupids and the Aphrodites in classical mythology—but this is not what the Christian means. His God is both a loving person (which makes sense) and also the perfection of lovingness (which does not, since persons are not abstractions). In saying that God is love, medieval Christianity adds a human warmth to the coldness of Platonic philosophy. The gain in poetry is very great, but the loss in logic is simply staggering. Santayana perceives this calamitous shortcoming as well as anyone can: "If in saying that God is love we understand that God is charity, we are led to certain consequences perhaps unwelcome to theology. For if the whole essence of deity were bounty, evidently the creator could not exist without the creation; and if the whole essence of deity were mercy, God would depend for his existence on the existence of suffering and sin. These implications are pantheistic; they are incompatible with Christianity, the religion of charity. But a more insidious consequence follows. If the impulse to give and to help were the very spirit of God (the occasion and demand for such charity being presupposed naturalistically) what would God be but goodness in ourselves, in so far as we are good? This insight may rather satisfy a moralistic and mystical piety, as the pantheistic insight satisfies dialectical wit: but if we say that God is nothing but the brotherly love that we feel for one another, it is clear that we are atheists."

In a sense, Luther and the caritas tradition fail for the same reason: they could not emancipate themselves from Plato's transcendentalism. The goal of Platonic eros was an ultimate, but nonexistent, entity—the Good. As the principle of perfection, it symbolized an important fact about man's moral nature: namely, that loving ideals means never being satisfied with any successes in the actual world. But by treating the Good as an object of love, Plato posits a *something* in which mortal yearnings cease, a metaphysical goal or destination, a particular terminus for all ideals unattainable elsewhere. In this wonderful culmination everything would fulfill itself. As the pure form that Aristotle intuits at the top of the hierarchy of being, the unmoved mover would be wholly self-sufficient, complete, needing nothing, wanting nothing, combining in its abstract generality all possible goods. In appropriating this conception, the Christians gave the highest form a supernatural existence and endowed it with a personality. Whatever love was available to man would have to be directed toward this perfect Person, whose unique essence completes all desires and satisfies the deepest inclinations of everything. By renouncing the distractions of a lesser domain, man might even achieve a loving oneness with this other Person. But since the Christian God was also the principle of goodness, love itself would have to originate with him. Only he could have the ability to bestow value or initiate anything as glorious as a joyful love between persons.

Modifying Platonism in this way, Christianity inherits a static view of man. It assumes that there must be a specific and determinate *completion* to human nature, a total satisfying of desires, a perfecting of what it is to be a man. Never finding the ideal in the realm of experience, it posits another world in which a perfect love would make a perfect man. Since that love *is* God, the finished product must be an image, or a likeness, of the divine original. But all of this presupposes that human beings are fixed entities, that man is like a question for which there must be a definite and prearranged answer, that by his very nature he cannot create anything new, that he cannot bestow value from within himself or love authentically as one among other organisms in nature. The medieval Christian realizes that the love of persons depends upon a free bestowal, but he cannot believe that man is capable of such awesome creativity. He therefore calls it *super*natural, identifies it with God, and perpetuates the static model that prevents him from understanding human nature. Not only does this violate the empirical phenomena in which the love of persons consists, but also it misconstrues the inherent incompleteness of man—the fact that perfection for a human being is always an ideal direction and never a goal. To see another as an essence is to see him dead, to destroy him, to make him into a perfection perhaps, but the perfection of nothingness. That is why the medieval concept of a person is so unsatisfactory. Since God is love and man fulfills himself only through love, the "real" human being must belong to a realm of pure spirits. The person in Christian dogma is never an empirical self; it is always a transcendental soul. But that is just another abstraction. It does not comport with the reality of man as we know him in experience.

In making these criticisms, I speak as a man of the twentieth century. But the sentiments I voice have been felt for hundreds of years. Throughout its history as the dominant religion in the Western world, Christianity has changed with the intellectual climate of its times. Since the Middle Ages, much of that climate has been determined by humanistic and naturalistic arguments such as the ones I have presented. These arguments need not deny that the medieval concepts were also beneficial. More than any prior doctrine, medieval Christianity recognizes the love of persons as the highest ideal. It gives the eros tradition an anthropomorphic, if not a human, object to desire; and it strengthens man's will to love by encouraging him to emulate that object. How the Christian God can need or desire anything may not be clear; but there is great wisdom in associating the love of God with the search for happiness and, in general, with the satisfying of human needs and desires. At the same time, the medieval attitude counters the eros tradition with the idea that love is a bestowal. So wonderful is this element in love that the Christian treats it as divinity and, endowing it with a will, idealizes sheer conformity above all else. What could this be but an act of love? In some ways it may be unwholesome love: for in some individuals it surely idealizes the sickly desire to be accepted in one's own self-hatred instead of learning how to love oneself and others as oneself. Yet the Christian concept of bestowal may also be defended. For unless we cherish and revere the creativity of love, unless we respond to the ever-present reality of its infinite possibilities, we shall never succeed in loving anything.

All this the medieval Christian portrays within a mythic picture of the universe. Later generations, both in and out of Christianity, would subject that picture to revision and reinterpretation. In the modern world we may only take it as an imaginative blueprint for the constructing of new societies. But even so, the fellowship of religious love prefigures all rational civilization—though modifications are always necessary. The good society is neither a merging nor a wedding, except as these contribute to a free interaction between self-orienting persons. What man requires is the opportunity to *exercise his powers* against a responsive environment: not to lose his personality or to glue it onto something else, but to live dynamically within the human surroundings of persons and things, ends and instruments, ideals and actualities. In trying to do so, modern man has sought to evolve within himself that loving community which Christians idealize as the kingdom of heaven. To a large extent, he has given up the hope of finding it outside of nature. For us the other world is this one idealized by the possibilities of human love, which entails living in the world and in our natural selves, accepting both as what they are. In this venture nothing is guaranteed—at least, no prior certitudes of the sort that the Middle Ages could take for granted.

Oscar Wilde said that there were two tragedies in life: not getting what you want, and getting what you want. Medieval Christianity turns them both into divine comedies. You get what you want by possessing the highest good and completing your nature in a world beyond this one. And you avoid the frustration of not getting what you want by no longer wanting it, by annihilating all inclinations other than those that God ordains (and therefore protects). This is a glorious dream, with love as the basic ingredient. But it is only a dream; and though rich in symbolism, it distorts what it also symbolizes. Medieval dogma establishes the dignity of the lowly, those who do not get what they want. But then it rewards them in heaven for their lowliness on earth. If it followed its own deepest inspiration, the traditional doctrine would have no such conception of heaven. It would merely bestow importance upon gentleness and humility as one of the ways in which a man may attain happiness.

Instead, the religious idealizations of the Middle Ages often combine servility with condescension, making the devout believer appear to be what Nietzsche called "an undeservedly favoured or elevated slave." Even the saint returns to the world from the height of a transcendental deity he wishes to imitate. Though he considers himself to be nought, the love that makes him into a saint shines *down* on other people. As Ortega says: "Thus, for the mystic and the accepted lover, everything is lovely and charming. What happens is that on returning, after his period of absorption, to peruse things once again, he sees them not as they are but as they are reflected in the only thing which exists for him: God or the beloved." And even as sympathetic a scholar as Rudolph Otto unwittingly touches upon the moral dilemma in Christian love: "The Christian consciousness of self has a double orientation: toward God and toward the rest of creation. Toward God it is humility. But toward the rest of creation it is pride and the sense of an exalted position, if the teaching that man, and man alone, is created in the image of God, is Christian."

Otto calls this disposition a "sublime self-consciousness." But many in the modern world have wondered whether it is an ideal worth pursuing. Since the Middle Ages, religious idealization has tried to find ways in which a saint might accept human beings *as* human beings, and nature as itself. Major aspects of the Judaeo-Christian religions are defeated by the challenge. But not those elements in them that are true to the nature of love. If only in their secular resurrections, these survive. The present cannot live without its past, or without a recognition of what earlier geniuses have wrought for it. I give the final word to Nietzsche:

> To love man *for God's sake*—this has been until now the most distinguished and exalted emotion that has been attained among men. That a love for man, apart from some ulterior object to hallow it, is a piece of folly and bestiality; that the propensity to this love for man must first receive from a higher propensity its measure, its elegance, its grain of salt and particle of ambergris—whoever the man was who first felt and "experienced" this, and however much his tongue may have stammered, when it tried to express something so delicate, let him be to us in all ages holy and venerable, as the man who of all men hitherto has flown highest and gone most splendidly wrong!

Conclusion
The Beginnings of
Courtly and Romantic Love

IN STUDYING THE PHILOSOPHY OF love from antiquity into the Middle Ages, this book will strike some readers as a kind of prehistory. In some respects they are right. The troubadours of the twelfth century sang of an ideal love that we have scarcely mentioned—a love between idealized human beings rather than man and God or man and the Good. And out of their poetry grew many of the ideas that have made the modern world. But the troubadours lived in a Europe that was dominated by the religious concepts we have analyzed. They considered themselves Christians; and few of them saw any threat to orthodoxy in their attitude toward love. By and large, these poets presuppose the caritas-synthesis and then duplicate its structural elements on the level of human relations. When the northern tradition of courtly love supplemented the Neoplatonism of the troubadours with Ovidian ideas about adultery and sexual freedom, the danger to ecclesiastical doctrine was obvious. The church condemned these movements as heresies, burned the principal texts, and thereby contributed to that division of the soul which is so evident throughout the later Middle Ages. In the work of Dante, courtly love submits to revisions that enable it to survive. It is given a place within the caritas-synthesis, its Neoplatonism subordinated to Christian dogma, and human love reestablished as a means of approaching the divine. In making these changes, Dante blunts the humanistic implications of courtly love. He turns its male and female lovers into ethereal abstractions. The movement takes its revenge—even in *The Divine Comedy*—by subtly affecting the character of religious love itself. Beginning with Dante and extending into the philosophy of thinkers like Ficino, the love of God becomes increasingly anthropocentric. Ficino says that man is "God upon earth," a microcosm that includes within itself the being of everything—even divinity. With the Italian Renaissance the eros tradition reappears as a Neoplatonism that even the troubadours could hardly match. Moving northward, it mingles with a post-Lutheran emphasis upon agapē at work among human beings. The combination eventually produces the ideas of Romantic love which still surround us.

The analysis of the concepts in this historical progression I leave for the second volume in this trilogy. The passage from courtly to Romantic love makes a unit in itself, though its dynamism largely consists of a series of reactions to the narrowness of medieval religious idealization. The church had condoned the sexual instinct but condemned all attempts to idealize sexuality. Marriage was holy, but only as a means of reproducing the species. It could not serve as the basis of an ideal love. That is why St. Paul says it is better to marry than to burn, but that chastity is best of all. According to St. Jerome, "an ardent lover of his wife is an adulterer." Confronted with this attitude, Western man had to decide whether the love of God required such exclusiveness; and whether some types of human love might not be preferable to the ideals of medieval religion. These ideals belonged to the same masculine society that Plato and Lucretius also represented. But even in the church, male dominance was being altered by the cult of the Blessed Virgin. Through the idealizations of courtly and Romantic love, the female sex was afforded new opportunities to assert itself. In courtly love, woman often takes the place of God or the Good. In much of Romantic love she displaces the male as the one who is truly capable of loving. But *what* is a woman in love? Is she a biblical Eve in league with the devil, as the church fathers thought, or a lovely angel through whom divinity expresses itself? Since the twelfth century, philosophers and poets have said both, even at the same time. In their ambivalence they manifest a similar uncertainty about the moral possibilities of human love in general, and of sex in particular. In courtly and Romantic love the ambivalences issue into a variety of idealizations. They are still to be resolved.

Notes

p. xi   *l.7*   (London: Boosey and Hawkes, 1951), p. 15.

p. 3   This chapter in particular (though others as well) benefited from the extensive criticism of Jason Epstein and Alice Mayhew. I have also used suggestions of Stephen N. Thomas.

p. 15   *l.11*   *The Man Who Died* (New York: Vintage Books, 1960), p. 202.

p. 18   *l.7*   *La Nouvelle Héloïse*, vol. 2 (Philadelphia, 1796), p. 90.

p. 20   *l.27*   John Donne, "The Ecstasy."

p. 23   I am grateful to Norman N. Holland for detailed criticism of this and other chapters.

p. 26   *l.15*   *Reason in Society*, in *The Life of Reason* (New York: Charles Scribner's Sons, 1954), p. 101.

p. 27   *l.11*   Ibid., p. 90.

p. 28   *l.35*   *On Narcissism: An Introduction*, in *The Standard Edition of the Complete Psychological Works of Sigmund Freud*, vol. 14 (London: Hogarth Press and the Institute of Psycho-Analysis, 1957–), p. 94. Freud's complete works are hereafter referred to as *SE*.

p. 28   *l.37*   *Three Essays on Sexuality*, in *SE*, 7:150.

p. 29   *l.5*   *Group Psychology and the Analysis of the Ego*, in *SE*, 18:112.

p. 30   *l.4*   *On Narcissism*, in *SE*, 14:88.

p. 30   *l.36*   *A General Selection from the Works of Sigmund Freud*, ed. John Rickman (New York: Anchor Books, 1957), p. 121. I prefer this translation of the quoted passage to the one in *SE*, 14:100.

p. 31   *l.10*   "The Resistances to Psycho-Analysis," in *SE*, 19:218.

p. 32   *l.27*   "A Special Type of Choice of Object Made by Man" (*Contributions to the Psychology of Love* I), in *SE*, 11:169.

p. 33   *l.5*   *Reason in Society*, p. 90.

p. 34   *l.4*   "Platonic Love in Some Italian Poets," in *Essays in Literary Criticism by George Santayana*, ed. Irving Singer (New York: Charles Scribner's Sons, 1956), p. 101.

p. 35   *l.9*   In *The Future of an Illusion*.

p. 39   *l.23*   Act V, scene 1.

p. 47   *l.20*   Charles Seignobos, quoted (and criticized) in Maurice Valen-
cy, *In Praise of Love* (New York: Macmillan, 1958), p. 1.

p. 47   *l.22*   Alfred North Whitehead, *Process and Reality: An Essay in Cos-
mology*, corrected edition, ed. David Ray Griffin and Donald W. Sher-
burne (New York: The Free Press, 1978), p. 39.

p. 49   *l.4*   *The Symposium*, trans. W. Hamilton (New York: Penguin Books,
1951), p. 36.

p. 49   *l.18*   Ibid., p. 97.

p. 51   *l.22*   Ibid., p. 62.

p. 51   *l.23*   Ibid., p. 64.

p. 52   *l.18*   *Beyond the Pleasure Principle*, in *SE*, 18:57.

p. 52   *l.36*   *The Symposium*, p. 85.

p. 53   *l.13*   Ibid., p. 86.

p. 55   *l.35*   Ibid., p. 92.

p. 56   *l.11*   Ibid., p. 93.

p. 56   *l.19*   Ibid., pp. 93–94.

p. 62   *l.20*   *Phaedrus*, in *Dialogues of Plato*, trans. B. Jowett, vol. 1 (New
York: Random House, 1937), p. 225. Hereafter referred to as *Dialogues*.

p. 63   *l.19*   *The Symposium*, p. 95.

p. 64   *l.4*   *The Republic of Plato*, trans. Francis Macdonald Cornford (New
York: Oxford University Press, 1941), p. 208.

p. 66   *l.5*   *The Symposium*, pp. 63–64.

p. 68   *l.15*   "Platonic Love in Some Italian Poets," in *Essays in Literary
Criticism*, p. 99.

p. 68   *l.23*   *The Symposium*, p. 86.

p. 74   *l.19*   *The Republic of Plato*, p. 6.

p. 74   *l.30*   Cf. Thomas Gould, *Platonic Love* (New York: The Free Press,
1963), p. 1.

p. 77   *l.18*   *Laws*, in *The Collected Dialogues of Plato*, ed. Edith Hamilton and
Huntington Cairns (New York: Pantheon, 1961), p. 1402. Some of the
wording in this paragraph has been revised in order to accommodate
remarks in Gregory Vlastos, *Platonic Studies* (Princeton: Princeton University Press, 1973).

p. 79   *l.31*   *On Creativity and the Unconscious* (New York: Torchbooks,
1958), p. 177. For a variant translation, see *SE*, 11:183.

p. 81   *l.34*   Quoted in Frank Harris, *Oscar Wilde* (New York: Dell, 1960),
pp. 175–76.

p. 88   For a recent analysis, see John M. Cooper, "Aristotle on Friendship,"
in *Essays on Aristotle's Ethics*, ed. Amélie Oksenberg Rorty (Berkeley:
University of California Press, 1980), pp. 301–40.

p. 88   *l.22*   *Ethica Nicomachea*, in *The Student's Oxford Aristotle*, vol. 5, trans.
W. D. Ross, 1156a.

p. 90   *l.1*   Ibid., 1156b.

p. 90   *l.7*   Ibid., 1155b.

p. 90   *l.19*   Ibid.

p. 92   *l.32*   Ibid., 1156b.

p. 93   *l.17*   Ibid., 1157b.

p. 93   *l.31*   Quoted in Denis de Rougemont, *Love in the Western World,* trans. Montgomery Belgion (Princeton: Princeton University Press, 1983), p. 198.

p. 94   *l.5*   *Pensées* (New York: Modern Library, 1941), no. 323, p. 109.

p. 95   *l.6*   *Ethica Nicomachea,* 1155a.

p. 97   *l.3*   Act II, scene 2.

p. 97   *l.25*   *Civilization and Its Discontents,* in *SE,* 21:102.

p. 97   *l.33*   Ibid., p. 109.

p. 98   *l.28*   *Ethica Nicomachea,* 1170b.

p. 100   *l.3*   Ibid., 1161b.

p. 100   *l.27*   Ibid., 1169a.

p. 101   *l.1*   Ibid., 1158b.

p. 101   *l.19*   Erich Fromm, *The Art of Loving* (New York: Harper and Row, 1962), p. 58.

p. 103   *l.18*   *Ethica Nicomachea,* 1156b.

p. 104   *l.18*   Act I, scene 3.

p. 105   *l.24*   In *Portrait of a Lady.*

p. 108   *l.22*   Book 12, Chapter 7, 1072b, 28–30.

p. 108   *l.28*   1159a.

p. 109   *l.8*   *Dialogues,* p. 43.

p. 109   *l.34*   1169b.

p. 111   *l.2*   In Plotinus, *The Enneads,* trans. Stephen MacKenna (New York: Pantheon, 1957), p. 1.

p. 111   *l.5*   Ibid., p. 17.

p. 111   *l.12*   Ibid., p. 2.

p. 111   *l.23*   Ibid., p. 625.

p. 112   *l.16*   W. R. Inge, *The Philosophy of Plotinus,* vol. 1 (New York: Longmans, Green, 1929), p. 15.

p. 113   *l.24*   Quoted in Porphyry's "Life of Plotinus," *The Enneads,* p. 15.

p. 114   *l.12*   *The Enneads,* p. 61.

p. 115   *l.12*   Ibid., p. 361.

p. 116   *l.17*   Ibid., p. 62.

p. 116   *l.31*   *The Enneads,* VI, 8, 15. MacKenna gives a variant translation, p. 608.

p. 117   *l.31*   *The Enneads,* p. 622.

p. 118   *l.7*   Elmer O'Brien, S. J., *The Essential Plotinus* (New York: Mentor Books, 1964), p. 22.

p. 118   *l.15*   *Dialogues Concerning Natural Religion,* Part III.

p. 119   *l.1*   *The Enneads,* p. 624.

p. 122   I am grateful to Winthrop Wetherbee for having encouraged me to revise this chapter. Its earliest version was published in *The Hudson Review* (Winter 1965–66): 537–59.

p. 123   *l.5*   *Three Essays on Sexuality,* in *SE,* 7:149n.

p. 123   *l.34*   F. A. Wright, *The Mirror of Venus* (London: G. Routledge & Son, 1925), p. 27.

p. 125 *l.35* Quoted in A. J. Denomy, *"Fin' Amors*: The Pure Love of the Troubadours, Its Amorality, and Possible Source," *Mediaeval Studies*, 7 (1945):174n.

p. 126 *l.25* *Metamorphoses* X, 245ff. Translations from Latin in this chapter were all made by Richard A. Macksey. It would be difficult to express sufficient gratitude for the help and encouragement which he has given me throughout the writing of this book. I have also used two references suggested by John M. Bullitt and Roy L. Perkinson.

p. 126 *l.33* Ibid., 256–58.

p. 127 *l.7* Ibid., 289–94.

p. 127 *l.23* *Metamorphoses* IV, 373–76.

p. 127 *l.31* A. R. Nykl in *Hispano-Arabic Poetry and Its Relations with the Old Provençal Troubadours* (Baltimore: J. H. Furst, 1946), p. 371.

p. 128 *l.19* *Metamorphoses* III, 3.

p. 128 *l.32* *Amores* II, XVII, 1–3.

p. 129 *l.1* *Ars amatoria* II, 109ff.

p. 129 *l.11* Ibid., 53–60.

p. 130 *l.16* *Fasti* IV, 91–102.

p. 132 *l.6* *De Rerum Natura* IV, 1052ff.

p. 132 *l.19* Quoted in Giorgio de Santillana, *The Origins of Scientific Thought* (New York: Mentor, 1961), p. 111.

p. 134 *l.12* *De Rerum Natura* IV, 1284–87.

p. 134 *l.36* Ibid., 1160–69. At this point, Richard Macksey comments, "As a pedantical footnote you might want to mention that this passage is a classical *topos*. The large number of Greek words in the Latin text suggests an earlier model, possibly contained in Epicurus' *Peri Erōtos*, though the source was more likely poetry. Plato *Republic* 474dff. deals with the same topic, and there are parallels to individual words and phrases in Theocritus (X, 25, etc.) and the *Anthology*. The Latin elegiac poets develop the same idea, as in Propertius II, 25, 41ff., Ovid, *Amores* II, 4, and the passage from the *Ars amatoria* which you quote. (Ditto Molière.)"

p. 135 *l.20* Act II, scene 5, trans. Richard Wilbur (New York: Harcourt, Brace, 1955), pp. 58–59.

p. 136 *l.17* *Ars amatoria* II, 641–48.

p. 137 *l.4* *De Rerum Natura* IV, 1079–83.

p. 137 *l.28* Ibid., 1110–13.

p. 138 *l.5* Ibid., 1173–74.

p. 138 *l.9* *Much Ado About Nothing*, Act II, scene 3.

p. 138 *l.11* *The Tempest*, Act III, scene 1.

p. 138 *l.16* *De Rerum Natura* IV, 1175–85.

p. 138 *l.38* Cf. "Love's Melancholy—Artificial Allurements," in Burton's *The Anatomy of Melancholy*, part III, section 2, member 2, subsections 3–4.

p. 140 *l.4* *Three Philosophical Poets*, in *Essays in Literary Criticism*, p. 25.

p. 141 *l.34* *Ars amatoria* I, 275–76.

p. 143 *l.1* *Remedia amoris* III, 323–28.

p. 144 *l.14* Cf. Brooks Otis, *Ovid as an Epic Poet* (Cambridge: Cambridge University Press, 1966).

p. 145 *l.5* *Ars amatoria* III, 789–90.

p. 146   *l.23*   *Metamorphoses* III, 433.

p. 147   *l.23*   Quoted in M.C. D'Arcy, *The Mind and Heart of Love* (New York: Meridian Books, 1956), pp. 78–79, 102.

p. 148   *l.4*   *Leviathan* (Oxford: Basil Blackwell, 1946), p. 63.

p. 148   *l.6*   Ibid., p. 32.

p. 148   *l.13*   Ibid., p. 63.

p. 149   *l.5*   "Because You're You," in *Heart Songs Dear to the American People* (New York: The World Syndicate Publishing Co., 1909), p. 499. Words by Henry Blossom, music by Victor Herbert.

p. 151   *l.7*   *Love Declared* (Boston: Beacon Press, 1964), pp. 7–8.

p. 151   *l.31*   Quoted in Abraham Kaplan, *The New World of Philosophy* (New York: Vintage Books, 1963), p. 252.

p. 152   *l.1*   Bhikshu Sangharakshita, *Survey of Buddhism* (Bangalore: Indian Institute of World Culture, 1957), p. 160. I am indebted to Huston Smith for calling my attention to various books, including this one.

p. 152   *l.4*   Kaplan, *New World of Philosophy*, p. 289.

p. 152   *l.18*   *The Republic*, in *Dialogues*, p. 632.

p. 152   *l.38*   Quoted in Alan W. Watts, *Psychotherapy East and West* (New York: Pantheon, 1961), p. 78.

p. 153   *l.10*   Ibid., p. 80.

p. 153   *l.31*   Walter Pater, *The Renaissance: Studies in Art and Poetry*, ed. Donald L. Hill (Berkeley: University of California Press, 1980), p. 164.

p. 161   *l.22*   From "The Rubáiyát of Omar Khayyám," trans. Edward FitzGerald.

p. 165   *l.8*   Quoted in Anders Nygren, *Agape and Eros*, trans. Philip S. Watson (Chicago: University of Chicago Press, 1982), p. 477.

p. 165   *l.10*   Ibid., p. 476.

p. 165   *l.13*   *The City of God*, XIV, 7. Here as quoted in John Barnaby, *Amor Dei, A Study of the Religion of St. Augustine* (London: Hodder & Stoughton, 1938), p. 95. For a variant translation, see *The City of God*, trans. Marcus Dods (New York: Modern Library, 1950), p. 449.

p. 166   *l.27*   Quoted in D'Arcy, *Mind and Heart of Love*, pp. 78, 102.

p. 169   *l.22*   Ibid., p. 98.

p. 169   *l.34*   Ibid., p. 79.

p. 175   *l.11*   From "An Epistle of Discretion," quoted in Evelyn Underhill, *Mysticism: A Study in the Nature and Development of Man's Spiritual Consciousness* (New York: E. P. Dutton, 1912), pp. 101–2.

p. 176   *l.23*   From Sermon LXXXII, 7, 8, quoted in Etienne Gilson, *The Mystical Theology of Saint Bernard* (New York: Sheed and Ward, 1940), pp. 151–52.

p. 177   *l.17*   From *Avisos: Puntos de Amor*, quoted in E. Allison Peers, *Studies of the Spanish Mystics* (New York: Macmillan, 1951), 1:195.

p. 177   *l.20*   *The Confessions*, book III, chapter 4.

p. 178   *l.28*   Nygren, *Agape and Eros*, p. 441.

p. 180   *l.9*   Cf. John R. Martin, *The Illustration of the Heavenly Ladder of John Climacus* (Princeton: Princeton University Press, 1954).

p. 180   *l.10*   Richard of Saint-Victor, *Selected Writings on Contemplation*, trans. Clare Kirchberger (London: Faber and Faber, 1957), p. 226.

p. 181 *l.12* Quoted in David Knowles, *The English Mystical Tradition* (New York: Harper and Row, 1961), p. 59.

p. 182 *l.15* *The Interpretation of Dreams*, in *SE*, 5:355.

p. 182 *l.17* Ibid.

p. 184 *l.27* Richard of Saint-Victor, *Writings*, p. 213.

p. 185 *l.19* Ibid., p. 223.

p. 186 *l.2* Ibid., p. 218.

p. 186 *l.15* Ibid., p. 220.

p. 188 *l.25* *Saint Bernard on The Love of God*, trans. the Rev. Terence L. Connolly (Westminster, Md.: Newman Press, 1951), p. 37. Hereafter referred to as *Saint Bernard*.

p. 189 *l.27* Ibid., p. 40.

p. 190 *l.32* Ibid., p. 44.

p. 191 *l.10* Ibid., p. 46.

p. 191 *l.26* Quoted in D'Arcy, *Mind and Heart of Love*, p. 99.

p. 191 *l.33* No. 420, *Pensées*, p. 132.

p. 192 *l.22* *The Bible Designed to be Read as Literature*, ed. Ernest Sutherland Bates (London: William Heinemann, n.d.), p. 975.

p. 196 *l.7* Richard of Saint-Victor, *Writings*, p. 232.

p. 196 *l.18* Ibid.

p. 198 *l.3* *Group Psychology and the Analysis of the Ego*, in *SE*, 18:135.

p. 200 *l.1* Ibid., pp. 138–39.

p. 200 *l.27* Cf. Gilson, *Mystical Theology of Saint Bernard*, pp. 8–13.

p. 203 *l.29* Part I, Q.37, in *Basic Writings of Saint Thomas Aquinas, Summa Theologica* (New York: Random House, 1945), pp. 353–54.

p. 205 *l.34* *Sermons on the Canticle of Canticles*, in *Saint Bernard*, p. 77. Hereafter referred to as *Canticle of Canticles*.

p. 207 *l.7* Quoted in Dom Cuthbert Butler, *Western Mysticism* (New York: E. P. Dutton, 1923), p. 139.

p. 207 *l.24* Ibid., p. 173.

p. 210 *l.20* *Canticle of Canticles*, p. 230.

p. 211 *l.5* Galatians 2:20.

p. 211 *l.7* Romans 11:27.

p. 211 *l.8* John 14:18.

p. 211 *l.10* *Epist. ad Parthos*, quoted in M. Eugene Boylan, O. Cist. R., *This Tremendous Lover* (Westminster, Md.: Newman Press, 1960), p. viii.

p. 212 *l.3* *Canticle of Canticles*, p. 106.

p. 212 *l.13* *A Commentary on St. Paul's Epistle to the Galatians* (London: J. Clarke, 1953), p. 79.

p. 213 *l.31* *Canticle of Canticles*, p. 231.

p. 214 *l.25* Quoted in Gilson, *Mystical Theology of Saint Bernard*, p. 136.

p. 214 *l.29* Ibid., p. 137.

p. 217 *l.10* From the *Brihadaranyaka Upanishad*, in *The Teachings of the Mystics*, ed. Walter T. Stace (New York: Mentor Books, 1960), p. 37.

p. 217 *l.21* From the *Katha Upanishad*, 4.15, quoted in Robert C. Zaehner, *Hindu and Muslim Mysticism* (New York: Oxford University Press, 1960), p. 46.

p. 218 *l.25* Quoted in Underhill, *Mysticism*, p. 509.

p. 219   *l.4*   *The Teachings of the Mystics*, p. 214.

p. 219   *l.23*   Gershom G. Scholem, *Major Trends in Jewish Mysticism* (New York: Schocken, 1941), p. 55.

p. 220   *l.4*   Cf. *Love in the Western World*, pp. 153ff.

p. 220   *l.20*   *Morals of the Catholic Church*, in *Basic Writings of Saint Augustine*, ed. Whitney J. Oates (New York: Random House, 1948), 1:329.

p. 220   *l.35*   Sermon LXXI, quoted in Butler, *Western Mysticism*, p. 167.

p. 221   *l.15*   "Ignitum cum Deo Soliloquim," Chapter 4, quoted in Underhill, *Mysticism*, pp. 511–12.

p. 221   *l.25*   *Enchiridion Symbolorum*, no. 510. For Eckhart's "Defense," see Raymond Bernard Blakney, *Meister Eckhart* (New York: Harper, 1941), pp. 258ff.

p. 221   *l.34*   *The Teachings of the Mystics*, p. 184.

p. 222   *l.12*   Ibid., pp. 184–85.

p. 222   *l.23*   Ibid., p. 188.

p. 222   *l.33*   *Spiritual Canticle*, XXII, 3.

p. 223   *l.6*   Quoted in Butler, *Western Mysticism*, p. 322.

p. 223   *l.19*   Richard of Saint-Victor, *Writings*, p. 192.

p. 223   *l.24*   Ibid., p. 189.

p. 223   *l.35*   Quoted in E. Allison Peers, *Mystics of Spain* (London: Allen & Unwin, 1951), p. 100.

p. 224   *l.14*   *The Teachings of the Mystics*, p. 172.

p. 224   *l.25*   Quoted in Rudolph Otto, *Mysticism East and West* (New York: Meridian Books, 1957), p. 12.

p. 224   *l.28*   *The Teachings of the Mystics*, pp. 173–74.

p. 225   *l.6*   In Otto, *Mysticism East and West*, pp. 182–83.

p. 227   *l.9*   Dante Alighieri, *The Divine Comedy*, trans. John D. Sinclair (New York: Oxford University Press, 1961), 3:483.

p. 227   *l.30*   (New York: Dover, 1952), 1:250–51.

p. 228   *l.16*   *The Realm of Spirit* (New York: Charles Scribner's Sons, 1940), p. 255.

p. 228   *l.37*   *Civilization and Its Discontents*, in *SE*, 21:64–65.

p. 229   *l.15*   Ibid., p. 66.

p. 231   *l.32*   *On Love: Aspects of a Single Theme* (New York: New American Library, 1957), p. 63.

p. 233   I am especially indebted to Michael Wager for many useful criticisms of this and the following chapter.

p. 233   *l.23*   *The Realm of Spirit*, pp. 230–31.

p. 234   *l.3*   *Civilization and Its Discontents*, in *SE*, 21:126.

p. 235   *l.15*   Ibid., p. 42.

p. 235   *l.30*   *Group Psychology and the Analysis of the Ego*, in *SE*, 18:113–14.

p. 236   *l.4*   Ibid., p. 114.

p. 239   *l.15*   *Agape and Eros*, p. 201.

p. 239   *l.23*   Douglas N. Morgan, *Love: Plato, The Bible, and Freud* (Englewood Cliffs, N.J.: Prentice-Hall, 1964), p. 71. Cf. William Graham Cole, *Sex and Love in the Bible* (New York: Association Press, 1959), passim. I have drawn on both of these useful books in various places.

p. 239   *l.25*   Ibid., p. 122.

p. 243   *l.5*   Bates, *The Bible as Literature*, pp. 580–81.
p. 244   *l.30*   Ibid., p. 107.
p. 244   *l.32*   Ibid., p. 661.
p. 245   *l.1*   Ibid., p. 402.
p. 245   *l.5*   Ibid., p. 578.
p. 245   *l.24*   1 Samuel 15:22.
p. 252   *l.15*   *The Idea of Christ in the Gospels* (New York: Charles Scribner's Sons, 1946), p. 109.
p. 254   *l.18*   Bates, *The Bible as Literature*, p. 701.
p. 254   *l.20*   Ibid., p. 702.
p. 255   *l.10*   Ibid., p. 752.
p. 255   *l.28*   Ibid., p. 562.
p. 255   *l.33*   Ibid., p. 570.
p. 256   *l.9*   Mark 12.
p. 256   *l.19*   Mark 11.
p. 256   *l.22*   Luke 6.
p. 256   *l.31*   Cf. Bertrand Russell, *A History of Western Philosophy* (New York: Simon and Schuster, 1945), pp. 319–20.
p. 260   *l.31*   Bates, *The Bible as Literature*, p. 942.
p. 261   *l.7*   Ibid., p. 412.
p. 263   *l.23*   *Civilization and its Discontents*, in *SE*, 21:102.
p. 263   *l.30*   Ibid.
p. 269   *l.1*   Act IV, scene 1.
p. 270   *l.36*   George Foot Moore, *Judaism in the First Centuries of the Christian Era, The Age of the Jannim* (Cambridge: Harvard University Press, 1927), 2:94–95. Hereafter referred to as *Judaism*.
p. 271   *l.29*   Ibid., p. 94.
p. 272   *l.4*   Quoted in Sarvepalli Radhakrishnan, *Hindu View of Life* (London: Macmillan, 1927), p. 89.
p. 272   *l.15*   Erwin Rohde, *Psyche: Cult of Souls and Belief in Immortality among the Greeks* (London: Routledge and Kegan Paul, 1950), p. 342.
p. 273   *l.36*   B. Z. Goldberg, *The Sacred Fire: The Story of Sex in Religion* (New York: Grove Press, 1962), p. 53.
p. 275   *l.34*   Matthew 5:45.
p. 277   *l.22*   *American Edition of Luther's Works* (Philadelphia: Muhlenberg Press, 1955), 31:57. Hereafter cited as *Luther's Works*.
p. 279   *l.23*   1 Corinthians 1.
p. 279   *l.26*   1 John 3:16.
p. 280   *l.20*   Matthew 20, in *The Four Gospels*, trans. E. V. Rieu (Baltimore: Penguin Books, 1953), p. 90. Hereafter referred to as *Four Gospels*.
p. 280   *l.28*   Luke 15, in *Four Gospels*, p. 164.
p. 281   *l.4*   Ibid., p. 165.
p. 285   *l.18*   Bates, *The Bible as Literature*, p. 564.
p. 285   *l.22*   Ibid., p. 644.
p. 285   *l.30*   Ibid., p. 798.
p. 286   *l.9*   *Agape and Eros*, p. 88.
p. 287   *l.14*   Cf. ibid., p. 72.
p. 287   *l.24*   Luke 15:7.

p. 288   *l.13*   In *Lord Jim*.
p. 288   *l.26*   Bates, *The Bible as Literature*, pp. 1194–95.
p. 290   *l.19*   *Summa Theologica*, 1:353.
p. 290   *l.23*   *Four Gospels*, p. 196.
p. 291   *l.27*   Quoted in Radhakrishnan, *Hindu View of Life*, p. 65.
p. 292   *l.37*   Bates, *The Bible as Literature*, p. 1028.
p. 293   *l.23*   Ephesians 1:4–5.
p. 294   *l.15*   Bates, *The Bible as Literature*, p. 1151.
p. 294   *l.18*   Ibid., p. 1149.
p. 294   *l.25*   Ibid., p. 1150.
p. 294   *l.37*   Ibid., p. 1149.
p. 295   *l.5*   Ibid.
p. 295   *l.10*   Ibid., p. 1115.
p. 295   *l.14*   Ibid., p. 1152.
p. 295   *l.21*   *Agape and Eros*, p. 124.
p. 295   *l.25*   Galatians 5:14.
p. 295   *l.27*   Romans 13:8–9.
p. 297   *l.33*   Ibid., 5:1–5.
p. 297   *l.36*   Galatians 2:20.
p. 298   *l.14*   1 Corinthians 13:2–3.
p. 298   *l.32*   Ibid., 12:4–7.
p. 299   *l.1*   Ibid., 13:13.
p. 299   *l.11*   1 John 2:15.
p. 299   *l.18*   The idea of making this comparison was given to me by Hubert L. Dreyfus.
p. 299   *l.19*   *The Symposium*, p. 82.
p. 299   *l.36*   1 Corinthians 13:4–8.
p. 300   *l.22*   Fromm, *The Art of Loving*, p. 65.
p. 300   *l.31*   Ibid., pp. 66–67.
p. 302   *l.14*   *Group Psychology and the Analysis of the Ego*, in *SE*, 18:94.
p. 302   *l.22*   John 13:34.
p. 302   *l.33*   *Group Psychology and the Analysis of the Ego*, in *SE*, 18:134–35.
p. 303   *l.19*   *Civilization and Its Discontents*, in *SE*, 21:109; in paperback (New York: W. W. Norton, 1962), p. 57.
p. 303   *l.32*   Ibid., p. 90.
p. 305   *l.29*   *The Realm of Spirit*, p. 238.
p. 306   *l.36*   Cf. Philip Rieff, *Freud: The Mind of the Moralist* (New York: Anchor Books, 1961), p. 168.
p. 307   *l.5*   *Group Psychology and the Analysis of the Ego*, in *SE*, 18:138–39.
p. 309   *l.34*   In *The Man Who Died*.
p. 310   *l.19*   *On Love*, p. 67.
p. 311   *l.3*   Act V, scene 1.
p. 312   I am indebted to George C. Anagnostopoulos for some of the quotations from Luther used in this chapter. Paul A. Lee was very helpful in criticizing an earlier draft.
p. 313   *l.11*   *Agape and Eros*, p. 210.
p. 315   *l.27*   For Augustine's discussion of these words, see *The City of God*, XIV (New York: Modern Library, 1950), pp. 448–49.

p. 316   *l.3*   Quoted in Nygren, *Agape and Eros*, p. 457.
p. 316   *l.5*   Ibid.
p. 316   *l.32*   Ibid., p. 495.
p. 318   *l.23*   Ibid., p. 528.
p. 318   *l.32*   Quoted in D'Arcy, *Mind and Heart of Love*, p. 77.
p. 319   *l.11*   Saint Thomas Aquinas, *On Charity* (*De Caritate*), trans. Lottie H. Kendzierski (Milwaukee: Marquette University Press, 1960), p. 17.
p. 320   *l.30*   Ibid., p. 24.
p. 321   *l.1*   Ibid., p. 21.
p. 321   *l.3*   Ibid., p. 22.
p. 322   *l.4*   Ibid.
p. 323   *l.12*   Ibid.
p. 325   *l.4*   *Luther's Works*, 24:342.
p. 325   *l.11*   *Table Talk* (London: George Bell & Sons, 1884), p. 117.
p. 325   *l.16*   Ibid.
p. 326   *l.14*   Quoted in Nygren, *Agape and Eros*, p. 686.
p. 326   *l.16*   *Luther's Works*, 26:176.
p. 326   *l.20*   Quoted in Nygren, *Agape and Eros*, p. 728n.
p. 326   *l.27*   Ibid., p. 702n.
p. 327   *l.27*   Ibid., pp. 694–95n.
p. 328   *l.4*   Ibid., p. 703n.
p. 328   *l.22*   Ibid., p. 724.
p. 328   *l.28*   *Luther's Works*, 31:57.
p. 328   *l.31*   Quoted in Nygren, *Agape and Eros*, p. 730n.
p. 329   *l.12*   *Table Talk*, p. 120.
p. 329   *l.20*   Quoted in Nygren, *Agape and Eros*, p. 735n.
p. 329   *l.31*   Philippians 2:12–13.
p. 331   *l.24*   Fromm, *The Art of Loving*, p. 67.
p. 332   *l.22*   Act I, scene 2.
p. 332   *l.26*   Quoted in Nygren, *Agape and Eros*, p. 733.
p. 333   *l.27*   Ibid., p. 720n.
p. 333   *l.34*   Ibid., p. 734n.
p. 333   *l.35*   Ibid., p. 719n.
p. 334   *l.5*   *Martin Luther: Selections from His Writings*, ed. John Dillenberger (New York: Anchor Books, 1961), p. 61.
p. 334   *l.20*   Daniel Cory, *Santayana: The Later Years* (New York: George Braziller, 1963), p. 71.
p. 336   *l.9*   Act I, scene 3.
p. 337   *l.25*   Quoted in Gilson, *The Mystical Theology of Saint Bernard*, p. 159.
p. 339   *l.6*   Quoted in *Mysticism East and West*, p. 180.
p. 339   *l.10*   Ibid., p. 195.
p. 339   *l.20*   Ibid., p. 200.
p. 339   *l.24*   Ibid., p. 194.
p. 339   *l.26*   "Preface to the Epistle of St. Paul to the Romans," in *Reformation Writings of Martin Luther*, ed. Bertram Lee Woolf (New York: Philosophical Library, 1956), 2:289.
p. 339   *l.31*   *Martin Luther: Selections from His Writings*, p. 102.

p. 341   *l.9*   Quoted in Nygren, *Agape and Eros*, p. 732.

p. 342   *l.31*   For further discussion of Nygren and concepts of Christian love in general, see Gene Outka, *Agape: An Ethical Analysis* (New Haven: Yale University Press, 1972), passim.

p. 344   *l.2*   *On Charity*, p. 69.

p. 344   *l.4*   *Morals of the Catholic Church*, in *Basic Writings of Saint Augustine*, p. 337.

p. 345   *l.22*   Quoted in Nygren, *Agape and Eros*, p. 506.

p. 346   *l.6*   Ibid., p. 454.

p. 347   *l.18*   Ibid., p. 679. The words are Nygren's. His reading of Ficino has been contested in James A. Devereux, S. J., "The Object of Love in Ficino's Philosophy," *Journal of the History of Ideas* (April-June 1969): 161–70.

p. 348   *l.19*   *Morals of the Catholic Church*, in *Basic Writings of Saint Augustine*, p. 339.

p. 349   *l.19*   *On Charity*, p. 61.

p. 350   *l.2*   Ibid., p. 62.

p. 350   *l.7*   Ibid.

p. 351   *l.14*   *Civilization and Its Discontents*, in *SE*, 21:110.

p. 354   *l.11*   Quoted in Nygren, *Agape and Eros*, p. 712.

p. 354   *l.20*   *Judaism*, 2:86.

p. 356   *l.3*   Dante Alighieri, *The Divine Comedy*, trans. John D. Sinclair, 3:51–53.

p. 356   *l.18*   From *Three Philosophical Poets*, in *Essays in Literary Criticism*, p. 47.

p. 357   *l.1*   *Divine Comedy*, 3:53.

p. 358   *l.24*   *The Realm of Spirit*, pp. 241–42.

p. 362   *l.18*   *On Love*, p. 67.

p. 362   *l.24*   *Mysticism East and West*, p. 136.

p. 363   *l.3*   *Beyond Good and Evil*, no. 60.

p. 365   *l.4*   Marsilio Ficino, *Theologia Platonica*, book XVI, chapter 6.

p. 365   *l.20*   St. Jerome, *Against Jovinian*, I. 49.

Index